Library of
Davidson College

Neither Kingdom
Nor Nation

Neither Kingdom Nor Nation

The Irish Quest for
Constitutional Rights,
1698–1800

∽

Neil Longley York

The Catholic University of America Press
Washington, D.C.

Copyright © 1994
The Catholic University of America Press
All rights reserved
Printed in the United States of America

The paper used in this publication meets the minimum requirements of American National Standards for Information Science—Permanence of Paper for Printed Library materials, ANSI Z39.48–1984.

∞

LIBRARY OF CONGRESS CATALOGING-IN-PUBLICATION DATA
York, Neil Longley.
Neither kingdom nor nation : the Irish quest for
constitutional rights, 1698–1800 / Neil Longley York.
  p.   cm.
Includes bibliographical references and index.
  1. Ireland—Politics and government—18th century.
  2. Ireland—Constitutional history. I. Title.
DA947.Y67 1994
320.9415—dc20
93-633
ISBN 0-8132-0782-7 (alk. paper)

To My Teachers;
For My Students

Contents

List of Illustrations ix
Acknowledgments xi

Introduction 1
1. Creating a Constitutional Tradition 8
2. Patriots and Popular Politics 39
3. Ireland and the American Revolution 74
4. Parliamentary Independence and the
    "Constitution" of 1782 109
5. The Limits of Democratic Reform 153
6. An End to "Independence" 195
7. Ireland and the Rebellious American Colonies:
    A Comparison 242

Bibliographical Note 265
Index 273

Illustrations

William Molyneux 21
Jonathan Swift 44
Charles Lucas 61
John Philpot Curran 123
1780 House of Commons 126
Henry Flood 133
Henry Grattan 137
Caricature of Grattan and Flood 139
Map of Parliamentary Constituencies 159
James Caulfield, earl of Charlemont 167
Francis Dobbs 171
Theobald Wolfe Tone 209
John Fitzgibbon, earl of Clare 225

Acknowledgments

This book began in a roundabout way. I started reading histories of Ireland's place in the British empire in order to create a larger context for the undergraduate and graduate courses I teach on Revolutionary American history. I eventually expanded from reading what others had said to wanting to say something myself. Although I have not set out to revise the findings of any particular historian, I have taken a different approach in tracing the Irish constitutional tradition.

In leaving the familiar landmarks of Revolutionary American history and crossing the Atlantic to the Irish past, I ventured into what were, for me, uncharted waters. Fortunately I had good pilots. Francis G. James, professor emeritus at Tulane University, and Maurice O'Connell, professor emeritus at Fordham University, offered excellent suggestions as I began my research and writing. Professor O'Connell took me under his wing when I traveled to Dublin and did his best to help me clarify muddled thoughts and garbled prose. J. C. Beckett, professor emeritus at Queen's University, Belfast, corrected factual errors and slips of the pen in chapters 1 and 7, and offered his views on my Irish-American comparison. J. I. McGuire of University College, Dublin, perused earlier versions of chapters 1 and 2 with a critical eye. John Phillip Reid, of the New York University School of Law, read chapter 3 and made incisive comments about the British constitution. Joseph S. Tiedemann of Loyola Marymount University put aside his writing to wade through the entire manuscript, aiding me at the expense of his own work. Just when I thought I had finished, Robert E. Burns of the University of Notre Dame helped me to pare the text and tighten my arguments, and Gerard O'Brien of the University of Ulster pointed me toward several sources and caused me to reconsider some of my conclusions. Susan Needham helped immensely with her skillful copy editing.

Past history department chairman James B. Allen supported me generously, as did the research committee for my college at Brigham Young University. My wife, Carole Mikita York, became a one-woman research foundation by signing over her tax refunds to support my archive hopping. With her largess and university funding, I was able to work at the Library of Congress in the spring of 1985, and the following year I read manuscripts and other sources at the British Library and the Public Record Office in London. In Dublin I paged through collections at the National Library of Ireland, the Royal Irish Academy, the Gilbert Library of the Dublin City Library, and the manuscripts room at Trinity College.

Kathy Hansen, John Higginbotham, and the interlibrary loan staff at the Harold B. Lee Library were swift and efficient in obtaining items from other libraries, including dissertations and theses as well as rare books and pamphlets. A. Dean Larsen authorized the purchase of materials that I could not obtain on loan, most notably the printed records (on microfilm) of the Irish Parliament.

A leave from teaching during the winter semester of 1987 freed me to write a first draft of this book. Julie Crandall, Kristie Jolley, Heather Nicholas, and history department secretary Mariel Budd indulged my aversion to sitting at a computer terminal and transferred my typewritten text to disk. Although I was on leave for a time, I was no less preoccupied with the past than usual, and for that I apologize to my wife and our daughters, Jennifer and Caitlin.

In "American Revolutionaries and the Illusion of Irish Empathy," *Eire-Ireland* 21 (Summer 1986): 13–30, I touched on some of the conclusions reached in chapter 3. Information used in that essay is repeated with the permission of the Irish American Cultural Institute.

Neither Kingdom
Nor Nation

Introduction

"Rights were taken seriously in the eighteenth-century British Empire," wrote John Phillip Reid recently; indeed, "people cherished them, championed them, defended them."[1] I agree. Consequently a discussion of rights—especially what the Irish thought were their "constitutional" rights—dominates the following pages. The Irish, or more properly those Irish of the Anglo-Irish Protestant Ascendancy, were as concerned as their contemporaries in Revolutionary America with questions of liberty and authority. They, too, debated the extent of individual freedom and the limits to governmental power. Like Revolutionary Americans, these Irish talked about rights handed down from God or derived from the law of nature, rights that had been legitimized by the passage of time or protected under common law, rights recognized by the Crown or formalized in legislative acts. Irish and American agitators and pamphleteers often drew from the same sources; they even quoted each other.

Revolutionary Americans eventually struck out on their own. They fought a war of independence and established a republic. The Anglo-Irish, all of their complaints about the empire notwithstanding, did not revolt and had no interest in replacing the time-honored arrangement now known as mixed and balanced government with new republican forms. The Anglo-Irish elite may have had the ingredients for a revolutionary ideology, but they stopped short of revolution. There they parted company with their revolutionary cousins across the Atlantic: ideological similarities were overshadowed by social and geographical differences.

Anglo-Irish "Patriots" of the 1760s and 1770s and Revolutionary Americans understandably thought that they had more in common than they really did. After all, Ireland and the American colonies were crucial outposts of empire. Some of those involved in failed New World enter-

---

1. John Phillip Reid, *Constitutional History of the American Revolution*, 3 vols. (Madison: University of Wisconsin Press, 1986–), 1:3.

prises during the 1580s had had their first colonizing experience in Ireland. That they considered Native Americans to be barbaric, savages not unlike those who opposed them in Ireland, has become a staple of recent writing.[2] More importantly, English failure to work out a plan of empire before England became imperialistic complicated both Irish and American affairs. So did later British attempts to bring greater uniformity and efficiency to the empire.

Eighteenth-century Ireland was distinct from the American colonies in the sense that it was called a "kingdom" rather than a colony, with a parliament *theoretically* more powerful than any legislative body in the colonies. Kingdom or not, Ireland was, like the American colonies, still caught up in a dispute over sovereignty that plagued the empire. "It is here that the problem of the British Empire exemplified the fundamental problem of international politics," observed Randolph Adams more than a half century ago. With both Ireland and the American colonies, Adams contended, can be seen the confusion produced by a failure "to work out a rational theory of sovereignty."[3] Disagreements over the locus of sovereignty, disagreements most often couched in the language of constitutionalism, eroded belief in a reciprocal empire and broke the spirit of cooperative enterprise, replacing them with jealousy and competitiveness.

Ireland had been a political problem for England from the moment in 1172 that it was linked to the English Crown. That political problem eventually became a constitutional problem as well. Treated as little better than conquered territory and referred to ambiguously—often simply as "the land of Ireland"—for centuries thereafter, from 1541 on it was more consistently called a distinct "kingdom" under the "imperial crown." In reality, as a subordinate part of an expanding empire, Ireland was not free to shape its own destiny, much less to choose its monarch.

---

2. See Howard Mumford Jones, *O Strange New World* (New York: Viking Press, 1964), 167–79; David Beers Quinn, *The Elizabethans and the Irish* (Ithaca: Cornell University Press, 1966), 23–33; and Nicholas P. Canny's, *The Elizabethan Conquest of Ireland* (Hassocks, Sussex: Harvester Press, 1976), 75–76, 126–30, 160–63; "The Ideology of English Colonization: From Ireland to America," *William and Mary Quarterly*, 3d ser., vol. 30 (1973): 575–98; and Canny's more sweeping observations about Ireland and America in *Kingdom and Colony: Ireland in the Atlantic World, 1500–1800* (Baltimore: Johns Hopkins University Press, 1988).

3. Randolph G. Adams, *Political Ideas of the American Revolution*, 3d ed. (New York: Barnes and Noble, 1958; orig. ed., 1922), 38. Also see Charles M. Andrews, *The Colonial Period of American History*, 4 vols. (New Haven: Yale University Press, 1934–38), 1:68–72; and Stephen Saunders Webb, *The Governors-General* (Chapel Hill: University of North Carolina Press, 1979), which takes issue with Andrews's emphasis on the commercial empire, but, like Andrews, notes Ireland's importance in the larger scheme of empire building.

Over the centuries the Irish became so divided along class, ethnic, and religious lines that socially and politically they did not constitute a single nation. Instead, they were a disunited and contentious people with a confused identity, living in a land that was a kingdom in name only.

English, and later British, imperialists complained about the Irish and their autonomous tendencies as much as they did about irascible Americans. Neither the Irish nor the Americans would conform to expectations, and both resisted efforts to make them more compliant.[4] Irish-American connections were strengthened by trade and by the immigration of many Irish, especially in the eighteenth century, to what appeared to be a more hospitable America. With deepening imperial crisis in the 1760s, the Irish followed American affairs closely, looking for signs of what lay ahead for themselves. When American colonists rebelled, there were those on both sides of the Atlantic who predicted that the Irish—with more justification and longer provocation—would soon follow. "In the new world, the spirit of independence first awoke from her long trance," wrote one historian at the end of the century, and "the genius of Liberty" soon "traversed" the ocean and "alighted upon the shores of Ireland."[5] The Irish were thereby swept into what R. R. Palmer has called "the age of the democratic revolution."[6]

Yet the Irish did not rebel in the 1770s, and if they were caught up in the same democratic movement that passed through Revolutionary America, the results were not as obvious. Without drifting off into what Crane Brinton warned is "the cloudland of metaphysics,"[7] I have tried to explain how the Irish and Americans used political ideology in ways that were at once similar and distinct. Important as ideas are, social setting helps determine which ideas will be most popular and how far actions based on or justified by those ideas will be taken. One does not have to believe that all thought is sired by experience to conclude that society fosters some notions and chokes off others. "Whether arguments

---

4. See Nicholas Canny, "The Permissive Frontier: The Problem of Social Control in English Settlements in Ireland and Virginia, 1550–1650," and Karl S. Bottigheimer, "Kingdom and Colony: Ireland in the Westward Enterprise, 1536–1660," both in K. R. Andrews, et al., eds., *The Westward Enterprise* (Liverpool: Liverpool University Press, 1978), 17–44, 45–64, resp.

5. Rev. James Gordon, *History of the Civil War in Ireland*, 2 vols. (Baltimore: Samuel Butler & Pickin & Frailey, 1805), 1:29.

6. R. R. Palmer, *The Age of the Democratic Revolution*, 2 vols. (Princeton: Princeton University Press, 1959, 1964); and idem, "The Revolution," in C. Vann Woodward, ed., *The Comparative Approach to American History* (New York: Basic Books, 1968), 47–61, though Palmer emphasized the distinctiveness of the "revolutionary" experiences in the United States and France, and Ireland's marginal involvement in both.

7. Crane Brinton, *The Anatomy of Revolution*, revised ed. (New York: Random House, 1965; orig. ed., 1938), 19.

command assent or not," Carl Becker once wrote, "depends less upon the logic that conveys them than upon the climate of opinion in which they are sustained."[8] Political ideas are often put to the service of society or some group within it, particularly by societies or groups or even individuals seeking to establish an identity.[9] Anglo-Irish Patriots were obliged to carve an identity for themselves as the rightful leaders of Irish society and as equal partners in the British empire. What J. G. A. Pocock has said about some seventeenth-century English thinkers—that they attempted "to understand themselves by understanding their past and their relation to it"[10]—was also true of the eighteenth-century Anglo-Irish.

Following the lead of their nationalistic predecessors, a group that included Catholics as well as Protestants, the eighteenth-century Anglo-Irish elite tried to locate their rights within a constitutional tradition, a past that, paradoxically, they themselves were helping to create. Issues that had been ignored or put aside in the aftermath of previous imperial crises came to a boil during the second half of the eighteenth century.

8. Carl Becker, *The Heavenly City of the Eighteenth-Century Philosophers* (New Haven: Yale University Press, 1932), 5.

9. George Rudé, *Ideology and Popular Protest* (London: Lawrence and Wishart, 1980), repeats Helvétius's comment that "our ideas are the necessary consequences of the societies in which we live" (15), but then goes on to discuss how the interaction of society and ideology is much more complex. As Lawrence Stone, "The Results of the English Revolutions of the Seventeenth Century," in J. G. A. Pocock, ed., *Three British Revolutions: 1641, 1688, 1776* (Princeton: Princeton University Press, 1980), 23–108, pointed out, it is possible for ideas to be socially ahead of their time, and to change their form and power even as society itself changes. Also see the discussion in Dominick LaCapra, *History & Criticism* (Ithaca: Cornell University Press, 1985), 15–44, 71–94, and Quentin Skinner, "Meaning and Understanding in the History of Ideas," *History and Theory* 8 (1969): 3–53. Historians working on the American Revolutionary era have become increasingly sensitive to the problem of connecting ideas to their social setting. Some have apparently been influenced by anthropologist Clifford Geertz's 1964 essay "Ideology as a Cultural System," reprinted in *The Interpretation of Culture* (New York: Basic Books, 1973), 193–233; others take exception to Geertz, or at least to the way his themes have been applied by their peers. See, for example, Robert E. Shalhope's discussion in "Republicanism and Early American Historiography," *William and Mary Quarterly*, 3d ser., vol. 39 (1982): 334–56; and Colin Gordon's "Crafting a Usable Past: Consensus, Ideology, and Historians of the American Revolution," *William and Mary Quarterly*, 3d ser., vol. 46 (1989): 671–95. Also see Gordon Wood's "Rhetoric and Reality in the American Revolution" *William and Mary Quarterly*, 3d ser., vol. 23 (1966): 3–32; the discussion of Wood's *The Creation of the American Republic, 1776–1787* (Chapel Hill: University of North Carolina Press, 1969) in *William and Mary Quarterly*, 3d ser., vol. 44 (1987): 549–640; Bernard Bailyn, "Political Experience and Enlightenment Ideas in Eighteenth-Century America," *American Historical Review* 67 (1962): 339–51; and the appendices to John P. Diggins, *The Lost Soul of American Politics* (New York: Basic Books, 1984), 347–65, where Diggins discusses the problem of determining whether ideas are truly "explanatory" or merely "expressive."

10. J. G. A. Pocock, *The Ancient Constitution and the Feudal Law* (Cambridge: Cambridge University Press, 1957; rev. ed., 1987), xiii.

In response, the Anglo-Irish strove to formulate a political ideology and put constitutional history to work for them, but the historical record was vague. The British often disagreed with their view of the past, and the Anglo-Irish themselves divided over questions of what was historically correct or constitutionally sound. Furthermore, those wanting to capitalize on nationalist political ideology could not always control ideas once they entered the marketplace. Talk about rights, in Ireland as in the American colonies, brought unexpected and sometimes unwanted results.

Anglo-Irish leaders during the American Revolutionary era hoped to secure their rights within the empire. Most of them also intended to restrict those rights to a property-owning Protestant electorate that in turn deferred to their will. Nonetheless, once constitutional issues were raised, the Anglo-Irish elite found it difficult to confine discussion within the limits they had set. Those in the Irish Parliament who characterized themselves as "Patriots," dedicated to preserving what they thought was the spirit of the British constitution as well as their liberties under a reified Irish constitution, were challenged by separatists wanting to leave the empire altogether and reformers advocating a democratic political leavening. Separatists and radical reformers took up ideas long articulated by the Anglo-Irish elite and carried them to their logical conclusion. Thus plans by one group to "restore" the constitution and salvage the empire led inadvertently to attempts by another to replace the constitution and chart an independent course.

Very few Irish who asserted their rights thought of themselves as revolutionaries, however, including those who challenged the ruling Anglo-Irish Protestant elite and condemned British policy. Even the United Irishmen of the 1790s swore that they had been moderate reformers pushed into radicalism by unresponsive Irish and British leaders. When they demanded independence from Britain and a more democratic political system, they still claimed that they had a moderate, even conservative, end in view: restoration of right as it once existed or as it should have existed all along. Like the Anglo-Irish elite whose leadership they came to resent and the Revolutionary Americans whose example they admired, they discovered that the quest for constitutional rights took unexpected turns.

In telling this story I have not tried to paint a complete social portrait of eighteenth-century Ireland. Nor have I given equal space to all of the players in eighteenth-century Irish politics. Others, whose works are cited in the notes or mentioned in the bibliographical essay, have already examined the period in much greater detail. I have concentrated on the constitutional tradition that Anglo-Irish Patriots of the American Revolutionary era used as the foundation of their rights. I therefore found it necessary to reconstruct that tradition, at least as they understood it, by going back to the twelfth century. For Anglo-Irish constitutionalists, unearthing the agreements reached by Henry II and Irish "kings" was far more important than perusing anything done in the reign of Henry VIII. Why? Because they claimed that their "constitution" dated from the twelfth, not the sixteenth, century. Anglo-Irish Patriots "constantly referred" to the "medieval precedents" that underlay their constitution, although we now know they often did so "incorrectly."[11]

Before discussing the crises leading to an Act of Union in 1800, I needed to sketch in arguments first made in the seventeenth century, when the Irish "constitution" took its basic form. What is usually, albeit misleadingly, characterized as Anglo-Irish constitutionalism was an extension of views expressed in the 1640s by Catholics and Protestants alike. I refer to the men who defined and defended that constitutional tradition as nationalists, for reasons that should become clear early on in the text, reasons that I further explain in the final chapter. Suffice it to say that I avoid the phrase "colonial nationalism" favored by some writers.[12] That characterization obscures rather than clarifies—because the Anglo-Irish denied that they were colonists, and because they believed that under their constitution they could be at once citizens of empire and the "free" residents of an "independent" kingdom. Historians of modern nationalism may take issue with my usage; seventeenth- and eighteenth-century Irish constitutionalists would have understood my meaning perfectly well.

In part I have returned to themes that interested an earlier generation of Irish historians.[13] At the same time, I have moved beyond those writers in discussing how constitutional disquisition doubled as polemic. If constitutional history is to be more than the mere explication of ideas, it must be treated in a wider context. And while it would be too simple

---

11. A. F. McC. Madden, "1066, 1776 and All That: The Relevance of English Medieval Experience of 'Empire' to Later Imperial Constitutional Issues," in John E. Flint and Glyndwr Williams, eds., *Perspectives of Empire* (London: Longman Group, 1972), 23.

12. See, for example, J. G. Simms, *Colonial Nationalism, 1698–1776* (Cork: Mercier Press, 1976); and J. L. McCracken, "Protestant Ascendancy and the Rise of Colonial Nationalism, 1714–1760," in T. W. Moody and W. E. Vaughan, eds., *A New History of Ireland*, vol. 4 (Oxford: Clarendon Press, 1986), 105–22.

13. Such as J. T. Ball, *Historical Review of the Legislative Systems Operative in Ireland* (Dublin: Hodges, Figgis, and Co., 1889); and J. G. Swift MacNeill, *The Constitutional and Parliamentary History of Ireland til the Union* (Dublin: The Talbot Press, 1917).

and most unfair to the dead to say that the Irish cynically "played politics" with constitutional issues, those issues became muddled in political debate, and with dire consequences. In a twist on an old adage, all of the Irish constitutionalists, most especially those who were part of the Anglo-Irish Protestant Ascendancy, became proof enough that those who live by the word can die by it too.

CHAPTER 1

Creating a Constitutional Tradition

> ... the land of Ireland is and at all times has been corporate of itself, by the ancient laws and customs used in the same, freed of the burthen of any special law of the realm of England, save only such laws as by the lords spiritual and temporal and of the said land had been in Great Council or Parliament held, admitted, accepted, affirmed and proclaimed, according to sundry ancient statutes thereof made.
>
> The Irish Parliament, 1460[1]

Historians often point to William Molyneux's 1698 tract, *The Case of Ireland Stated*, as a watershed in Irish constitutional history, and with good reason. Molyneux's *Case* infuriated English politicians at the time and, as reprinted by a later generation of Anglo-Irish parliamentary "Patriots," it came back to haunt Whitehall and Westminster. It did not, however, mark the beginning of Irish constitutionalism. On the contrary, Molyneux's arguments were the culmination of views dating back over two centuries and the outgrowth of political problems stretching back another three. Unlike his predecessors, Molyneux did not talk about vague Irish rights; rather, he wrote explicitly of an Irish "constitution," an unwritten and yet somehow tangible, fundamental testament of higher law as sacred and venerable as the English constitution that served as its model. Ironically, this reified Irish constitution, so much a creature of the English constitutional tradition, eventually became more of an obstacle than an aid to English empire-building. Under it, Irish constitutionalists characterized their island as a "kingdom" inhabited

---

1. Henry F. Berry, ed., *Statutes and Ordinances and Acts of the Parliament of Ireland*, 3 vols. (Dublin: Alexander Thom & Co., 1907–14), 1:645 (38 Henry VI c.6).

by a "free people" who were subject only to the "imperial crown" and laws passed by their own parliament.

On the surface, at least, Molyneux's Ireland was thoroughly anglicized. A ruling elite later to be known as the Anglo-Irish Protestant Ascendancy bestrode the island like a colossus. By 1698 the Anglo-Irish virtually monopolized political power and public life. Although Catholics would not be completely disfranchised until 1728, they had ceased to sit in the Irish House of Commons by 1692.[2] The Irish Parliament, so essential to the *Case* made by Molyneux, had first emerged at the end of the thirteenth century and, following the lead of its English counterpart, evolved into lords and commons, created many of the same offices and observed most of the same practices and ceremonies. Irish government had a privy council to assist a royally appointed lord deputy or lord lieutenant similar to the English privy council that advised the Crown. English law courts like king's bench and common pleas were as ancient as the parliament in Ireland and did their part in gradually anglicizing the island.[3]

As in England, the parliament in Ireland took on more and more legislative and judicial responsibilities over the centuries and with that became increasingly jealous of its prerogatives. It in fact had the audacity in 1460 to claim legislative autonomy, contending that the only laws binding Ireland were those it had passed. That assertion of parliamentary right was in turn based on the assumption that the Irish were a distinct people living in a distinct land, all ties to England notwithstanding. Since Ireland from the twelfth through the fifteenth centuries had been a backwater of empire and the Irish had become accustomed to a

---

2. For Catholic loss of power see Maureen Wall, *The Penal Laws, 1690–1760* (Dundalk: Dundalgan Press, 1976), reprinted in Gerard O'Brien, ed., *Catholic Ireland in the Eighteenth Century* (Dublin: Geography Publications, 1989), 1–60; idem, "The Age of the Penal Laws (1690–1778)," in T. W. Moody and F. X. Martin, eds., *The Course of Irish History* (New York: Weybright and Talley, 1967); J. G. Simms, *The Williamite Confiscation in Ireland, 1690–1703* (London: Faber & Faber, 1956); and idem, "Irish Catholics and the Parliamentary Franchise, 1692–1728," *Irish Historical Studies* 12 (1960): 28–37, reprinted in D. W. Hayton and Gerard O'Brien, eds., *War and Politics in Ireland, 1649–1730* (London: The Hambleton Press, 1986), 225–34; and Thomas Bartlett, *The Fall and Rise of the Irish Nation* (Savage, Md.: Barnes & Noble, 1992), for a historiographical review as well as Bartlett's own insights into the "Catholic Question" in Irish politics from 1690 to 1830.

3. J. T. Ball, *Historical Review of the Legislative Systems Operative in Ireland*, and J. G. Swift MacNeill, *The Constitutional and Parliamentary History of Ireland til the Union* (Dublin: Talbot Press, 1917), cover much of this story, as do Edward and Annie G. Porritt, *The Unreformed House of Commons*, 2 vols. (Cambridge: University Press, 1903, 1909), 2:185–529; Henry Joseph Monck Mason's brief *Essay on the antiquity and constitution of the parliaments in Ireland* (Dublin: W. Folds, 1820), which carried through the reign of Charles I; and the first two chapters of Alfred Gaston Donaldson, *Some Comparative Aspects of Irish Law* (Durham: Duke University Press, 1957).

great deal of self-rule, "practice seems to have supported what was then turned into a principle."[4]

At the end of the fifteenth century the English finally tried, rather halfheartedly, to alter the "practice" that had given life to the "principle." When the English determined to bring the Irish to heel, it was less because of the assertiveness of the Irish Parliament than for the independent tendencies of some lords deputy, especially those who were themselves Irish. Henry VII dispatched Englishman Edward Poynings to replace the Irish earl of Kildare as lord deputy in 1494 because Kildare was too unmanageable and a Yorkist sympathizer. If Henry VII gave the Irish Parliament much thought, it was because he did not want it to become the Yorkist preserve it had been as recently as 1487, when it proclaimed a Yorkist king, or twenty-seven years before that, when, with Commons leading the way, it had asserted its legislative prerogatives at the urging of a deposed and attainted Yorkist lord deputy. One of the laws that Poynings pushed through a hastily convened parliament at Drogheda specified that no Irish parliament could meet without the king's formal permission, nor could it consider any legislation that had not been approved in advance by the king in council. Yet when Poynings left after a relatively short stay Kildare was reinstated. Henry VII, like all of his predecessors on the English throne going back to Henry II, found it best to work through accommodation as well as intimidation, by negotiation as well as coercion.[5] He did little after passage of Poynings' Law to push Ireland into line. The "principle" that the Irish Parliament asserted in 1460 was not quashed by a more vigorous or more consistent imperial government.

Henry's son and successor, Henry VIII, gave similarly mixed signals. In order to strengthen the titular English hold, Henry VIII had himself proclaimed "king" of Ireland by the Irish Parliament. His predecessors had ordinarily been called "lord" of Ireland, so the 1541 proclamation helped eliminate any lingering doubt over what title was most appro-

---

4. J. F. Lydon, *The Lordship of Ireland in the Middle Ages* (Dublin: Gill and Macmillan, 1972), 265. Also see the somewhat different view in H. G. Richardson and G. O. Sayles, *The Irish Parliament in the Middle Ages* (Philadelphia: University of Pennsylvania Press, 1952), 260–63; Art Cosgrove, "A Century of Decline," in Brian Farrell, ed., *The Irish Parliamentary Tradition* (Dublin: Gill and Macmillan, 1973), 56–67; and Cosgrove's discussion, "Parliament and the Anglo-Irish Community: The Declaration of 1460," in Art Cosgrove and J. I. McGuire, eds., *Parliament and Community* (Belfast: Appletree Press, 1983), 25–41.

5. For the text of Poynings' Law see *The Statutes at Large*, 20 vols. (Dublin: George Grierson, 1786–1801), 1:44 (10 Henry VII c. 4), and the comments about it in Edmund Curtis, *History of Ireland* (London: Methuen, 1936), 150–52; Richardson and Sayles, *Irish Parliament*, 273–79; and the overview, "English Government in Ireland, 1470–1543," in Stephen G. Ellis, *Reform and Revival* (Woodbridge: Boydell Press, 1986).

priate. Through a policy of surrender and regrant, Henry VIII was able to coax various dynastic Irish lords into swearing fealty to him in exchange for recognition of their estates and power. Even so, the primary impetus for proclaiming Henry king came from Irish councillors anxious to consolidate control. They wanted to silence the malcontents who believed that the English Crown held title to Ireland only through the sufferance of the pope. With the 1534 Act of Supremacy, the pope, insofar as the English were concerned, had been removed from the political picture. Henry's Irish allies wanted it made clear that the king's title had never been contingent on papal approval anyway.

Such were Henry's belated efforts. He acted hesitantly and inconsistently, and it is hard to see how his change in the royal style can stand as proof of what historian Brendan Bradshaw called a "constitutional revolution" in sixteenth-century Ireland.[6] True, Ireland, which was only occasionally referred to in English statutes or royal proclamations as a "kingdom" before 1541, was more consistently referred to as such from that point on. Whatever Henry VIII's intentions, William Molyneux did not call attention to his policies, nor did the other seventeenth-century Irish constitutionalists who preceded him. If anything, Henry's attempts to tighten English domination bolstered later Irish constitutionalist arguments. His formal assertion of kingship was used to reaffirm that Ireland was a distinct kingdom tied to England through the same monarch, with a parliament separate from and equal to the parliament in England. Representation in the Irish Parliament expanded under Henry with the shire system to include new areas brought under control, ideally to enhance the king's power and further the process of anglicization. Yet the larger and more inclusive the Irish Parliament was, the more faction ridden and jealous of its power it could also become. Near the end of Henry's reign, Poynings' Law was suspended to allow the Irish greater legislative efficiency, which understandably would be used by subsequent Irish constitutionalists as evidence of Parliament's rightful auton-

---

6. Brendan Bradshaw, *The Irish Constitutional Revolution of the Sixteenth Century* (Cambridge: University Press, 1979), 3–13, 189, and 264–67; also idem, "The Beginnings of Modern Ireland," in Farrell, ed., *Irish Parliamentary Tradition*, 68–87. Although Darcy and Molyneux did not dwell on Henry VIII, his severing of ties with the Vatican did eliminate one potential dispute. So long as England was tied to the Vatican, title to Ireland was problematic. In 1472 the Irish Parliament affirmed that Pope Adrian IV had held title to Ireland, which he then passed on to Henry II "and to his heirs for ever" (Berry, ed., *Statutes*, 3:437, 439, at 7 & 8 Edward IV c. 8). Therefore Catholic prelates in Ireland were subject to the English Crown and, resolved the Irish Parliament, they would be excommunicated if they went against it. Parliament thus opened the way for jurisdictional disputes between church courts and common law courts, disputes that could extend to London and the Vatican. For Ireland's being referred to as a kingdom well before 1541, see I Henry III (for the year 1216) in ibid., 1:7, 11, 19.

omy. Furthermore, by trying to unite the Irish under English rule Henry added to his kingly duties, reinforcing the view of those Irish who believed that their English connection carried as many rights as responsibilities.

Constitutional debates grew out of political disputes: the more crucial the political dispute, the more heated the constitutional debate. It is no coincidence, then, that the first clear articulation of what the Irish considered their constitutional rights came during the great political crises of the 1640s, setting the stage for Molyneux's tract of a half-century later. Stuart pacification in Ireland, more aggressive than anything that had come before, made perennial disputes that had before been only intermittent. Matters came to a head under Charles I. By the middle of the 1630s Charles's lord deputy, Sir Thomas Wentworth, had managed to alienate many Catholic and Protestant members of the Irish Parliament by struggling with them over issues of legislative prerogative.[7] Wentworth was determined to humble the Irish and, as Aidan Clarke put it, his application of Poynings' Law "became the cornerstone of a general design to reduce Parliament to the subordinate status of a legislative agency obediently giving statutory effect to executive policy."[8] From 1633 to 1640 the contest surged. Wentworth tactlessly referred to Ireland as a "conquered nation"; the Irish Parliament remonstrated to Charles I that Ireland "should be governed according to the municipal and Fundamental Lawes of *England*," and that "*Magna Charta*, or the Great Charter of the Liberties of *England* and other laudable Laws and Statutes, were in several Parliaments here enacted and declared."[9] Parliament won by default when Wentworth was recalled and, within a year, executed.

---

7. Hugh F. Kearney, *Strafford in Ireland, 1633–1641* (Cambridge: Cambridge University Press, 1989; orig. ed., 1959), covers Wentworth's disputes with the Irish Commons in great detail. Revolutionary era American writers like "The Centinel" in *The Massachusetts Spy*, 3 October 1771, made Wentworth the exemplar of a long train of imperial abuse.

8. Aidan Clarke, "Historical Revision: XVIII the History of Poynings' Law, 1615–1641," *Irish Historical Studies* 18 (1971): 214. Also see Clarke's *The Old English in Ireland, 1625–1642* (Ithaca: Cornell University Press, 1966), and Clarke's essays in T. W. Moody, F. W. Martin, and F. J. Byrnes, eds. *A New History of Ireland*, vol. 3 (Oxford: Clarendon Press, 1976), 233–88; and David B. Quinn, "The Early Interpretation of Poynings' Law, 1494–1534," *Irish Historical Studies* 2 (1941): 241–54.

9. The 7 November 1640 resolution is in the *Journals of the House of Commons of the Kingdom of Ireland*, 20 vols. (Dublin: George Grierson, 1796–1802), 1:162. Also see John Nalson, *An Impartial Collection of the Great Affairs of State*, 2 vols. (London: Tho. Dring, et al., 1682–83), 2:44, and Wentworth's "Conquer'd Nation" opinion, repeated in 1641, 2:20, 108–9.

Wentworth's disgrace and condemnation were only in part for his Irish policy. His opponents in the English Parliament attacked him for his "treasonous" actions, not for his ideas about Irish subordination, which, as he noted in self-defense, they shared with him. He fell primarily as a royalist, the victim of his own mistakes in Ireland and, more importantly, his loyalty to a king locked in a growing struggle with the English Parliament and a rebellion in Scotland that presaged civil war in Ireland and England—civil war that Wentworth's master eventually lost.

In the aftermath of their confrontations with Wentworth, leaders in the Irish Commons, including Audley Mervin, an English Protestant recently arrived in Ulster, and Patrick Darcy, a recusant from an old County Galway family, sought to defend their parliamentary powers. By 1641 they had been nudged into formally defining those powers as they dealt with the question of subsidies and the aftershock of their protests against Wentworth. In February they compiled a list of twenty-one "Queries"; in June, after a group of Irish judges gave a very equivocal response to a House of Lords directive to review those queries, Commons stated its position. Darcy was apparently the primary spokesman, though it must be remembered that the House formally endorsed his contentions the next month. Perhaps the Irish M.P.s had been emboldened by Wentworth's demise so that Darcy could mimic, on a smaller stage and for different purposes, John Pym at Westminster.

Darcy spoke in the dining hall of Dublin Castle to the Commons and a committee from Lords, and drew from his close reading of Irish history. A large man and noted debater in the House, Darcy was a barrister who had studied at the Middle Temple. He took the twenty-one "Queries" that Commons passed on to Lords, and Lords to the judges, and answered them. To the most important question—"Whether the Subjects of this kingdom be a free people, and to be governed only, by the Common Lawes of England, and Statutes of force in this kingdom?"—he gave an emphatic "yes." In reality, the questions had been rhetorical. Darcy and other members of Commons already thought they knew the proper answer; they had just wanted the judges to uphold their views and were chagrined when those judges did not. Their combativeness was embodied in their statement as to why the queries had been made at all:

the unlawfull actions and proceedings of some of his Majesties Subjects, and Ministers of Justice of late Yeares, introduced and practised in this kingdome, did tend, to the infringing and violation of the lawes, liberties, and freedome, of the said Subjects of this kingdome, contrary to his Majesties Royall and pious intentions. Therefore the Knights, Citizens, and Burgesses in Parliament assembled, not for any doubt, or ambiguity, which may be conceived, or thought of, for, or concerning the premisses, nor of the ensueing questions, but for the manifestation and declaration of a cleere truth, and of the said Lawes and Statutes already planted, and for many ages past, settled in this kingdome.[10]

Irish common law freedoms, the rights of the Irish Parliament, and the limits to royal prerogative were stressed throughout Darcy's *Argument*. It stated that the Irish could be bound only by laws passed in their own parliament, an explicit assertion of Irish parliamentary independence. There was even an implicit argument for Irish parliamentary supremacy over the Crown in a passage stating that quo warranto proceedings against parliamentary boroughs, even if issued by the Court of King's Bench, were illegal. Inclusion of this particular claim was no minor point. Years before, Wentworth had tried to interfere with borough affairs to pack Commons with Protestants and reduce the power of Catholics. Putting aside their own anti-Catholic fears, some Protestant M.P.s, appalled by this meddling, had joined with the recusants to protest, which Darcy remembered quite well. Judges were also subordinate to Parliament, continued the *Argument*: "Judges are and ought to be bound by resolutions in Parliament, and not Parliament by them." Buried more deeply was an argument for popular sovereignty, not just in the characterization of the Irish as a "free people," but in the contentions that jurors were the sole judges of fact in a trial and that they could not be punished for their decisions. This passage might have been included because Darcy had seen jurors from Galway jailed in 1636 when they refused to find for Wentworth and his planned Connacht plantation. Darcy allowed the king his prerogative, to be sure, but the most proper use of that prerogative was to protect the liberty of the people. Government was ultimately a compact:

The trust betweene the King and his people is threefold: First as betweene Soveraigne and Subject, Secondly, as betweene a Father and his Children, *unde Pater*

---

10. Patricke Darcy Esquire, *An Argument* (Waterford: Thomas Bourke, 1643), 4. Also see William A. O'Malley, "Patrick Darcy, Lawyer and Politician, 1598–1668" (M.A. thesis, University College, Galway, 1973), which James I. McGuire pointed out to me; and O'Malley's "Patrick Darcy, Galway Lawyer and Politician, 1598–1668" in Diarmuid n Cearbhaill, ed., *Galway: Town and Gown, 1484–1984* (Dublin: Gill and Macmillan, 1984), 90–109, kindly sent to me by Gerard O'Brien. Also see Patrick J. Corish, "The Origins of Catholic Nationalism" in Corish, ed., *A History of Irish Catholicism*, vol. 3, no. 8 (Dublin: Gill and Son, 1968). R. F. Foster, *Modern Ireland, 1600–1972* (London: Allen Lane, 1988), 84n, gave Darcy his due by noting that he preceded Molyneux and that his *Argument* "remained the linchpin of constitutional nationalist thought until the fall of Isaac Butt in 1877." If Foster mentions Darcy without exploring his ideas or explaining the complexities of Darcy's form of constitutionalism, at least he does mention him in the same breath with Molyneux. Many other writers purporting to discuss the origins of Irish nationalism do not mention Darcy at all.

Creating a Constitutional Tradition 15

Patriae; Thirdly, as betweene Husband and Wife, this trust is comprehensive of the whole body politicke, And for any Magistrate or private person to advise, or contrive the breach of this trust in any part, is of all things in this world the most dangerous.[11]

Much of what Darcy said in 1641 was repeated in documents issued by the Kilkenny Confederates from 1642 to 1649. Darcy sat on the Supreme Council and might have had a hand in drafting them, as he did in writing the "constitution" under which the confederation was governed. If the Confederates were at all consistent, it was not in their behavior or their attachment to the king but in their demands that certain rights be restored or recognized anew. Central among those demands lay their claim to common law protections and their requirement that the Irish Parliament be acknowledged as an independent body. They resubmitted their 1643 list of necessities (given their ostensible loyalty to the Crown, they had to be careful not to make outright demands) in various forms throughout their negotiations with Charles I, insisting:

That whereas this your Majestie's kingdome of Ireland in all successions of ages, since the raigne of King Henry the Second, sometimes King of England and Lord of Ireland, had Parlyaments of their owne, composed of Lords and Commons, in the same measure and forme, qualified with equall liberties, powers, priviledges and immunities with the Parlyament of England, and only dependant of the King and Crowne of England and Ireland: and for all that time noe prevalent record or authentique president cane be found, that any statute made in England could or did bind this kingdom before the same were here established by Parlyament.[12]

In effect, the Confederates made the same basic claim in 1643 as the Irish Commons made two years before. The Confederates, not Parliament, financed the first printing of Darcy's *Argument*. Civil war notwithstanding, when Darcy and some two score others left Parliament to

---

11. Darcy, *Argument*, 94–95. Also see Charles H. McIlwain, *The American Revolution: A Constitutional Interpretation* (New York: Macmillan, 1923), 29–78, and Robert Livingston Schuyler, *Parliament and the British Empire* (New York: Columbia University Press, 1929), 41–43, for very different views of these assertions. Thomas L. Coonan, "Irish Antecedents of the American Revolution," *The Historical Bulletin* 25 (1947): 51–52, 63–66, 71–72; and, more expertly, Barbara A. Black, "The Constitution of Empire: The Case for the Colonists," *University of Pennsylvania Law Review* 124 (1976): 1174–91, discuss the McIlwain-Schuyler debate.

12. The text of this petition of 17 March 1643 (mislabeled as 1642) is in [John Curry], *Historical Memoirs of the Irish Rebellion in the Year 1641* (London: J. Williams, 1767), 190–211; quote from p. 205. Compare this with the resolution passed by the General Assembly at Kilkenny on 24 October 1642, the text of which is in Richard Bellings's narrative in the *History of the Irish Confederation and the War in Ireland*, 4 vols., ed. John T. Gilbert (Dublin: M. H. Gill & Son, 1882–88), 2:73–84.

join and help form the Kilkenny confederation, they did not take and make exclusive to themselves the ideas of the *Argument*. The constitutional case articulated in that *Argument* had nothing to do with the differences that separated Protestants from Catholics, or supporters of Charles I from adherents of the English Parliament. By 1644 there had appeared a "Declaration" that circulated through the Irish Parliament and made the same assertions as those made by the Confederates at almost the same moment.[13] Both were in line with Darcy's *Argument*.

The "Declaration's" authorship is shrouded in mystery: Darcy or other Confederates might have written it to challenge the power of the English Parliament, just as the *Argument* had been written to question the prerogatives of the Crown, lord deputy, and Irish judges. Darcy was in Dublin at about the time that the "Declaration" appeared. True, his *Argument* had just been published, but the perilous times and shift in emphasis might have been incentives to take up the pen again. Lord Chancellor Richard Bolton, who was no friend to the Confederates and had not done much heretofore to defend Irish parliamentary rights, could also have been the author. Regardless of who wrote it, the "Declaration" appears to have enjoyed a certain popularity even though it was

13. "A Declaration setting forth how and by what means the Lawes and Statutes of England from time to time came to bee of force in Ireland" was first published in Walter Harris, ed., *Hibernica: Or, some Ancient pieces relating to Ireland* (Dublin: John Milliken, 1770; orig. ed., 1747–50), Part II, 9–45. Two manuscript copies are in the Trinity College, Dublin (hereafter TCD) manuscripts collection (MSS. 647 and 843). Both are dated 1643 and ascribed to Sir Richard Bolton, by different hands. Hugh Howard's two-volume manuscript history of Parliament, written from 1772 to 1774, in the Gilbert Library, Dublin City Library, has a note on the inside cover of Volume I stating that Richard Bolton was the presumed author of this "Declaration." Certain details in this note only add to the confusion. See the comments on Howard's history by John T. Gilbert in the Historical Manuscripts Commission (hereafter HMC), *Third Report* (London: Eyre & Spottiswoode, 1872), appendix, 432–34. Harris worked from the TCD copies and believed that Darcy was probably the real author of the "Declaration." Bolton, most historians now agree, was an unlikely author. That does not mean that we are left with Darcy, although O'Malley, "Patrick Darcy," 192–200, 239–54, makes a good circumstantial case for him (and other Confederates). Bolton may not have been a likely author, yet Samuel Mayart, who was in a position to know, stated in his response that the "Lord Chancellor"—Bolton—was in fact the author (Harris, ed., *Hibernica*, Part II, p. 48). Darcy had joined with others who wanted to impeach Bolton during the battles between Wentworth and Commons. The ideas expressed in the "Declaration," like those in *An Argument*, seem to have been widely held, at least by members of the Irish Commons. Nevertheless, if Darcy was the author, or if it had been written by another Old English recusant, that would help to explain why Domvile and Molyneux did not want to draw attention to it. Even if it was written by a member of the "legitimate" Irish Parliament, Domvile might not have wanted to tie himself too closely to a group that supported the regicides of Charles I. For allusions to a "book" being circulated in the Irish Parliament in April 1644 that was no doubt the "Declaration" see the *House of Commons Journal*, 1:323, 326, 327.

not officially endorsed. Neither was it censored or ordered to be destroyed; on the contrary, more manuscript copies were made.

In any event, its appearance was seen by some as threatening enough to require a response—hence Samuel Mayart's counterblast. Mayart, a justice on the court of common pleas, sought to dismantle the primary contentions of the "Declaration."[14] He had been one of the seven judges who responded to the House queries of 1641, subsequently published by the Kilkenny Confederates with Darcy's *Argument*. Mayart's treatise was much more detailed than the "Declaration" and in some ways better argued. The "Declaration" contended that Ireland had been a distinct kingdom since the time of Henry II. Henry, according to its reading of the past, had in fact parted with his title before he died, bequeathing it to his son John. John had not only eventually become king of England; for a time he had been lord of Ireland, while his father was still living—thus showing that the kingdoms and thrones of England and Ireland were separable and equal. Mayart countered that the record was not so clear, on this point and others. Mayart's search of the past showed that Henry had not really given control of Ireland to John. Mayart also turned up no convincing proof that the Irish Parliament was independent or that English laws were binding in Ireland only if passed through the Irish Commons and Lords first. If the "Declaration" could show that the Irish Parliament had asserted its legislative independence periodically ever since the fifteenth century, Mayart could respond that over that same period the Irish Parliament had accepted as law acts first passed in the English Parliament. He dismissed the "Declaration's" claim that the Irish could not be taxed by the English Parliament because they had no M.P.s sitting there; he retorted that they were virtually represented at Westminster.

In the end Mayart's rejoinder probably changed no minds, and the same is true of Darcy's original *Argument* and the subsequent "Declaration." Moreover, Mayart could not use precedent to establish principle any better than those he criticized. Consequently the indecisive 1644 debate did not end attempts to rummage through Irish history to find a usable past. And unfortunately the historical record was so vague that each side could find evidence to support its respective view.

Even more damaging was the splitting of Irish constitutionalists into rival political camps. Native Irish and Old English recusants were thoroughly discredited in the eyes of Irish Protestants, who lumped together

---

14. Mayart's response is in Harris, ed., *Hibernica*, Part II, 46–231.

the Ulster outbreak of 1641 and the activities of the Kilkenny confederation into one conspiratorial whole. As far as most of those who led the Anglo-Irish Protestant Ascendancy in the eighteenth century were concerned, the Confederates played no legitimate role in the articulation of Irish constitutional rights. Disdained as the dupes of Charles I, or worse, of the pope, they had been no more subservient to either than the legitimate Irish Parliament ended up becoming to the English Parliament during the 1640s. Indeed, there is evidence that some Confederates contemplated actually declaring independence.[15] But the more that Catholics were excluded from public life, the more difficult it was for them to promote their view of the past. Their support of James II in 1689 not only hastened their political decline, it further distanced them from what Protestants considered constitutional legitimacy. To Protestants, the so-called "Patriot Parliament" that met under James was a final, fleeting example of Stuart highhandedness, and its proceedings were expunged from the official record.

Therefore a tract like *Ireland's Case Briefly Stated* was doomed to obscurity in the age of a William Molyneux. It appeared anonymously in 1695, just three years before Molyneux's own treatise, and has been attributed to Hugh Reilly, a Catholic who served in a minor post under James II's shortlived Irish government. Reilly argued that the Irish in general, not just Irish Catholics, had been grievously wronged by the English over their history. In doing this he was trying to stimulate national pride and unity, a sense that all of the Irish, regardless of ethnic or religious differences, shared the same past. Irish Protestants nonetheless would have taken umbrage at much of what he wrote. He blamed them for the 1641 rebellion and held up the Kilkenny Confederates as true defenders of Irish liberties. English as well as Irish Protestants would have been offended by his biting comments about English policy in Ireland and his allusion to Elizabeth as the "bastard" queen. Stuart sympathizers would not have appreciated his arguments either, since he dismissed Charles II as a weak king who permitted "wicked" acts against Irish Catholics to be committed in his name.[16]

Some or even most of what Reilly wrote may have been true; that is less important than how his arguments were received. They were undoubtedly attractive to many Irish Catholics, yet Catholics were fast

---

15. See MS. 24 O 18 at the Royal Irish Academy (hereafter RIA), a partial transcript of a document apparently prepared for the Kilkenny confederation, ca. 1645, arguing that the English Crown had no title to Ireland and therefore no proper claim to Irish lands. For context see D. F. Cregan, "The Confederation of Kilkenny: Its Organization, Personnel and History" (Ph.D. thesis, University College, Dublin, 1947).

16. [Hugh Reilly], *Ireland's Case Briefly Stated* (1695).

losing what political power remained to them, and their view of the past could be and was discredited by rising Anglo-Irish Protestants. Reilly's *Case* was no worse as constitutional history than the much more famous *Case* written by Molyneux. But Anglo-Irish Protestants could ignore Reilly's tract as a Catholic polemic, an example of invalid history. Molyneux's book, on the other hand, would eventually be embraced by the Anglo-Irish as the distillation of historical truth.

A fourth-generation Irishman, Molyneux was actually of French Huguenot descent. He attended Trinity College, Dublin, the Middle Temple, and sat in the Irish Commons from 1692 until his death six years later. Only forty-two when he died, during his short life he established himself as one of the leading Irishmen of his generation, a friend and correspondent of John Locke, a cosmopolite of varied interests and activities: mathematics, engineering, astronomy, optics and philosophy. Member of the Royal Society of London, he also helped found the Dublin Philosophical Society.[17] His *Case of Ireland Stated* reflected his deep interest in Irish politics; he did not simply "sit" in the House of Commons. The *Case* demonstrated Molyneux's skills as a synthesizer rather than as a daring, original intellect, for most of what Molyneux wrote in that *Case* had already been said before, in the preceding generation by Darcy and by the author of the "Declaration," and even more recently by his own father-in-law, Sir William Domvile.

Domvile penned an unpublished manuscript, "A Disquisition," from which his son-in-law drew freely. He addressed this rather brief tract—the *Case* would be considerably longer—to Charles II at the time of the Stuart Restoration in 1660. Apparently Domvile drafted it at the behest of a special convention composed of Protestant leaders anxious to secure Irish rights and work out an accommodation with the new king. Domvile was made attorney general for Ireland, though not because of his "Disquisition"; he was fortunate that Charles probably never read what he wrote.

Domvile claimed to have searched "the Historians, and Writers of Elder Times" as well as more contemporary records and statutes; for example, his discussion of Ireland under the Normans relied heavily on the chronicle of Sylvester Giraldus Cambrensis, and his historical interpretations were reminiscent of those made in the 1644 "Declaration."[18]

17. J. G. Simms, *William Molyneux of Dublin, 1656–1698* (Dublin: Irish Academic Press, 1982).
18. As James Ivan McGuire, "Politics, Opinion and the Irish Constitution, 1688–1707" (M.A. thesis, University College, Dublin, 1968), pointed out, 8–39, Domvile may also have drawn from the then-unpublished *Modus tenendi Parliamenta in Hibernia* (Dub-

He professed to be objective, not to be writing for any one faction or interest. Yet he also made it clear that his history was didactic, designed to show the danger of "Innovations in the fundamentals of Government." Having stated his method and purposes he opened with what was in effect a conclusion:

Now in Reading the Historys of Ancient times wee shall Clearly finde that England could have no Jurisdiction over the Kingdome of Ireland, for that Ireland is a more Antient Separate, and Distinct Kingdome, having never been subject to the Roman Yoke. Whereas England and all other Kingdoms in the Christendome, now in being, which were subjected to the Romans had theire rising from ye fall of that Empire. But Ireland being never brought under the Roman Yoke hath Adorned the English Crown in that respect with Titles of no less Splendor, than Antiquity.[19]

Domvile did conclude that Henry II and subsequent English monarchs had "an absolute Direct Dominion over the Kingdome and people of Ireland," but only after emphasizing that the "Submission of all the Nobility, and Gentry of Ireland" to Henry had been "voluntary" as well as "absolute." The key, then, was the contractual nature of the connection. Ireland did not "belong" to England and the existing tie between the two was not based on conquest. Furthermore, the tie was only through the king, not through the English Parliament. "Neither was it ever in the minde or Intention of the Nobility and Clergy in Ireland by those voluntary" submissions "to prostrate themselves and their Posteritys their Lives and fortunes unto the Lords and Commons of England."[20] In short, the original tie had been made by consent, through the

---

lin, 1692), which was an "ancient record," dating back well before 1613, supposedly to the original parliamentary *Modus* sent over by Henry II. G. O. Sayles, "Modus Tenendi Parliamentum: Irish or English?" in James Lydon, ed., *England and Ireland in the Later Middle Ages* (Kill Land: Irish Academic Press, 1981), 122–52, contends that the Irish *Modus* dates from sometime after the middle of 1382, and that the English text was derivative, based on the Irish version. Molyneux referred to the *Modus* in his *Case*. Molyneux's nephew, Samuel Dopping, son of the bishop of Meath, had given him a copy. Dopping's father had had it printed on the eve of the opening of a new Parliament in 1692. The *Modus* fell into the bishop's hands when it was bequeathed "as a legacy" from Domvile. The *Modus* was not an explicit defense of Irish parliamentary independence; rather, it detailed how a parliament should be called and who should attend. Since it paralleled procedures used in England, Irish constitutionalists inferred that Henry II saw the two parliaments as co-equal and that, in its very antiquity, the Irish Parliament existed by right.

19. Sir William Domvile, "A Disquisition touching that great Question Whether an Act of Parliamt made in England shall binde ye Kingdome, & people of Ireland without theire Allowance & Acceptance of such Act in the Kingdome of Ireland," 1660, MS. 890 TCD (autograph copy), p. 1. There are two other copies bound with this one, and there is another, more difficult to read, copy at the National Library of Ireland (hereafter NLI), MS. 40. The TCD copies are bound with two manuscript copies of Molyneux's *Case*.

20. Domvile, "Disquisition," 8.

William Molyneux as bewigged man of vision, by P. Simms.
Courtesy of the National Library of Ireland.

person of the king, and it had established "Ireland as a Separate and Distinct Kingdome from England" with an autonomous Parliament. Pursuing an argument that the "Declaration" had made previously, Domvile asserted that Henry had passed full title to his son John as "lord" of Ireland. That the connection continued to be through the English Crown was because Richard I, John's elder brother, died childless and John succeeded him to the throne. Otherwise John would not have been king of England, but he still would have had title to Ireland. Ireland might then have passed from the royal line. Thus Domvile contended that the king of England actually wore two distinct crowns: one as king of England, the other as king of Ireland. The actions of Henry VIII in 1541 as well as those of Henry II earlier, he felt, confirmed his view.

Domvile did not originate the distinction between crowns. The Irish Parliament had made it in its November 1640 remonstrance to Charles I and it was implicit in the 1644 "Declaration." Henry VIII would not have interpreted the clause in his 1541 decree describing Ireland "as united and knit to the imperial crown of the realm of England" in quite the same way. The only question is if Domvile knew how far he strayed from Henry's original intent.

Pressing on, Domvile contended that Poynings' Law bound Ireland only because it had passed the Irish Parliament. Under Poynings' Law, any statutes passed at Westminster should not be applicable to Ireland unless the Irish Parliament ratified them by passage. Even acts passed by the English Parliament that referred specifically to Ireland should not be binding unless, again, the Irish Parliament subsequently approved them, recent practices to the contrary notwithstanding. English common law had been extended to Ireland by Henry II, it had been reaffirmed by John and the extension to Ireland of Magna Carta, and it was in no way affected by the actions of Sir Edward Poynings. Domvile was certain that Henry II had implicitly recognized the independence of the Irish Parliament from that in England by sending instructions to the Irish that were similar to the regulations governing the calling and organization of Parliament in England. Because "no one thing can be both supreme and Subordinate," reason dictated that the Irish Parliament had to be independent or there was no logic to its even existing. To believe otherwise "is so Repugnant to Reason, and Natural Equity and so directly ag.t all those freedoms and Libertys contained in Magna Charta, and King John's greater Charter, and the Common Liberty of a People, and the Laws both of England and Irel.d as no Rationall Man will Contest for it."[21]

21. Ibid., 24.

Molyneux's repetitiously long *Case* expressed identical sentiments. "*That* Ireland *should be Bound by Acts of Parliament made in England,*" concluded Molyneux, "*is against Reason, and the Common Rights for all Mankind.*"[22] Molyneux denied the right of the English Parliament to tax him or his countrymen. "To *Tax* me without Consent, is little better, if at all, than *down-right robbing me,*" he chided.[23] He echoed Domvile on the rights and longevity of the Irish Parliament, and the extension to Ireland of English common law. He also defended the appellate authority of the Irish House of Lords against any claim to that power made by the English lords. Basing his arguments on natural rights, the common law tradition of England as it had been extended to Ireland, and legal and historical precedent, Molyneux found no fewer than ten justifications for his argument. What has usually caught the most attention are his many allusions to natural rights, a reflection of his association with Locke and his place in what has been called the Whig "commonwealth" tradition. As he stated in one oft-quoted passage:

That the Right of being subject Only to such Laws to which Men give their *own Consent,* is so inherent to all Mankind, and found on such Immutable Laws of Nature and Reason, that 'tis not to be *Alien'd,* or *Given up,* by any Body of Men whatsoever: For the End of all Government and Laws being the Publick Good of the Commonwealth, in the Peace, Tranquility and Ease of every Member therein; whatsoever Act is contrary to this End, is in it self void, and of no effect.[24]

Of course Molyneux's bold assertion of natural rights appealed to those who accepted the validity of natural right theory and Molyneux's application of it to the Irish situation. But natural right theory was not universally accepted; nor was it necessarily seen as applicable to Ireland in the manner Molyneux attempted, even by those who did not reject the theory outright. Molyneux's combination of political philosophy

---

22. William Molyneux, *The Case of Ireland's Being Bound by Acts of Parliament in England Stated* (Dublin, 1698; reprint ed. Dublin: Cadenus Press, 1977), 116. Also see the introduction by J. G. Simms, who edited the reprint edition, and the afterword by Denis Donoghue. See pp. 42–45 for Molyneux's reference to Domvile and the origins of the *Modus* (also see n. 18 above). Isolde Louise Victory, "Colonial Nationalism in Ireland, 1692–1725: From Common Law to Natural Right" (Ph.D. dissertation, Trinity College, University of Dublin, 1985), discusses Swift as well as Molyneux but tries too hard to trace a progression from common law to natural right. Justifications were jumbled together—whether by Swift and Molyneux, or earlier by Darcy and later by Henry Grattan. On Molyneux's importance to the parliamentary Patriots of Grattan's generation, see Patrick Kelly, "William Molyneux and the Spirit of Liberty in Eighteenth-Century Ireland" *Eighteenth-Century Ireland* 3 (1988): 133–48.
23. Molyneux, *Case,* 130.
24. Ibid., 93.

and historical understanding had many problems. The *Case* was not just the "tissue of error, contradiction and fallacy" that one twentieth-century American historian labeled it, yet it could be and was countered by critics who mustered countervailing evidence—as had happened with the "Declaration" in 1644.[25]

The philosophical and historiographical debates between Molyneux and his critics demonstrate rather clearly the very unclear nature of the empire. The empire was not static; it had changed continually over the centuries and those manifold changes rendered impossible the finding of historical and legal precedents to settle all constitutional disputes. Time had not stood still, and Molyneux was not the only one trapped by that fact. His father-in-law argued in 1660 that, politically, Ireland was by right as distinct from England as was Scotland. Domvile did not foresee the 1707 Act of Union that would undo that contention. He also argued that the king was supreme over the English Parliament; understandably, he did not foresee the Glorious Revolution in 1688–89 and the theoretical as well as practical primacy of parliamentary power that it ushered in.[26]

With the advantage of hindsight we can see that it was futile as well as anachronistic to view the original twelfth-century English-Irish tie through a seventeenth-century constitutionalist lens. From 1172 to his death in 1189, Henry II had been called both "lord" and "king" of Ireland.[27] So too with his son John from 1177 until John's death in 1216, including the years when John's elder brother Richard was king of England. John did not have full authority over Ireland when his father was alive or when Richard sat on the throne, so the matter of title could easily become perplexing. Moreover, from its inception the Irish Parlia-

---

25. Schuyler, Parliament and the British Empire, 85. Caroline Robbins, *The Eighteenth-Century Commonwealthman* (Cambridge: Harvard University Press, 1959), 140, also noted that Molyneux's arguments had problems, but she is more charitable than Schuyler. Robbins in fact included Molyneux in her group of "Real Whigs," men of genuine constitutional concerns. W. Atwood, *The History, and Reasons, of the Dependency of Ireland upon the Imperial Crown of England* (London: Dan. Brown, 1698), critiqued Molyneux's interpretation of Irish history and offered in its place one that was not necessarily any better. There were simply too many lacunae in the historical record for either side to present simple, incontrovertible proof of its case. Atwood studied law at Gray's Inn before joining the Bar; he went on to become chief justice of New York. Even though he was unsympathetic to Irish claims of right—and those of Scottish nationalists—he was a "Whig" defender of English liberties for Englishmen.

26. Domvile, "Disquisition," 15, 24.

27. Marie Therese Flanagan, *Irish Society, Anglo-Norman Settlers, and Angevin Kingship* Oxford: Clarendon Press, 1989), 254, 255, 281. Flanagan also points out that if Henry II had invaded Ireland in 1155, as he considered doing, he might have bestowed the island on his brother William afterward (p. 39), but it is doubtful that he would also have given up overlordship.

ment referred to Henry's successors as "King of England and France and lord of Ireland," a reference that could be read to mean that there truly was a distinction between king and lord. But those later monarchs were also referred to as "our lord sovereign the King," which diminished the distinction if it did not make it altogether meaningless.[28]

In all likelihood Henry II probably intended to keep the Angevin empire a single entity, insofar as possible, given his need to accommodate old or potential enemies and stave off disaffection. He teetered between diplomacy and conquest, in Ireland as elsewhere, when he felt threatened or sought to expand. Accordingly, he continued to treat Rory O'Connor as "king" of Connacht, and O'Connor dealt with lesser "kings" in the areas that he claimed as his own even after he submitted to Henry's authority in 1175. The tie of O'Connor and other Irish leaders to Henry II is not necessarily explicable in feudal terms. The conditions under which titles and lands were granted were vague and poorly understood, and ignored by the Anglo-Normans and Irish alike when it suited their purposes. Furthermore not all Irish landholders were mere vassals to Henry; some were themselves liege lords. To further confuse matters, Henry's Anglo-Norman vassals who had taken title to estates in Ireland may have held those lands under yet another understanding that could have differed from the ties that bound them to Henry in Wales or England.

Constitutional scholars have noted that some jurists in medieval England drew a distinction between *gubernaculum*, the king's right and power to govern, and *jurisdictio*, the existence of laws that bound him, laws theoretically beyond his autocratic control.[29] A king like Henry II exercised a personal *imperium* and saw himself as the fountain of justice as well as the source of legitimate authority. At the same time there was an expectation—if only from opportunistic rivals and a handful of jurists—that the king would not act arbitrarily even if he was absolute; he was pressured to observe the law that he helped define and enforce.

Institutionalization of the common law and growth of parliamentary power reinforced the tendency to set limits on the royal prerogative. And yet all of this occurred over centuries. The parliamentary procedures

---

28. Berry, ed., *Statutes*, 3:259 (3 Edward IV c. 102), where Edward IV is referred to both ways, in the same sentence. Also see the famous Kilkenny Statutes of 1366, where Edward III is referred to throughout as "our lord the King" in ibid., 1:431–469 (40 Edward III).

29. Charles Howard McIlwain, *Constitutionalism: Ancient and Modern*, rev. ed. (Ithaca: Cornell University Press, 1947), 67–92, who in discussing *gubernaculum* and *jurisdictio* followed in the footsteps of Henry de Bracton, a thirteenth-century English jurist.

pointed to by Domvile could not have dated back to Henry II because the first Irish Parliament did not sit until the end of the thirteenth century, long after Henry's death. If changes can be said to have been already well under way by the reign of Henry II, they still had not reached full definition by the seventeenth century. The growth of constitutionalism, the notion that there are some inherent rights beyond the reach of Crown or Parliament, is difficult enough to trace in England alone. When placed in the context of English-Irish relations, the question of constitutionality becomes just that much more complicated. Appeals to the sanctity of custom or the immanence of Irish rights depended on an easily explicable past that did not exist. Those who pursued constitutional solutions to political problems could stumble into a labyrinth of false leads and dead ends.

Still, Irish constitutionalism was no sudden invention of William Domvile or William Molyneux or those who followed them. Anglo-Irish Protestants in the eighteenth century placed themselves firmly within a constitutional tradition established long before, dating back at least to the Irish Parliament in 1460 and more deeply entrenched in the seventeenth century by Patrick Darcy and other Catholics as well as by Protestants. Darcy did not once use the word constitution in his published *Argument*. His contentions, however, incorporated most components of what Irish constitutionalists through the next century came to view as the Irish constitution, to wit: that from 1172 on Ireland had been a commonwealth as well as a kingdom, governed by the rule of law; that Ireland's legal tradition was linked to Magna Carta and rights enjoyed under common law, custom, royal proclamation, and parliamentary statute; that the Crown and all royal officials were bound to honor those rights; and, finally, that the Irish were a free people entitled to their own parliament, which had the sole power to legislate for them.

The 1644 "Declaration" did not talk expressly of a constitution either, but it repeated Darcy's assertions, including the notion that Ireland, with the spread of English common law to its shores in the twelfth century, was protected by customs "beyond the memory of man."[30] Adding a refinement not found in Darcy's *Argument*, the "Declaration" distinguished between the crowns of England and Ireland, a distinction that it claimed dated from the reign of Henry II. For the "Declaration" as for Darcy, Henry's reign was crucial, both for the original tie to England and for Ireland's status as a kingdom; neither drew attention to Henry VIII's 1541 proclamation. So too with William Molyneux in

---

30. "Declaration," Harris, ed., *Hibernica*, Part II, p. 13.

Creating a Constitutional Tradition 27

1698. Granted that under Henry VIII the title became *Rex Hiberniae*; as far as Molyneux was concerned, *Dominus Hiberniae*, the title used by monarchs from Henry II until Henry VIII, could be understood to mean "lord" or "king." The difference was of little consequence, a mere formality.

Quoting from the English jurist Thomas Littleton, the 1644 "Declaration" had stipulated that English common law, as extended to Ireland by Henry II, was based upon reason and God's law in addition to immemorial custom, thereby injecting into Irish constitutionalism a transconstitutional element. It only remained for Molyneux to cap this discourse on Irish rights with the word "constitution." Molyneux's Irish constitution, like the English constitution that inspired it, was not a written document. What fell within its purview was determined by those who believed in its existence. Having formalized the constitutional arguments of his predecessors, Molyneux later became the most-quoted authority among eighteenth-century Anglo-Irish leaders who took ideas once articulated by Catholics as well as Protestants and made them their own. Molyneux's *Case* also became a veritable lightning rod for counterarguments.

Like his constitutionalist predecessors, Molyneux tried to find meaning in what were very loosely applied terms; he sought certainty in what were vaguely defined and constantly changing relationships dating back some five centuries. Even as late as the seventeenth century, the Irish Parliament did not have a pure, unbroken pedigree. It had ceased to exist for a short period during the 1650s, when the Irish were given minimal representation in the "Barebones" Parliament. After the Restoration, Charles II had seen fit not to call the Irish Parliament into session for most of his reign. By Molyneux's own admission there were at least two times when the English Parliament had rightfully legislated for Ireland: in 1660 and 1689. In both cases, Molyneux contended, the Irish Parliament was not sitting because Irish affairs were unsettled and the English Parliament had, in effect, legislated to return Irish life to normal—which meant that Ireland, once it regained its composure as a kingdom, would be outside the English Parliament's purview. Acts passed at other times by the English Parliament, or even in 1660 or 1689 if they were not in Ireland's best interests, were void unless specifically recognized by the Irish Parliament.[31] That English parliamentarians would see this argument as vexing if not specious should not be too surprising.

If Molyneux's contentions about the Irish Parliament did not per-

---

31. Molyneux, *Case*, 85–86, 91–93.

suade English readers, neither did his discussion of Ireland's connection through the Crown. Like the "Declaration" and Domvile's "Disquisition," Molyneux devoted special attention to Henry II's tie to the Irish "people," their entitlement to the *"Liberties of England,"* and the passing of title to John. The Irish people, he concluded (as had the two earlier tracts), had been tied to Henry II through voluntary submission, and Henry had passed on dominion to John.[32] As Samuel Mayart had shown in response to the "Declaration" in 1644, and as Molyneux's critics would repeat in 1698, the historical record was spotty. If John held title to Ireland before he was king, how could Ireland be a kingdom? And besides, even allowing Molyneux's title transfer argument, what would happen to it if the current monarchs, William and Mary, chose to grant title to the English Parliament? Henry II had not sought Irish permission when he "gave" Ireland to John, so would William and Mary now need permission to part with it? Since the Glorious Revolution had altered the connection between the Crown and Parliament, with the Crown now "in" Parliament, what did that mean for Irish claims that Ireland was a distinct kingdom connected to England only through the person of the king (or queen)?

Molyneux tripped over himself again and again, and won no friends in Westminster and Whitehall, even if many fellow members of the Irish Parliament ignored or could not see the inconsistencies of his *Case*. They were not sitting at the time and did not publicly support Molyneux, perhaps because they guessed how the *Case* would be received in London. The English House of Commons determined that the book was "of dangerous Consequence to the Crown and People of England" and ordered that its author be punished. "The consequences of such positions and proceedings will be so fatal to this kingdom, and even Ireland itself," the English Commons concluded, that "they need not be enlarged on, or aggravated."[33] Commons was convinced that the type of thinking

32. Ibid., 47–48, for the people and their liberties; 52–53, for passage of title to John. Molyneux also talked about rights by conquest, but only after establishing their secondary importance and, taken alone, their inadequacy.
33. William Cobbett et al., eds., *The Parliamentary History of England*, 36 vols. (London: T. C. Hansard, 1806–20), 5:1182. There is apparently no hard evidence that the English Commons ordered the *Case* to be burned. Even so, a later generation of Anglo-Irish Patriots would state as fact that the public burning took place, and they used that "fact" in their criticisms of British policy. Walter Hussey Burgh referred to the burning in a 10 October 1775 speech in the Irish Commons, as did Henry Grattan in (one version of) his famous Commons speech of 16 April 1782, and Henry Flood the year before. They had not invented the story. On 10 February 1766, during debate in the British House of Lords on the bill that would become the 1766 Declaratory Act, the earl of Mansfield, no

represented in the *Case* had prompted the Irish Parliament to "re-enact" a statute that had recently passed the English Parliament and been applied to Ireland. Furthermore, the Irish House of Lords had at the same moment sought to define and defend its appellate rights. In English and perhaps Irish minds, these two very real challenges to English power in Ireland were linked to the theoretical threat presented in the *Case*.[34] From the English perspective, its timing as well as its tone could not have been worse.

Molyneux died soon after the *Case* was printed, so he escaped possible censure. The Irish Parliament that assembled in September 1698 after publication of the *Case* took no action against him. Its members reaffirmed their loyalty to the king and their attachment to the empire. They said nothing about the *Case,* nor were they pressed by Whitehall or Westminster to do anything about it. The hope in both London and Dublin was that the issues Molyneux raised would fade away. But they did not. Some Irish leaders at least silently assented to Molyneux's claims. Molyneux lived on in memory as the leading spokesman for Anglo-Irish Protestant constitutionalism. He wanted to defend what he took to be Irish constitutional rights and find some underlying justification to support his view. He searched the Irish past primarily as a lawyer attempting to make his case, an advocate seeking forensic evidence rather than a historian with a more detached view. Too good a man to simply fabricate his arguments, he was also too selective in his use of evidence and had no doubt reached his conclusions before he had even begun to do his research. If that was a major failing, it was one he shared with most others before and after him who searched through Irish history for "facts" to justify their constitutional opinions.

Molyneux's primary concern all along was to protect Irish interests and provide Ireland with some sort of constitutional guarantees and representative government. The *Case* barely mentioned strictures against the wool trade pending in the English Parliament, but its timing was influenced by fears of what the Woolens Act would do to Irish economic

---

friend to Irish parliamentary pretensions, alluded to Molyneux's book being burned. See Cobbett et al., eds., *Parliamentary History,* 16:177. Kelly, "Molyneux and the Spirit of Liberty," 138–39, states that Charles Lucas helped popularize the story in 1749, and that rumors of the burning first cropped up thirty years before that.

34. See the discussion in McGuire, "Politics, Opinion and the Irish Constitution," 140–53, which stresses that King's actions and arguments in the House of Lords were every bit as important as the position taken by Molyneux and the feelings of members in the Irish Commons. Also see Simms, *William Molyneux,* 102–19, for the *Case,* its reception in 1698, and subsequent use by Irish nationalists, and idem, *Colonial Nationalism, 1698–1776* (Cork: Mercier Press, 1976).

life. Molyneux knew that the Irish were at a disadvantage so long as they were in the empire but with little say in imperial legislation. A separate but equal Irish Parliament would, he probably hoped, make the empire more truly reciprocal. He was not anti-empire, just as he was not anti-English. If the *Case* was bold it was also diffident in its language, with Molyneux appealing as a supplicant to William III. Though he was not a supplicant to the English Parliament, he did his best to avoid offending "that August Senate," going so far as to pledge his "Submissive Acquiescence" to whatever Westminster decided about the merits of his *Case*.[35] He was strongly attached to the principles of the Glorious Revolution, and he was equally attached to an Anglo-Irish Protestant Ascendancy that depended on English power for its continued survival. Therefore, he might not have objected to a parliamentary union with England if he had felt that would have been the best way to secure constitutional guarantees of basic rights, representative government, and the protection of Irish economic interests.

Bishop William King, who had taken the lead in pushing the issue of appellate rights in the Irish House of Lords in 1698, had similar views. King and Molyneux are linked in that their first loyalty was to Irish rights, at least insofar as they applied to Anglo-Irish Protestants. They were not so different from others who, though they felt as strongly the need to protect Ireland, thought that the *only* way to do that was through parliamentary union. For example, Irish Jacobite Thomas Sheridan, author of a 1677 *Discourse,* called for parliamentary union between England, Ireland, and Scotland.[36] At least one Englishman, William Petty,

---

35. Molyneux, *Case,* 24, for his "Acquiescence." On pp. 83–84, he noted that there had been times when the Irish had been represented in the English Parliament and the English Parliament had during those periods legislated for Ireland. He then observed: "If from these last mention'd Records, it be concluded that the Parliament of England may *Bind Ireland*; it must also be Allow'd that the People of Ireland ought to have their Representatives in the Parliament of England. And this, I believe we should be willing enough to embrace; but this is an Happiness we can hardly hope for" (84). This passage is often cited as evidence that Molyneux would have looked favorably on a parliamentary union between England and Ireland. It proved embarrassing enough to the champions of Irish parliamentary independence in 1782 that they had it struck from the edition published that year. But perhaps Molyneux, realizing full well that the English had no interest in having the Irish sit with them in Westminster, included the statement to accentuate his moderate tone; it might even have been added (as in the manuscript copy it appears to have been inserted as an afterthought) as an ironic twist, or as a sop to potential critics. Molyneux wanted to believe in the possibility of a single English-Irish interest, yet he also seemed to think that Ireland could—and should—be responsible for its own legislation. Indeed, his paragraph on p. 83, where he talks about Ireland in the early days, seems to be saying that the time when Ireland could or needed to be represented in the English Parliament had passed.

36. [Thomas Sheridan], *A Discourse on the Rise and Power of Parliaments* (London, 1677; reprint ed., Port Washington, N.Y.: Kennikat Press, 1970; from the text edited by Saxe Bannister in 1870).

concurred. Petty had made his way to Ireland during the 1650s and rose to prominence in the same fashion as had his more famous predecessor, Sir John Davies. Petty conducted the "Down Survey" to facilitate distribution of confiscated lands that he, like Davies many years earlier, also obtained for himself. Petty knew of Davies and thought a great deal of him. Like Davies, he saw the need to break the back of native Irish Catholic power and build up Anglo-Irish Protestantism in its place. He agreed, as had Davies, with programs designed to redistribute offices and privileges as well as land. He emphasized kindly incentive more than Davies had, however: he wanted the Irish and English to intermarry and he wanted them to trade as equals. Most important, he urged:

That if both Kingdoms, now two, were put into one, under one Legislative Power and Parliament, the Members whereof should be in the same proportion that the Power and Wealth of each Nation are, there would be no longer danger such a Parliament should do anything to the prejudice of the English interest in Ireland; nor could the Irish ever complain of Partiality, when they shall be freely and proportionably represented in all Legislatures.[37]

Anglo-Irish parliamentary union, just one theme in the Sheridan and Petty tracts, was the sole subject of a pamphlet that appeared in 1703. This brief treatise, attributed to Irish M.P. Henry Maxwell, argued that without a union the Irish would be forever resentful and Ireland would have to be ruled perpetually as a conquered province.[38] Maxwell made what were by then the usual arguments about the benefit of union to both parties, emphasizing that parliamentary union could pave the way for the elimination of trade restrictions; that in turn would bring more commerce, increased manufacturing, higher rents, and less poverty. Greater anglicization, too, would follow, thereby bringing an end to disruptive cultural differences. Maxwell even played on English fears of standing armies by contending that, so long as Ireland bubbled with discontent, troops would have to remain there. Maintaining a standing army over a people with diminished freedoms would prove hazardous to the English themselves, he warned.

A parliamentary union did take place in 1707—between England and

---

37. Sir William Petty, *The Political Anatomy of Ireland, with the Establishment for that Kingdom and Verbum Sapienti* (London: D. Brown and W. Rogers, 1691), 31. In his 1687 "A Treatise of Ireland," written fifteen years after *The Political Anatomy*, but not finally published until 1899, Petty recommended that most of the Irish be removed to England, with the island being converted into what in effect would be a huge cattle ranch. The Anglo-Irish elite would not have cared for this at all.

38. [Henry Maxwell], *An Essay Towards an Union of Ireland with England* (London: Timothy Goodwin, 1703). If Maxwell was the author, he wrote as if he were an Englishman.

Scotland, not England and Ireland. The Maxwells, Sheridans, and Pettys had not been persuasive enough, it would appear. For its part, the Irish Parliament had been receptive to the idea. Receptive to union did not necessarily mean enthusiastic about its prospects, however. The House of Commons "representation" to the queen in 1703 was much more ambiguous in its wording than the text produced by the House of Lords. The peers congratulated Anne on her accession to the throne, swore their loyalty, noted the many problems besetting their land, and concluded, "[A]s we are sensible, that our Preservation is owing to our being united to the Crown of England, so we are convinced it would tend to our further Security and Happiness, to have a more comprehensive and intire Union with that Kingdom."[39] Commons did not draft its resolution until October 20, almost three weeks after passage of the resolution in Lords. Commons expressed loyalty to Anne and noted the same problems, especially the dangers posed by the "Papists," but worded its resolution differently because it embraced the idea of union much more reluctantly. Parliamentary union, in fact, appeared to be a second choice. First choice was more frequent meetings of the Irish Parliament and a restoration to "a full Enjoyment of our Constitution."[40] Commons, making a distinction that Lords did not, also characterized the existing English-Irish tie as being through the "Imperial Crown of England," showing that members were still concerned with the intricacies of constitutional disquisition and were familiar with Molyneux's arguments as well as the stand taken by their forerunners in 1640. They were much more ambivalent about union than were their colleagues in the upper house, although by their willingness to go along with union—if it came—they were less attached to their seats than a later generation would be.

The Irish Parliament was not in session when the Act of Union joining the English and Scottish parliaments was rushed through, although that mattered little. Scotland was in a much stronger position than Ireland and could force the issue; Ireland could not. English M.P.s had been reluctant to allow the Scots to sit in Westminster and were in no mood to dilute their power further.[41] Ireland would remain isolated and its

39. *Journals of the House of Lords of the Kingdom of Ireland*, 8 vols. (Dublin: William Sleater, 1779–1800), 2:8.
40. *House of Commons Journal*, 2:342. As Francis Godwin James, *Ireland in the Empire, 1688–1770* (Cambridge: Harvard University Press, 1973), 27, pointed out, the Irish Parliament might have been more assertive in the 1690s if it had not been so dependent on English support. Anglo-Irish Protestants lost control from 1689 to 1690, and their fears had not dissipated by 1703. Indeed, the most restrictive penal laws were yet to be passed.
41. McGuire, "Politics, Opinion and the Irish Constitution," 164–76.

status confused. Some viewed it as: a "sister kingdom" to England, equal (theoretically, anyway) in rights and prerogatives; others considered it a kingdom, but a kingdom subordinate to England (now Great Britain with the Act of Union); and still others dismissed it as a mere colony, no more, no less, than other colonies like those in America.

Anglo-Irish Protestants, therefore, took on an almost schizophrenic personality. They were very conscious, even proud, of their English heritage, and in Ireland they wore their Englishness as a badge of cultural superiority. Most were realistic enough to know that their tie to Britain could not safely be severed. Because of Ireland's very nearness, and because of its importance as a source of raw materials and as a market for exports, the British would not let it go without a fight—a fight that Anglo-Irish Protestants did not want anyway because they knew that their fate in Ireland hinged on a British policy that propped them up. They needed the places, the pensions, the trade, even the troops whose presence they often resented, in order to maintain themselves as overlords of an increasingly disenfranchised, underprivileged Catholic majority.

At the same time they were very jealous of their rights and prerogatives, those they enjoyed and those that they believed they were being denied. Men like William Molyneux supported the Glorious Revolution and styled themselves as Whigs in the English fashion. And yet the Glorious Revolution had not, they felt, been fully extended to them. Molyneux's *Case*, the contemporaneous claims of the Irish Commons to "re-enact" legislation sent over from London, and the Irish lords' defense of their appellate rights came after the Glorious Revolution, after Ireland had been freed of Stuart "tyranny." The lord lieutenant appointed by William and Mary prorogued the Irish Parliament in 1692 because Commons, much to his dismay, claimed the sole right to originate a money bill. In so doing it seemed to be indirectly challenging Poynings' Law and Crown prerogative. Molyneux's tract six years later and the positions taken by the Irish Lords and Commons were part of a continuum; they were the unavoidable outcomes of unresolved constitutional issues and clashing interests.

Their many frustrations and resentments notwithstanding, the Anglo-Irish stopped short of challenging Crown power too forcefully; they even moderated their tone, except on rare occasions, when dealing with the English (after 1707, British) Parliament. By the end of the seventeenth century, they had begun to emphasize the powers and privileges of their own Parliament, and they had begun to see that Parliament as the primary repository of their wider constitutional rights. But members of the

Irish Parliament had not yet begun to equate their rights as a people with the rights of their Parliament; otherwise, they would not have voted for a parliamentary union in 1703. And the constitutionalists among them did not speak with one voice. If, for example, Molyneux could not accept that Ireland was a subordinate kingdom, author and judge Richard Cox could, yet Cox considered himself no less a defender of Irish rights. He differed from Molyneux on what rights Ireland should insist upon.[42] Ironically enough, the English Parliament helped swing Irish opinion to Molyneux's side and brought upon itself the agitation leading to Grattan's Parliament in 1782. By avoiding parliamentary union with Ireland in 1707, the English helped push the Anglo-Irish into viewing their Parliament as the basic protector of their rights.

Molyneux believed that there could be a united English-Irish interest, a single imperial community. Part of that belief stemmed from his conviction that Celtic and Catholic Ireland would be absorbed in the process of anglicization. Assimilation would be so complete, he wanted to believe, that Ireland really would become a mirror of England. Molyneux, William King, and their associates supported penal laws and Catholic exclusion, under the assumption that Catholicism was more a superstition than a genuine religion and that it would disappear as enlightened Protestantism spread across the land. They were wrong. They misread the resiliency of Roman Catholicism and the survival of an Irish sense of distinctiveness that was not identical to their own. Ethnicity, by the end of the seventeenth century, had been eclipsed by religion as the primary dividing line separating those in power from those left out. But that was only because Irish with a Celtic or Old English background could, if they renounced their non-English, Catholic ways, become a part of the Anglo-Irish Protestant ruling class. Exclusion was the price paid by those who did not put aside their Irishness: religious difference became the most convenient, most detectable, sign of cultural difference.

Anglo-Irish Protestants denied Irish Catholics any part in the true constitutionalist tradition. Molyneux defended the rights of Anglo-Irish

---

42. Richard Cox, *Hibernia Anglicana*, 2d ed. (London: Joseph Watts, 1692), characterized the stand taken by the Irish Commons in 1641 as "fruitless Declarations" and "needless Queries" (Part II, p. 74), yet in so doing did not see himself as an enemy to Irish liberties. Also see the *Aphorisms relating to the Kingdom of Ireland* (London: Joseph Watts, 1689), attributed to Cox. They were presented to the English parliament in 1689 in a bold attempt to curry favor. Here Cox, as he would in 1692, emphasized Irish subordination to England and the need of a strong English presence in Ireland. (At the time he wrote *Aphorisms*, James II still controlled Ireland. Cox wanted William III to send troops over to defeat him.)

Protestantism, but he had little sympathy for those outside that protective umbrella. He did not link the Kilkenny Confederates to his own generation of men who were at once nationalists and loyal citizens of empire.[43] If writers like Molyneux did see an Irish revolutionary tradition, they equated it with the rebelliousness of the 1641 Ulster uprising. They tried to distance themselves from such dangerous radicalism. Ironically, so too had most of the Kilkenny Confederates. Not since the fourteenth century had there been a sizeable group committed to the revolutionary act of fighting for independence. Virtually all, from the native Irish and Old English recusants of the seventeenth-century Kilkenny confederation to the Anglo-Irish Protestants of the eighteenth-century Ascendancy, tried to style themselves as moderates, nationalists protecting their constitutional rights within the British empire.

Should Anglo-Irish Protestants have tried to develop a nationalistic spirit at all? One of the English critics of Molyneux's *Case* thought not. He urged Anglo-Irish Protestants to drop their pretensions and consider themselves colonists instead. To do so would not only be a better reflection of historical reality, it would also better protect their present and future interests. The logic of Molyneux's own reasoning dictated that he condemn Henry II's "invasion" and call on the native Irish to throw off the English yoke, because they had seen their power erode ever since the twelfth century. Eventually they lost it altogether to Anglo-Irish Protestants who, working hand-in-glove with the English, had squeezed the native Irish off of their land and out of public life by the end of the seventeenth century.

> If Ireland was granted [by Henry II] to the Native Irish and Old English, as an Absolute, Independent Kingdom, and was never since re-conquered by England; the right of administering the publick Affairs of that Government (under the King) ought to remain in them, since 'twas never given up to you by their Consents; and then they have no reason to consider you otherwise, than as having no Title more than Usurpers and Oppressors, and that you may justly be treated as such whenever they are in a condition to do it.[44]

43. Molyneux was friends with and seemed to share the views of Edmund Borlase, whose *The reduction of Ireland to the crown of England* (London: R. Clavel, 1675) sharply condemned the "rebels" of 1641 and had little good to say about the Kilkenny Confederates. See the transcript of Molyneux's letter to Borlase of 22 November 1679 in the Borlase Papers, MS. 190, Gilbert Library, Dublin City Library. Molyneux's father fought against the Confederates in the 1640s. Molyneux himself was driven from office by Tyrconnell in the 1680s and left for London when James II came to Ireland. Cox, *Hibernia Anglicana*, was also sharply critical of the 1641 rebellion and attached little significance to the Kilkenny confederation. Here Cox and Molyneux were not very far apart in their thinking.

44. *An Answer to Mr. Molyneux* (London: Rich. Parker, 1698), in "The Epistle Dedicatory."

This author had his own interpretive problems, especially in assuming that the Anglo-Irish would be better off and happier as colonists—like those contented Americans, he seemed to think. But he did raise an important point. Irish nationalism as it had matured by the end of the seventeenth century was too exclusive and too contradictory. It was based on natural rights arguments and claims to freedoms that under an encompassing Irish constitution were not universally accepted; it made allusions in theory to a popular sovereignty that it denied in practice; it was based on an overly selective and thereby faulty reading of the past; it was too imprecise in defining a national interest.[45]

What is more, Anglo-Irish constitutional nationalists could not completely separate themselves from the radical, revolutionary side of their ideology. This difficulty is readily apparent in a pamphlet debate between two Anglo-Irish clergymen, one a high Tory, a defender of the Stuarts and the divine right theories of Robert Filmer, the other a Whig defender of the Glorious Revolution and the ideas of John Locke. Both anonymously wrote pamphlets soon after James II was driven from Ireland by troops serving William III. The Whig, William King, was rising in stature and power, soon to become a leading voice in the Irish House of Lords. Charles Leslie, the Tory, was on the decline, like the deposed monarch he defended; he spent years on the run for his caustic attacks on the Williamite accession.

45. For example, "A Declaration," Domvile's "Disquisition," and Molyneux's *Case* all referred to Sir Edward Coke's *Institutes* and most often to his ruling in Calvin's Case. Yet they picked and chose what they wanted to accept and reject, concluding that Coke was right here or wrong there—depending upon whether Coke's view supported or contradicted their own. They probably did not think that they were distorting the past; on the contrary, they seem to have been convinced that they were right and that their historical editing was valid. For the anomalies in Coke's arguments see Black, "Constitution of Empire," and J. W. Gough, *Fundamental Law in English Constitutional History* (Oxford: Clarendon Press, 1955), 30–47. Even Coke's sympathetic biographer, Catherine Drinker Bowen, conceded in *The Lion and the Throne* (Boston: Little, Brown, 1956), 293, that if "legal consistency is a virtue, then Coke did not have it." Martin Stephen Flaherty, "The Empire Strikes Back: *Annesley v. Sherlock* and the Triumph of Parliamentary Supremacy," *Columbia Law Review* 87 (1987): 593–622, builds on Black and contends that the subordination of the Irish Parliament to Westminster implicit in the Glorious Revolution was not realized until the aftermath of the *Annesley* case, when the Irish Lords were stripped of their appellate rights. From then on the "Cokean" view, where a local parliament could argue that it was tied to Whitehall directly with no subordination to Westminster, lost out to what became Blackstone's position. Also see J. G. A. Pocock, *The Ancient Constitution and the Feudal Law* (Cambridge: Cambridge University Press, 1957; revised ed., 1989), and the revisionist essay by Martyn P. Thompson, "The History of Fundamental Law in Political Thought from the French Wars of Religion to the American Revolution" *American Historical Review* 91 (1986): 1103–28. For the real and mythical place of Magna Carta in all of this, see William H. Dunham Jr., "Magna Carta and British Constitutionalism," in Samuel E. Thorne et al., *The Great Charter* (New York: Pantheon Books, 1965), 20–47.

King's tract defended those Irish who had opposed James II, and it denounced the doctrine of passive obedience. King quoted Dutch jurist Hugo Grotius; he even tried to turn the arguments of those who adhered to passive obedience, to show that "if a King designs to root out a People, or destroy one main part of his Subjects in favour of another whom he loves better, that they may prevent it by opposing him with Force." That is what had happened with James II in Ireland and that is why James lost the right to rule and why the people were obliged to oppose him. "The mischiefs of tamely submitting to the tyranny and usurpation of a Governor," King opined, "may be worse and have more dangerous consequences to the Commonwealth, than a War." King was careful to qualify the right of rebellion with "in some cases" and to indict James with a sweeping charge: that he had "designed to destroy and utterly ruin the Protestant Religion, the Liberty and Property of the Subjects in general, the English Interest in Ireland in particular, and alter the very Frame and Constitution of the Government."[46] By his reasoning, Irish supporters of the Glorious Revolution had not been revolutionaries at all; rather, they had restored constitutional government and re-established the proper relationship of rulers to ruled.

Leslie countered that King erred in promoting "the old Rotten, Rebel, Commonwealth Principles." Any notion "[t]hat all Power is from the People: That Kings are but their Deputies, and therefore are accountable to the People, and may be deposed by them" was not only wrong but, worse, dangerously foolish. Such thinking "is calculated for the Destruction of Mankind," he preached, "by setting up such Principles as countenance Eternal Rebellions, and afford Pretences for War and Confusion to the end of the World."[47] Leslie's protests were as shrill as King's contentions were self-justifying. Leslie's own philosophical shortcomings notwithstanding, he raised a key point. By King's own argument, the rebels of 1641 had had the right to rise up; by the same logic, those Irish who followed James II in 1689 had the right to choose their monarch. Like the 1641 rebels, they should not be condemned for fighting to defend what they took to be their constitutional rights. Leslie did not believe that the 1641 rebellion had been justified. King did not either;

---

46. [William King], *The State of the Protestants of Ireland Under the Late King James's Government*, 3d ed., (London: Samuel Roycroft, 1692); quotes from pp. 2, 5.

47. [Charles Leslie], *An Answer To a Book, Intituled, The State of the Protestants of Ireland* (London, 1692); quotes from pp. 1–3. Leslie may also have written *Considerations of Importance to Ireland* (1699), which agreed with Molyneux's basic thesis but criticized Molyneux's acceptance as binding of a 1691 act passed by the English Parliament that served to exclude Catholics from the Irish Parliament. He believed that Molyneux had undercut his own argument.

he dismissed it as a "wicked" uprising, which Leslie undoubtedly knew. King supported the land confiscations that followed it, just as he supported the further erosion of Catholic power in the aftermath of the Glorious Revolution.

Leslie caught King in the same trap in which Molyneux's critics would snare him six years later. By insisting on their constitutional rights, Anglo-Irish nationalists embraced a theory of revolution, even if they did so unwittingly and even if they claimed to resist London's authority only to protect old rights and old freedoms, not to introduce new ones. By emphasizing government as a contractual relationship between the governed and their governors, by emphasizing their right to representation and a protection of their interests, and by characterizing themselves as a free people living in a real kingdom, they fostered and added to ideas that could be appropriated by others. Without realizing it, they had paved the way for the United Irishmen of the 1790s and the Catholic nationalists of an even later generation—the very groups that would spurn their brand of constitutionalism and try to bring their progeny down.

CHAPTER 2

Patriots and Popular Politics

WHOEVER *takes the Trouble of inquiring, will find, all the* English *Parlements, who have* presumed *to* impose laws *upon* Ireland, without the consent of the People, *were of the* slavish *and* corrupt *stamp . . . and the* Irish Parlements, *at the same time, were not much better.*
Charles Lucas, 1748.[1]

W. E. H. Lecky characterized Ireland at the opening of the eighteenth century as a society divided against itself, a powder keg ready to explode. The Glorious Revolution "had thrown all the resources and government of Ireland into the hands of a small Protestant minority, but it had not given that minority any real security," he observed. "The ruling class" of the Anglo-Irish Protestant Ascendancy, he continued, "were thinly scattered among a hostile population" and their position was "exceedingly precarious." The "hostile" Catholic population was biding its time, waiting for the right moment to rebel. "Though all active resistance had ceased, the passions and memories of a succession of ferocious civil wars still burnt fiercely beneath the surface of Irish society."[2]

Dramatic stuff, this, but somewhat misleading. The actual scene was more complicated and less volatile than what Lecky painted. Lecky wrote about the beginning of the eighteenth century with the end of that century in mind. By 1700 the English government had worked for Anglo-Irish "security" as much as any distant government could that

---

1. Charles Lucas, *The Political Constitutions of Great-Britain and Ireland*, 2 vols. (London, 1751), Address X, p. 128.
2. William Edward Hartpole Lecky, *A History of Ireland in the Eighteenth Century*, 5 vols. (London: Longmans, Green, and Co., 1913–16; orig. ed., 1892), 1:136.

was trying to rule more by persuasion than by force, though it did not satisfy those Anglo-Irish leaders who felt that the 1691 Treaty of Limerick failed to sufficiently punish Catholics, and who therefore delayed ratification until they could exact a heavier toll. If Protestants lacked security, it was as much because of internal divisions as for lack of London support, and because they had waited too long to share power with their erstwhile enemies. Security was not really London's to give.

Anglo-Irish Protestants were not always uniform in their approach to Catholic rights, but they were more united on that issue than they were on most others. Presbyterians in Ulster were generally Scots-Irish as well as Protestant, yet they were penalized for their religious beliefs—if not as harshly as Catholics, then enough to keep them restive. They and other Dissenters resented being discriminated against. Neither were the ranks of the religiously orthodox, those who were at least nominally members of the Church of Ireland, necessarily tight and well-formed. There were power struggles between those associated with the London-appointed administration and those in opposition, an Irish version of "court" and "country" divisions in England, and there were factions that revolved around great families and the seats they controlled in the Irish Parliament. A further complicating feature by the 1740s would be the rising political aspirations of the merchant and artisan classes in Dublin, who were by and large Protestant and had no religious score to settle with the ruling class.

Catholics no doubt harbored deep resentments, but they did not always define political issues in religious terms. Some joined the established church and thereby escaped repressive legislation. The repressive legislation itself was enacted gradually.[3] By design the Williamite confiscations further eroded Catholic power, as did subsequent penal laws, which eventually excluded Catholics from sitting in parliament and voting in parliamentary elections. Through most of the eighteenth century, however, the typical Catholic response was hope for improvement through peaceful means and under Protestant direction. Catholics hoped that, just as loss of power had been gradual, some power would gradually be returned to them. For that to happen, they knew that they had to show they no longer posed a threat to Protestants and that religious divisions would therefore not impinge on public policy. To do that they had to avoid taking a threatening stance.

Still, even if Lecky overstated and oversimplified, he was correct in noting that eighteenth-century Ireland had many pressing problems. By

---

3. See J. G. Simms, "Irish Catholics and the Parliamentary Franchise, 1692–1728," *Irish Historical Studies* 12 (1960): 28–37.

the latter half of the century, it had become clear to a growing number of British and Irish politicians that the basic question of Ireland's constitutional relationship to Britain had to be answered. It was also clear that the prevailing British and Irish views were incompatible. Passage of the Woolens Act in 1699 had only deepened Irish longing for greater economic autonomy; passage of the Declaratory Act of 1720 only pushed the Irish toward a desire for greater political freedom. The Declaratory Act proved especially offensive to Anglo-Irish constitutionalists, stating that

the said kingdom of Ireland hath been, is and of right ought to be, subordinate unto and dependent upon the imperial crown of Great Britain, as being inseparably united and annexed thereunto, and that the king's majesty, by and with the advice and consent of the lords spiritual and temporal and commons of Great Britain in parliament assembled, had, hath, and of right ought to have full power and authority to make laws and statutes of sufficient force and validity to bind the kingdom and people of Ireland.[4]

Poynings' Law had been designed to keep the Irish executive in line. This Declaratory Act was passed primarily to strip the Irish House of Lords of its appellate jurisdiction in the aftermath of *Annesley v. Sherlock,* in which the British Lords had intervened and ruled on a case originating in Ireland. Neither piece of legislation had been intended to control the Irish Commons. After the Declaratory Act's passage, there were those in London who toyed with the idea of eliminating the Irish Parliament altogether, but British politicians made no move to do so until the end of the century, and then only when certain of support in Dublin. British power over Ireland, even British power in Ireland, had grown over the centuries; nonetheless, a sense of distinctiveness remained and grew apace among the Anglo-Irish. In the ensuing competition between British imperialists and anglicized Irishmen, those Irishmen expressed their grievances in constitutional terms. The continued existence of an Irish Parliament, regardless of how limited in power, insured that Irish constitutionalists would have a forum for their arguments and an institution around which they could rally.

English reaction to Molyneux's *Case* did not, in Irish eyes, discredit Molyneux's argument. In protesting against the British Lords acting as an appellate court in *Annesley v. Sherlock,* the Irish peers—with the "lords spiritual" rather than the "lords temporal" taking the lead, interestingly enough—resorted to the same constitutional language as

---

4. (Great Britain), *The Statutes at Large,* 47 vols. (London: M. Barkett, et al., 1769–1809) at 6 George I c.5.

Molyneux. Contending that the British peers encroached upon royal authority as well as their own, they complained that "if the Power of Judicature may, by a Vote of the *British* Lords, be taken away from the Parliament of *Ireland,* no reason can be given, why the same Lords may not, in the like Manner, deprive us of the Benefit of our whole Constitution."⁵ Significantly, the Declaratory Act did not change their understanding of what was constitutionally correct. Obviously, despite their undeniable political subordination, there were those in the Irish Lords and Commons who clung to the notion of a constitutional tie based on equal partnership in the empire. They continued to call Ireland a kingdom, not a colony; they continued to argue that the only constitutional tie was through the "imperial" Crown; and they continued to contend that the Irish Parliament was by right independent. Some even warned that British policy would drive Irish Protestants and Catholics to combine in a common cause.⁶

The British were not completely unresponsive, though the responses they made often added to the problem. Presaging their reaction to the American crisis in the 1760s, leading British politicians seemed to think that Irish constitutional concerns would shrink in importance as Ireland was more fully incorporated into the commercial empire. Constitutional quibbling, concluded many, stemmed from economic grievances; eliminate one and the other would soon cease. Thus, they reasoned, the Irish could be turned to the manufacture of linen from the manufacture of

---

5. *Journal of the House of Lords of the Kingdom of Ireland,* 8 vols. (Dublin: William Sleater, 1779–1800), 2:655–60, quote from p. 659 of this "humble REPRESENTATION" of 17 October 1719.

6. Francis Godwin James, *Ireland in the Empire, 1688–1770* (Cambridge: Harvard University Press, 1973), 107–9. For two protests of the Declaratory Act, see *A Letter from a Member of the House of Commons of Ireland to a Gentleman of the Long Robe in Great Britain* (Dublin: E. Waters, 1720), and [John Toland?], *Reasons most humbly offered to the Humble House of Commons, Why the Bill sent down to them from the Humble House of Lords . . . Should not pass into a Law* (London: R. Franklin, 1720). Also see Isolde Victory's "The Making of the 1720 Declaratory Act," in Gerard O'Brien, ed., *Parliament, Politics and People* (Dublin: Irish Academic Press, 1989), 9–29, which stresses that the act "was as much a product of political conditions at Westminster as its repeal was to be in 1782" (27). For an example of desires for greater economic freedom, see Samuel (son of William) Molyneux, "Hibernia Notitia," an unfinished and unpublished work, MS. 888/1, TCD. For an overview of Irish politics in the first half of the eighteenth century, see the essays in T. W. Moody and W. E. Vaughan, eds., *A New History of Ireland,* vol. 4 (Oxford: Clarendon Press, 1986), by J. G. Simms, "The Establishment of the Protestant Ascendancy, 1691–1714" (1–30); J. L. McCracken, "The Political Structure, 1714–1760" (57–83), and "Protestant Ascendancy and the Rise of Colonial Nationalism, 1714–60" (105–22). Robert E. Burns, *Irish Parliamentary Politics in the Eighteenth Century,* 2 vols. (Washington, D.C.: The Catholic University of America Press, 1989–90), covers the intricacies of castle and parliamentary maneuverings, and in an appendix to volume 2, 325–37, critically reviews "Some Historians of Early and Mid-Eighteenth Century Irish Parliamentary Politics," most notably J. L. McCracken.

wool. With the spread of linen, Irish dissidents would soon forget about the wool trade, come to believe that the empire truly was reciprocal, and leave behind their constitutional obsessions. So the British hoped.

Such was not to be. The Anglo-Irish continued their love-hate relationship with the British empire. No one better embodied the extreme form of a confused Anglo-Irish identity that could result than did Jonathan Swift, satirist par excellence. Swift is a puzzle, a man who dismissed and lamented his Irish birth as a perfect accident and his Irish career as a life spent in exile. He has been depicted as a philosophical Whig whose partisan politics were Tory, as a man of great though frustrated ambitions, as an iconoclast, a cynic, even a misanthrope, and as all of them rolled together. One thing is certain: Swift was never comfortable with his Irishness; he sought to escape it and the land of his birth for much of his life. He wrote in 1719 that he was marooned "in a most disagreeable country, and among a most profligate and abandoned people," sentiments he echoed fifteen years later in deciding, "We are all Slaves, Knaves, and Fools, and all but Bishops and People in Employments, Beggars."[7]

Yet for all of this, Swift made his mark as a champion of Irish rights and became, for a short while, a hero to a "people he despised."[8] Swift established his views, though not his reputation, with his first tract on Irish affairs, *The Story of the Injured Lady*, written at the time of the English-Scottish parliamentary union but not published in Swift's lifetime. The subtitle to the story told its moral: "Being a true PICTURE of Scotch Perfidy, Irish Poverty, and English Partiality." *The Injured Lady* was a brief allegory about a gentleman suitor (England) and the two objects of his desire (Scotland and Ireland) as told by the one (Ireland) who was wronged in this romantic triangle. The gentleman had pressed his suit vigorously with the more virtuous of the two maids (Ireland) as well as with the other (Scotland), a foul slut who cared nothing for the gentleman but wanted to share his fortune. The gentle-

---

7. Letter to the Count de Gyllenburg, 2 November 1719, and letter to Francis Grant of 23 March 1734 in Herbert Davis et al., eds., *The Prose Works of Jonathan Swift*, 14 vols. (Oxford: Basil Blackwell, 1957–68), 5:11 and 13:112, respectively. I agree with J. C. Beckett, who believed that if Swift's "hopes had been fulfilled, if he had received the English preferment that he looked for, it is unlikely that we should have heard anything from him of the claims and miseries of his native country." See Beckett, "Literature in English, 1691–1800," in Moody and Vaughan, eds., *New History of Ireland*, 4:434.

8. A. L. Rowse, *Jonathan Swift* (New York: Charles Scribner's Sons, 1975), 138; also see J. A. Downie, *Jonathan Swift: Political Writer* (London: Routledge & Kegan Paul, 1984), and the discussion of Irish writers from Swift through Wolfe Tone in Beckett, "Literature in English, 1691–1800," in Moody and Vaughan, eds., *New History of Ireland*, 4:424–70, and Joseph McMinn, "A Weary Patriot: Swift and the Formation of an Anglo-Irish Identity," *Eighteenth-Century Ireland* 2 (1987): 103–13.

A placid, even contented Jonathan Swift, by Charles Jervas. Courtesy of the National Gallery of Ireland.

man promised to marry the virgin maid even as he consorted with the unprincipled wench. "Overcome by Love, and to avoid Noise and Contention, I yielded to all his Usurpations," the good maid repined, and he took a share of her estate. He appointed a new steward (king) to manage her lands and replaced many of her tenants with his own (land confiscations). He became more and more demanding, allowing her and her tenants fewer and fewer freedoms (commercial restrictions), and all the while he continued to court the other woman. Through it all, the virtuous maid remained loyal and pledged to stand by the gentleman and overlook his unseemly conduct.

The gentleman and the other woman married despite their incessant squabbling, leaving the virtuous and naively trusting maid cheated and betrayed. "Yet, in the Midst of this my Situation, I cannot but have some Pity for this deluded Man," she sighed, urging him to cast away "an infamous Creature, who, whatever she pretendeth, I can prove, would this very Minute rather be a Whore to a certain Great Man . . . if she might have her Will" (referring to Scottish Jacobitism). The good maid only wished "to be free from the Persecutions of this unreasonable Man, and that he will let me manage my own little Fortune to the best Advantage." The friend to whom she wrote recommended that she gather her tenants, agree to four resolutions, and submit them to the gentleman:

First. That your Family and Tenants have no Dependence upon the said Gentleman, further than by the old Agreement, which obligeth you to have the same Steward, and to regulate your Household by such Methods as you shall both agree to. Secondly. That you will not carry your Goods to the Market of his Town, unless you please, nor be hindered from carrying them any where else. Thirdly. That the Servants you pay Wages to shall live at Home, or forfeit their Places. Fourthly. That whatever Lease you make to a Tenant, it shall not be in his Power to break it.[9]

The resolutions expressed allegorically four longstanding Irish claims: that Ireland was tied to England through the Crown; that the Irish could be bound only by laws to which they consented; that they should be allowed free trade; that officeholding absentees should live at home on their Irish estates. *The Injured Lady* had little impact after it was pub-

---

9. *The Story of the Injured Lady* (London: M. Cooper, 1746); in Davis et al., eds., *Works of Swift*, 9:11. For a similar allegory and one that anticipates the story line used by American writer Francis Hopkinson in his *A Pretty Story* (1774), see Jonathan Swift, *The Intelligencer* (London: Francis Cogan, 1730), no. 16, "The Adventure of the Three Brothers, George, Patrick, and Andrew," 203–4. Swift's collaborator in the series, Thomas Sheridan (namesake and nephew of the Jacobite author mentioned in the preceding chapter), apparently wrote this piece.

lished, yet it is important, perhaps even more important than some of Swift's more famous pieces, in reflecting dissident Irish attitudes.

Swift knew William Molyneux's brother Thomas, and he studied at Trinity College under St. George Ashe, one of William Molyneux's old friends, but that does not mean that Swift was consciously setting himself up as Molyneux's disciple. Molyneux, after all, did not originate most of the arguments that had appeared in the *Case*. Both men based their defense of freedoms on natural rights as well as constitutional guarantees. But with Swift, much more than with Molyneux, can be seen the veiled threat of force. The friend to whom the "injured lady" confided closed by stating that if the gentleman did not respond favorably to the four resolutions, "perhaps I may think of something else that will be more effectual." Swift did not push any further; what he meant by "more effectual" he preferred to leave to the reader's imagination. On the surface he seemed to be saying that all would work out: the empire could be reciprocal. Assuming the gentleman agreed to the injured lady's stipulations, she would contribute to "all parish and country charges." In real terms, if Britain gave Ireland greater autonomy within the empire, Ireland would help to defray the costs of imperial administration.

Swift repeated ideas first expressed in *The Injured Lady* in his later writings. In his many pamphlets and even from the pulpit as Dean of St. Patrick's, he railed against restrictions on the Irish economy and infringements of Irish constitutional rights. He harangued readers and listeners alike about the evils of indulgence in luxuries, landlord absenteeism, and public indolence.[10] Although he saved his sharpest criticism for the British policies he opposed, he could also be hard on the Irish people. His writing about political economy culminated in one of his bitterest satires, the *Modest Proposal* of 1729. Noting that children of the Irish poor were so numerous that they were a great burden to society, he suggested that the vast majority of them be sold to the wealthy and suckled until they were plump. Once fattened they would be slaughtered like livestock, each one providing enough meat for four meals and "carcasses" that could be made into gloves. "I GRANT this Food will be somewhat dear, and therefore very *proper for Landlords*," he fumed, "who, as they had already devoured most of the Parents, seem to have the best Title to the Children."[11]

10. See, for example, Swift's *A Proposal for the universal Use of Irish Manufacture* (Dublin: E. Waters, 1720), or the sermon reprinted in Davis et al., eds., *Works of Swift*, 9:199–209; and *A Short View of the State of Ireland* (Dublin: S. Harding, 1728).
11. *A Modest Proposal for preventing Children of Poor People from being a Burthen to their parents or the Country and for making them beneficial to the Publick* (Dublin: S. Harding, 1729) in Davis et al., eds., *Works of Swift*, 12:112.

Unlike Molyneux, who had avoided tying economic complaints to constitutional grievances, Swift joined the two whenever he could, most notably with his anonymously authored "Drapier" letters. These essays were precipitated by a monopoly that had been granted by the British Privy Council to Englishman William Wood to make copper halfpence and farthing coins for Ireland. Sprinkled throughout are objections on economic grounds: that, for example, an influx of new coins would debase the currency and disrupt Ireland's already-declining trade. More prominent were Swift's objections on constitutional grounds, especially in the third and fourth letters. In his own blunt and abrasive style, Swift made the same claims that Molyneux, Darcy, and others before him had made in more restrained language.

WERE not the People of Ireland born as free as those of England? HOW have they forfeited their Freedom? Is not their Parliament as fair a Representative of the People, as that of England? And hath not their Privy Council as great, or a greater Share in the Administration of publick Affairs? Are they not Subjects of the same King? Does not the same Sun shine over them? And have they not the same God for their Protector? Am I a Free-man in England, and do I become a Slave in six Hours, by crossing the Channel?[12]

Capping his arguments he proclaimed:

For in Reason, all Government without the Consent of the Governed, is the *very Definition of Slavery* . . . by the Laws of GOD, of NATURE, of NATIONS, and of your own Country, you ARE and OUGHT to be as FREE a People as your Brethren in England.[13]

Here was the great triad of justifications—law of nature, law of man, and law of God—that had been and would continue to be used by Irish constitutional nationalists for years to come, just as they would be seized upon by American pamphleteers in the 1760s and early 1770s.

As the "Drapier," Swift became genuinely popular for one of the few times in his career. The Irish Parliament, still fretting under the Declaratory Act, voiced its own protest; feeling threatened, the Irish Privy Council chimed in as well, as did the general public. Swift could feel victorious, in that Wood surrendered his monopoly. With that the furor died down and Swift's popularity slipped. Naturally, his views had not

---

12. M. B. Drapier, *Some Observations upon a Paper, call'd, the Report of the Committee of the most Honourable the Privy-Council in England, Relating to WOOD's Half-Pence* (Dublin: John Harding, 1724), as cited in Davis et al., eds., *Works of Swift*, 10:31.

13. Idem, *A Letter to the WHOLE People of Ireland* (Dublin: John Harding, 1724), as cited in Davis et al., eds., *Works of Swift*, 10:63. Also see Burns, *Irish Parliamentary Politics* 1:134–216, for a detailed treatment of this business.

been popular in Britain, and his constitutional arguments were no better received there than Molyneux's had been. As one Swift biographer put it, here was "Molyneux's thesis of legislative independence expressed with an insolence Molyneux would not have dared."[14] The king, if he had had the "Drapier's" letters read to him, would not have been pleased by the thinly veiled questioning of Crown prerogative and Swift's emphasis on limited monarchy and the rights of the people. Swift had tried to style himself as one of the people by taking on the identity of a draper, but he was no populist. The Irish Parliament and Privy Council carefully kept their complaints distinct from those of the "Drapier." The Privy Council in fact censored the fourth letter for its seditiousness. Fortunately for Swift, a grand jury refused to hand down an indictment.

Swift was too mordant, too impudent, too large a bundle of contradictions to remain the darling of the public for very long. It was incongruous for someone who had wanted so badly to leave Ireland for a post in England to condemn opportunists when he himself was an office seeker, and it was difficult to tell if he was any more anti-English than he was anti-Irish. His views were caught up in his own ambitions and frustrations. His anti-Whig, anti-Walpole political ideas might have been shaped as much by his not getting lucrative office as they were by genuine aversion to Whig partisan politics.

Swift is not representative of Irish critics of the empire in the first half of the eighteenth century. While his political complaints and constitutional theories were not unique to him, his way of expressing them put him on the fringe. Most other constitutional nationalists of his age and for decades to come would not be so caustic in their criticism. It was not that Molyneux would not have "dared" to be so insolent; his affection for England was more genuine than Swift's, as was his desire not to offend. Molyneux, Robert Molesworth, John Trenchard, and other members of what Caroline Robbins has called the "commonwealthman" tradition no doubt considered themselves to be as protective of Irish freedoms as Swift, but they eschewed Swift's carping style. They thought that Catholicism would eventually die out if the Protestants were wise; they believed that there truly could be a single Irish-English interest; they determined that a parliamentary union would benefit Ireland and help ease the growing problems of empire. They were much more moderate in tone and more circumspect in their assertions.

Sitting in the British House of Commons, Molesworth voted against the Declaratory Act, perhaps because he (like Molyneux) considered

---

14. Oliver W. Ferguson, *Jonathan Swift and Ireland* (Urbana: University of Illinois Press, 1962), 119.

parliamentary union preferable to parliamentary subordination. Notably, Swift respected Molesworth enough to address one of his "Drapier" letters to him. Trenchard, in the widely read *Cato's Letters* that he coauthored with Scotsman Thomas Gordon, criticized the way that Ireland had been treated and urged reform in British imperial policy. He singled out the cattle acts and the Woolens Act as mistaken legislation that hurt the English as well as the Irish. He observed that Ireland was treated as a colony even if it was called a kingdom, and there were "but two Ways in Nature" to keep colonies from rising up and throwing off their dependence: "one to keep it out of their Power, and the other out of their Will." The Irish were

> too powerful to be treated as a Colony; and . . . if we design to continue them Friends, the best Way to do it, is to imitate the Example of Merchants and Shopkeepers; that is, when their Apprentices are acquainted with their Trade and their Customers, and are out of their Time, to take them into Partnership, rather than let them set up for themselves in their Neighborhood.[15]

For Trenchard and other Irish critics of British mercantilism as it stood in the 1720s, then, the solution was not greater agitation on the part of the aggrieved but better understanding, better cooperation, and a more informed policy. They tried, as had Molyneux, to keep their criticisms balanced and palatable to a British audience. Some put the burden on the Irish themselves to be better citizens of empire, to be more industrious, to pursue livelihoods that would complement rather than compete with those in Britain. In the *Querist*, George Berkeley went so far as to chide his countrymen for "hankering after the Woollen Trade" and blaming the British for their economic woes. Berkeley's "queries" sought to remind the Anglo-Irish elite that they owed much to their British tie. Berkeley asked whether "the Protestant Colony in this Kingdom can ever forget what they owe to England?" whether "we can propose to thrive, so long as we entertain a wrongheaded Distrust of England?"[16] Where Berkeley only hinted at the need for parliamentary

---

15. [John Trenchard and Thomas Gordon], *Cato's Letters*, 4 vols., 3d ed., 1733 (New York: Russell and Russell, reprint ed., 1969), 4:12. Also see the discussion in Caroline Robbins, *The Eighteenth-Century Commonwealthman* (Cambridge: Harvard University Press, 1959), 143–76. According to the British Library copy, Trenchard wrote *A Letter from a souldier to the Commons of England* (London: E. Mallet, 1702), which argued that those who advocated Irish parliamentary independence were basically looking for a way to legitimize their desire for confiscated land. Trenchard, one of the commissioners involved in the confiscations, seems to have been more critical than Molyneux ever was of his countrymen's motives.

16. [George Berkeley], *The Querist, Containing Several Queries, Proposed to the Consideration of the Public* (Dublin: R. Reilly, 1735–37), Part II, queries 76 and 78, resp.

union, friend and fellow essayist Samuel Madden closed his 1738 *Reflections and Resolutions* by endorsing Trenchard's call made some sixteen years before.[17]

Madden, Berkeley, and Trenchard are all proof that Irish constitutional nationalism could express itself under a number of guises. Madden, unlike his uncle William Molyneux, did not equate Irish parliamentary independence with the protection of Irish interests and Irish rights. He was nevertheless concerned that those interests and rights be protected, and that is what qualifies him and Berkeley as constitutional nationalists. Moderates in their criticism of British mercantilism, they believed that the Irish—a thoroughly protestantized, anglicized Irish—could join with the British to produce one people. To them the best future for Ireland was for the island to cease to have a separate political identity. The goal of these nationalists, paradoxically, was to protect their society by absorption into another political culture.

Their assumption, their undying hope, was that the British would be responsive. They were therefore shrewd enough to point out that, if the Irish had to change, so too did the British. In addition to their call for frugality and greater industry on the part of the Irish, they called on the British to respect Irish needs and broaden their thinking enough to treat the Irish as fellow citizens of empire. Or, as Berkeley asked in his Queries, "Whether *Great Britain* ought not to promote the Prosperity of her Colonies, by all Methods consistent with her own?"—indeed, "Whether the remotest Parts from the Metropolis, and the lowest of the People, are not to be regarded as the Extremities and Limbs of the political Body?"[18] Madden might have written that the Irish had brought many

---

Also see J. M. Hone and M. M. Rossi, *Bishop Berkeley* (New York: Macmillan, 1931), 199–204; and A. A. Luce, *The Life of George Berkeley, Bishop of Cloyne* (London: Thomas Nelson and Sons, 1949), 25–26.

17. Samuel Madden, *Reflections and Resolutions Proper for the Gentlemen of Ireland, As to their Conduct for the Service of their country* (Dublin: R. Reilly, 1738), pp. 119–25. See also A. D. [Arthur Dobbs], *Some Thoughts Concerning Government in General: And Our Present Circumstances in Great Britain and Ireland* (Dublin: S. Hyde, 1731); and *An Inquiry into Some of the Causes of the Ill Situation of the Affairs of Ireland* (Dublin: Geo. Grierson, 1731), for other examples of pamphlets that urge the Irish to work more industriously to prove to the British that they deserved better consideration. Though both Madden and Dobbs put much of the burden on the Irish, both also emphasized that government was supposed to serve public needs. Since they assumed that the British as well as the Irish would be responsive and real improvement would follow, their language was not threatening. The major difference between these tracts and those that would appear in the commercial crisis of 1779 was the tone of the writing; by 1779 pamphleteers were becoming more insistent and more critical of the British, and less critical of the Irish.

18. [Berkeley], *The Querist*, Part III, queries 304 and 305, resp.

of their problems on themselves by "the Wildness of our Extravagance, on the one Side, and the most stupid want of Care and Industry of the other"; yet he also echoed his uncle when he described England as

> our true Parent and Protector, on whose Prosperity our own immediately depends, who must wound herself whenever, through inadvertence she hurts us; and must in Interest, as well as Justice, take care not to sacrifice the Ease and Welfare of the Younger Child to the Grandeur and Splendor of the eldest.[19]

Through the middle of the eighteenth century, Irish nationalists seldom moved beyond the positions taken by John Trenchard and George Berkeley, by Arthur Dobbs and Samuel Madden. The Irish Parliament during that same period was more or less quiescent. It left behind the Wood halfpence controversy and showed itself to be a bastion of Anglo-Irish domination, concentrating its efforts on consolidating power and keeping Catholics in an economic and political nether world. John, Lord Carteret, proved to be an astute lord lieutenant. Arriving in the aftermath of the halfpence dispute, by the time he left in 1730 he had restored administration control. A surface calm prevailed in Irish affairs well into the 1740s. The war that raged in Scotland resulting from Jacobite support for The Pretender did not spread to Ireland, and Ireland was almost as untouched by the 1745 Scottish rebellion as it had been by the 1715 outbreak.

Nonetheless, if the Irish Parliament was quiet, it was because British policy, more than ever during the Walpolean era, was to rule by persuasion or manipulation rather than through coercion. Generally speaking, British politicians attempted to build a solid political foundation in Ireland through more effective use of patronage. New Irish peerages were made, places were awarded and names were added to the pension list. The undertaker system was more fully developed, with powerful Irish families being courted as allies to assist in the implementation of British policy, not only by pushing legislation through the Irish Parliament, but by keeping the opposition in line when Parliament was not meeting and the lord lieutenant was not in residence.

Still, the Irish Parliament never became a perfect reflection of British interests, and Anglo-Irish priorities could be different from those of London. "Apart from pressing for the appointment of Englishmen to key positions in Irish church and state offices during the early and middle 1730s," Robert Burns has concluded, the British government "had no

19. Madden, *Reflections and Resolutions*, 109, which is very similar to William Molyneux's appeal to the king in his *Case*; also see 111.

consistent strategy for managing the Irish parliament or governing the country during this period."[20] For the British politicians of Walpole's generation, Irish affairs were of secondary importance and often enmeshed in party struggles that pitted Whigs against Tories at Westminster as well as rival factions in Dublin. Political maneuvering in both places actually undercut the very undertaker "system" upon which the British had to rely. Those who, as lords justice, acted as undertakers exacted a price for their loyalty: increased patronage. In the hands of cunning politicians like Speaker of the House Henry Boyle and, in Lords, Archbishop of Armagh George Stone, patronage could be used to build powerful parliamentary followings. A middling lord lieutenant like the earl of Harrington, in office from 1746 to 1750, would have accomplished even less than he did had he not worked out an accommodation with Boyle and Stone. The same holds for those who preceded him to the Castle.

During the 1730s, the Irish Parliament had moved into a new home—"a truly most august pile"—facing College Green.[21] This architecturally impressive building featured a piazza with ionic columns, separate chambers for Lords and Commons, and stately elegance throughout. Its construction coincided with the rising power of legislatures throughout the British empire. As Francis G. James has noted, these legislatures "grew in prestige, in experience, and in independence. The Irish Parliament was no exception."[22] Parliament House stood as a monument to the growing aspirations of the Irish Parliament. Its distance from the Castle underscored Parliament's heightened sense of self and desire for autonomy. Its ornateness, like that of the largest country houses—Castletown, Russborough, Carton, and Powerscourt—testified to both the pride and the insecurity of Ireland's ruling class.

Parliamentary leaders reveled in their oratorical skills. One M.P. boasted that the Irish Commons "contained as much character, as much eloquence, and as much sincerity, as any popular assembly since the most brilliant era of the Roman republic."[23] The House of Lords closed

20. Burns, *Irish Parliamentary Politics*, 2:334–35. See also David Hayton, "Walpole and Ireland," in Jeremy Black, ed., *Britain in the Age of Walpole* (London: Macmillan, 1984), 95–119; and idem, "The Beginnings of the Undertaker System," in T. Bartlett and D. Hayton, eds., *Penal Era and Golden Age* (Belfast: Ulster Historical Foundation, 1979), 41–50.
21. As described by Englishman Philip Luckombe, *A Tour Through Ireland*, 2d ed. (London: T. Lowndes, 1783; orig. ed., 1780), 8.
22. James, *Ireland in the Empire*, 139, and the general discussion of Ireland and imperial politics from 1727 to 1760 on pp. 134–89, which differs from that in Burns's *Irish Parliamentary Politics*, with Burns stressing more the shifting, unstable nature of the so-called undertaker "system."
23. Jonah Barrington, *Rise and Fall of the Irish Nation* (New York: D. & J. Sadlier,

its sessions to public view; not so Commons. A gallery overlooking its chamber could be packed with visitors when controversial issues came up for discussion. The opening of a new parliamentary session was one of the grandest public events in all of Ireland and was carried off with much pomp and ceremony. Parliament met biennially through most of the eighteenth century, with sessions opening in October and, depending on the amount of business, ending in early spring or carrying through the summer. Beginning in 1785 there were annual sessions that usually opened in July, an arrangement continued until the 1800 Act of Union. Active members took themselves very seriously. When they sat, the lord mayor was expected to divert wheeled traffic from moving past Parliament House during the middle of the day, so their proceedings would be undisturbed. Both houses often had evening as well as morning sessions, and when a touchy subject was being addressed, debates could drag on through the night and into the next morning.

Despite all the real changes that had come since the thirteenth century, the Irish Parliament was still technically at the king's beck and call. Through the lord lieutenant, the Crown determined when a session opened and closed, and, under Poynings' Law, what business would be handled. The Declaratory Act explicitly stated what had been implicit all along. Yet, so long as the Anglo-Irish did not press constitutional issues and British policy did not harm (or was not perceived to harm) Irish interests, no crisis erupted.

The imperial quiet ended in the 1750s. Constitutional issues were once again raised, and raised vociferously with the emergence of so-called "Patriots." These members of the Irish Parliament styled themselves as the best defenders of the national interest and the true voice of the people. Their rise also threatened the system of deference and political horse trading upon which a smooth running of government had depended during the preceding half century. Moreover, there was a threat to deference on another level: popular politics in Dublin that mixed municipal and imperial issues with the growing ambitions of the Protestant electorate.

The controversy that erupted in the Irish Parliament in 1753 showed how tenuous the connection between Britain and Ireland could be and how undertakers rarely managed Irish affairs to the satisfaction of the British or the Irish. This crisis revolved around the use of surplus funds

---

1885; orig. ed., 1833), 37. Here, as elsewhere in his writings, Barrington was perhaps self-serving. For Parliament House, see Maurice Craig, *Dublin, 1660–1860* (Dublin: Allen Figgis, 1969), 164–201; and J. T. Gilbert, *A History of the City of Dublin*, 3 vols. (Dublin: James Duffy, 1861), 3:58–180.

in the Irish exchequer. George II had suggested two years earlier that the money be used to help pay off the public debt. Through evasive language and avoidance of controversy in both Dublin and London, the 1751 session passed quietly into the record. Not so in 1753, when the question of surplus funds resurfaced. Commons objected to the king's granting his "consent" for such use, preferring instead to state that it was following his "recommendation." The lord lieutenant and administration men in the Irish Parliament wanted it made clear that funds could be spent only with the king's permission; the Patriots opposing them argued that Commons had the right to dispose of funds as it saw fit. At the same time, Patriots accused the administration of permitting graft and corruption when awarding contracts for the construction of new, and the repair of old, barracks. The Irish House submitted a bill that did not refer to Crown consent; the British Privy Council returned it with the right of consent firmly stated; a Patriot-led Irish House rejected it. The battle raged in the press as well as in Parliament House through 1756. Henry Boyle, speaker of the House, and Anthony Malone, the prime serjeant, led the opposition, despite Boyle's supposed pro-administration role as a lord justice and undertaker.[24]

This small episode precipitated a constitutional crisis; much significance was attached to it at the time and for years after, when the Irish Parliament became even more headstrong. "This is the last Struggle and Effort the People of Ireland have left for Freedom," warned one pamphleteer in 1753, "and should we now miscarry in this, we may sit down and idly show our Affections for our ruined Country, and fruitlessly bewail the loss of our liberties, but shall never meet with another Opportunity of exerting ourselves in its Defence."[25] Lamenting what had happened, the earl of Shelburne wrote that the "foundation was thus laid, and may be easily traced from that time to the total emancipation of the legislature of Ireland from that of Great Britain, and the complete Revolution which has since taken place in regard to the fundamental laws of Ireland."[26]

Irish opposition M.P.s, who would lead the fight for parliamentary

---

24. See the *Journal of the House of Commons of the Kingdom of Ireland*, 20 vols. (Dublin: George Grierson, 1796–1802), 5:167, 169, for the different wording of the king's message and Commons' response; the overview in J. L. McCracken, "The Conflict between the Irish Administration and Parliament, 1753–6," *Irish Historical Studies* 3 (1942): 159–79; and the lengthier, more complex discussion in Burns, *Irish Parliamentary Politics*, 2:120–219.

25. *The Patriot* (Dublin, 1753), Letter I, p. 4. This is a collection of seven "letters" written from October to December 1753.

26. Edmond Fitzmaurice, *Life of William, Earl of Shelburne*, 3 vols. (London: Macmillian, 1875–76), 1:348, written sometime after the Act of Union.

Patriots and Popular Politics 55

"independence" in the early 1780s, agreed with Shelburne on the controversy's significance, though they viewed it from a different perspective. "The question of 53, was the beginning, in this country, of that Constitutional spirit which asserted afterwards the privilege of the Commons, and guarded and husbanded the essential right of a free Constitution" declared Henry Grattan.[27] His friend and patron the earl of Charlemont went even further:

> ... the people were taught a secret of which they had been hitherto ignorant, that government might be opposed with success, and, as a confidence in the possibility of victory is the best inspirer of courage, a spirit was consequently raised in the nation, hereafter to be employed to better purposes. Men were likewise accustomed to turn their thoughts to constitutional subjects, and to reflect on the difference between political freedom and servitude. . . . They were taught to know that Ireland had, or ought to have, a constitution. . . . In a word, Irishmen were taught to think, a lesson which is the first and most necessary step in the acquirement of liberty.[28]

There were various other, more minor crises through the 1750s, all of which weakened the inherently unstable undertaker system and highlighted differences separating the Anglo-Irish from the British. Although the Patriots did not hold together as a solid group (much less as an organized party), they still raised objections to the awarding of pensions and places and found other ways to obstruct government. Oppositionism had become so endemic by 1757 that Edmund Sexton Pery, Boyle's successor as speaker of the House, warned the new lord Lieutenant, the duke of Bedford, that Commons had been taken over by a "cabal."[29]

There was also a fair amount of agitation outside Parliament. Poynings' Law was again subjected to scrutiny and criticism, but far more important was the public reaction to rumors of an impending parliamentary union between Britain and Ireland.[30] Malachy Postlethwait's lengthy tome, *Britain's Commercial Interest Explained and Improved*,

---

27. Henry Grattan, Esq., *An Answer to a Pamphlet, entitled, The Speech of the Earl of Clare, on the Subject of a Legislative Union between Great Britain and Ireland* (London: G. G. and J. Robinson, 1800), 40.

28. Historical Manuscripts Commission, *The Manuscripts and Correspondence of James, First Earl of Charlemont*, 2 vols. (London: Eyre and Spottiswoode, 1891, 1894), 1:7, from Charlemont's autobiography.

29. Idem, *Eighth Report* (London: Eyre and Spottiswoode, 1881), Part I, p. 175, a letter from Pery to the duke of Bedford, sometime in 1757.

30. A Gentleman of Ireland, *Remarks upon Poyning's Law, and the Manner of Passing Bills in the P—t of I—d* (Dublin, 1758), attributed in some places to Robert Hellen, a judge on the Irish court of common pleas, and in others to John Monck Mason, a barrister and later M.P. The author argued, as had earlier writers, that the law had been twisted over the years—it was not a bad law, it just had been misapplied. The author called for clarification rather than repeal.

went through a Dublin edition in 1758, the year after it was printed in London, and may have helped to bring on a panic. An Englishman, Postlethwait wrote from his country's perspective. He undoubtedly did not think that that made him anti-Irish. Citing approvingly *Cato's Letters*, he called for parliamentary union as the only real solution to commercial problems, the first and unavoidable step in commercial reform. Talk of union took up much space in his book, and the benefits of union were argued from an imperial angle; thus he warned of growing French and Spanish power and the need for British imperial solidarity. He thought that the Irish wool trade should once again be stimulated (if necessary) to steer the Irish away from contacts outside the empire, but in other places he seemed to be arguing that Irish commerce had to be controlled to prevent the Irish from competing with the British.

Apparently he provoked discussion in the Irish Parliament and on Dublin street corners.[31] Some Irishmen disturbed by Postlethwait may have recalled two pamphlets that had appeared in 1751, one anticipating Postlethwait's arguments, the other warning against any move toward union. The second pamphlet, *An Alarum*, cautioned that the Irish would have too small a voice in Westminster and would not be able to prevent passage of discriminatory legislation: there would be no practical gain and a great deal lost. Ireland, the pamphlet contended, would be better off to insist on its rights as a sister kingdom with an independent parliament.[32]

If the idea of union had once been popular, it was no longer so in the 1750s. Fearing a French invasion, the administration sponsored a bill making it easier for the Crown to assemble Parliament during an emergency. Stories soon circulated that even more was intended: a parliamentary union. Surly crowds began milling around Parliament House in November 1759, when rumors that union was being considered were rife, despite disclaimers that the "Report of a Union between Great-Britain and Ireland is without the least Foundation."[33] Popular agitation grew to such a state that on December 3 rioting broke out suddenly in Dublin, "the fiercest ever known in the metropolis."[34] Members in both

---

31. Malachy Postlethwait, *Britain's Commercial Interest Explained and Improved*, 2 vols. (Dublin: J. Flin, 1758), especially 1:188–283.

32. *A Proposal for Uniting the Kingdoms of Great Britain and Ireland* (London: A. Millar, 1751), sometimes attributed to Arthur Hill, earl of Hillsborough; and N. Archdall, *An Alarum to the People of Great-Britain and Ireland: In answer to a Late Proposal for Uniting these Kingdoms* (Dublin: George Faulkner, 1751). Archdall was no friend of the Catholics; he dismissed them as bigots.

33. *Dublin Journal*, 24 November 1759.

34. J. G. Swift MacNeill, *The Constitutional and Parliamentary History of Ireland til*

houses of Parliament who were thought to be in favor of union were waylaid and accosted. A crowd outside Commons forced members, before they were allowed to enter, to swear an oath that they would vote against union. Another crowd actually burst into and ransacked the Lords's chambers. Several members were pelted in their carriages, others were jostled or pulled from their horses, and still others had their lives threatened. Through this all, the lord mayor and sheriffs did virtually nothing; with the appearance of a detachment of regulars sent from the Castle by the lord lieutenant, the crowd trickled away virtually unpunished, after doing a fair amount of damage.

Administration men cried out against "anarchy" and speculated about French intrigue. Both opposition and administration leaders attempted to distance themselves from the rioting and lambasted the participants as mobocrats drawn from the dregs of society. Outraged House members voted, without a dissenting voice, to condemn those who had attempted to intimidate them and, they felt, destroy the rule of law.[35] Nevertheless, the bill introduced by the chief secretary, interpreted by some to be a first step toward union and thought to have triggered the tumult, was withdrawn, and the city soon quieted down.

The Irish Parliament was not contemplating union in 1759 any more than it had been in 1751, when Nicholas Archdall's previously mentioned *An Alarum* was published. Archdall was an M.P. for County Fermanagh when he wrote the pamphlet, as he was when the rioting broke out eight years later. If he was in Dublin at the time, he was probably appalled by the crowd activity and may well have joined with the other members of Commons in censuring the mob. If so, then Archdall was blind to the fact that his pamphleteering had helped bring the crowd to life. Irish leaders had for years appealed to the public, trying to enjoy the benefits of political popularity without diminishing their monopoly

---

the Union (Dublin: Talbot Press, 1917), 87, basically follows Lecky, *History*, 2:435–36. Also see Burns, *Irish Parliamentary Politics*, 2:268–72; Sean Murphy, "The Dublin Anti-Union Riot of 3 December 1759," in O'Brien, ed., *Parliament, Politics and People*, 50–68; and Jim Smyth, *The Men of No Property* (New York: St. Martin's Press, 1992), 121–39, who puts crowd activity into the context of politicized common folk. Burns sees this episode as more important than the 1753–56 crisis in stimulating Anglo-Irish interest in constitutional issues.

35. For the reactions of Parliament see the *House of Commons Journal*, 6:156, 157; and *House of Lords Journal*, 4:165. The proposed bill providing for defense in case of French invasion was printed several times in the *Dublin Journal* (such as on 27 November 1759) to quiet the public and show that no union was planned. Also see the letter of the Irish lord chancellor in HMC, *Report on Manuscripts in Various Collections*, 6 vols. (London: John Falconer, 1901–9), 6:71–2; and the account in Henry Grattan, Jr., *Memoirs of the Life and Times of the Rt. Hon. Henry Grattan*, 5 vols. (London: Henry Colburn, 1849), 1:72–79.

on political power. Archdall did not write his *Alarum* just for fellow M.P.s; he wrote it for voters as well. Archdall can be numbered among those who had come to equate the protection of Irish constitutional rights with the prerogatives of the Irish Parliament. At the same time, he also seemed to equate Commons with the people: the "people" spoke only through that body. In December 1759 the "people" spoke spontaneously and more violently than even the Patriots had intended or wanted. But the mob responded to fears that M.P.s like Archdall planted when they warned that parliamentary union would result in Ireland being reduced to a "wild desart."

Furthermore, Patriots in Parliament were not alone; there were also extra-parliamentary "patriots" who formed local organizations, perhaps with the encouragement of some M.P.s. The Patriot Club of Antrim formed in 1753; it was followed by one in County Armagh in 1758. Members of these clubs gathered in meetings, discussed pressing issues, and expressed their commitment to protecting the constitution and parliamentary rights. Even administration supporters appealed to the people, if only to counteract the opposition in Parliament and neutralize their popular appeal. They produced pamphlets denouncing parliamentary Patriots as self-serving and petty, and clubs like that in Antrim as iniquitous dens of republican agitation.[36]

Patriot clubs might have been more in sympathy with the parliamentary opposition, they might even have been organized through the instigation of Patriot M.P.s, but they could take on their own identities and draw up their own agendas. Both the opponents and supporters of government paid lip service to the belief that the people were the foundation of all government and that the primary purpose of government was to protect the people's constitutional rights. They did not anticipate the expansion of this idea to include the notion that, as one pamphleteer put it, members of parliament were "trustees" of the people or, as the Patriot Club of Antrim had pledged in 1757, "That the freeholders and freemen of Ireland may ever exert their *constitutional right* of judging the conduct of their representatives."[37]

36. See the attack in *Advice to the Patriot Club of the County of Antrim* (Dublin: Robert Freeman, 1756) and the defense in *Remarks on a Late Pamphlet entitled, Advice to the Patriot Club of the County of Antrim* (Dublin, 1756).

37. *A Letter from a Free Citizen of Dublin to a Freeholder in the County of Armagh* (Dublin, 1753), 6; and Henry Joy, *Historical Collections relative to the Town of Belfast* (Belfast: George Berwick, 1817), 100; with similar sentiments being expressed the year before (98). Derek Hirst, *The Representative of the People?* (Cambridge: Cambridge University Press, 1975), 161–66, 178–88, notes that some English M.P.s were accustomed to receiving instructions—though they were not necessarily bound by them—from their

Patriots and administration men alike tried to carefully direct the electorate. They wanted to mobilize the people and then send them home after they had served their purpose. Parliamentary Patriots tried to manipulate what was still an inchoate "public opinion"; they were elitists who dabbled in democratic politics without understanding the implications of their actions. Yet they had little choice but to follow that course. They, like British imperialists having to promote a certain amount of local power, could be trapped; the source of their power could also become a check on it. If British imperialists had had to deal with the problem since the twelfth century, Anglo-Irish politicians had to deal with their version of it intermittently from the 1740s on. This can be seen quite dramatically with the rise of Charles Lucas.

Lucas first gained prominence in Dublin city politics, making his name as a critic of the mayor and aldermen, and as a champion of the rights of the freemen. Lucas himself had become a freeman in 1735 by joining the barber surgeons guild.[38] At that time Dublin had a population of perhaps 130 thousand, of whom some three thousand or so enjoyed freeman status. Only freemen could vote in city elections or hold office, and only they could vote in parliamentary elections for the two Dublin city seats in Commons. Since 1672, Dublin's mayor had been chosen from the ranks of twenty-four aldermen. Together they formed the upper house of the common council. The lower house was composed of fifty sheriffs and "sheriffs peers" and ninety-six representatives of the city guilds. Merchants held thirty-three of the guild seats; the rest were spread among various trades, including the barber surgeons. Guild representatives were "elected" every three years; that is to say, the ninety-six members were chosen from a list of one hundred ninety-two submitted to the mayor and aldermen. Thus the mayor and aldermen, acting as the upper house of the common council, could exercise considerable control over the lower house. Moreover, election of the mayor and sheriffs had to be approved by the lord lieutenant. City politics and national politics were thereby inextricably intertwined. The lord lieutenant was obliged to take an interest in Dublin municipal issues, and the freemen of Dublin determined the outcome of parliamentary elections in the city.

---

electors as early as the 1640s. Also see Edward and Annie G. Porritt, *The Unreformed House of Commons,* 2 vols. (Cambridge: Cambridge University Press, 1903, 1909), 1:263–72, and Paul Kelly, "Constituent Instructions to Members of the Parliament in the Eighteenth Century," in Clyve Jones, ed., *Party and Management in Parliament, 1660–1784* (Leicester: Leicester University Press, 1984), 169–89.

38. For Lucas's politics, see Sean Murphy's excellent "The Lucas Affair: A Study of Municipal and Electoral Politics in Dublin, 1742–9" (M.A. thesis, University College, Dublin, 1981); as well as Burns, *Irish Parliamentary Politics,* 2:101–10.

Enter Lucas. He gave some indication of his future behavior when he joined the barber surgeons. An apothecary by trade, he refused to associate with his fellow pharmacists because, he charged in his first pamphlet, they were guilty of fraud. By the time he was put up for election to the common council as a representative for the barber surgeons, he had moved on to bigger game. He criticized the "New Rules" of 1672 as a violation of the city's original charter, particularly the provision allowing aldermen (with the mayor) to choose their own successors instead of calling together both houses of the common council. He also criticized various policies and programs of city government.

His three-year term expired in 1744, and when his name was submitted for a second term, the mayor and aldermen made sure that it was not among the four taken from the list of eight returned by the barber surgeons. They did not silence Lucas by this ploy, however. He continued his guild activities and expanded his range of interests. He began to write pamphlets focusing on national affairs, and he gained enough of a following among the freemen of Dublin in general to make it likely he would be elected as one of Dublin's two M.P.s in 1749.

Alas for him, he was forced to flee the country before the election. He had continued to offend the mayor and aldermen and added the lord lieutenant and many members of Parliament to his growing list of enemies. His writings proved so offensive that he was in danger of being tried and imprisoned for seditious libel. He left Ireland and did not return for over a decade, yet he had stirred up controversies and stimulated public discussion about important issues that did not end with his leaving.

Lucas has been called "in some ways the harbinger of a new age," and he certainly was that.[39] He took the arguments of Molyneux and other nationalists within the constitutional tradition and stripped them of their moderate tone. He was more insistent, more truculent—a Swift without Swift's misanthropic tendencies. It was difficult to tell how much Swift cared about the issues he examined, so harsh were his views of human nature and so frustrated was he with his public life. Lucas was not as pessimistic, and his politics were his passion.

In his pamphlets he worked his way through the Irish past to show, as had Molyneux, that Ireland was a distinct kingdom; that its tie to England was voluntary and only through the king; that therefore the

---

39. R. B. McDowell, *Ireland in the Age of Imperialism and Revolution, 1760–1801* (Oxford: Clarendon Press, 1979), 211. Porritt, *Unreformed House of Commons*, 2:324–31, presents the New Rules of 1672 as important reform legislation—a different view from that of Lucas.

Charles Lucas as statesman and defender of the people, by William Jones. Courtesy of the National Library of Ireland.

Irish Parliament was independent from and not subordinate to the British Parliament; and that the Irish were entitled to constitutional rights and had been since the reign of Henry II. "The Laws of our Country expressly declare, We are FREE and INDEPENDENT of all Legislatures, but our OWN," he wrote. "We can be bound by no Laws, but such as are, or shall be made by *our own* free and voluntary Consent, in OUR LEGISLATURE, consisting of the KING, or his *Viceregent*, the LORDS and COMMONS of the Realm in PARLEMENT assembled."[40]

Lucas tried to connect himself to Molyneux, whose arguments he noted approvingly again and again, but his language betrayed him. He was not really a resurrected Molyneux. He was much more critical, much more irreverent; he was obviously not as enamored as Molyneux had been of either the Irish Parliament or the English tie, despite his defense of both. Biting words gushed from his pen. He condemned Poynings' Law as "preposterous," a "Monstrous Production" in which "there is not a single Sentence consistent with Justice, Reason or the Constitution of our Country."[41] Those who talked of Ireland as a subordinate kingdom did so "falsely and wickedly"; the Declaratory Act of 1720 was unjust and unconstitutional and reduced the Irish to "Dupes and Slaves."[42] Lucas seemed to find corruption and callous disregard for Irish freedoms everywhere he looked. He professed to be attached to the Glorious Revolution, yet he stressed how William III had done little to advance Irish interests. He defended the idea of an independent Irish Parliament even as he argued that the Irish Parliament had failed in its task. Sprinkled throughout his many pamphlets are allusions to "servile ministers" and "selfish Slaves" on both sides of the Irish Sea and over the full course of Irish history. His readers might well have come away thinking that a conspiracy had been hatched to subvert their liberties.

Few escaped Lucas's censure. Many Irish M.P.s probably squirmed at the thought of his taking a seat among them, and British imperialists dismissed his contentions. Most disturbing, perhaps, were his appeals to the "people" as reflected in the title of pieces like *Free Will to Freeholders* and his insistence that:

---

40. Charles Lucas, *An Address to His Excellency William Earl of Harrington* (Dublin: James Esdall, 1749), 5. Copies of most of the pamphlets written by Lucas or attributed to him can be found in the Royal Irish Academy as well as the National Library of Ireland; a fair number are also in the British Library.
41. Idem, *Political Constitutions*, Address XV, p. 229. This is a collection of Lucas's essays originally published between 1748 and 1750, which Lucas had reprinted while he was in exile in London, before he left for the Continent to study medicine.
42. Ibid., Address X, p. 113; and Address XI, pp. 143–44.

OUR GOVERNMENT is declared and confessed, by the greatest of our Lawyers, Legislators and Kings, to be a *Common-Wealth,* not a Monarchy. We are not to judge of the Power or Prerogative of our Crown, by Things, claimed or possessed in *Absolute Monarchies,* under the Civil Law, a System of Government, which never yet subsisted in *Great-Britian,* or Ireland. Our Government may, with equal Propriety, be called a *Democracy,* or an Aristocracy, as a Monarchy: It is truly a mixed Government, composed of each of these Forms; and has more of the true *Republic,* in it's Composition, than any of those, that now bear the Name of Republic.[43]

On the surface, what Lucas wrote here is a reiteration of Whig commonwealth ideology in a more jumbled, even garbled, form. But then "commonwealth" men like Trenchard and Gordon had not literally called for the replacement of mixed government with a republic.[44] Lucas's preferences were not as clear, perhaps not even to himself. His arguments seemed to challenge the very notion that mixed government could work, because it had historically done such a miserable job of securing the people's liberties. The people had to be more politically active, they had to act as the ultimate check on the conscience of government. "I disdain the Thought of representing a People, *who dare not be free*" Lucas proclaimed.[45]

Lucas moved well beyond Molyneux in describing the dangers to Irish liberties. "LIBERTY, my Brethren, the best Gift of Heaven, is your inheritance," but, "your excellent Constitution has been poisoned, your most wholesome Laws openly violated; your sacred Rights invaded, your Means and Bounds beaten down, and your goodly Heritage ravaged and laid waste," he exclaimed.[46] He tried to heighten the sense of crisis and played to Irish insecurities. Where others had talked about the need for the people to elect responsible men to Parliament, he emphasized that the responsibility—and power—of the people did not end there. Indeed, Lucas was somewhat of a leveler. Attacked for presumptuously standing for Parliament when he had little experience in government and even less to recommend him socially, he countered that any man could aspire to office if he prepared himself for public service. Virtue, he contended, was the best qualification for office. Whether voting for representation in Dublin guilds or for members of Parliament, "our

---

43. Ibid., preface, xvi.
44. See Gordon's comments on Trenchard's ideas in his preface to *Cato's Letters,* liii–lv.
45. Lucas, *Political Constitutions,* Address XI, p. 148.
46. Idem, *Divelina Libera: An Apology for the Civil Rights and Liberties of the Commons and Citizens of Dublin* (Dublin: James Esdall, 1744), 5.

Choice should be determined, according to the weight of the Man's essential Abilities for the Office to be confer'd, and not according to the weight of the Ornaments, that might illustrate such Abilities and set them forth in great Lustre."[47] What is more, he asserted that all who sat in government, from the king down, were directly answerable to "the Voice of the People."[48] He not only rebuked placemen and pensioners, something commonly done by parliamentary Patriots, he urged that all members of Parliament be required to live in their districts and not hold offices where there was a possible conflict of interest. This the parliamentary Patriots were not at all inclined to do. And they no doubt flinched at Lucas's depiction of them as trustees of the people, bound to answer the popular will.

Lucas brewed a storm of controversy in Dublin and national politics. Admirers revered him as the "palladium of constitutional liberty," and detractors reviled him as the "Wilkes of Ireland."[49] He returned from exile in 1761 after obtaining a medical degree at Leyden and opening a practice in London. The indictment against him had been dropped and some of the reforms he agitated for in Dublin municipal government had been carried out in his absence. Vindicated, he sat in the House of Commons for a decade, before his death in 1771. His funeral was a major occasion in Dublin, with the lord mayor and aldermen obligingly joining with guild members and the general citizenry to pay their respects. The earl of Charlemont marched in the procession, as did "Divers of the Nobility and Gentry" and "two hundred of the young gentlemen of Trinity College, in their gowns, two and two."[50] The *Freeman's Journal*, a paper Lucas founded, eulogized him as "a gentleman of unblemished honour . . . as a Senator, unbiased in judgement, invariable in conduct, and incorruptible in integrity."[51] Eight years later, a white marble statue of him would be placed in the newly constructed Royal Exchange. On the pedestal was carved a bas-relief of Liberty, with rod and cap.[52] Ed-

---

47. Idem, *Lucas Against the World, and the World Against Lucas* (1748), 5.
48. Idem, *Political Constitutions*, Address IX, p. 97. Also see John Fleming, *The Country Gentleman's Letter to the Citizens of Dublin* (Dublin: James Esdall, 1749); and the series of ten letters that began with *An Occasional Letter from The Farmer to the Freemen of Dublin* (Dublin: George Faulkner, 1749), both of which show that Lucas was not alone in his thinking on this and other subjects.
49. *Freeman's Journal*, 6 November 1771, from Lucas's obituary, for Lucas as "palladium"; and Murphy, "The Lucas Affair," 231, for Townshend on Lucas as Wilkes; and ibid., 3, 211, for Lucas's significance.
50. From the account reprinted in the *Boston Gazette, and Country Journal*, 9 March 1772.
51. *Freeman's Journal*, 6 November 1771; reprinted in the *Boston Evening-Post*, 3 February 1772; also see the briefer notice in the *Dublin Journal*, 5 November 1771.
52. See the description in Gilbert, *History of Dublin*, 2:55–61.

ward Newenham, one of the more liberal members of Commons, paid for a memorial erected to Lucas in St. Michan's churchyard. The lengthy inscription praised Lucas mightily and extolled his virtues, concluding:

> LUCAS! Hibernia's Friend, her Joy and Pride.
> Her Powerful Bulwark, and her skilful Guide,
> Firm in the Senate, steady to his Trust.
> Unmov'd by Fear, and obstinately Just.[53]

There were also those who preferred that Lucas be forgotten and who wished that his populist politics had never been introduced. Edmund Burke, for one, was disturbed by his irreverent, combative style. "I do not understand that spirit which could raise such hackneyed pretences and such contemptible talents as those of Dr. Lucas to so great consideration," he complained to a close friend, "not only among the mob, but as I hear on all hands, among very many of rank and figure."[54] Even those who admired Lucas could be ambivalent about what he had done. Despite their hopes, leaders of the parliamentary opposition could not completely control him or the manner of politics to which he helped give birth.[55]

Lucas tried to place his views within what he took to be the proper historical framework. Like Domvile and Molyneux, he searched the Irish past to establish legitimacy. He condemned the "New Rules" of 1672 for the conduct of Dublin government as a violation of the original corporate charter. To Lucas the historical record spoke plainly. Unfortunately, Dublin's corporate past was actually as confused and difficult to follow as that of Ireland itself. Precedents were not clear, because the city had changed drastically over the centuries. It had received numerous charters, and it altered its governmental forms and practices many times. The history of Dublin could no more be used to prove constitutional rights and lawful prerogatives than could the history of Ireland. Lucas's critics noted that fact and dismissed him as a firebrand stoking the people with delusive ideas.[56]

---

53. *The Dublin Journal*, 19 June 1777. The *Freeman's Journal*, 8 June 1776, had lamented that Lucas was being forgotten and urged the city corporations to raise money for a monument to him.

54. Thomas W. Copeland, et al., eds., *The Correspondence of Edmund Burke*, 10 vols. (Cambridge: Cambridge University Press, 1958–78), 1:139, letter from Burke to Charles O'Hara of 3 July 1761. Murphy, "The Lucas Affair," 175–81, asserts that Burke was not as vehemently anti-Lucas as it is usually thought.

55. See the earl of Charlemont's letter of 9 April 1767 to Henry Flood in the Henry Flood Correspondence, British Library, Add. MS. 22,930, where Charlemont tried to reassure Flood that Lucas could be useful to their group in Parliament. Also see the sketch of Lucas in Grattan, *Memoirs*, 1:81–92.

56. See, for example, *The Cork Surgeon's Antidote, Against the Dublin Apothecary's*

Others accused Lucas of being inconsistent, of seeking office while he condemned office seekers. In truth, Lucas was not above taking posts that were little better than sinecures, prompting one critic to call him the "three penny patriot" for a duty he was supposed to collect as a city-appointed customs collector.[57] Admittedly Lucas was not as pure as his supporters wanted to believe and as his writings and speeches encouraged them to think. Yet purity was a scarce commodity in Irish politics.

Lucas fretted in exile when the 1753 crisis erupted and the Patriots organized themselves in Parliament. He scoffed that they were not really patriots; rather, they were men jealous of their power, who sought only to protect themselves. Lucas ended up being as critical of the Patriots as were defenders of the administration.[58] No one could deny that Henry Boyle and Anthony Malone, leaders of the Patriots in 1753, were afterward reconciled to the administration. Boyle became the earl of Shannon and accepted a pension; Malone eventually became chancellor of the exchequer. To observers like Lucas, these men had sold their services to the court: like Judas they surrendered to their greed.

Still, there were those who conceded that the Patriots and disgruntled undertakers had not been selfless but that they had nonetheless advanced the cause of Irish rights.[59] Besides, the "Patriots" were not necessarily insincere simply because they switched sides. Politicians as well as statesmen, they could do little if they were out of power, and they had no hope of gaining and keeping power if they were too anti-administration, too unyielding in their demands, too unwilling to taint themselves by taking office. Lucas himself behaved like a politician. He condemned the Parliament for its shortcomings, yet he sought to be a member of it.

Like the Patriots he judged so harshly, Lucas was part of a political movement he helped to create but did not fully understand. For all of

---

Poyson for the Citizens of Dublin (Dublin: Peter Wilson, 1749), which is often attributed to Richard Cox, grandson and namesake of the chancellor. Cox was pro-administration at the time this pamphlet was written. By 1753 he had shifted to the Patriot side and is thought to have written *The True Life of Betty Ireland* (London: J. Robinson, 1753), an allegory somewhat similar to Swift's *Injured Lady*. This pamphlet was not the first to use the "Betty Ireland" motif, nor would it be the last. There were also many other allegories floating around, such as *A Fragment of the History of Patrick* (London, 1753), a throwback to the tale in Swift's *Intelligencer*.

57. See Murphy, "The Lucas Affair," 140–41, for this.
58. Charles Lucas, *Charles Lucas's Prophecy, concerning the Mock-Patriots of Ireland* (London, 1756); and similar sentiments in George Macartney, *An Account of Ireland in 1773* (London, 1773), 29–35. Macartney had been chief secretary to Lord Lieutenant Townshend and had little regard for Lucas.
59. HMC, *Charlemont*, 1:6.

his criticisms of the Irish Parliament's failings and the inadequate safeguards of mixed government, he did not come out and condemn Parliament as an irredeemable institution; nor did he call for the overthrow of mixed government and the creation of a republic. He denied that he was a radical or revolutionary, calling himself instead a defender of age-old constitutional and charter rights. He likewise denied that he was anti-British or a separatist, or that he was inciting the people to violence with his talk of the dangers of becoming "enslaved." He did, however, foster a greater democratization of politics. To that extent, the critics who scourged him as the "Wilkes of Ireland" were not so wrong. His attempt to mobilize the freemen of Dublin anticipated by over a decade what Wilkes would do on a more ambitious scale in London.[60] He was no literal democrat, but then again, neither was John Wilkes. If he appealed to the "people," he also attempted to lead and instruct them. He could not conceive—nor could he accept—their spurning him. He did indeed have demagogic tendencies, as his political opponents were quick to point out.

Despite all his shortcomings and inconsistencies, Lucas gave the people a greater sense of their power. He called for "free and frequent elections." He sought to redefine the relationship between elector and elected. He urged voters in parliamentary as well as municipal elections to require candidates to make pledges, sign formal declarations, and swear that they were not attached to any faction, that they would abide "upon true, and disinterested patriot Principles."[61] He even hinted that members of Parliament should be bound by their constituents' instructions and turned out of office if they violated their trust. Lucas made the people the lifeblood of politics, and he was echoed by a growing number of writers through the 1750s. As one pamphleter avowed:

We have nothing to fear, but among ourselves. We are in the Hands of those who represent Us; the present and future Happiness of Ireland depends on *their* Behaviour, and that, in the greatest Degree, on the spirit of the People.[62]

Another writer was more direct and more emphatic:

Wherefore, when we elect Persons to represent Us in Parliament, we must not be supposed to depart from the smallest Right which we have deposited with

---

60. For Wilkes see George Rudé, *Wilkes and Liberty* (Oxford: Clarendon Press, 1962).
61. Lucas, *Political Constitutions*, Address III, p. 398.
62. *Common Sense: In a Letter to a Friend*, 4th ed. (Dublin, 1755), 44. Also see *A Letter from a Free Citizen of Dublin, to a Freeholder in the County of Armagh* (Dublin, 1753), which argued that M.P.s were obliged to follow the instructions of their constituents.

them. We make a Lodgment, not a Gift. We entrust, but part with Nothing. And, were it possible that They should attempt to destroy the Constitution which We had appointed them to maintain, They can no more be held in the Rank of our Representatives, than a Factor, turned Pirate, can continue to be called the Factor of those Merchants whose Goods he had plundered and whose Confidence he had betrayed.[63]

Lucas is important, too, for the numerous causes he championed. An outspoken advocate of a free press, he also founded two newspapers: the shortlived *Censor* and the *Freeman's Journal*; the latter was for three decades the leading opposition paper in Dublin. He also defended freedom of conscience and argued against the power of the clergy over the laity. Though not an outspoken advocate of Catholic political rights, at the same time he was not as anti-Catholic as some have contended. He believed that Catholics were entitled to the "full Protection and Benefit of the Law," and he even conceded that Catholics—before the Reformation, at least—had defended Irish constitutional rights.

Yet Lucas also seemed to think that Catholics were not as independent minded as Protestants and had shown that they could fall under the "*despotic Sway* of a *foreign Bishop*."[64] In some ways Lucas was not so different from Molyneux, Swift, and others who defended Irish constitutional rights but did so in an Anglo-Irish Protestant context. Molyneux had little to say about Catholics; although Swift criticized Dissenters more than he did Catholics, he was no champion of downtrodden Catholics.[65] Swift, like Lucas, sympathized with Catholics at those few times when he saw that there was a distinction between the Church in Rome and Catholicism as it was practiced in Ireland.

By and large, Catholics were still excluded from the constitutional nationalist tradition as Swift, Lucas, and leaders of the Anglo-Irish Ascendancy defined it. They took their cue from William Molyneux, the Protestant, not Patrick Darcy, the Catholic, although Darcy had made the same basic defense of Irish constitutional rights. Two Catholic writ-

---

63. *Liberty and Common-Sense to the People of Ireland, Greeting* (Dublin, 1759), 3–4. The author of this pamphlet contended that citizens had the right to defend their liberties but at the same time they had the obligation to act responsibly, not hysterically. The pamphlet was intended to quiet the people, reassure them that union was not intended and get them to cease their rioting. Thus, interestingly, the author had to use the rhetoric of popular politics in an attempt to control its effects. See RIA Haliday pamphlet 256 for the 4 page *A Catalogue of Political Pamphlets* (1756?) that lists 30 entries for the years 1751–1755. Most administration critics were countered by administration defenders. The sheer number of pamphlets demonstrates the frequency with which political issues were debated in public.

64. Lucas, *Political Constitutions*, "A Letter, &c.," 443.

65. For Swift, see his 1717 sermon "Brotherly Love" in Davis et al., eds., *Works of Swift*, 9:172–74.

ers, John Curry and Charles O'Conor, led an unsuccessful campaign to restore Catholics to their role in that tradition. Curry was descended from an "ancient" family in County Cavan. He studied medicine at the University of Paris and practiced for many years in Dublin. He was also a self-styled revisionist historian, whose treatises were loaded with notes and documents to make his case. He argued against the notion, accepted by Anglo-Irish Protestant historians as indisputable truth, that Catholics could not be trusted and that in 1641 they had proved as much when they rose up in an unwarranted and wanton rebellion. From his first brief essay in 1746 to his two volume magnum opus nearly thirty years later, Curry attempted to rewrite Irish history, especially the prevailing view of events in 1641. He contended that Catholics then had had legitimate grievances and had rebelled only after exhausting all efforts at constitutional redress. They had been subjected to oppressive confiscations and restrictions on their worship and had been victimized by greedy men like Thomas Wentworth. They were driven to rebel, despite their heartfelt desire to be good, loyal citizens. Curry did not justify the brutalities that had taken place, but he assembled reams of evidence to prove that Catholics had not been any more brutal than were Protestants. He contended that Catholic motives and actions had been misrepresented by successive generations of writers seeking to rationalize Protestant exclusionism.[66]

Curry's close friend Charles O'Conor expressed similar sentiments. O'Conor spent most of his life on the remnant of what had once been his family's vast estate of Belanagare, in County Roscommon. Even Protestant historians respected O'Conor for his prodigious research into Irish antiquities. He tried to assuage what he knew were deep-seated fears among Protestants. He therefore distinguished between Catholics in Ireland and the Church in Rome, arguing that Catholics could also be good citizens, because they did not subscribe to the theory of papal infallibility in temporal affairs. The pope was not supposed to mix in the secular affairs of Ireland and, when he had in the past, he had been in error. O'Conor called for reason to replace passion and for Protestants to step outside the narrow understanding of the Irish past that they had when they focused on the 1641 rebellion. He, like Curry, called for repeal of the penal laws, the welcoming of Catholics to full citizenship,

---

66. [John Curry], *A Brief Account from the Most Authentic Protestant Writers of the Causes, Motives, and Mischiefs of the Irish Rebellion on the 23rd Day of October 1641* (London, 1747); [idem], *Historical Memoirs of the Irish Rebellion in the Year 1641* (London: J. Williams, 1767; orig. ed. 1758); and idem, *An Historical and Critical Review of the Civil Wars in Ireland,* 2 vols. (Dublin: Luke White, 1786; orig. ed. 1775).

and recognition that "we are as much indebted to our Popish Ancestors for our *Liberties* as for our *Existence*."[67] Catholics would be loyal to any government that protected their rights, he insisted; political orthodoxy could be achieved without insisting on religious homogeneity; the time for sectarian divisions in Irish society had passed.

Both O'Conor and Curry walked a historiographical tightrope. They tried to show where Catholics had been wronged and where Catholics themselves had erred. They tried to criticize without making blanket condemnations, hoping that their readers would see that all of the Irish, throughout their history, had been the victims of needless pain and suffering. They hoped to close old wounds as well as promote healthy new policies.

Their writings enjoyed wide circulation, though not necessarily much popularity outside Irish Catholic circles. Protestant antiquarian Walter Harris dismissed Curry's depiction of the 1641 rebellion as "Monstrous" and "Atrocious" and "destitute of the least foundation of truth."[68] O'Conor's call for repeal of the penal laws was answered by critics countering that, because the Catholics had not yet proved they could be trusted, the penal laws were a matter of Protestant self-preservation.[69] Protestant readers were no doubt much more attracted to the view of history presented in Henry Brooke's *Farmer's Letters*, published in 1745, and Thomas Leland's 1773 three-volume history of Ireland. Leland attemped to strike a stance of scholarly detachment; his text was thus not as impassioned as that of Brooke. Their basic conclusions were nonetheless quite similar: Catholics had not proved that they were part of the true Irish constitutional nationalist tradition, and they could not yet be trusted to participate as equals in Irish society.[70] Curry

---

67. [Charles O'Conor], *The Case of the Roman-Catholics of Ireland* (Dublin: P. Lord, 1755), 20.

68. Walter Harris, Esq., *Fiction Unmasked: Or, An Answer to a Dialogue lately Published by a Popish Physician* (Dublin: Edward Bate, 1752), vii. Harris, by his anti-Catholic intemperance, seemed to violate his own code explained in *Hibernica* (Dublin: John Milliken, 1770; orig. ed., 1747), "An Essay on the Defects in the Histories of Ireland," 255–87, where he argued for a greater appreciation of the Irish past and a better historical method. Charles O'Conor complained to his friend, Dr. John Curry, about Harris's "malice," concluding—sarcastically—"were it worth the while, he ought to be gutted up and gibetted for the good of the public," in a letter of 2 June 1756 in Robert Ward, et al., eds., *Letters of Charles O'Conor of Belanagare* (Washington, D.C.: The Catholic University of America Press, 1984), 14.

69. A Protestant, *Remarks on a Late Pamphlet, entitled, The Case of the Roman Catholics of Ireland* (Dublin, 1755).

70. [Henry Brooke], *The Farmer's Letters to the Protestants of Ireland* (Dublin: George Faulkner, 1745); and Murphy, "The Lucas Affair," 118–20 for a critique of

and O'Conor kept up in their fight in the historiographical trenches even after Leland's history appeared, albeit without much success.

Religious divisions in mid-eighteenth-century Ireland remained strong. Penal laws were not always enforced (otherwise Curry, for example, could not have practiced medicine), but they were still on the books and would remain there for some time to come. Anglo-Irish Protestants like George Berkeley and Samuel Madden, who recognized that Catholics were suffering and needed to be better integrated into Irish society, had also wanted Catholics to solve the problem themselves by becoming Protestants.[71] To them, Catholicism did not qualify as a legitimate religion. For years to come, the Irish Parliament would continue to observe an October "Thanksgiving Day for the Deliverance from the horrid Rebellion" of 1641. Each November 4 brought an even grander occasion, with the lord lieutenant, his ministers, and city officials parading from the Castle to the statue of William III opposite College Green. Volleys were fired and huzzas were shouted, all to celebrate the Glorious Revolution and the victory in Ireland of Anglo-Irish Protestant liberalism over Catholic Stuart oppression.

Even so, it would be inaccurate to say that Ireland at the accession of George III in 1760 was politically no different from what it had been at the beginning of the century. Anglo-Irish Protestants had indeed strengthened their position over these years, excluding the Catholic majority from political participation and keeping them out of many economic pursuits. From one angle, Anglo-Irish Protestants had never been more united, and sectarian divisions had never been more pronounced. From another angle, the view is strikingly different. Parliamentary leaders frequently divided among themselves and politics were often lively—sometimes, as from 1753 to 1756, and again in 1759, almost brutal. Places, pensions, and new peerages had not created lasting alliances between the Castle and Parliament. There were no formal political parties, but there were numerous factions with shifting memberships that organized in response to a multitude of issues, some of only domestic con-

---

Brooke and his views, and his connection to Charles O'Conor. Thomas Leland, *The History of Ireland from the Invasion of Henry II*, 3 vols. (London: J.Nourse, 1773); and the critique by [John Curry], *Occasional Remarks on Certain Passages in Dr. Leland's History of Ireland, relative to the Irish Rebellion of 1641* (London: J. Johnson, 1773). Englishman Ferdinando Warner produced a history that was better balanced and more sophisticated than Leland's; see Warner's *The History of the Rebellion and Civil-War in Ireland* (London, T. Cadell, 1768).

71. [Berkeley], *The Querist*, Part III, query 289; Madden, *Reflections and Resolutions*, 92–106.

cern, some tied to larger questions of empire. The Irish Parliament had become more, not less, insistent about defending its perceived constitutional rights and prerogatives, and it had left behind its earlier lukewarm receptiveness to the idea of union. By mid-century the stage was set for the emergence of a Henry Grattan and the thrust toward parliamentary independence.

Grattan and other inheritors of the mantle handed down by the Patriots of the 1750s did not have a free hand at home, however. At the very moment when Parliament appeared to be most powerful, its leaders were in fact being challenged from without. Men like Charles Lucas had brought a democratic leavening, a movement toward open-air, street-corner politics. Lucas had not intended a political revolution, to be sure; neither, for that matter, had Jonathan Swift, George Berkeley, or the Patriots of 1753. Yet by their talk of constitutional guarantees, their defense of basic freedoms, their emphasis on government by consent, their attempts to mobilize public opinion, and their use of the press, they paved the way for later groups like the Volunteers and United Irishmen that were even more attracted to republican ideas.

The democratic politicians of Lucas's generation denied that they were separatists. Disingenuous or not, Lucas always styled himself as a loyal member of the British empire seeking to restore lost constitutional rights and ensure Irish freedoms. In that sense he was a nationalist in the same way as a Molyneux or Berkeley, though he employed more caustic language and a less deferential approach. If he could deny that he was a revolutionary because he was no separatist, it was harder to escape the revolutionary side to his domestic politics. He challenged the power of the Anglo-Irish elite by emphasizing, as few had before, the rights of the middling sort, the "people" who traditionally had been excluded from the mainstream of political life, even by those who called themselves their representatives and who celebrated the people as the foundation of all legitimate government.

Lucas and others like sometime-ally, sometime-opponent James Digges Latouche revitalized and reconstructed Dublin politics and, through their rhetoric and tactics, Irish politics in general. But Lucas and his allies did not combine with Catholics to form an incipient popular front. They were ambivalent about allowing Catholic political involvement and hesitant to press for Catholic rights. And yet they could not forever ignore the inconsistency of their agitation for more rights and greater freedoms while excluding Catholics, just as parliamentary leaders could not ignore them as spokesmen for middle class Anglo-Irish Protestants.

Besides, religious lines had been blurred a bit in the attempt to build national pride. Curry and O'Conor might not have had much influence as historians, but as activists involved in founding the Catholic Committee in Dublin during the late 1750s, they helped to give Catholics an unofficial political voice. That voice was moderate in tone, requesting and petitioning rather than demanding. Moreover, they helped to stimulate a renewed interest in Irish constitutional history. Although Leland and O'Conor did not agree on how the past should be viewed, they did share manuscripts and ideas; so too had O'Conor and Henry Brooke some years before.[72] Walter Harris, who frowned with such disdain on the Catholic rebels of 1641, was responsible for getting the 1644 "Declaration" into print, although he believed that Patrick Darcy—a Catholic—had written that most important constitutional nationalist tract. In the 1760s there were still a Catholic view and a Protestant view of Irish history, yet Catholics and Protestants alike sought to defend as well as define Irish constitutional rights. Their differences notwithstanding, both groups furthered the development of Irish constitutional nationalism.

The Protestant-Catholic division was only the most obvious rent in Irish society. Defenders of Irish constitutional rights themselves divided along many lines. All were nationalists to one degree or another, but virtually all shunned any association with revolutionary tendencies. By the 1750s, there were more constitutional nationalists than ever before. Members of Parliament were joined by Protestants from modest backgrounds with higher expectations and Catholics hoping to benefit from the growing concern for Irish rights. For another thirty years these Irish nationalists could ignore the revolutionary implications of their constitutional arguments. They preferred instead to look for change through reform, within the empire and the parameters of the Anglo-Irish Protestant Ascendancy.

---

72. Walter D. Love, "Charles O'Conor of Belanagare and Thomas Leland's 'Philosophical' History of Ireland," *Irish Historical Studies* 13 (1962): 1–25. Also see Ned Lebow, "British Historians and Irish History," *Eire-Ireland* 8 (December 1973): 3–38; Francis G. James's suggestive "Historiography and the Irish Constitutional Revolution of 1782," ibid., 18 (Winter 1983): 6–16; and Jacqueline R. Hill, "Popery and Protestantism, Civil and Religious Liberty: The Disputed Lessons of Irish History, 1690–1812," *Past and Present*, no. 18 (February 1988): 96–129.

CHAPTER 3

Ireland and the American Revolution

We fear that the same arm of power that is first stretched out against our brethren and fellow-subjects in America, to abolish their Charters, will violate the great Charter of this land.

Freeman's Journal, 1774

A voice from America shouted to liberty! the echo of it caught your people as it passed along the Atlantic, and they renewed the voice till it reverberated here.

Henry Flood, 1782[1]

George III has the misfortune of being remembered as the king who lost thirteen American colonies. It would be stretching the truth to say that he came close to losing Ireland as well. Nevertheless, perennial Irish problems worsened during the American Revolutionary era, causing George III, his closest ministers, British parliamentary leaders, and their Irish supporters a great deal of worry. Even though Irish problems predated the American crisis that emerged in the 1760s, Irish affairs and attitudes during the latter half of the eighteenth century were shaped in part by what went on across the Atlantic, just as American developments were influenced, though not as much, by what happened in Ireland.

A new generation of Patriots in the Irish Parliament would be more insistent than those who came before and they would draw lessons from what they saw as British tyranny in America to warn of what could

---

1. *Freeman's Journal*, 30 June 1774; Flood from his speech in Commons of 14 June 1782 in Henry Grattan, Jr., ed., *The Speeches of the Right Honourable Henry Grattan*, 4 vols. (London: Longman, Hurst, Rees, Orme, and Brown, 1822), 1:321.

happen in Ireland. Their forerunners, the Patriots of 1753, had gradually been reabsorbed into the mainstream of Irish parliamentary politics. Ireland appeared to be peaceful enough, even prosperous, when George III began his reign in 1760. Appearances, as the old saying goes, can be deceiving. Elections were held, a new session of Parliament opened in October 1761, and with that the undertaker system-Castle alliance was once again wrenched. It did not take long for fissures to appear and for constitutional issues and sundry grievances to be raised. The most basic differences were still unresolved, as George Townshend discovered during his stormy lord lieutenancy from 1767 to 1772.

Townshend, a veteran army officer who had fought alongside Wolfe on the Plains of Abraham outside Quebec, had his mettle tested again as viceroy. It seems only fitting that the name Townshend should be associated with imperial crisis on both sides of the Atlantic. Charles Townshend became a villain to Americans protesting the revenue-raising program that he shepherded through the British Parliament in 1767, the same year that his older brother George became lord lieutenant in Ireland. Charles's death spared him from the turmoil that his policies provoked in the American colonies; George would not be so lucky. His lord lieutenancy saw yet another strain in Irish-British relations, this one tied to a prolonged crisis that helped bring revolution in America and a renewed questioning of the imperial tie among the Irish.

Townshend fell prey to the instability of British politics, the indecisiveness of the British government, the ambitions of the Irish Parliament, and his own shortcomings. He was the sixth lord lieutenant since George III had taken the throne; his appointment reflected the rise and fall of ministries across the Irish Sea and the desires of George III and his advisers to check the power of "Whig oligarchs" in the British Parliament as well as undertakers in Ireland.[2] Townshend was expected (though not obliged) to reside in Dublin—even when the Irish Parliament was not in session—in order to bring the undertakers into line. As a symbol of more vigorous Crown government, he was bound to offend Irish leaders jealous of their power and their own claims on the patron-

---

2. See the traditional view of the Townshend viceroyalty offered in J. L. McCracken, "The Irish Viceroyalty, 1760–1773," in H. A. Cronne, et al., eds., *Essays in British and Irish History* (London: Frederick Muller, 1949), 152–68; and the somewhat different view in Thomas Bartlett, "The Townshend Viceroyalty, 1767–1772" (Ph.D. dissertation, Queen's University of Belfast, 1976), much of which is summarized in Bartlett's "The Townshend Viceroyalty, 1767–72" in T. Bartlett and D. Hayton, eds., *Penal Era and Golden Age* (Belfast: Ulster Historical Foundation, 1979), 88–112. Also see Bartlett's "Opposition in Late Eighteenth-Century Ireland: The Case of the Townshend Viceroyalty," *Irish Historical Studies* 22 (1981): 313–30.

age system. House speaker John Ponsonby and prime serjeant John Hely-Hutchinson had been willing to work with Townshend when he first arrived, as were other parliamentary leaders. They soon went into opposition, and not simply because of Townshend's mandate as a resident lord lieutenant. Townshend was inept at courting them, and he did not really have a free hand or a precise policy to enforce—a failing of Whitehall and Westminster and a reflection of the larger malaise of British politics. British policy continued to be irresolute. It lacked consistency and cohesiveness, despite British recognition that the Anglo-Irish, ostensibly their partners in empire, had separatist tendencies. The resident lord lieutenant was expected to check those tendencies as they had developed during the 1750s. And yet the American crisis of the 1760s, culminating in open rebellion by April 1775, further distracted British attention from Ireland. Townshend and his successors were destined for trouble.

The Irish Parliament had been pressing a number of issues before Townshend's arrival, including a habeas corpus act, restrictions on places and pensions, more secure tenure for judges, and a septennial act for parliament modelled on that used in Westminster. The general election in 1760 had been the first in Ireland since 1727, when George II took the throne. Patriots in Commons chafed at a system that allowed elections to be tied to the death of old and coronation of new monarchs. Until George II died they had no way of knowing when the next general election would occur. They had to settle for an octennial act in 1768, good for the Irish Parliament, but not necessarily passed for that reason. In one of his rare sarcastic asides, the earl of Charlemont later observed that the Irish Commons pressed for a septennial bill only because its members feared the popular protest that could result if they did not. Commons, according to Charlemont, hoped that the Irish privy council would quash it. But the privy council, insulted that Commons went ahead with its proposed bill and courted popular favor, sent the bill on to London, assuming that it would be tabled there. British privy councillors were upset by all of this but decided to change the septennial act into an octennial act; they sent it back to the Irish Parliament with the stipulation that, once the bill was signed, that session of Parliament would be ended immediately. Instead of refusing to accept the altered bill—as the British privy council expected—Lords and Commons in Ireland passed it, because, Charlemont contended, the members looked forward to more money and more power from the more frequent sale of borough seats. Thus a good law was entered on the books, a law wanted and needed by the people, though it had not really been passed for them; it passed because of political ambition and factional maneuvers.[3]

There was undoubtedly more to it than that, but Charlemont did have a point. The Irish Parliament was not above shifting its ground on constitutional questions. Constitutional issues could not be divorced from politics, and because of that the Irish Parliament did not always act consistently. It overlooked the fact that the septennial act had been altered in London because of anticipated benefits at home. (Less than three years later, the Irish Commons would refuse to pass a money bill altered by the British privy council, claiming that the council had trespassed on its rights.) Undeniably, many Commons members were ambivalent about more frequent meetings of Parliament, because more frequent elections meant greater expenses and increased power for the electorate. For those controlling numerous seats, there was money to be made and influence to be peddled, considerations that might have counterbalanced their fear of more frequent elections.

For all of his troubles, Townshend managed to survive, despite battles over augmentation (enlarging the military establishment from twelve thousand to over fifteen thousand) and increasing the number of revenue commissioners, and despite the accusations of opponents like Hely-Hutchinson that the lord lieutenant's "ill-placed partialities and ill-founded resentments will greatly and unnecessarily involve and embroil the affairs of the country."[4] Hely-Hutchinson was peeved that he had not been made lord chancellor; that did not stop him from accepting another sinecure. He and others who attacked Townshend for "abuse" of the civil list and the awarding of new pensions and peerages often themselves sought office. Their own ambitions and rivalries, as much as Townshend's buying off of the opposition, kept them from presenting a united front. Ponsonby eventually resigned as speaker when he found that, as late as 1771, Townshend could still assemble a majority, despite the widespread muttering against his administration.

Townshend did have defenders and they justified his pushing the augmentation bill and proroguing Parliament following the money bill dispute. They pointed out that he had supported the octennial bill and other

3. Historical Manuscripts Commission, *The Manuscripts and Correspondence of James, First Earl of Charlemont*, 2 vols. (London: Eyre amd Spottiswoode, 1891, 1894), 1:25–27. Also see J. Steven Watson, *The Reign of George III, 1760–1815* (Oxford: Clarendon Press, 1960), 129.

4. Hely-Hutchinson to Lord Hertford in 1769, HMC, *The Manuscripts of the Duke of Beaufort, K.G., the Earl of Donoughmore, and Others* (London: Eyre and Spottiswoode, 1891), 265.

issues that came up in Parliament, and they insisted that his administration was not corrupt, nor did it behave unconstitutionally.[5] Nonetheless, Townshend's critics were even more vehement and vocal. The most vocal, the most irksome to Townshend of them all, was Charles Lucas. Lucas had returned from exile in 1761 unrepentant, his politics unchanged. Elected to the House of Commons as one of the representatives for the city of Dublin, he remained so until his death in 1771. He came back an aged man, his hair grey and his body tormented with arthritis and gout, so crippled that he was carried into the House chambers and almost never rose to speak. No matter: his tongue and his quill were still sharp.

Wanting to get back into the thick of Irish politics and knowing that parliamentary elections would be held, Lucas had fired off some *Seasonable Advice* soon after the coronation of George III. He tactfully described George as a "GREAT, a PATRIOT KING" before he went on to ridicule the last lord lieutenant appointed by George II for acting "more like an Oriental Nabob, or a Turkish Captain Basha, than the representative of a free people." As far as Lucas was concerned, the Irish people continued to be wronged "by lawless governors, corrupt counsellors, ignorant and servile judges, and packed perpetual parliaments." His description of George III as "heaven's vice-regent" notwithstanding, he also noted that "so sacred is the liberty of every individual, that there exists no power, that can wrest it from the meanest of subjects." He called for Irish electors (especially those in Dublin) to elect virtuous, honest men (meaning him) to office, men who would restore vigor and integrity to government, who could head off "that most violent and desperate remedy, which you now so justly dread, an Union."[6]

Once ensconced in the Irish Commons, Lucas agitated for a septennial act; had he had any hope of success, he would have pressed for a triennial act instead. His insistence on a more responsive Parliament, and his continued reference to M.P.s as trustees of the people, sparked rebuttals by other pamphleteers. Reacting to Lucas's assertion that elec-

---

5. For Townshend's defense, see two pamphlets attributed to James Caldwell: *An Essay on the Character and Conduct of His Excellency Lord Visc. Townshend* (1771) and *An Address to the House of Commons of Ireland: By a Freeholder* (n.d.), both copies in the BL. Also see Bartlett, "Townshend Viceroyalty," appendix D, 354–55, listing Townshend's appointments and disbursements of places and pensions—outlays that were not unusually large, Bartlett noted. For a more damning portrait of Townshend, see Henry Grattan, Jr., *Memoirs of the Rt. Hon. Henry Grattan*, 5 vols. (London: Henry Colburn, 1849), 1:172–73, 191–92.

6. Charles Lucas, *Seasonable Advice to the Electors of Members of Parliament at the ensuing General Election* (London: T. Davies, 1760), quotes from pp. 11, 8, 22, 23, and 27–28, resp.

tors had the right to instruct M.P.s, one critic countered that the notion *"that all power is derived from the people* is absolutely false, false in theory, and false in fact."[7] To this writer, and no doubt to others as well, Lucas was a dangerous man with even more dangerous ideas.

By the time that Townshend arrived in 1767, Lucas had managed to elbow himself to the front of opposition politics. When Townshend prorogued Parliament in 1769 after Commons refused to pass a money bill drafted by the Irish privy council, Lucas again took up his pen. He mocked Townshend by the very politeness of his tone. After the appearance of this first Lucas pamphlet, Townshend endeavored to stop the publication of a second—to no avail. In these writings "to promote the knowledge and cause of truth," Lucas chastised the lord lieutenant for abusing his executive powers. As he had from the beginning of his career, Lucas stretched the use of constitutional history to prove his argument that only the Irish Commons, not the lord lieutenant and not the Irish privy council, had the right to introduce money bills, because the people could be taxed only by their representatives. Poynings' Law, he contended, in no way altered that fact. He sprinkled his texts with allusions to natural and constitutional rights. The title page of the first pamphlet featured a picture of a hand thrust out of the clouds clenching Magna Carta, to add a divine dimension.[8]

Lucas's criticisms of Townshend's administration came on the heels of essays that had been even more mocking and caustic but were written by M.P.s whose politics were not as radical as Lucas's. The essays were first published in the *Freeman's Journal,* the newspaper that Lucas helped found; they began as a series in January 1768 that ran irregularly for several years. They were eventually collected and published separately as *Baratariana.*

Hercules Langrishe, M.P. for the borough of Knocktopher, County Kilkenny, was apparently the primary author in this collaborative effort. Henry Flood and his friend Gervase Parker Bushe, also members of Commons, lent a hand. Born in 1732, the illegitimate son of the chief justice on the Court of King's Bench for Ireland, Flood was fast becoming a leading voice among the reorganized parliamentary Patriots. He had attended Oxford after studying at Trinity College, Dublin. From Oxford he moved on to the Inner Temple and was soon after sworn to the Irish Bar. Entering Commons before the age of thirty, he was highly

---

7. Philopator, *The Question about Septennial, Or, frequent new Parliaments, Impartially Examined in Two Letters* (Dublin, 1761), 27.
8. Charles Lucas, *The Rights and Privileges of Parliament* (Dublin: Thomas Ewing, 1770), and idem, *The Usage of Holding Parliaments* (Dublin, 1770).

regarded for his mastery of the classics and skills in debate. In a daring, even reckless, move in 1766 he criticized Poynings' Law and urged that it be repealed; the administration blocked him easily.

Bushe was soon to marry the older sister of yet another of the *Baratariana* authors, Henry Grattan, a young man not yet sitting in Commons and still studying law at the Middle Temple.[9] Grattan's father, James, had been recorder for the city of Dublin at the time that the reforms Lucas advocated were finally made, and he served with Lucas as M.P. for Dublin. The elder Grattan and Lucas were not overly friendly, but that did not stop the younger Grattan from admiring Lucas's work. Langrishe and Henry Grattan were tied by a lifelong friendship, the older Langrishe playing an avuncular role for Grattan. At this point in their careers Flood and Grattan were close, and they shared a respect for Charles Lucas. Flood helped Grattan become a protégé of the earl of Charlemont. Lucas was Charlemont's personal physician.

Like Flood, Langrishe and Bushe were noted debaters in Commons and had sometimes opposed Townshend; still, they were not implacable foes of the administration or the aristocratic system of parliamentary politics that Lucas found so reprehensibly oligarchical.[10] Langrishe held government posts throughout his career and sat for a borough whose elections he easily controlled. Bushe and Flood also sat for boroughs with small electorates. Flood had purchased his seat in Commons, was longing to buy a seat in the British Parliament, and would become a

---

9. *Baratariana: A select Collection of Fugitive Political Pieces, Published during the Administration of Lord Townshend in Ireland*, 2d ed. (Dublin, 1773; orig. ed. 1772). For authorship see the *Dictionary of National Biography* sketches of Flood, Grattan, and Langrishe; Grattan, *Memoirs*, 1:185–88; and idem, ed., *Miscellaneous Works of the Right Honourable Henry Grattan* (London: Longman, Hurst, Rees, Orme, and Brown, 1822), 1. W. G. Carroll, editor of John Hely-Hutchinson's *The Commercial Restraints of Ireland* (Dublin: M. H. Gill, 1888; orig. ed., Dublin, 1779), included Philip Tisdal and Barry Yelverton among the authors. Tisdal was opposed to Townshend early on, but Carroll presents no evidence of authorship. Indeed, Carroll admits that Tisdal was parodied as "Don Phillip the Moor" (his nickname was "Black Phil"). Tisdal was an inveterate foe of Hely-Hutchinson, who was also parodied in *Baratariana*. Yelverton would become one of Grattan's allies in Parliament, at least through 1782, but I have seen nothing to link him with Grattan and *Baratariana*. The *Pennsylvania Chronicle*, 8 November 1773, reprinted one of the essays and identified Flood, in effusively flattering terms, as the "supposed" author.

10. See David Large, ed., "The Irish House of Commons in 1769," *Irish Historical Studies* 11 (1958): 18–45, which includes a list of Commons members compiled in 1769 that categorizes Bushe and Langrishe as "Doubtful against" government, Flood as "Doubtful govt.," and Charles Lucas as "Against. Always against." Also see Edith Johnston's list in appendix C, 368–77, of *Great Britain and Ireland, 1760–1800* (Edinburgh: Oliver and Boyd, 1963). Johnston included M.P.s who sat from 1768 to 1776 and divided them into pro- and anti-government categories, based on her reading of voting records.

vice-treasurer under Townshend's successor. He and the others were less offended by the system of government than by what they considered Townshend's abuses of that system. They denounced Townshend and the Irish privy council on the money bill issue for taking "a point-blank shot, let fly directly against the bulwark of our constitution, the democratic part of our senate." Appealing to the people, they proclaimed, "Let us cast off the yoke of slavery, and vindicate our freedom and independence. Let us no longer be rid, rather than ruled, as we have been too long, by men who have neither heads nor hearts."[11]

Despite the popular appeals and constitutional allusions, most of the essays in *Baratariana* concentrated on lampooning Townshend, "Sancho" in the cast of pseudonymous characters. Britain came under fire as "La Mancha," and one of the most severe criticisms levelled at Townshend was that he had become "the miserable instrument of English tyranny." The authors of *Baratariana*, then, went beyond Lucas in their criticism of the Townshend administration to question the very nature of the imperial tie. Later essays scolded George III for appointing Lord North his chief minister. North, the authors huffed, had answered the king's "expectations. Ireland is in a flame; and he may now hug himself in the thought, that every part of his domain groans under the iron rod of oppression."[12] Furthermore, *Baratariana* linked the troubles of Ireland with those of imperial administration in general, especially those that had brought crisis to the American colonies. The very first letter in the series was "From a Native of Barataria, to His Friend" in Pennsylvania and warned that "the same arts, which may be capable of destroying our liberties, must certainly operate more strongly against yours." For indeed:

You are happily, at too great a distance from ministerial tyranny to fall an immediate sacrifice to the politics of despotism; therefore the essay has been commenced nearer home. We have been treated, of late, not as the children, but the bastards of our mother country; and all our expectations of an equal distribution of inheritance are considered, not as claims of right, but as pretenses of contumacy, and presumption. Your circumstances and ours then, being exactly the same, the difference of our situations can possibly gain you but the poor respite of Ulysses' petition to Polyphemus, of being devoured the last.[13]

11. *Baratariana*, Letter IV, p. 39. The authors also warned that the Townshend administration was plotting a move for union, which Lucas had also claimed of an earlier administration in his 1760 *Seasonable Advice*. Union had become anathema; conjuring it up as evidence of an administration conspiracy was a common ploy from the 1750s onward, which may help to explain why the anti-union reactions were so strong and emotional in 1799–1800. For some it was ingrained behavior.
12. *Baratariana*, Letter XXIX, p. 233.
13. Ibid., Letter I, p. 2: also see the ballad in Letter XXXVI, pp. 291–99.

Bushe and Langrishe did not confine their criticisms to the essays and letters of *Baratariana*. Bushe, it appears, wrote a brief, anonymous critique of Anglo-American relations, and Langrishe followed with his own, longer—and also anonymously written—pamphlet. Bushe argued that Americans were not represented in the British Parliament, that they had the right to tax themselves through their own representative assemblies, and that they were entitled to all the rights of British citizens, regardless of their many differences and the varieties of their charters. Parliament had at most a superintending power over commerce, he continued; this, along with his slap at virtual representation, may help explain why this little tract was so rapidly reprinted in the American colonies.[14]

Langrishe acknowledged and seconded the arguments made by Bushe. He took issue with a pamphlet just written by William Knox recommending that Ireland and the American colonies carry a larger burden of the costs of empire. He countered that Ireland could not afford to pay any more because its economy was already depressed, to some extent because of Britain's navigation system. He called for commercial relief, with Ireland and the American colonies to be treated as equal trading partners. Like Bushe, he tried to argue from the position of self-interest, noting that flourishing trade would help Britain as much as it would the colonies. And, like Bushe, he made constitutional considerations secondary. Both authors allowed the British Parliament a superintending power over commerce within the empire, Ireland included. And both avoided calling Ireland a sister kingdom, realizing that such insistence could alienate British M.P.s, their intended readers. Neither employed the abrasive, inflammatory language of *Baratariana*, perhaps because they wanted to appear judicious or, equally possible, because they still wanted to believe that a community of interests could be created within the empire, making further agitation unnecessary. "Give them *freedom,* and they will adhere to you," Langrishe pleaded, "give them *commerce,* and they will enrich you."[15]

William Knox would not have disputed Langrishe on that point. He too felt that the Irish—and the Americans, for that matter—should be

14. [Gervase Parker Bushe], *The Case of Great-Britain and America, addressed to the King, and both Houses of Parliament* (Philadelphia: William and Thomas Bradford, 1769). It has also been attributed to George B. Butler; it went through three editions within one year in Boston.

15. [Hercules Langrishe], *Considerations on the Dependencies of Great Britain with Observations on a Pamphlet entitled The Present State of the Nation* (London: J. Almon, 1769), quote from p. 84. Langrishe's authorship has not been proved or disproved. I have accepted the claim that Langrishe was indeed the author, as I did for Bushe (above).

made full commercial partners. Thus, although he advocated a land tax in Ireland to help raise revenue there, he also wanted an easing of all trade barriers within the empire. The gains made by the Irish through increased trade, he believed, would more than offset the drain brought by a new land tax.[16] Knox certainly did not consider himself anti-Irish; of Scots-Irish descent, he was born and raised in County Antrim. Nonetheless, he wrote from a London rather than a Dublin perspective.

He and other advocates of reform like Thomas Pownall were imperialists even if they were reform-minded. They tried to tiptoe around political issues and constitutional questions, hoping that an easing of commercial restrictions would diminish the frequency and stridency of political disputes. Pownall had called for "a grand marine dominion, consisting of our possessions in the Atlantic and in America united into a one interest, into a one center where the seat of government is." He and Knox were liberals insofar as they could see the need for change and greater accommodation. In the reciprocal empire they envisioned, Britain would "nourish and cultivate" as well as "protect and govern the colonies."[17] If they were liberal on economic issues, however, on political issues they could be rather conservative. Their expressions of concern for the "colonies"—probably anticipating the reaction of Irish readers, Knox was careful to call Ireland a "kingdom"—were not insincere, but they still considered all of the colonies and the "kingdom" of Ireland to be subordinate to the mother country, and more specifically, to the British Parliament.

By 1774, amid a deepening American crisis, Pownall blamed Britain for making colonial policy a partisan issue and the colonists for shifting their ground and casting British actions in the worst possible light. His solution to the confusion over sovereignty was to call for "a mixed im-

---

16. [William Knox], *The Present State of the Nation* (London: J. Almon, 1768); and [idem], *The Controversy between Great Britain and her Colonies Reviewed* (London, J. Almon, 1769).

17. [Thomas Pownall], The Administration of the Colonies (London: J. Wilkie, 1764), quotes from pp. 6, 24. On Knox, see Leland Bellot, *William Knox* (Austin: University of Texas Press, 1977). For one view of Pownall (and Knox), see Richard Koebner, *Empire* (Cambridge: Cambridge University Press, 1961), 173–92, and Randolph G. Adams, *Political Ideas of the American Revolution* (New York: Barnes and Noble, 1958; orig. ed., 1922), 56–58; for another, see John Shy, "Thomas Pownall, Henry Ellis, and the Spectrum of Possibilities," in Alison Gilbert Olson and Richard Maxwell Brown, eds., *Anglo-American Political Relations, 1675–1775* (New Brunswick: Rutgers University Press, 1970), 155–86. For another tract on reforming the empire, see *An Application of some General Political Rules to the Present State of Great Britain, Ireland, and America* (London: J. Almon, 1766). Also see Jack P. Greene, et al., eds., *Magna Charta for America* (Philadelphia: American Philosophical Society, 1986), for James Abercromby's two hitherto unpublished tracts (of 1752 and 1774) calling for imperial reform.

perium of *colonial government*."[18] This in itself was a convoluted notion and could not mask the fact that Pownall believed, as did Knox, that ultimate sovereignty over Ireland as well as over the American colonies lay with the British Parliament.

Neither advocated parliamentary union, and Pownall tried to soften his arguments by allowing the Irish Parliament and colonial American assemblies a certain amount of localized power, but both ultimately accepted the interpretations of Sir William Blackstone. Blackstone's *Commentaries*, the culmination of some twenty years of lectures on the law at Oxford, were published during the latter part of the 1760s, when the Irish and Americans were becoming more restive and when Bushe, Langrishe, Knox, and Pownall had begun their pamphleteering. Blackstone made an emphatic defense of parliamentary sovereignty, stating that the "power of parliament is absolute and without control." Since the British Parliament was composed of three distinct branches—king, Lords, and Commons—that represented the three basic, irreducible political tendencies—monarchy, aristocracy, and democracy—Parliament embodied the ideal of mixed and balanced government. All parts of the empire were subordinate to the British Parliament, Ireland no less than the American colonies. "As to Ireland," Blackstone concluded, "that is still a distinct kingdom; though a dependent, subordinate kingdom." Consequently, "the king's majesty, with the consent of the lords and commons of Great Britain in parliament, hath power to make laws to bind the people of Ireland."[19]

Blackstone contended that England had title to Ireland by right of conquest; he also emphasized that the tie was strengthened, even validated, through government by compact, where the Irish consented to an imperial connection and were entitled to the rights of Englishmen. His assumption, of course, was that the Irish, like the Americans, would

18. Thomas Pownall, *The Administration of the British Colonies*, 5th ed., 2 vols, (London: J. Walter, 1774), 2:45.
19. William Blackstone, *Commentaries on the Laws of England*, 4 vols. (Chicago: University of Chicago Press, 1979; facsimile of the orig. 1765–69 ed.), quotes from 1:157, 98, 101. Blackstone was not always consistent, notably on what he said about the right of revolution and the relationship of the British Parliament to the British constitution. For the problems inherent in Blackstone's attempt to impose order on what had begun as imperial anarchy, see A. Berriedale Keith, *Constitutional History of the First British Empire* (Oxford: Clarendon Press, 1930); A. E. Dick Howard, *The Road from Runnymede* (Charlottesville: The University Press of Virginia, 1968); and the classic "debate" between Charles H. McIlwain, *The American Revolution: A Constitutional Interpretation* (New York: Macmillan, 1923). and Robert Livingston Schuyler, *Parliament and the British Empire* (New York: Columbia University Press, 1929). Barbara A. Black, "The Constitution of Empire: The Case for the Colonists," *University of Pennsylvania Law Review* 124 (1976): 1158–74, discusses McIlwain and Schuyler's rival views.

accept the British Parliament as he had defined it as the final arbiter and defender of those rights. The Irish probably took little solace in his conclusion that they, unlike the American colonists, were specifically entitled to common law protection. He stripped their Parliament of virtually all powers of consequence, concluding that, technically, under Poynings' Law it could only vote on bills presented to it by the lord lieutenant and Irish privy council. Pownall would not have disagreed; he simply would have expressed himself more tactfully. But greater tact did not count for much. Irish Patriots found Pownall's views as unattractive as Blackstone's. Many Americans took little satisfaction in Pownall's sop that the British Parliament had the obligation to "fix in the most perfect security, the *free-will absolute of the Colonies, so far as it is consistent with subordination.*"[20] And neither the Irish nor the Americans looked forward to paying higher taxes, as Knox and Pownall thought they should, to help defray the greater costs of empire after 1763.

It should not be surprising that Irish and American pamphleteers saw themselves as being trapped in a similar predicament. Critiques of the empire, some written by Irish authors, some by Americans, and some even by Britons, linked affairs on both sides of the Atlantic: thus the pamphlets by Bushe and Langrishe, as well as their collaboration on *Baratariana* to castigate Townshend. To opposition leaders, Townshend's augmentation scheme was an ill-concealed attempt to raise troops that could be used against the Americans. "The unfortunate and fatal American contest was already begun," reminisced the earl of Charlemont some years later, "and Ireland, justly, naturally, and wisely favourable to her oppressed brethren, saw with disgust and apprehension the use which was making, and likely to be made of the British forces." For Ireland, he concluded, "every augmentation of her own army was in effect raising troops against those to whose cause she must be partial, since it, in some degree resembled her own."[21]

With the Stamp Act crisis, more and more writers in Ireland and the American colonies began to draw parallels between their situations. And it was an Anglo-Irish member of the British Parliament protesting

20. Pownall, *Administration of the British Colonies*, 5th ed., 2:76–77.
21. HMC, *Charlemont*, 1:32. Also see Vincent T. Harlow, *The Founding of the Second British Empire, 1763–1793* (London: Longmans, Green and Co., 1952), 512–13; R. Coupland, *The American Revolution and the British Empire* (London: Longmans, Green and Co., 1930), 97; and Lawrence Henry Gipson, *The British Empire before the American Revolution*, 15 vols. (New York: Alfred A. Knopf, 1936–70), 13:18, who noted, "It would appear that the growing spirit of independence and self-assertiveness in the American colonies had made the British Ministry apprehensive that Ireland would follow a similar trend unless steps were taken to bind the country more closely to Great Britain."

against the Stamp Act, Isaac Barré, who referred to Americans as "sons of liberty." Barré, in turn, probably borrowed that phrase from Charles Lucas, who had used it several times in his appeals to Irish voters.[22] Lucas, in fact, had been one of the first to claim that there was a conspiracy on the part of British ministers to subvert the liberties of both Ireland and America, doing so in 1756 when he was still exiled in London.[23] In 1756 he was almost alone in making such a charge; within a decade his voice was only one of many.

Americans were susceptible to the fears of conspiracy that the historian Bernard Bailyn has traced;[24] so too were the Irish. Revolutionary Americans exaggerated the dangers posed by what they viewed as British plots to oppress them, and yet it would be misleadingly simple to conclude that they—or the Anglo-Irish in their protests—fabricated their grievances, that they cut their arguments from whole cloth. Some Irish politicians heard that the stamp duty passed for the American colonies would soon be extended to Ireland. Although that rumor proved false, the British could do little to reassure the Irish. This was especially so after the Irish learned that George Grenville had asserted that Britain's Parliament had the right to impose taxes on Ireland if it chose to do so, just as it did in America.[25] Grenville reinforced the tendency among Irish Patriots to look for analogies between their situation and that of the Americans. His talk, his actions and those of other British M.P.s provided grist for the mill of Irish dissatisfaction. If most Americans were relieved when the Rockingham ministry engineered a repeal of the Stamp Act in 1766, others were worried by the wording of the Declaratory Act that accompanied repeal and claimed for the British Parlia-

---

22. William Cobbett et al., eds., *The Parliamentary History of England*, 36 vols. (London: T. C. Hansard, 1806–1820), 16:39, for Barré's statement of 6 March 1765 in the British Commons; and Charles Lucas, *Political Constitutions of Great-Britain and Ireland*, 2 vol. (London, 1751), Address IV, 26, and idem, *Seasonable Advice*, 21, where Lucas referred to the Irish as "sons of liberty," in 1748 and 1760, resp.

23. Charles Lucas, *An Appeal to the Commons and Citizens of London by Charles Lucas, the last freeman of Dublin* (London, 1756), 5. Some American patriots, at least, knew of Lucas. *A Letter from the Town of Boston to C. Lucas, esq.* (Dublin: Tho. Ewing, 1770), was sent to tell the "truth" about the Boston Massacre and some colonial newspapers—notably the *Pennsylvania Gazette*, 13 February 1772, and the *Boston Gazette, and Country Journal*, 3 February 1772—reprinted the obituary for Lucas that had run in Dublin.

24. Bernard Bailyn, *The Ideological Origins of the American Revolution* (Cambridge: Harvard University Press, 1967), 144–59, which should be contrasted with Robert H. Webking, *The American Revolution and the Politics of Liberty* (Baton Rouge: Louisiana State University Press, 1988), 5–15, 153–75.

25. See the letter from W. G. Hamilton to Edmund Pery of 7 March 1765 in HMC, *Eighth Report* (London: Eyre and Spottiswoode, 1881), Part I, p. 190, which comments on Grenville's assertion.

ment power over the colonies similar to that asserted in the Declaratory Act of 1720 for Ireland. Therefore, some Americans and Irish feared that the British Parliament leaned more toward coercion than reform. Even the limited commercial freedoms advocated by Pownall and Knox were not granted. No wonder one Englishman wrote in 1770 to a relative sitting in the British Commons that "[b]etween America, Ireland, and our own dissensions I see no end to our troubles."[26]

A reprint of Molyneux's *Case* appeared in 1770; equally significant, Darcy's 1643 *Argument* had been reprinted six years earlier, for the first time since its original publication. American writers, notably John Dickinson, were cited in the Irish press and had their tracts reprinted in Dublin.[27] Reciprocally, the *Boston Gazette* ran excerpts from Molyneux's tract, "with very little Variation, to adapt them to the present State of American Affairs."[28] In his *Letters from a Farmer in Pennsylvania*, Dickinson used British abuses in Ireland as an indication of what Americans could expect for themselves if they did not defend their liberties. "We may perceive, by the example of *Ireland*," he warned, "how eager

---

26. HMC, *The Manuscripts of the Earl of Buckinghamshire, the Earl of Lindsey, the Earl of Onslow, Lord Emly, Theodore J. Hare, Esq., and James Round, M.P.* (London: Eyre and Spottiswoode, 1895), 303, letter from Thomas Falconer to Charles Gray, of 20 January 1770. It has often been noted that the Rockinghamites were simultaneously assertive and evasive in the 1766 Declaratory Act (6 George III c. 12). They did not use the word "tax," even as they stipulated that the American colonies were "subordinate unto, and dependent upon, the Imperial Crown and Parliament of *Great Britain*," and even as they claimed Parliament's right to "make Laws and Statutes" for the colonies "in all cases whatsoever." Had Parliament been sloppy, sly, or unaware of the danger of ritualized, routinized language, when in 1720 (6 George I c. 5) it asserted the "Dependency of the Kingdom of *Ireland* upon the Crown of *Great Britain*," with Parliament only giving "Advice and Consent"? In the 1766 act, the "Dependency" of the American colonies was explicitly on Crown *and* Parliament. Not so for Ireland. Even the 1782 act of repeal (22 George III c. 53) and the 1783 act of renunciation (23 George III c. 28) were phrased to make the king supreme in Ireland, acting with Parliament's "advice" and "consent"—despite the prevailing view, as articulated best by Blackstone, that the king ruled only "in" Parliament. The 1766 use of "Imperial Crown" also shows—if its authors were concerned about the language they used—that the phrase did not mean what Anglo-Irish constitutionalists claimed. The American colonies, too, were described as being under an "Imperial Crown."

27. *Modus tenendi Parliamenta in Hibernia* (Dublin: J. Millikin, 1772) was also reprinted—see chapter 1, n. 18. The defense of Molyneux's *Case* as both "valid" and relevant to Americans by "Valerius Publicola" that appeared in the *Boston Gazette*, 28 October 1771, has been attributed to Samuel Adams and is reprinted in Harry Alonzo Cushing, ed., *The Writings of Samuel Adams*, 4 vols. (New York: G. P. Putnam's Sons, 1904–8), 2:256–64. Also see Edmund O'Brien, "The Declaration of Independence," *Lawyer and Banker and Central Law Journal* 21 (1928): 298–309, for Molyneux's popularity with and importance to the Americans, including the use of ideas and language in the Declaration of Independence. For the Dublin edition of John Dickinson's *Letters from a Farmer in Pennsylvania*, see Paul Leicester Ford, ed., *The Writings of John Dickinson* (Philadelphia: The Historical Society of Pennsylvania, 1895), 293.

28. *Boston Gazette*, 24 August 1771.

ministers are to seize upon any settled revenue, and apply it in supporting their own power." Condemning the civil list that Charles Townshend wanted to create in the American colonies, he argued that Ireland had already been corrupted and treated "cruelly" by the use of places and pensions, and Americans could expect as much to happen to them if Townshend had his way. Like the Irish, Americans had to stand up for their constitutional rights. "I am astonished to observe such a love of liberty still animating that LOYAL and GENEROUS nation," he marveled.[29] Dickinson returned to his Irish theme in later writings, sometimes to show how Irish and American conditions were similar, sometimes to show how they were different, but always to demonstrate that British policy endangered American and Irish freedoms. James Otis, James Wilson, and other American pamphleteers from the mid-1760s into the early 1770s did the same.[30] "Ireland, groaning under Egyptian-like bondage, is stretching forth her hands, and calling to us for help and relief," preached one New England minister.[31] He and other writers "drew wonderful propaganda from the sufferings of the Irish," linking those "sufferings" with their own.[32]

They were bolstered by English writers like Granville Sharp and James Burgh. "And as all British subjects, whether in Great-Britain, Ireland, or the Colonies, are *equally free* by the law of Nature," proclaimed Sharp in 1775, "they *certainly* are *equally* entitled to the same Natural Rights that are essential for their own preservation."[33] Styling himself

---

29. [Dickinson], *Letters from a Farmer*, in Ford, ed., *Writings of John Dickinson*, quotes from pp. 375, 376, 380. Also see Dickinson's 1774 "letter" in ibid., p. 484, the third of a series of four published anonymously in the *Pennsylvania Journal* (this one on 8 June 1774), contending that the 1766 Declaratory Act for America was far more dangerous than the 1720 act for Ireland.

30. James Otis, *The Rights of the British Colonies Asserted and Proved* (Boston: Edes and Gill, 1764), 43, 45; and James Wilson, *Considerations on the nature and the extent of the legislative authority of the British Parliament* (Philadelphia: William and Thomas Bradford, 1774), where Wilson critiques Blackstone and also shows a willingness to use constitutional arguments to transcend historical precedent.

31. Peter Whitney, *The Transgression of a Land punished by a multitude of Rulers* (Boston: John Boyle, 1774), 68–69. John Phillip Reid called this pamphlet to my attention.

32. John Phillip Reid, *In a Defiant Stance* (University Park: The Pennsylvania State University Press, 1977), 15. For an example, see SCAEVOLA, "To the Commissioners appointed by the EAST-INDIA COMPANY, for the SALE of TEA, in AMERICA" (n.p., n.d.).

33. Granville Sharp, *A Declaration of the People's Natural Right to a Share in the Legislature* (London: B. White, 1775), 21; James Burgh, *Political Disquisitions*, 3 vols. (Philadelphia: Robert Bell, 1775; orig. ed., London, 1774–75); and the discussion in Robert E. Toohey, *Liberty and Empire* (Lexington: University of Kentucky Press, 1978), 53–80. Edmund Burke linked Irish and American affairs in his speech (22 March 1775) in the British Commons on reconciliation. See *The Writings and Speeches of Edmund Burke*, 12 vols. (Boston: Little, Brown and Co., 1901), 2:145–48. Also see John Cartwright's pamphlet, listed in chapter 6, n. 69.

"Junius," another writer not only linked American, English, and Irish grievances against the empire, he urged English reformers to "attend to the grievances of our fellow-subjects in Ireland and second the complaints they may bring to the throne."[34]

By 1774, Lucas's old paper, the *Freeman's Journal,* was following American affairs closely, never failing to point out what were perceived to be direct threats to American liberties and indirect threats to those of the Irish. Other Irish papers carried American news but none were as inflammatory. It even outstripped most American newspapers before 1776 in its criticisms of British imperialism, notably in the "Free Press" editorial column that ran on the front page of almost every edition. Many issues had more news on what was happening across the Atlantic than what was happening at home, and that news was bad:

The situation of our brave, virtuous and suffering fellow-subjects throughout the continent of AMERICA is truly alarming; on the one hand, if they yield up their inherent right of *internal* taxation, their boasted liberty is gone; and on the other, if a stroke is given or blood shed, the *English* parliament will immediately be convened, and they declared rebels. Thus, whatever step they take is crucial. They have no choice but of *freedom* and *slavery*.[35]

After fighting erupted at Lexington and Concord, the paper lamented:

The innocent *blood* of our suffering brethren in *America* which has been shed in the *defence* of their *rights* and freedom, calls aloud to *us* for *revenge*. There we see the most unparalleled acts of tyranny and barbarity, exercised upon a *free people,* under the reign of a King, who is indebted for his very crown to the free and *patriotic* spirit of our fathers.[36]

---

34. John Cannon, ed., *The Letters of Junius* (Oxford: Clarendon Press, 1978), quote from no. 10. See no. 39 for a linking of American, English, and Irish affairs. The "Junius" letters appeared in the London *Public Advertiser* from 1769 to 1772. At one time Grattan and Flood had been mentioned as possible authors (though neither one was a likely "Junius"). Whoever the author was, Irish and American affairs were less pressing to him than were English politics and a defense of John Wilkes. Thomas R. Adams, "The British Pamphlet Press and the American Controversy, 1764–1783" *American Antiquarian Society. Proceedings* 89 (1979): 33–88, includes Irish authors and gives a concise overview of the immense (microfilm) collection he assembled with Colin Bonwick, *British Pamphlets Relating to the American Revolution, 1764–1783* (East Ardsley, England: Microform Ltd. 1972). Adams's *The American Controversy: A Bibliographical Study of the British Pamphlets about the American Dispute, 1764–1783,* 2 vols. (Providence: Brown University Press, 1980) should be used with that microfilm collection.

35. *Freeman's Journal,* 18 August 1774; see the *Hibernian Journal,* 19 January 1774, for an example of the pro-American sentiment sometimes expressed in that paper. The *Freeman's Journal* covered events in Massachusetts throughout 1774 very thoroughly, even reprinting town meeting resolutions and provincial convention proceedings.

36. *Freeman's Journal,* 17 June 1775; also see "An Alphabet for Little Masters and Misses" in the 2 September 1775 issue.

The Continental Congress tried to capitalize on the putative mutual grievances tying Ireland to the American colonies. Congress included Ireland in the non-intercourse resolution it passed in September 1774, a fruitless attempt to strong-arm support from abroad.[37] With the failure of economic coercion and the widening of the breach separating the mainland American colonies from the mother country, Congress took more positive, less punitive, action to attract Irish support the following spring. In June 1775 it formed a special committee to compose an address to the "people" of Ireland. The document that the committee drafted and Congress approved was addressed to "Friends and Fellow-Subjects" and ticked off a litany of constitutional violations committed by the British Parliament. The Irish people, stated the address, "had ever been friendly to the rights of mankind"; what is more, "*your* nation has produced patriots, who have nobly distinguished themselves in the cause of humanity and America."[38]

Other committees were organized to compose similar addresses to the residents of Canada, Jamaica, and Great Britain. In each case, Congress tried to appeal directly to the citizenry, bypassing their respective governments. Parliament was criticized but George III was not; malicious ministers were taken to task but the people at large were not. Members of Congress like John Adams and Benjamin Franklin were convinced that such appeals could be effective. Adams sat on the committee that drafted the appeal to the people of Ireland; Franklin included Ireland in his scheme for a new government for the American colonies drawn up at approximately the same time.

Adams had previously used his study of Irish affairs to make a case against parliamentary rule in the colonies. In his *Novanglus* letters he argued that, since the American colonies were not part of the realm of England, they were not subject to the British Parliament. The only proper tie to the empire was through the person of the king. The Irish were joined more directly to the Crown, and somewhat less directly to Parliament, because they had been conquered and because they later consented to formal ties. The Americans could not be bound by parliamentary statute or Crown decree because they had not been conquered; nor had they given consent to any such relationship. Even if the Irish

---

37. Worthington C. Ford, ed., *The Journals of the Continental Congress*, 34 vols. (Washington, D.C. Government Printing Office, 1904–37), 1:42–43, 51–52; also see the comments of Robert Treat Paine in Paul H. Smith, ed., *Letters of Delegates to Congress, 1774–1789*, 20 vols. (Washington: The Library of Congress, 1976–), 1:146–49.
38. Ford, ed., *Journals of Continental Congress*, 2:219.

situation was different in strictly legal terms, Adams contended, it was quite similar constitutionally. Both the Irish and Americans were entitled to government by consent, and they could not be legislated for in a British Parliament where they had no representatives. If England with its six million inhabitants was entitled to some five hundred seats in the House of Commons, then the mainland American colonies with their three million should have at least half that many and "Ireland, too, must be incorporated, and send another hundred or two members."[39]

The purpose of Adams's constitutional hair-splitting, of course, was not to win seats in the British Parliament for either Ireland or the American colonies. His use of Irish history was—consciously or unconsciously—selective and, as in his depiction of American conditions, his arguments based on Irish history were often strained. No doubt, some Irish who sympathized with Adams's intention would have taken exception to his understanding of the Irish past. Accurate or not, Adams was satisfied that Ireland served as an example of how *not* to run an empire and as a warning to Americans of what awaited them if they did not force a change. Like Franklin, he also believed that the Irish were ripe for rebellion.

Franklin had decided years before the outbreak of hostilities in April 1775 that the Irish sympathized with American protests. Franklin made but one short, six-week trip to Ireland (in 1771) and then only to the eastern fringe around Dublin. He arrived during the augmentation controversy, met with Charles Lucas while he was in Dublin, and may have been influenced by Lucas's views on the empire as well as on Ireland. Franklin concluded that the widespread poverty and misery so evident in the Irish countryside were due to imperial restrictions that kept an abundant land and resourceful people in a wretched state. His reading, his social contacts, and his limited Irish experience reinforced his feelings that Ireland and America had much in common.[40] In 1770, when he sent a copy of Molyneux's newly reprinted *Case* to a friend, he observed, "Our Part is warmly taken by the Irish in general, there being

---

39. John Adams and Jonathan Sewall [Daniel Leonard], *Novanglus and Massachusettensis* (Boston: Hews & Goss, 1819), 80.

40. See Franklin's letter to Lord Kames of 25 February 1767 in Leonard Labaree et al., eds., *The Papers of Benjamin Franklin*, 30 vols. (New Haven: Yale University Press, 1959–), 14:62–71; and the account in J. Bennett Nolan, *Benjamin Franklin in Scotland and Ireland, 1759 and 1771* (Philadelphia: University of Pennsylvania Press, 1938). Also see Franklin's testimony before the House of Commons on 13 February 1766, in Labaree, ed., *Papers of Franklin*, 13:153, where Franklin stated that the "Colonies are not supposed to be within the realm; they have assemblies of their own, which are their parliaments, and they are in that respect, in the same situation with Ireland."

so many Points in Similarity in our Cases."[41] This despite Molyneux's insistence that Ireland was not and had never been a British "colony."

Franklin conceded that the Irish and American situations were in some ways different. The colonies, he realized, had never been a "kingdom," a status that was in part recognized by the British, even in Blackstone's *Commentaries*. Franklin also understood that Irish society had different problems and, compared with the American colonies, less potential for rapid change. Nevertheless, he felt that they had one major characteristic in common: both the Irish and the Americans had been victimized by the British Parliament. That shared experience with British oppression made them alike. In linking the two cases, Franklin blurred the distinctions to make his larger point and in so doing nearly contradicted himself. Adams had done pretty much the same.

Perhaps because of the similarity he saw in Irish and American conditions, Franklin wrote Ireland into his July 1775 plan of government for a partially independent America. He proposed that the "United Colonies of North America" press their legislative independence and join together in a "firm league of friendship" with other portions of the British empire in the Americas and, notably, Ireland as well. Under Franklin's scheme, Ireland was allowed thirty members in "Commons" and ten in "Lords," and the American colonies (Canada included) and the West Indies between them would have had fifty in Commons and ten in Lords. The Lords in America would be created "by the royal Prerogative"; the Irish Lords would be chosen from among existing peers. This inter-colonial parliament would be concerned with imperial affairs only and would leave purely domestic matters to the colonial assemblies and Irish Parliament.[42] Congress, unwilling to come out for such a plan,

---

41. Labaree, ed., *Papers of Franklin*, 17:124, letter to Samuel Cooper of 14 April 1770. Franklin had the year before sent Cooper copies of Langrishe and Bushe's tracts, as well as Knox's *Present State* and a pamphlet by Edmund Burke (*Papers of Franklin*, 16:117–20; letter of 27 April 1769).

42. Papers of the Continental Congress, 1774–1789 (Washington, D.C.: Government Printing Office, 1959, 204 reels microfilm), item 9, pp. 1–6 (reel 22); and Albert H. Smyth, ed., *The Writings of Benjamin Franklin*, 10 vols. (New York: Macmillan, 1905–7), 10:291–92. Franklin had blown hot and cold on the subject for nearly twenty years. See his letter of 9 May 1766 to Cadwalader Evans in Labaree, ed., *Papers of Franklin*, 13:268–69, where he sounds very pessimistic about the prospects of a truly representative imperial parliament. In the aftermath of the Stamp Act crisis, there appeared *A College Exercise, Delivered 16 December 1765* (London: J. Almon, 1769), which urged a parliamentary union that would include the mother country as well as Ireland and the American colonies, as did an anonymous *A Plan of Union, by Admitting Representatives from the American Colonies, and from Ireland into the British Parliament* (Philadelphia, 1770); and, earlier, *Observations and Propositions for an Accommodation between Great Britain and her Colonies* (1768). Englishman Samuel Clay Harvey's (1775?) plan excluded Ireland. It is reprinted in Peter Force, ed., *American Archives*, 9 vols. (Washington, D.C.: M. St. Clair, 1837–53), 4th series, 1:1204–1208.

balked at Franklin's suggestion and filed it away without official comment. The scheme had basically been a revised, enlarged version of Franklin's old Albany Plan, except that it carried with it the threat that if the British did not concur, the Americans would go ahead anyway.

Although most members of Congress thought Franklin went too far in moving toward formal legislative independence, few if any thought his ideas about Irish sympathies fanciful. Franklin and Adams were only two of the more obvious patriots who took an interest in Irish affairs and thought they could find in the Irish experience examples of British misconduct relevant to their own troubles. As a result, they likewise saw the Irish as potential converts to their cause, and there were clear signs of Irish sympathy.

The citizens of Cork sent provisions at their own expense to the patriot forces at Cambridge in 1775, and a brisk trade in smuggling was carried on in Cork and Dublin throughout the war.[43] American newspapers reprinted pieces from Irish newspapers or Irish correspondents supporting the Americans and condemning the British, and excerpts from Irish parliamentary debates showing that Irish sympathy for the Americans extended into the highest circles. "Here are none but rebels," lamented one Irishman, who observed that "the King is reviled" and "the ministry cursed," while another noted enthusiastically, "We are all Americans here except such as are attached servilely to the Castle Papists."[44] Indeed, "Irish and American patriots," commented historian Richard B. Morris, "were quick to perceive how closely their respective situations paralleled each other and were alert to demonstrate how each suffered alike from discriminating trade legislation and a denial of a role in decision-making within the empire."[45]

---

43. Building on the foundation laid in Francis Godwin James, "Irish Colonial Trade in the Eighteenth Century," *William and Mary Quarterly*, 3d ser., 2 (1963): 274–84, Thomas M. Truxes, *Irish-American Trade, 1660–1783* (Cambridge: Cambridge University Press, 1988) lays out in great detail the nature of Irish-American commercial ties through the War of American Independence.

44. The Rev. Philip Skelton to William Knox, 22 November 1777, in the "Additional Manuscripts of Captain H. V. Knox" in HMC, *Report on Manuscripts in Various Collections* 6 vols. (London: John Falconer, 1901–9), 6:446; and Lord Midleton to Thomas Townshend, 16 August 1775, in the Sydney Papers, MS. 52, vol. 2, Packet K, National Library of Ireland. Townshend was a Rockingham Whig opposed to North's ministry; Midleton, his nephew, had similar views and was not really familiar with the area, although the family estate was located there.

45. Richard B. Morris, *The Emerging Nations and the American Revolution* (New York: Harper and Row, 1970), 82, which follows the thinking of Michael Kraus, "America and the Irish Revolutionary Movement in the Eighteenth Century," in Richard B. Morris, ed., *The Era of the American Revolution* (New York: Columbia University Press,

It is relatively easy to search through Irish newspapers, magazines, and contemporary correspondence to find evidence of pro-American sentiment, so easy, in fact, that readers even now could be misled, as were readers then. The Irish were undeniably restive, and American Revolutionaries fastened on any form of Irish discontent as the prologue to greater revolutionary activity. Intelligence brought in from Ireland often told American Revolutionaries exactly what they wanted to believe. There were stories of how provisions intended for British troops stationed in America were destroyed, of how recruiting parties were harassed, and "that those employed therein met with little success." Some reports claimed that "the People at large heartily wish Us Success & some even say that it is Time for Ireland to follow our Example."[46] Information from the British Parliament reinforced that view: George Johnstone, speaking in the House of Commons in October 1775, estimated that "three to one in *Ireland*" sided with the Americans.[47]

In sum, many Americans, many of their Irish contemporaries, and even some Englishmen were convinced that Irish identification with the American cause was dangerously real and potentially catastrophic to the empire. Hence the subsequent fame of a rumor repeated by Horace Walpole in 1776 that "all Ireland is 'America mad'" and the conclusion reached by W. E. H. Lecky over a century later that "there were great numbers in Ireland who regarded the American cause as their own."[48] These opinions have to be taken with a grain of salt, however. Walpole and Johnstone hardly qualified as objective observers. Both were sharp critics of the North ministry and used whatever sources they could to discredit it. Lecky wrote much later, though as a critic not all that different from Johnstone and Walpole. He too highlighted the failures of

---

1939), 332–48. Owen Dudley Edwards, "The Impact of the American Revolution on Ireland," in *The Impact of the American Revolution Abroad* (Washington, D.C.: The Library of Congress, 1976), 127–58, takes issue with Morris and Kraus and writers like Pauline Maier, *From Resistance to Revolution* (New York: Alfred A. Knopf, 1972), who did not question the accuracy of Revolutionary American assumptions about the supposed similarities of the Irish and colonial American experiences. Also see Maurice O'Connell, "The American Revolution and Ireland," *Eire-Ireland* 11 (Fall 1976): 3–12, and John A. Murphy, "The Influence of America on Irish Nationalism," in David Noel Doyle and Owen Dudley Edwards, eds., *America and Ireland, 1776–1976* (Westport: Greenwood Press, 1980), 105–15; and John Phillip Reid, *Constitutional History of the American Revolution*, 3 vols. (Madison: University of Wisconsin Press, 1986–), 2:89–91, 153–57, and 3:200–206.

46. Smith, ed., *Letters of Delegates*, 2:390, 269; also see *Pennsylvania Gazette*, 18 October 1775; and Force, ed., *American Archives*, 4th ser. 3:168–69, 619–20, 1553; and 2:1672–73, for other examples.

47. Cobbett, ed., *Parliamentary History*, 18:751.

48. W. S. Lewis, ed., *Horace Walpole's Correspondence*, 48 vols. (New Haven: Yale University Press, 1937–1983), 32:296; Lecky, *History of Ireland*, 2:153.

mercantilism and unrest against what he disdained as inept rule. Given their own predispositions, it is understandable why American Revolutionaries read too much into the Irish reaction to their plight. They were tempted, as Owen Dudley Edwards has explained, "to remake Ireland in their minds to the concept of it they wished to have."[49]

Ireland did not rebel; Ireland and the rebellious American colonies were at once similar and distinct. Irish and American developments had not really "paralleled each other," the beliefs of American Revolutionaries and some later historians notwithstanding. If many American Revolutionaries misread Irish affairs, some Irishmen, at least from 1774 to 1776, likewise misread the nature of the American crisis. Both tried too hard to draw parallels and find analogies. Little did they realize that the ideological origins of the American Revolution had taken root in a different soil. Ireland was not really in danger of following the American example.

No one could have been more relieved that Ireland was not on the verge of rebellion than Townshend's replacement as lord lieutenant, Simon, Earl Harcourt. An old and experienced courtier at Whitehall, Harcourt was released from his duties as ambassador to France to strengthen the Irish administration. Townshend had managed to keep a majority in Parliament at the time of his leaving in 1772, but that majority was very slim and could easily be lost, given the unrelieved tensions in Irish affairs and growing imperial crisis. Harcourt was a more astute diplomat than Townshend, and for the first two years of his residence gradually built up Castle influence and administration power. If, as rumored, he had been sent to push for a parliamentary union, he was wise enough to abandon what would have been an immensely unpopular proposition that might in fact have brought ruin to his administration.[50]

---

49. Owen Dudley Edwards, "The American Image of Ireland: A Study of Its Early Phases," *Perspectives in American History* 4 (1970): 200.

50. See Thomas Francis Moriarty, "The Harcourt Viceroyalty in Ireland, 1772–1777" (Ph.D. dissertation, University of Notre Dame, 1963), for an overview; and the analyses of parliamentary divisions in M. Bodkin, ed., "Notes on the Irish Parliament in 1773," *Royal Irish Academy. Proceedings* 48–49 (1942–44): 145–232; and William Hunt, ed., *The Irish Parliament, 1775* (New York: Longmans, Green and Co., 1907). Judging by these lists, which were probably compiled at Harcourt's request (perhaps by John Blaquiere or an assistant), Harcourt had added significantly to the number of government supporters by the time Parliament opened in October 1775 and the American issue was addressed. If he had not, the debate might have been more heated and the outcome less satisfactory to Harcourt and Whitehall. Also see Johnston, *Great Britain and Ireland*, appendix C, 331–37, for a discussion of these lists and the other ten Johnston found that had been compiled between 1770 and 1791. The rumors that Harcourt had been sent to bring about a union spread across the Atlantic, where they were printed in the *Virginia Gazette* (Purdie and Dixon), most notably in the 31 December 1772, 25 March 1773, and 8 April 1773 issues.

Harcourt scored a major victory in persuading Flood to leave the opposition and accept a post as vice-treasurer. Flood's former associates among the Patriots were gravely disappointed, and Flood was vilified in the press. Once called "the brightest ornament of the Irish Parliament," Flood's reputation was now tarnished.[51] Winning over Flood did not gain Harcourt very much. He spent lavishly to attract others as well and has been accused of standing "unrivalled" for his "expense and prodigality."[52] He had little choice: patronage was the best, even if an unsure, way to form alliances. He awarded a key post to Flood, even though he thought Flood was a meddlesome opportunist. Thus, too, his unremitting—if only partially successful—efforts to woo powerful men like the duke of Leinster and George Ponsonby, who between them controlled over twenty seats in the Irish Commons.[53]

Harcourt was not without his critics, and his chief secretary, John Blaquiere, made many enemies in and out of Parliament. Still, Harcourt could claim during his first parliamentary session that "we have carried every Point hitherto in spite of any Opposition." By the middle of his second year, he had grown even more confident. "I have every Reason to be satisfied with the Turn that things have taken," he reported, "for more Busyness has been transacted, more Advantages have been obtained for the Crown, & for the People, than at any Period, between this & the Revolution."[54] Harcourt did have a tendency to magnify his accomplishments, and he always sought to put the best face on his adminstration, yet his claims were not groundless. As he soon discovered, however, his greatest challenges lay ahead.

The Irish Parliament had been prorogued on 2 June 1774, and did not begin a new session until 10 October 1775. Much had happened during the intervening months. Agitation in the American colonies had finally led to revolt, a revolt followed very sympathetically in the *Hibernian Journal* and Walker's *Hibernian Magazine,* as well as the *Freeman's Journal.* Large numbers of Irish had emigrated to the colonies during recent decades, especially from Ulster, and those who remained behind naturally took an interest in what happened to them after they

---

51. "Brightest Ornament," in [Bushe], *Case of Great-Britain and America,* 15; Flood was criticized in the *Freeman's Journal,* 23 April 1774, and the "Poet's Corner" of the *Hibernian Journal,* 4 February 1774; Harcourt had earlier been parodied in the same place—see *Freeman's Journal,* 15 March 1773.

52. Grattan, *Memoirs,* 1:207.

53. For Harcourt's patronage difficulties see the Harcourt Papers, MSS. 73 and 74, Gilbert Library, Dublin City Library, especially vol. 2 (MS. 74), chap. 1, pp. 31–35, and vol. 2, chap. 10, pp. 141–43.

54. Letter of 27 May 1774 in the Harcourt Letters, 1772–1775, MS. 5161, NLI.

left. Irish trade ties with the American colonies had never been stronger; many feared that war would interrupt what had become a very lucrative connection. Irish leaders, whether they were pro- or anti-adminstration, could not help looking to see what implications American actions and the British response had for them. The British knew all of this, and opponents of George III and North's ministry were quick to criticize unpopular policies. "Ireland never was in the situation of real honour and real consequence in which she now stands," Edmund Burke wrote excitedly. "She has the Ballance of the Empire and perhaps its fate for ever, in her hands."[55] Burke exaggerated, but he was not wrong in guessing that the king and his ministers were anxious to see what a new Irish parliamentary session would bring.

Parliament opened in the usual grand ceremony, with the Lords assembled in their chamber, bedecked in their formal robes and awaiting Harcourt's arrival. Harcourt entered, even more ornately attired and attended, and proceeded to the canopied Chair of State. The Lords remained standing until he was seated; only then were the members of Commons ushered in. They stood about to hear the formal "message from the throne" that opened every session, with the lord lieutenant speaking as the king's representative. Harcourt intoned:

I am persuaded you entertain a grateful Sense of the Blessings you enjoy under the mild and firm Government of the best of Sovereigns, and his Majesty relies on the known Zeal and Loyalty of his Subjects of *Ireland*, that whilst his Government is disturbed by a Rebellion existing in a Part of his American Dominions, you will be ready to shew your inviolable Attachment to his Person and Government in the Assertion of his just Rights, and in the Support of his legal Authority.[56]

As evidence of the king's "tender concern for the Welfare of this Kingdom," Harcourt pointed out that Irish fishing rights had been extended and a bounty on imported flax seed to help the linen industry had been passed by the British Parliament. Harcourt then withdrew, followed by the members of Commons, who went to their chambers to draft a response. The members of Lords recessed to remove their formal robes, then reassembled to offer their reply.

---

55. Burke to the duke of Richmond, 26 September 1775, in Thomas Copeland et al., eds., *The Correspondence of Edmund Burke*, 10 vols. (Cambridge: Cambridge University Press, 1958–78), 3:218.

56. *Journal of the House of Commons of the Kingdom of Ireland*, 20 Vols. (Dublin: George Grierson, 1796–1802), 9:169. Also see the general account in R. B. McDowell, *Irish Public Opinion, 1750–1800* (London: Faber and Faber, 1944), and Maurice O'Connell's indispensable *Irish Politics and Social Conflict in the Age of the American Revolution* (Philadelphia: University of Pennsylvania Press, 1965).

It was proposed that the Lords respond by thanking the king for his concern and by reassuring him of their support for his American policy. Before the proposal could be approved, peers sympathetic to the Americans offered an amendment:

> we the Lords Spiritual and Temporal in Parliament assembled, cannot see, without the utmost Concern, the unhappy Differences which now subsist between the Parliament of *Great Britain* and your *American* Colonies, and which are now grown to such a Height, as to threaten Consequences fatal to all your Majesty's Dominions.[57]

Noting that Lords had been "hitherto absolutely silent" about the dispute, the amendment urged that the American crisis "be Terminated without further Effusion of Blood." It was defeated soundly, thirty to four. The next day, Lords passed a more strongly worded response than originally proposed in support of the king and his suppression of the American rebellion, "which we cannot hear of but with the utmost Abhorrence and Indignation."[58] Twenty-six peers approved this response; only Charlemont, Leinster, Powerscourt, and two others opposed it.

The more strongly worded phrase had been borrowed from a resolution introduced in Commons by administration supporters the day before. Not coincidentally, the amendment proposed in Lords on October 10 urging an end to the war was identical to an amendment proposed by opposition leaders in Commons at the same time. It is obvious, then, that members of Lords and Commons engaged in cloakroom politics. Anticipating what Harcourt would say, they had had their responses ready, administration supporters and administration critics alike.

Opposition members of the House seem to have been especially well-organized. Some of them ardently opposed any resolution that condemned the Americans. George Ponsonby, Thomas Conolly, Gervase Parker Bushe, and a half dozen others argued against mentioning American conditions, George Ogle observing that "if we take the part of the Americans we irritate England, and if we assist Britain we thereby vote away our liberties."[59] Ogle referred here to what Conolly had noted before; namely, that the British Parliament believed it had the right to tax Ireland directly, "without our consent." Edward Newenham, Lucas's old associate and self-styled friend of the Americans, conceded that it

---

57. *Journal of the House of Lords of the Kingdom of Ireland*, 8 vols. (Dublin: William Sleater, 1779–1800), 4:791.
58. Ibid., 4:793.
59. *Freeman's Journal*, 12 October 1775; and *House of Commons Journal* 9: 170–72.

would be better not to refer to the rebellion, but if they did, they should advise "his Majesty to suspend the operations of war, and to order his Ministers to form a just and impartial plan of reconciliation."[60]

Administration supporters were not about to be deterred by Newenham and his colleagues. Chief secretary John Blaquiere countered that a rash British M.P., not the whole British Parliament, had claimed the right to tax Ireland, and that it was difficult to call the Americans anything other than rebels since they were in rebellion. He led the way in pushing through a supportive response to Harcourt's message that expressed "Abhorrence" and "Indignation" over the American "rebellion," using words borrowed soon after by his allies in Lords. A majority sided with him. The friends of America were defeated handily, and the pro-administration response carried by an even larger margin, ninety to fifty. Opponents to the response tried again the next day when it came up for a final vote. They introduced first one amendment, then another, to delete any mention of rebellion or expressions of Irish disapproval. They lost again, and so the matter ended.

Harcourt got what he wanted. Publicly he gave no hint that he had ever doubted the outcome; privately he expressed his relief, confiding to the earl of Rochford that he had taken a calculated risk in referring to American affairs in his speech. "I saw the Moment approaching, when this important Question, would have been pressed upon me by the Opposition to the King's Government in this Country," he explained, "who were dayly gaining Strength upon this Ground with such Advantages, as I should have had great Difficulty in resisting it." He warned that the Presbyterians in Ulster were "in their Hearts . . . Americans" and that the Irish in general had been stirred up "by designing Men, whom I could name, from your Side of the Water"—a veiled reference to Burke, no doubt—to "engage Ireland to take an Adverse Part in the Contest." He felt that he had squelched any move within the Irish Parliament to use American affairs as a means to blackmail Whitehall. "For my own Part I shall confess to you," he closed, "that I feel such a Glow of Mind upon this Occasion, & the Advantage that has been obtained, that I have in My Life, never past moments so happy, as those have been, since this Question was determined."[61] For the veteran diplomat, this had been his finest hour.

He did have to weather one more crisis in connection with American affairs, and that came the very next month. Whitehall wanted to transfer

60. Ibid.
61. Harcourt to Lord Rochford, 11 October 1775, in the Public Record Office/State Papers (Ireland) 63, 449:87–88; contrast this with the official report on p. 81.

four thousand troops from the Irish establishment to America; it proposed to replace them with "foreign Protestant Troops." Some who had opposed condemning the Americans as rebels the month before were even more vehement in their opposition to sending reinforcements to, as George Ogle put it, "cut the throats of their *American* brethren."[62] It was decided that troops from Ireland would be sent to the colonies but that they would not be replaced by foreign mercenaries. Harcourt and Whitehall were satisfied, and American affairs rarely came up again in the Irish Parliament, except on questions involving a vote on supplies and when members thought it necessary to reaffirm their attachment to the Crown.

Edmund Burke, once so sanguine that the Irish would benefit from the American disturbance, was disappointed that the rebellion there seemed to have so little impact on his homeland. "Ireland has missed the most glorious opportunity ever indulged by heaven to a subordinate state, that of being the safe and certain mediatrix in the quarrels of a great empire." Regrettably, he complained, "she has chosen instead of being the arbiter of peace, to be a feeble party in the war waged against the principle of her own liberties."[63] Where Burke was disgusted, Harcourt was practically elated. He stepped down as lord lieutenant in 1777 feeling immensely satisfied. He retired to his estate in England, only to die in a freak accident, drowning in a well as he tried to save the dog trapped inside.[64]

Historian J. A. Froude rarely let slip an opportunity to deride the "Patriot" leaders of the Anglo-Irish Ascendancy; their actions—or rather inaction—during the American Revolution, he felt, fully proved his point. He compared them most unfavorably with the Americans. Unlike the Americans, who were willing to fight for what they wanted, the Anglo-Irish "expected to obtain the privileges which are the only prize of the brave and noble by eloquence and chicanery." Froude was no admirer of the American rebels, but he gave them grudging respect for having been true to their principles. The Anglo-Irish were, quite simply in his view, too cowardly, too concerned with protecting what little they had.[65]

---

62. *House of Commons Journal* 9:219, 220–21, 223; and the discussion in Moriarty, "Harcourt Viceroyalty," 326–411.
63. Burke to the earl of Charlemont, 4 June 1776, in HMC, *Charlemont* 1:334.
64. Harcourt's death was noted in the *Dublin Journal*, 13 September 1777; see the Harcourt Papers, vol. 2 (MS. 74), appendix 2, for a list of parliamentary loyalties in 1777, compiled for Harcourt just as he was leaving—no doubt to substantiate his claims for a successful administration.
65. James Anthony Froude, *The English in Ireland in the Eighteenth Century*, 3 vols.

Ireland and the American Revolution

Froude was typically too harsh. Some Irish leaders did take a stand on principle. Charlemont, Leinster, Powerscourt, and three other peers signed a very strongly worded protest in November 1775 over sending troops from the Irish establishment to the colonies. "We are prohibited by the Principles upon which the glorious Revolution was founded from adjudging Resistance to Royal Authority in all possible Cases, Rebellion." In the case of the Americans, war against them was not justified, and these peers felt constrained to "condemn its Object and lament its Duration."[66] As they saw it, sending more troops to subdue the Americans would only further alienate them and make reconciliation between Britain and the colonies more difficult. To say that Charlemont and the others were also concerned about Ireland and their own welfare does not mean that they were somehow petty, motivated solely by self-interest. It was only natural for them to worry about how American affairs would affect Ireland, since Ireland, logically enough, was their primary concern. This can be seen in the speech made by Walter Hussey Burgh on 10 October 1775, when he protested the response to Harcourt's message that referred to the American "rebellion" and

expressed his Terror of the consequences that would result from joining in an Address which supported sanguinary Measures and urged a vindictive Administration to proceed to the last Extremities. If the Americans were brought on their Knees to the Minister, as had been the favourite Expression, they could expect nothing but Slavery. A Conqueror, when he held his Sword over the head of the Vanquished, has, indeed, been known to spare his Life, but never to give him Liberty. To keep the subdued Colonies in a State of Subjection would require a standing Army, and these Troops would be ready, whenever required, to come over and destroy the Liberties of other Subjects. Ireland would then be enslaved, since those who are Slaves, themselves are fittest to enslave others, and Great Britain itself would then become only the Seat of a wide extended Despotism. It is evident Britain has not relinquished her Design of destroying the rights of this Kingdom; she has torn off already one of the valuable Principles of a free Nation, An Appeal to the House of Lords; and the Book written by Molyneux, in Defence of Irish Rights, was burnt by the Hands of the common

---

(London: Longmans, Green, and Co., 1872–74), 2:84, though in fairness to Froude he noted (2:71, 189–90) that Irish problems were caused by inept British policy as well. Indeed, Froude contended, the British should have realized that a parliament in Ireland "was at all times a curse to Ireland and not a blessing" and that their trade restrictions on Ireland were an "iniquity." Thus, Froude seemed to feel, if the British had been more generous with and less fearful of the Irish, the Irish would not have gotten so attached to the idea of parliamentary independence, which ultimately benefited neither Ireland nor the empire.

66. *House of Lords Journal* 4:804.

Hangman. They only wait an Opportunity, and it would be wrong to give them the least Handle for one."[67]

Hussey Burgh employed the same rhetoric as American Revolutionaries. He warned of the dangers of standing armies, he complained of a conspiracy to enslave the free, and he used history to chronicle the wrongs committed by Britain. He and other Irish leaders drew from the same stock of ideas as the Americans; by their speeches and writings they, like the American Revolutionaries, would even add to them. But rhetorical similarity should not obscure the dissimilarities of the Irish and colonial American experiences. The Irish could sympathize with the rebellious Americans, but they could not truly empathize with them, and the same is true of Americans who took an interest in the Irish.

Only with the publication of *Common Sense* could Irish Patriots finally see that their situation was not analogous to that of the Americans. At the same moment that Paine's now famous pamphlet was being printed in the colonies, the *Freeman's Journal* denied that the American revolt against British oppression was also a revolution for independence. "AMONG the numberless absurdities and delusive assertions thrown by the present minority to prejudice the people against the free and brave Americans," the paper editorialized, "none have been more violently and falsely urged than that the Americans contend for absolute independence on Great Britain." If that were true, the column continued confidently, all those in Ireland as well as Britain "warmly attached to constitutional supremacy, would approve co-ercive measures."[68] At this point, as far as the Irish knew, the Americans were not pushing for independence. Reconciliation still seemed to be the Americans' goal (as the Continental Congress had professed in its July 1775 "Address"), provided it brought better protection of their constitutional rights as citizens of the empire. When copies of *Common Sense* began to make their way into Ireland in the spring of 1776, the *Freeman's Journal* was at first inclined to belittle it, both for its advocacy of American independence and for its condemnation of monarchy and mixed government. The paper nonetheless ran the full text of *Common Sense* in several installments, without any marked criticism. What comments there were tended to be friendly.

Consequently, by the time the Irish learned of the Declaration of Independence, they had been prepared to expect it. Irish leaders knew that

---

67. *Hibernian Journal*, 11 October 1775. For the purported "burning" of Molyneux's *Case*, see n. 33 of chapter 1.
68. *Freeman's Journal*, 11 January 1776.

Common Sense was popular in American patriot circles and that American leaders had endorsed Paine's arguments, although they were reluctant to come out openly for independence, and many were slow to abandon their tie to monarchy just because they had been ruled by a "bad" king. The Irish heard rumors that the Americans had declared their independence months before the fact, but the *Freeman's Journal* ran no attacks like the one it had printed in January. When the formal Declaration was printed, the editors simply observed that it "is looked upon as the best explanation of the Rights of the People which has been published in this age. It clearly points out the Duty of the Governor to the Governed."[69] This was a friendly note, yet it lacked the fervor of the comments made in earlier years, when Anglo-Irish Patriots looked to form a common cause with the Americans. The Americans had left them behind in pressing for independence and beginning an experiment in republican government that the Irish, especially the Anglo-Irish elite, had no interest in imitating.

Not realizing this some Americans continued to look for a revolution in Ireland. It is difficult to know what American newspaper readers following Irish affairs noticed most, the official stand taken by the Irish Parliament in 1775 referring to the American war as a "rebellion" or the many protestations of sympathy for the Americans made by leaders of the parliamentary opposition.[70] Franklin and more especially Adams hoped that the Irish would rise up, even as late as 1782. Each outbreak of civil disobedience or anti-administration stand in the Irish Parliament seemed to them to portend a larger disaster for British interests. Adams predicted that the Volunteer movement would push the Irish down the road to rebellion; it did not. He predicted that the Irish move for parliamentary independence anticipated a move for complete independence from British rule.[71] He was wrong there as well. Although he persisted

---

69. Ibid., 24 August 1776. It should be noted that Walker's *Hibernian Magazine* 4 (1774): 101–3, had carried excerpts from a Josiah Tucker tract, where Tucker predicted that the Americans would push for independence, and an essay by an anonymous author who concluded that the Americans would be better off independent (pp. 154–57). The essays were printed without any editorial comment.

70. The October 1775 debates in the Irish Commons on the American war were reprinted without comment in the *Pennsylvania Gazette*, 10 and 17 January 1776, and were at least noted in other papers.

71. See Paul Leicester Ford, ed., *An Address to the Good People of Ireland, on Behalf of America* (Brooklyn: Historical Printing Club, 1891), a pamphlet that Franklin wrote in October 1778, smuggled into Ireland, and had reprinted in the *Hibernian Journal*, 4 November 1778. Even if by 1783 Franklin no longer believed that the Irish would rebel, his reports from France could leave readers with the opposite impression. See Samuel Hardy's letter to Benjamin Harrison of 5 March 1784 in Edmund C. Burnett, ed., *Letters of Members of the Continental Congress*, 8 vols. (Washington, D.C.: Carnegie Institution,

in misreading Irish affairs, there were others who did not. The Continental Congress had by 1779, if not earlier, given up any hope that Ireland would assist its cause much less follow its lead.

Franklin and Adams erred, but their misreading of Irish affairs is understandable. Franklin's Philadelphia had seen large numbers of Irish immigrants pass through it during the preceding half century. Early in the War of Independence, Lord Lieutenant Harcourt had worried that even more Irish were leaving their homeland for the express purpose of joining in the fight against Britain.[72] As one critic of British policy in Ireland claimed in 1780, "Our countrymen, whose high spirit could not brook oppression, and who fled to America for protection, first sounded the alarm, and it is perhaps not a strained assertion, that AMERICA WAS LOST IN IRELAND."[73] Historians who have emphasized the pro-American sentiment of the Irish in Ireland, especially many American historians of Irish descent, agree. The Friendly Sons of St. Patrick in Philadelphia have boasted that their fraternal order almost unanimously supported the patriot cause.[74] Franklin associated with Irish immigrants like Charles Thomson and John Dunlap who, as secretary and printer, respectively, to the Continental Congress, had indeed been leading patriots. Some historians have gone so far as to argue that fully half of the patriot military forces during the war were Irish immigrants or their descendants, and that a disproportionate number of political as well as military leaders came from an Irish background.

Although it is not true, as one overly enthusiastic writer claimed, that "in America every Irishman was a patriot," the Irish were undeniably well-represented in the revolutionary cause.[75] That they were is as much

---

1921–36), 7:463. For Adams, see his letter of 4 April 1780 in the Papers of the Continental Congress, item 84, vol. 1, pp. 405–7 (reel 111). Other Americans were much more realistic—see, for example, the letter of George Washington of 20 August 1780 in ibid., item 152, vol. 9, pp. 83–100 (reel 170).

72. Harcourt to Rochford, 1 September 1775, Public Record Office/State Papers (Ireland) 63, 448:159.

73. *Sketches of the History of Poynings' Law* (Dublin: S. Colbert, 1780), 9; author unknown. David Ramsay used almost the same language in his *The History of the American Revolution*, 2 vols. (Trenton: James J. Wilson, 1811; orig. ed. 1789), 2:396.

74. There are a number of works celebrating the contribution to the American Revolution made by the Friendly Sons of St. Patrick, from Samuel Hood's *A Brief Account of The Society of the Friendly Sons of St. Patrick* (Philadelphia: Hibernian Society, 1844) to John Hugh Campbell's massive *History of the Friendly Sons of St. Patrick and of the Hibernian Sons of St. Patrick* (Philadelphia: Hibernian Society, 1892), to Owen B. Hunt's more recent *The Irish and the American Revolution* (Philadelphia: Owen Hunt, 1975).

75. Thomas Hobbs Maginniss, *The Irish Contribution to America's Independence* (Philadelphia: Doire, 1913), 91. There has been a virtual historiographical cottage in-

a commentary on the differences separating Irish and American society as it is evidence of an innate tendency toward rebelliousness on the part of the Irish. There is really no proof that those who came to America would have been radicals or revolutionaries had they remained in Ireland, just as there is no proof that those who remained in Ireland and chose to work for reform within the empire would—or would not— have become revolutionaries had they gone to America.[76] Furthermore, the tendency of an Adams to misread Irish affairs becomes even more understandable when it is remembered that the Irish themselves were not always sure what was going on in their own land. Some of them too predicted that the Volunteer movement would lead to separation from Britain if not to anarchy and chaos.

One thing is certain: the American Revolution—not just the War of Independence—had an important impact on Irish affairs. The various legislative programs enacted by the British Parliament between 1764 and 1774 and the retaliatory non-intercourse agreements entered into by Americans disrupted the Irish economy. All of Ulster, especially the town of Belfast, was hurt by the loss of American markets closed because

---

dustry for studies tracing the Irish contribution to American independence, from the impassioned tomes by Maginniss and Michael J. O'Brien, *A Hidden Phase of American History* (New York: Devin-Adair, 1919), to briefer, more suggestive pieces like Homer L. Calkin's two articles: "The American Revolution in Ireland," *National Historical Magazine* 79 (1945): 299–301, and "American Influence in Ireland, 1760 to 1800," *Pennsylvania Magazine of History and Biography* 71 (1947): 103–20. David Noel Doyle's *Ireland, Irishmen and Revolutionary America, 1760–1820* (Dublin: Mercier, 1981), is better balanced and less impassioned than most other books and articles on the subject. Enthusiasts about the number of Irish immigrants who fought on the Patriot side need to remember that many Irishmen served in the British Army and fought against the Americans. Oliver Snoddy, "The Volunteers of Ireland," *The Irish Sword* 7 (1965): 147–59, discusses a corps of Irish immigrants raised in the American colonies for service in the British Army. See Kerby A. Miller, *Emigrants and Exiles* (Oxford: Oxford University Press, 1985), for an overview of the Irish-American immigrant experience and pp. 131–92 for the colonial and early national period.

76. For example, Francis Alison and George Bryan were both Irish immigrants who took up residence in Pennsylvania and in 1768 teamed with John Dickinson (who eventually became an honorary member of the Friendly Sons of St. Patrick) to write "The Centinel," a series of essays warning against the establishment of an Anglican episcopacy in the colonies. Bryan had come from Dublin, but he was of Presbyterian stock; Alison too was Presbyterian, from Donegal. They did not consider themselves "revolutionaries" in 1768, however, and did not try to tie their Irish heritage and experience to American affairs in these essays. It is impossible to tell what they would have done politically had they not emigrated. For their "Centinel" essays, see Elizabeth Nybakken, ed., *The Centinel* (Newark: University of Delaware Press, 1980). Of course some Irish immigrants may have had their ideas shaped by their understanding of the Irish experience. See Jack N. Rakove, *The Beginnings of National Politics* (New York: Alfred A. Knopf, 1979), 164–76, who suggests that Thomas Burke's fears of overcentralized power could have been derived in part from his perception of the Irish past.

of the economic warfare between Britain and the colonies. Unemployment within the linen industry helped to breed dissatisfaction that would in turn lead to the "free trade" agitation of 1779. Urban depression spread to rural areas, with those renting lands feeling squeezed by landlords wanting to charge higher fees. By 1771 bands of dispossessed tenant farmers calling themselves the "Hearts of Steel" were roaming the Ulster countryside. The lawlessness of this group, coupled with the depredations of the "Whiteboys" farther south that had been occurring for a full decade, alarmed Irish leaders and added to friction between the administration and opposition Patriots.

In November 1775, when the Irish Parliament debated the sending of four thousand troops to serve in America, George Ogle pushed for a national militia act to provide for greater internal security. The administration was not sympathetic at all, fearing that militia could become the tool of the Anglo-Irish gentry and a threat to imperial power. By 1778 fear of French invasion would be added to the worries about internal discord. Because there were not enough regular troops and no militia to mobilize, the administration acquiesced in raising a potentially even more dangerous force, independent military units that called themselves the "Volunteers."

American revolutionary agitation in the 1770s helped to set the timing of agitation in Ireland, just as two centuries later the American civil rights movement would help to trigger a civil rights movement in Northern Ireland. But in each case there were limits on how far ideas could be transplanted because social conditions were not the same. And, as with the divisions in Northern Ireland in this century, the problems besetting Ireland in the eighteenth century were disturbing enough that something similar would have occurred there, even without the American example.

What was most important for Ireland in the last quarter of the eighteenth century is that the American crisis served as a rallying cry among disgruntled Irishmen, inside Parliament and out. Few if any Irish Patriots would have disputed James Madison's claim that "Ireland is reaping a large share of the harvest produced by our labours."[77] The Irish Parliament successfully insisted on trade concessions in 1779 and three years

---

77. Madison to Edmund Pendleton, 23 July 1782, in William T. Hutchinson, et al., eds., *The Papers of James Madison*, 15 vols. (Chicago and Charlottesville: University of Chicago and University of Virginia presses, 1962–), 4:432. I am indebted to Francis G. James for calling this to my attention. Also see Benjamin Franklin's letter to R. R. Livingston of 25 June 1782 in Francis Wharton, ed., *The Revolutionary Diplomatic Correspondence of the United States*, 6 vols. (Washington, D.C.: Government Printing Office, 1889), 5:511.

later finally received formal British recognition of its independence. Irish Catholics would use the American crisis to demonstrate their loyalty and dependability as the first step toward improving their station. Most Catholic leaders (publicly, that is) rallied behind the British government and Dublin Castle, hoping that their reward would be an easing of restrictions. Their gambit paid off in 1774, 1778 and 1782, and again in 1793, though they were far from being accorded equal status.[78] And if they gained they also lost by incurring the resentment of Patriot leaders who still did not trust them and were trying to press their own claims against the Castle and Whitehall.

In the short run, the heightened political sensibilities of middle class Protestants loom even larger in importance. As members of the Volunteers, these men enjoyed an organizational opportunity unimaginable in the days of a Charles Lucas. They too eventually presented their own political agenda, inspired by the actions of their American cousins.

The parliamentary Patriots of this generation enjoyed a fleeting solidarity in part because of the American Revolution. For example, in 1769 both Bushe and Langrishe allowed the British Parliament a superintending role over Irish commerce, and Langrishe made the same distinction between internal and external legislation that Franklin had made and William Pitt had accepted when discussing American rights. Langrishe and Bushe left that ambiguous position behind for a more emphatic defense of Irish parliamentary independence by 1782. They thought alike on these issues, though not on others. In 1775 Bushe opposed Harcourt's reference to the American rebellion in his speech from the throne; Langrishe did not. Langrishe eventually drifted away from the Patriots, though he took a liberal stand on some issues; Bushe's ties to the Patriots were stronger. Bushe, Langrishe, and the other Patriots never were singleminded in purpose. Their joining together, if only temporarily, in 1782 has too often obscured that important point.

For an all too brief moment Henry Grattan and Henry Flood would lead a seemingly united push for parliamentary independence. Grattan frequently referred to the American struggle and its significance for the Irish. By 1782 he could insist on one objective—parliamentary independence under a "restored" constitution—as the key to national security. Unfortunately, parliamentary independence did not bring the peace or prosperity Grattan had wanted: his was a delusive dream. He and other Irish Patriots might have eliminated the problem of having no real focus to their political energy, but what they focused on did not give

---

78. See Eamon O'Flaherty's "Ecclesiastical Politics and the Dismantling of the Penal Laws in Ireland, 1774–1782," *Irish Historical Studies* 26 (May 1988): 33–50.

them greater or clearer vision. They could construct a continuous line of constitutionalist thought traced through Molyneux and Swift to themselves, eliminating as inconsequential any inconsistencies that might have been noted, yet they could not eliminate the basic problems with their form of constitutional nationalism. Indeed, by insisting on parliamentary independence they seemed to be denying that there truly could be a unified British-Irish interest; and that, ultimately, was the only sound justification for an imperial tie connecting the two "kingdoms."

CHAPTER 4

Parliamentary Independence and the "Constitution" of 1782

> *When Grattan rose, none dared oppose*
>   *The claim he made for freedom:*
> *They knew our swords, to back his words,*
>   *Were ready, did he need them.*
> *Then let us raise, to Grattan's praise,*
>   *A proud and joyous anthem;*
> *And wealth, and grace, and length of days,*
>   *May God, in mercy grant him.*
>   *Thomas Davis, ca. 1845*[1]

Looking back on the events culminating in Irish parliamentary "independence" in 1782, lawyer-cum-historian Francis Dobbs exclaimed that "it was on the plains of America, that Ireland obtained her freedom."[2] Irish agitators for imperial reform might not have had any intention of doing as the Americans had done, but that did not stop them from taking advantage of the American revolt. They advocated commercial relief in the "free trade" movement of 1779, and from there Parliament pushed on to make a formal declaration of its independence

---

1. Thomas Davis, "Song of the Volunteers of 1782," *The Poems of Thomas Davis* (Dublin: James Duffy, 1846), 156.
2. Francis Dobbs, *A History of Irish Affairs, from the 12th of October, 1779, to the 15th September, 1782, the Day of Lord Temple's Arrival* (Dublin: M. Mills, 1782), 7–8. Also see the overviews in R. B. McDowell, "Colonial Nationalism and the Winning of Parliamentary Independence, 1760–1782," in T. W. Moody and W. E. Vaughan, eds., *A New History of Ireland*, vol. 4 (Oxford: Clarendon Press, 1986), 196–235; Theresa Margaret O'Connor, "The More Immediate Effects of the American Revolution on Ireland, 1775–1785" (M.A. thesis, Queen's University, Belfast, 1938); and Maurice O'Connell, *Irish Politics and Social Conflict in the Age of the American Revolution* (Philadelphia: University of Pennsylvania Press, 1965), passim.

three years later. In each case the British gave in grudgingly and, had it not been for the American crisis, they might not have given in at all.

What no doubt aggravated some British leaders is that the Irish pressed their claims even as they swore fealty to the empire. Indeed, the Irish Parliament had made a point of reaffirming its attachment to the Crown in 1778, when France entered the war, and again in 1781, after news was received of Cornwallis's surrender at Yorktown. Yet Denis Daly and Henry Grattan, Commons members who helped draft the 1778 resolution, were leading Patriots, outspoken in the cause of commercial relief, and sharp critics of British trade policies. Likewise Barry Yelverton, author of the 1781 motion proclaiming that "our interests are become inseparably united with those of *Great Britain*," was an opposition leader who, at the same moment he professed loyalty to George III, worked for a partial repeal of Poynings' Law and greater freedom for the Irish Parliament. It appears that most Patriots backed Yelverton's motion even though Grattan—in what some might have thought "bad taste"—did not. Perhaps Yelverton and the others better understood that Yorktown would help bring an end to the very policies they had protested so futilely six years earlier.[3] As one administration supporter groused, men like Yelverton and Grattan were not rebels, but they were perfectly willing to make the "best use" of the American rebellion to further their own ends.[4]

The North ministry understood that Harcourt could do only so much and that, once he left, a new lord lieutenant would have to scramble to build Castle support and retain power. North had a difficult time finding a replacement for Harcourt and settled finally on John, earl of Buckinghamshire, politically experienced but also somewhat naive. The earl was willing to go and, more importantly, he had powerful family connections in Ireland. His wife was the sister of Thomas Conolly, a leading spokesman for the Ascendancy elite and sometime member of the opposition in Commons. Conolly, for his part, advised his brother-in-law not to take the post, knowing what he would be up against. Unpersuaded by Conolly, Buckinghamshire remained enthusiastic and confident. "He is in high spirits, they tell me, and expects nothing but sunshine," wrote Harcourt's son to his father, "although the world is

---

3. *Journal of the House of Commons of the Kingdom of Ireland*, 20 vols. (Dublin: George Grierson, 1796–1892), 9:450–51 (for the 23 March 1778 resolution) and 10:270 (for 4 December 1781); Grattan and "bad taste" suggested in Gerard O'Brien, *Anglo-Irish Politics in the Age of Grattan and Pitt* (Dublin: Irish Academic Press, 1987), 50.

4. John Beresford to Thomas Allan, 14 October 1777, in William Beresford, ed., *The Correspondence of the Right Hon. John Beresford*, 2 vols. (London: Woodfall and Kinder, 1854), 1:17.

convinced that, all things considered, he will in a very short time see threatening clouds, which will burst in thunder over his head."[5]

Buckinghamshire intended to rule "without faction or corruption" and thereby escape the charges directed at his immediate predecessors, Townshend and Harcourt, that they spent too lavishly and corrupted their administrations through excessive influence-peddling. The North ministry encouraged the new lord lieutenant in his plans because of the need for financial retrenchment. What pleased North did not necessarily please his Irish supporters, however. Administration men like John Beresford found little to respect in Buckinghamshire. They saw his reluctance to dispense patronage as unrealistic and his attempts to court independent and opposition members of the Parliament as weak and vacillating. Opposition leaders were not enthusiastic; neither were they especially hostile. While North could be pleased that Buckinghamshire was genuinely liked by some in Parliament and even seemed to be popular with the people, he still expected Buckinghamshire to be an effective administrator. Not overly astute to begin with, Buckinghamshire was caught in the middle, trying to meet the expectations of Whitehall that he keep Ireland quiet and the frustrations of Irish leaders looking for change. Eventually he failed.

First and foremost, Conolly had urged Buckinghamshire to be sensitive to the need for commercial relief. "It is certainly in the Power of Gt. Britain to make this Kingdom of much greater use to the British Empire, than she has hitherto been," wrote Conolly as his brother-in-law prepared to leave for Dublin. Conolly, like so many other Irish leaders who believed they had been denied their rightful place in the empire by petty British policies, complained that British M.P.s listened too much to a "Few Cities and Towns, whose Trade might be Injured by any Advantage given to" Ireland, "forgetting that Ultimately, any Wealth this Kingdom should acquire, would all settle in Great Britain."[6] Buckinghamshire would be put under intense pressure to do something about this.

The American war disrupted Irish trade, which by the time of Buckinghamshire's arrival had slipped into the doldrums. Harcourt, acting

---

5. Letter of 3 October 1776 in Edward William Harcourt, ed., *The Harcourt Papers*, 12 vols. (Oxford: James Parker, 1880–1905), 3:122. For Buckinghamshire's administration in general, see Thomas M. Molloy, "The Irish Executive and the North Ministry, 1777–1782" (Ph.D. dissertation, Fordham University, 1971).
6. Conolly to Buckinghamshire, 27 November 1776, in the Heron Papers, MS. 13,034, National Library of Ireland. Also see the characterization of Conolly in Falkland [John Robert Scott?], *A Review of the Principal Characters of the Irish House of Commons* (Dublin, 1789), 22–24.

on instructions from Whitehall, ordered an embargo in February 1776 on all provisions sent out of Ireland, except those sent to Britain and specified destinations within the empire. Although Irish smugglers kept at their illicit trade with the continent and even with the rebellious Americans, other merchants and members of the Irish Parliament were affronted by the move. An embargo made sense to the British but not to the Irish, who had already seen much of their linen market eliminated with the American rebellion and now had to add the beef and butter shipped to ports in France. To them British policy seemed to be intentionally rather than incidentally crippling. Irish finances were already in a bad state, and a commercial downturn only worsened them.

Economic issues, from the granting of supplies to the length of the pension list to the decline of commerce, could spark a constitutional crisis, as the British well knew. Buckinghamshire had been warned that "the leaders in Parliament are so accustomed to avail themselves of their own importance that you must expect some unreasonable demands" to be made.[7] Sure enough, Denis Daly called for a review of trade policy and launched into a diatribe against the North ministry in November 1777. "We have already seen our scanty trade persecuted by prerogative," he complained, "and we can discern no end to the oppression." He argued that the American colonies had been "enslaved," Ireland had been "plundered," and the Irish could not trust the British to protect them, so "that no relief is to be expected without our interposition."[8] Few were willing to use such harsh words, and most shied away from the threat implicit in "interposition," but Daly's desire to hasten commercial relief was widely shared.

Buckinghamshire had urged the North ministry to take action months before Daly's impassioned speech. North professed to be sympathetic and even suggested a number of areas where restrictions could

---

7. Note written by Chief Secretary Richard Heron, based on a letter from George Germain to Buckinghamshire on 12 February 1777, in Add. MS. 34,523, fo. 180, British Library. Also see the reports on British-Irish trade relations in Historical Manuscripts Commission, *Report on the Manuscripts of the Marquis of Lothian* (London: Eyre and Spottiswoode, 1905), 301–4, 306–10.

8. Daly in the Commons on 1 November 1777, as recorded in vol. 1, container 4 of Parliament, House of Commons Debates, 1776–89, a manuscript account owned by the Library of Congress (MS. 16, 363.1). Sir Henry Cavendish is thought to have been the author. Whoever the author was, he sat as a member of Commons, took shorthand notes, and later transcribed them, trying to record some proceedings verbatim. See Peter D. G. Thomas, "The Authorship of the Manuscript Irish Parliamentary Diary (1776–1789) in the Library of Congress," *English Historical Review* 77 (1962): 94–95. Cavendish was once described as having a tendency to be pro-administration, but he was "no steady partizan"; see Falkland, *Review of the Principal Characters*, 158–62. Cavendish joined the anti-administration Whig Club in 1789.

be eased. But North's willingness to open the African trade or remove penalties on the export of oats and wheat to England showed his evasiveness on larger issues and his unwillingness to court Irish favor at the expense of British opinion. For over two years his ministry made no real move to answer Irish complaints.[9] North was not, at least in his view, being inflexible or unfair. By the time that M.P.s like Denis Daly became more demanding his power was ebbing anyway. The American rebellion had mushroomed into a world war, with the French threatening to cross the channel and strike England or Ireland as well as send fleets and troops to the Americas. Weariness sapped the war effort at home, and North's critics in the British Parliament, never silent, became even more vocal.

By the spring of 1779, opposition leaders in the British Parliament like Charles James Fox and Edmund Burke in Commons and the marquess of Rockingham and earl of Shelburne in Lords were badgering North to make trade concessions to Ireland. "The American war had commenced upon less provocation than this country had given Ireland," claimed Shelburne when pointing an accusing finger at North.[10] Himself Irish-born, though taking no pride in that fact, Shelburne and others attacking the North ministry, whether they acted out of genuine concern for Ireland or were simply using Irish unrest as a way of discrediting the government, helped bring to life the "free trade" movement in Ireland.

When a new parliamentary session opened in Dublin in October 1779, there were more M.P.s willing to talk as Daly had two years earlier, and they could speak with greater confidence, given the seeming support they enjoyed among the British opposition. Finding that Ireland was so distressed and that the king and his ministers had been so unresponsive, "It is, therefore, evident that the people cannot support the King, nor the King the people," charged Daly's friend Henry Grattan in the Irish Commons; "We must therefore look to ourselves," Grattan

---

9. See Charles Jenkinson's letter to Buckinghamshire of 2 May 1777 in the Heron Papers, MS. 13,035, NLI; North to Buckinghamshire on 28 July 1777, in ibid., for expressions of sympathy on the part of the ministry; and Herbert Butterfield, *George III, Lord North, and the People, 1779–80* (London: G. Belland and Sons, 1949), 138–61, for ministerial foot-dragging. That North, while slow, even considered commercial relief as early as 1777 proves wrong the Volunteer claim that the British had been absolutely unmoving until they (the Volunteers) forced their hand, although the American war is what made North flexible in the first place. Also see O'Connell, *Irish Politics*, 159.

10. William Cobbett et al., eds., *The Parliamentary History of England*, 36 vols. (London: T. C. Hansard, 1806–20), 20:667, Shelburne in Lords on 2 June 1779; Rockingham in ibid., 11 May 1779, 20:639–40; and Butterfield's observations in *George III*, 86–99. For a complaint that Shelburne was disingenuous in his professed concern for Ireland, see the letter from Lord Lucan to Edmund Sexton Pery of 7 December 1779 in HMC, *Eighth Report* (London: Eyra and Spottiswoode, 1881), Part I, 206.

concluded in deliberately inflammatory language.[11] In the most famous speech of his career, Hussey Burgh condemned the "usurped authority of a foreign Parliament" that had passed "the most wicked laws that a jealous, monopolizing, ungrateful spirit could devise." Making the most of his oratorical moment, Hussey Burgh threatened that the "English have sown their laws like dragon's teeth, and they have sprung up in armed men."[12]

Taking their tactics from American protesters in the decade before Lexington and Concord who had signed non-intercourse agreements and formed associations, Irish protesters outside of Parliament tried to flex their political muscle as well. As in so many crises before, Irish parliamentary leaders tried to mobilize and channel their support. Grattan and his backers in Commons marched to the Castle to deliver their resolution for free trade personally to Buckinghamshire. They passed through crowds lining the street to cheer them on. Men who were supposedly the "Friends of Government" like Henry Flood and the duke of Leinster refused to resist the demands being made in Commons or to condemn the public demonstrations, at least those that did not get out of hand. (In 1779, as in 1759, crowds became unruly and accosted some members of Parliament when it was rumored that no commercial relief would be forthcoming.)[13]

Numerous pamphlets denounced British policy and promoted the cause of "free trade"—which in reality was little more than a desire for fuller participation in the British mercantile system. Trinity College provost and Cork M.P. John Hely-Hutchinson wrote one of the more popular tracts, condemning British acts from the middle of the preceding century on that resulted, he claimed, from an unfounded fear of Irish competition. He contended that nature had blessed Ireland with a temperate climate, good soil, natural harbors, and an energetic people want-

---

11. Henry Grattan, Jr., ed., *The Speeches of the Right Honorable Henry Grattan*, 4 vols. (London: Longman, Hurst, Rees, Orme, and Brown, 1822), 1:23. See note 41 in this chapter for the problem with Grattan's "speeches" in this edition.

12. As taken from Henry Grattan, Jr., *Memoirs of the Life and Times of the Rt. Hon. Henry Grattan*, 5 vols. (London: Henry Colburn, 1849), 1:403. Also see the tribute to Hussey Burgh by "Hibernicus Senior" in the *Freeman's Journal*, 5 February 1780.

13. For Leinster and Flood see Heron's note of 13 October 1779 in Add. MS. 34,523, fo. 192, BL. See George O'Brien, ed., "The Irish Free Tade Agitation of 1779," *English Historical Review* 38 (1923): 564–81 and 39 (1924): 95–109, for the reports submitted to Buckinghamshire by Flood, Langrishe, Hussey Burgh, and others that were forwarded to London; and the discussion in David Lammey's "The Free Trade Crisis: A Reappraisal," in Gerard O'Brien, ed., *Parliament, Politics and People* (Dublin: Irish Academic Press, 1989), 69–92, and "A Study of Anglo-Irish Relations between 1772 and 1782, with Particular Reference to the 'Free Trade' Movement" (Ph.D. thesis, Queen's University of Belfast, l984).

ing to work and deserving to prosper, but kept from doing either by a paranoid Britain. "Suffer no longer, respected sister, the narrow jealousy of commerce to mislead the wisdom and impair the strength of your state," he counseled.[14] Another pamphleteer observed:

> As *England* and *Ireland* are one dominion, though two kingdoms, it is the greatest absurdity imaginable to suppose, that what injures a part, can benefit the whole; that a measure which enfeebles, depopulates, and depresses one third, can render the aggregate strong, populous, and flourishing.[15]

The British Parliament finally acted before the end of the year, and, for the moment, most Irish leaders appeared to be satisfied with the greater commercial freedoms they would enjoy. They could once again export woolens and other goods to England, and they were given greater freedom of trade with the rest of the empire. Although Buckinghamshire disliked the tactics used by the free trade agitators, he did not oppose commercial relief and probably breathed easier in December than he had in October. Having gained their objective, opposition M.P.s like Denis Daly discontinued their fiery rhetoric. According to one administration supporter, Daly and Gervase Parker Bushe used their influence "both publicly and privately, to keep opposition within proper bounds; for it wanted only their encouragement to let loose confusion."[16] British observers were equally relieved that the commercial crisis ended; as Horace Walpole put it, the Irish had had "much the air of Americanizing."[17] Whitehall feared that constitutional issues would be raised, and with good reason. North, the target of so much obloquy, beseeched Buckinghamshire:

> For God's sake, Let the prudent friends of Gt. Britain & Ireland, keep out of sight the constitutional queston about the validity of the British Statutes. I will endeavour to do it on this side of the Water, but if we do not take care, we may split on that rock still & there are people enough in this country ready to raise a flame between us.[18]

---

14. [John Hely-Hutchinson], *The Commercial Restraints of Ireland* (Dublin: M. H. Gill, 1888; orig. ed., 1779), 163.

15. James Caldwell, *An Enquiry* (London: Henry Mugg, 1779), 31, the same James Caldwell thought to have written the anonymous pamphlets in defense of Townshend's administration (see chap. 3, n. 5). Caldwell took issue with Postlethwait's arguments twenty years before that a parliamentary union would bring an easing of trade restrictions (see chap. 2, n. 31 for Postlethwait).

16. Beresford, ed., *Corres. of John Beresford*, 1:104, letter from Beresford to John Robinson of 3 December 1779.

17. W. S. Lewis, ed., *Horace Walpole's Correspondence*, 48 vols. (New Haven: Yale University Press, 1937–83), 24:473, letter to Horace Mann of 9 May 1779.

18. North to Buckinghamshire, 9 December 1779, in Add. MS. 34,523, fo. 329, BL; also see R. B. McDowell, *Ireland in the Age of Revolution, 1760–1801* (Oxford: Clarendon Press, 1979) 270–72.

Some Irish leaders, notably the duke of Leinster, were inclined to agree with North on this point and wanted no further agitation. What worried North was that during the free trade controversy, the sovereignty of the British Parliament and its right to legislate for Ireland had again been questioned. He knew that some members of the Irish Parliament, unlike Leinster, wanted to re-examine Poynings' Law and review other issues that had been avoided or left unresolved. He had in fact been sent an open letter by a barrister, Francis Dobbs, informing him that many Irish were disappointed that trade restrictions had been lifted as a matter of expediency rather than principle. They resented having to beg for what the rebellious Americans had been offered in 1778 by the Carlisle commission. Furthermore, Dobbs's *Letter* noted, the Irish were not asking for an indulgence; they were claiming a constitutional right. "I do not deceive you when I say, we are attached to England, and seek a connection with her, in preference to the rest of mankind," Dobbs assured North. "But, my Lord, our first attachment is to FREEDOM, and every other is a secondary consideration."[19] As North had discovered in his dealings with the Americans, economic grievances and constitutional issues were inseparably tied; it was impossible to treat one and ignore the other.

Thus it was in the middle of the free trade movement that Charles Francis Sheridan wrote his critique of Blackstone's view of parliamentary sovereignty. Sheridan's essay was by no means the first rebuttal to Blackstone. James Burgh took Blackstone to task in his 1774 *Political Disquisitions,* as did James Wilson's *Considerations,* and Jeremy Bentham subjected him to a longer and more critical review two years later.[20] But none of these writers was primarily concerned with the question of Ireland's constitutional tie to Britain, and it was that question that Sheridan sought to answer. Both Charles James Fox and the earl of Shelburne referred favorably to Sheridan's *Observations* during debates in the British Parliament over commercial relief for Ireland, Shelburne calling it "a very able and masterly pamphlet."[21] One might well wonder

---

19. Francis Dobbs, *A Letter to the Right Honourable Lord North, on his Propositions in Favour of Ireland* (Dublin: M. Miles, 1780), 13.

20. James Burgh, *Political Disquisitions,* 3 vols. (Philadelphia: Robert Bell, 1775; orig. ed., London, 1774–75), 3:275; James Wilson, *Considerations on the nature and extent of the legislative authority of the British Parliament* (Philadelphia: William and Thomas Bradford, 1774), passim; and [Jeremy Bentham], *A Fragment on Government* (London: T. Payne, 1776), although Bentham and Sheridan focused on different issues, with Bentham devoting most of his attention to the second and third sections of Book 1 (the nature of law and the laws of England) and Sheridan most of his to section 4 (countries subject to the laws of England).

21. Cobbett, ed., *Parliamentary History,* 20:667; and ibid., 20:875–76 for Fox.

if Shelburne had read it closely, because Sheridan attacked "the uncontrolled, absolute, despotic power" of the British Parliament and challenged Blackstone on some points that Shelburne would not have, had he been given to constitutional disquisition.

Sheridan was the older brother of playwright Richard Brinsley Sheridan, whose *The School for Scandal* made him the toast of London. The older Sheridan studied law at Lincoln's Inn and would be called to the Irish Bar the year after his pamphlet was published. Unlike his brother, Charles chose Irish over British society, but he benefited from his brother's connections to obtain posts within several Irish administrations. At the time he wrote his *Observations*, he sat in Commons for the borough of Belturbet in County Cavan. He had already shown an interest in history by writing a study of Swedish politics based on his brief tour in Stockholm as a diplomatic secretary. In his *Observations* he alluded to Molyneux's *Case* and accepted Molyneux's view of the Irish past. Noting events that transpired since Molyneux had written, he singled out for criticism the Declaratory Act of 1720 as a violation of fundamental Irish freedoms. Unlike Molyneux, who touched on natural right theory and Lockean ideas but emphasized history to make his *Case*, Sheridan brushed lightly over Irish history. He concentrated on defending Lockean notions of natural right and applying them to Ireland.

Sheridan pointed to what he thought were Blackstone's logical inconsistencies, particularly in the "spurious" doctrine of the "supremacy and omnipotence" of the British Parliament. "The King, Lords, and Commons are *not* the constitution, they are only the *creatures* of the constitution," Sheridan contended.[22] The survivability of the constitution depended on the virtue and patriotism of the people, not the omniscience of parliamentary government. In the case of Ireland, the people there were entitled to constitutional protections but had been denied them by the usurpations of a British Parliament that did not represent them, its pretensions to proper authority notwithstanding. Trying to use Montesquieu to bolster his view that the empire was ideally composed of confederated states joined only through the Crown, he insisted that Ireland was *"connected with"* rather than *"dependent upon"* Britain. Looking past the North ministry, which he satirized in a postscript, Sheridan called for a new government with a more enlightened policy.

22. Charles Francis Sheridan, Esq., *Observations on the Doctrine Laid Down by Sir William Blackstone respecting the Extent of Power of the British Parliament, particularly in relation to Ireland* (Dublin: The Company of Booksellers, 1779), quotes from pp. 71, 20, resp. Gerard O'Brien notes the importance of this essay in his *Anglo-Irish Politics*, 39–42.

He hoped that "juster notions of liberty" would prevail so that Britain could leave behind the bad judgment that "has already cost us thirteen provinces."[23]

Blackstone also suffered at the hands of Frederick Jebb, whose *Letters of Guatimozin* were first published in the *Freeman's Journal* beginning in April 1779 and were then reissued under separate cover with the letters of "Causidicus." These tracts, along with barrister Joseph Pollock's *Letters of Owen Roe O'Nial*, written in 1779–80, apparently circulated even more widely than Sheridan's *Observations*. They drew "the attention of the people to their situation" so that "patriotism began to diffuse itself through every patriot breast."[24]

All of these "letters" were published anonymously. Jebb, a Dublin physician, apparently wrote those from Guatimozin alone and then teamed with Robert Johnson (like Pollock, a barrister) to produce Causidicus. Jebb and Johnson called for greater guarantees of Irish constitutional freedoms; they contended that the Irish were entitled to the rights of Englishmen as those rights had been extended to Ireland; they stated matter-of-factly that the Irish Parliament was by right independent and sovereign; they called on their countrymen to practice economic nationalism. Their criticism of Britain could be very pointed, with Jebb as Guatimozin writing that Ireland "hath been united to an unnatural sister" for some six hundred years, from whom "she had experienced nothing but adversity and opposition." He denounced the British Parliament for the "tyranny" it had "deliberately exercised" at least since 1698 with the "infernal compact" of killing the wool trade to promote linen in its place. Showing that he had read Molyneux's *Case* and perhaps even the 1644 "Declaration" (printed, finally, in 1750), he argued that the Irish had been entitled to the rights of Englishmen since the time of Henry II, when they agreed to accept Henry as their king. "What are the liberties of Englishmen?" Jebb asked; simple enough, he answered, "to be governed by LAWS to which they have given consent, either by themselves, or their Representatives in Parliament."[25] A parliamentary union would not solve Irish problems, he continued.

As to an union now with England, I confess I am doubtful of its expediency. Time was that it would have been a glorious proposition to Ireland—but to unite

---

23. Sheridan, *Observations*, 64, 30, resp.
24. Dobbs, *History*, 11.
25. [Frederick Jebb], *The Letters of Guatimozin, on the Affairs of Ireland . . . to Which are added, the Letters of Causidicus that accompanied the Essays of Guatimozin in their First Appearance* (Dublin: R. Marchbank, 1779), Letter I, pp. 1–2; Letter II, p. 12, resp. For Johnson, also see chap. 7, n. 27.

ourselves to the vices and the decay of England, when her prosperity has taken flight with her virtues, is an experiment of which no man can promise good consequences.[26]

Critics of Guatimozin condemned him for his harsh tone and for what they took to be his separatist tendencies. Guatimozin denied the charge of being a radical or a separatist and professed his loyalty to George III, even as he rebuked the British Parliament. Nonetheless, he also defended Ireland's *"independent national rights"*; his critics were not overreacting if they thought there was a revolutionary side to Guatimozin's position. Although he claimed not to be advocating violence, he also wrote, "I confess that, as an Irishman, I feel considerable gratification in the checks, which the progress of England's usurpations hath received in America."[27] He denied that calling for non-importation associations was rebellious, since rebellion could only be against lawful government. And he appealed directly to the Irish people:

But, though the monster is brought to light by a single strength, it is only in the activity of the many to hunt him *even unto death*. To speak in plainer terms, it is in the people only, and the people *united* in their efforts, to rid themselves of the tyrannic disposition in this *sovereign legislative parliament*.[28]

As Owen Roe O'Nial, Pollock was no kinder and even more impassioned and sarcastic. Like Guatimozin, whose arguments he endorsed, Pollock expressed little faith in British good will and threaded his way through the past to show that, as he put it, the Irish had been to the English what the helots had been to the Spartans. He echoed Jebb in denying that parliamentary union would solve anything, calling instead for clear-cut Irish parliamentary independence. "It would be singular enough if the same period which established American independence," he proclaimed, "shall be found to have destroyed the usurpation of the British Parliament over the legislative rights of Ireland."[29] Though he denied that he was being a radical or revolutionary, and made a point—like Jebb—of professing his attachment to the "imperial" Crown, he had almost nothing good to say about the British-Irish tie.

If Pollock complemented Jebb and Johnson, and if the three of them in turn only stated more emphatically and for a popular audience what

26. Ibid., Letter VII, p. 56.
27. Ibid., Letter II, p. 5; Letter III, p. 19, resp.
28. Ibid., Letter XII, p. 76 (by "Causidicus"—Jebb and Johnson).
29. [Joseph Pollock], *Letters of Owen Roe O'Nial* (Dublin: W. Jackson, 1779), 19n. Three "letters" were included here. Letters 5–9 were printed on the front page (in most cases) of the *Freeman's Journal*, in installments between 2 March and 27 April 1780. Apparently the fourth letter did not run as planned.

Sheridan had written, it was no coincidence. Not long after they began writing their tracts, all four men became members of the Monks of the Order of St. Patrick, a fraternal society organized in September 1779. This "order," whose members sometimes referred to themselves as "Monks of the Screw," was "partly political and partly convivial."[30] It was more than a dinner club and something less than a political caucus.

Clubs and fraternal societies were common during these years, especially in London. The most notorious of the London societies was the Brotherhood of Saint Francis of Wycombe—better remembered as the "Hell-Fire Club"—whose most famous member was John Wilkes.[31] The Monks of St. Patrick, like the more familiar London club, mocked Catholic ways with titles like "abbot" and "prior" and the dark robes worn by its members. Unlike the "monks" of St. Francis, however, the Monks of St. Patrick did more than eat, drink, and carouse. According to one of its members, its "general object was a co-operation of men, who held, or professed at least to hold, a general similarity of political principles, and resolved to maintain the Rights and Constitution of their Country."[32] Apparently they met every Saturday during law term, each garbed in a "black tabinet domino." They kept no record of their meetings, they passed no formal resolutions, but in public, acting as individuals, they were, Thomas Davis gushed, "the wisest, best, and most brilliant spirits of the island." When they gathered, "it was a union of strong souls, brought together, like electric clouds, by affinity, and flashing as they joined."[33] Davis indulged in romantic excess, and yet there was something to what he said; the Monks were a distinguished group.

30. From a note written by member Edward Hudson to the son of John Philpot Curran, William Henry Curran, which the younger Curran had printed along with the list of fifty-six members in his *The Life of the Right Honourable John Philpot Curran* (Chicago: Union Catholic Publishing Co., 1882, ed. by R. Shelton MacKenzie; orig. ed. 1819), 80n–82n. Hudson prepared this list for Curran ca. 1819, some forty years after the Monks were organized, and Hudson's memory was not perfect. For example, ten of the men he listed as being M.P.s were not sitting in Commons at the time the Monks were organized. Hudson may not have erred in his listing of members, however, even if he was wrong about their parliamentary political status in 1779. His list included only "professed brothers"; there were others who associated with them. The like-minded political views of the members should not be discounted. Their activities may not have been coordinated, but it was no coincidence that they joined the same "club." It is interesting, however, that Lord Townshend, the former lord lieutenant, was invited to join as well.

31. Donald McCormick, *The Hell-Fire Club* (London: Jarrolds, 1958).

32. Francis Hardy, *Memoirs of the Political and Private Life of James Caulfield, Earl of Charlemont*, 2 vols. (London: T. Cadell, 1812; orig. ed., 1810), 2:197. Hardy was one of those Hudson incorrectly placed in Commons (he did not take a seat until 1782). Hardy connected this club to the Whig Club founded in 1789; about a dozen Monks ended up in the Whig Club.

33. Thomas Davis, *The Life of the Right Hon. J. P. Curran* (Dublin: James Duffy, 1846), 26. Davis admired Curran immensely; he reproduced the list of Monks that first appeared in the biography by Curran's son.

Over fifty men enrolled as members of the Monks. Of those whose politics are known, not one was a strong supporter of the Buckinghamshire administration. Of the fifteen or so sitting in Commons, many were notable leaders of the opposition and free trade advocates. They included Barry Yelverton, who carried the title of "Founder" and seems to have organized the "Monks," and Yelverton's associates Walter Hussey Burgh, George Ogle, George Ponsonby, Denis Daly, John Forbes, and Henry Grattan. Four peers were members, including the earl of Arran and the earl of Charlemont, both of whom often took antiadministration stands. Of the 1779 Monks, Frederick Jebb was the only physician member; Edward Hudson was the lone dentist in the society. By far the largest number—well over thirty—were barristers, some of whom were not yet sitting in Commons but would be within the next few years.

Naturally not all of the Monks were brilliant, witty, and dynamic, despite Davis's flattering portrait. Henry Hartstonge was once called the "Jack Pudding" of Commons, and fellow M.P. Richard Martin was dismissed as an "odd, absurd character."[34] Sir Edward Newenham, whose dabbling in popular politics dated back to the days of Charles Lucas, was also thought to be a bit odd, possibly even by his friends.

Yet most were men of great standing. The earl of Charlemont was respected for his steady principles and moderation; he was an interesting mix of conservative and liberal tendencies. Seven years before the Monks first gathered, Charlemont had played host to the Society of Granby Row, which met in his elegant Dublin home and included Yelverton, Daly, Hussey Burgh, and Grattan. This early society, too, had had political as well as convivial purposes. Like others in the order who favored reforming as well as defending the Irish Parliament, Charlemont wanted the people to defer to their leaders in determining what changes should be made and when they should come. He sympathized with Catholics to the extent that he favored an easing of the penal laws and welcomed Arthur O'Leary, a Capuchin monk, as an honorary member of the society; still, he was not a champion of Catholic equality. Ogle had gained fame as a "popular and flashy speaker" in Commons; Daly was almost universally admired for his "sound judgement" and great learning. He and Charlemont might have had the finest personal libraries on the is-

---

34. Hartstonge and Martin on p. 255, and Newenham—"a man of no respect"—on p. 246 of G. O. Sayles, ed., "Contemporary Sketches of the Members of the Irish Parliament in 1782," *Royal Irish Academy. Proceedings* 56, sect. C (1953–54): 227–86. Falkland, *Review of the Principal Characters*, 93–95, is somewhat kinder to Newenham. Shevawn Lynam, *Humanity Dick: A Biography of Richard Martin, M.P., 1754–1834* (London: Hamish Hamilton, 1975), is much kinder in assessing Martin.

land, with Daly's running over one thousand titles and featuring the works of Aristotle and Plato, Cicero and Seneca, in original Greek and Latin as well as translations.[35] Yelverton could be a formidable presence in the House and "one of the first lawyers of the Bar." John Philpot Curran, "prior" of the Monks, was rising as a barrister and would eventually become a powerful voice in Commons and the nemesis of John Fitzgibbon.

Of all the Monks of St. Patrick, none became more famous and, for a short time, seemingly more powerful, than Henry Grattan. Grattan entered the Irish Parliament in December 1775, taking the borough seat opened by the drowning of Charlemont's son. The earl had long been the patron of Henry Flood and became attached to Grattan while Grattan was still studying law. Born in 1746, Grattan had attended Trinity College and went from there to the Middle Temple in 1767. He later admitted spending as much time listening to debates in the British House of Commons as he did studying law. He found law divorced from politics tedious and far preferred Milton and Pope to Coke and Blackstone. Whatever ideas he had formed about politics during his early Dublin years (when his father sat as a Dublin M.P. with Charles Lucas) were further refined by his sojourn in London. The first speaker he heard in the British Commons was George Grenville, and what Grenville said disturbed him deeply. "He talked of American taxation, and of the indisputable law of the realm that gave that right; and he extended this to Ireland," Grattan later reported. "It impressed on my mind a horror of this doctrine," he continued, "and I believe it was owing to this speech . . . that I became afterwards so very active in my opposition to the principles of the British Government in Ireland."[36]

Grattan venerated the British constitution, but that did not make him a slavish admirer of the British system of government and politics. He followed imperial affairs closely and tried to keep abreast of developments in Ireland and, with *Baratariana,* made his first political foray

---

35. Daly died suddenly in 1792, and his personal library was put up for sale, the titles of which are listed in *A Catalogue of the Library of the Late Right Honourable Denis Daly* (Dublin: John Archer, 1792). There were over 1400 individual titles or sets, close to half of which were classics, some in English translation, more in Greek and Latin. Daly's library and the list of books owned by the earl of Charlemont in the Charlemont Papers, RIA MS. 12R, give a rare look into the literary tastes and intellectual life (and pretensions) of the Anglo-Irish elite. Also see the characterizations of Daly, Charlemont, Grattan, Hussey Burgh, and most of the other leaders in the Irish Parliament in Barrington, *Rise and Fall of the Irish Nation.* Barrington was a younger contemporary of these men; he first sat in Commons in 1790 and stayed on to become a vehement opponent of union in 1799–1800. He was very opinionated, as is obvious from the impassioned tone of his writing.

36. Grattan, *Memoirs,* 1:136.

John Philpot Curran: barrister, M.P., leading Patriot, by Thomas Lawrence. Courtesy of the National Gallery of Ireland.

before he formally began his political career. He spent most of his time in London preparing himself for what he hoped would be his future at home, having no doubt already set his sights on a seat in the Irish Parliament. Impressed by the oratorical power of the elder William Pitt, he even practiced soliloquies as he walked through Windsor Forest, not for use in court but for floor debate in Commons. Thus this thin, somewhat ungainly man, whose awkward gait had earned him the nickname "elastic body" at Trinity College, prepared to become an orator and champion of Irish constitutional rights.[37]

Grattan sided with the opposition when he entered Commons, arguing against Harcourt's embargo in February 1776 and for free trade in 1779. Unlike many of his colleagues, he was not content with the easing of commercial restrictions. He wanted to make an explicit assertion of Irish constitutional rights, and his intentions were well known to an unreceptive administration. Buckinghamshire was instructed to see to it that no demands beyond "free" trade were made; George III and his ministers expected the Irish to be content with what they had already won and not insist on "constitutional innovations."[38] But Grattan was not to be deterred, despite the unpopularity of his plans among many members of the opposition as well as administration supporters. He apparently circulated the text of his address well in advance, which one administration supporter feared "is the signal for commencing hostilities in the country. I hope I am mistaken."[39]

Grattan rose on 19 April 1780 to give what he later considered his finest speech. He had prepared carefully for this moment, to him the most important, the most dramatic, of his career. He had even visited Marlay Abbey, where Jonathan Swift consorted with Vanessa. As Grattan's son wrote wistfully many years later, here, with Swift as his inspiration, Grattan "planned his measures for the independence of Ireland."[40] His day chosen, he moved that Commons pass a "Declaration of Right" stating "That the King's most excellent Majesty and

---

37. Ibid., 1:119 for solioquies; Walker's *Hibernian Magazine* 12 (August 1782): 422–23, for the description of Grattan.
38. Lord Hillsborough to Buckinghamshire, 28 March 1780, in Grattan, *Memoirs*, 2:31. Also see Edmund Pery to Buckinghamshire, 28 March 1780, in HMC, *Manuscripts of the Earl of Buckinghamshire, the Earl of Lindsey, the Earl of Onslow, Theodore J. Hare, Esq., and James Round, M.P.* (London: Eyre and Spottiswoode, 1895), 157.
39. Sir John Blaquiere to John Beresford, 11 March 1780, in Beresford, ed., *Correspondence of Beresford*, 1:128; also see ibid., 1:128–34, Beresford to John Robinson, at roughly the same time.
40. Grattan, *Memoirs*, 1:40. Whether Grattan really was inspired by Swift at that moment or, instead, simply invented this "reminiscence" later has caused historians no end of frustration.

the Lords and Commons of Ireland, are the only power competent to make laws to bind Ireland."

He introduced his motion with a rambling diatribe against the obsequiousness of the Irish Parliament as well as the tyrannic usurpations of Westminster. "Deny the claim of the British Parliament to make law for Ireland" he pled, "and with one voice lift up your hands against it."[41] He read the Declaratory Act of 1720 and condemned it utterly for having enslaved the country. He read a letter sent by the Carlisle commission to the Continental Congress to show that the British had offered to the rebellious Americans what they were denying to Ireland. He intended no criticism of the Americans; rather, his purpose was to expose British duplicity and remind his listeners of the opportunity afforded them by the American war. He denied that he was calling for a constitutional innovation, that his demands were "insatiable," or that he was claiming anything to which Ireland was not entitled. "You have done too much not to do more; you have gone too far not to go on," he admonished; "you have brought yourselves into that situation, in which you must silently abdicate the rights of your country or publicly restore them." He tried to embarrass his colleagues into supporting his motion, claiming that they had failed to protect their constitutional rights. "You have not been a parliament, nor your country a people," he chided. Improved commerce was nice:

But liberty, the foundation of trade, the charters of the land, the independency of Parliament, the securing, crowning, and the consummation of every thing, are yet to come. Without them the work is imperfect, the foundation is wanting, the capital is wanting, trade is not free, Ireland is a colony without the benefit of a charter, and you are a provincial synod without the privileges of a parliament.[42]

Grattan used the past to make his case, but in two different, even contradictory ways. He argued for the relevance of history by noting

---

41. Grattan, ed., *Speeches of Grattan*, 1:38–53, for the entire speech; quote from p. 39; the resolution itself is on p. 53. We will never know exactly what Grattan said in Commons on that occasion or any other. As Richard Koebner, "The Early Speeches of Henry Grattan," *Bulletin of the Institute of Historical Research* 30 (1957): 102–14 noted, Grattan only rarely wrote his speeches in full before giving them, and he went back over them in later years and added embellishments. There is nothing in the *House of Commons Journal* for 19 April 1780 even to indicate that Grattan introduced his motion; likewise with the MS. Parliamentary Debates, which records nothing between 3 March and 21 April. The *Freeman's Journal*, 22 April 1780, gave highlights of the debate and Grattan's speech. Thus, although I have enclosed excerpts from Grattan's "speech" in quotation marks, those were not necessarily his exact words. Grattan's *Memoirs* and *Speeches*, and more especially the writings of Jonah Barrington, are perhaps less important as documents showing what actually happened then as fundamental texts in the creation of myths about the Anglo-Irish Ascendancy.

42. Grattan, ed., *Speeches of Grattan*, 1:42.

Francis Wheatley's painting of the Irish House of Commons in 1780, with Henry Grattan proposing his "Declaration of Right." Gervase Parker Bushe sits at Grattan's right, and Walter Hussey Burgh is behind him, just off Grattan's shoulder. Denis Daly is on Grattan's left. Behind him are Barry Yelverton (on the left) and George Ogle (on the right). John Fitzgibbon sits in the second row, far right. *Courtesy of Lotherton Hall (Leeds City Art Galleries).*

that the rights of Englishmen had been extended to Ireland by "the compact of Henry" and "the charter of John." He did not bother to cite Molyneux or others to support his view, feeling, perhaps, that no one present would disagree with his interpretation of the past. Yet he also knew that, historically, those Irish "rights" had not included recognition of an independent parliament. He then attacked the notion that historical precedent was in any way binding. By the laws of nature, the laws of God, and the just intent of the British constitution, he asserted, the British Parliament had no power over Ireland. History, then, was both relevant and irrelevant to the defining of Irish freedoms. What is more, Grattan reaffirmed the contractual nature of the compact between the two kingdoms and the right of the people to choose their governors, by rebellion if necessary.

> The King has no other title to his crown than that which you have to your liberty; both are founded, the throne and your freedom, upon the right vested in the subjects to resist by arms, notwithstanding their oaths of allegiance, any authority attempting to impose acts of power as laws, whether that authority be one man or a host, the second James or the British parliament.[43]

Grattan's long speech was followed by an even longer debate, carrying the evening session into the wee hours of the next morning. Grattan was called on to withdraw his motion; he declined. He was asked to postpone introducing it; he refused even that. His friends and fellow "Monks" Yelverton, Hussey Burgh, Ogle, Forbes, Edward Newenham, and Peter Metge voted with him, as did some ninety others. Staunch administration supporters, joined by fence sitters and members of the opposition offended by the tone and timing of the speech, easily outnumbered them. Grattan's brother-in-law, Gervase Parker Bushe, sat next to him but voted nay. Hercules Langrishe and Henry Flood, who like Bushe had collaborated with Grattan on *Baratariana* a decade before, also opposed the motion. Although Flood had begun to drift away from the adminstration, he was reluctant to drift too far. Close friend and fellow "Monk" Denis Daly voted likewise, as did Charles Francis Sheridan and Thomas Conolly. Daly had often taken the lead in criticizing British policy and Sheridan had challenged Blackstone in his *Observations*, but neither man would endorse Grattan's strident declaration.[44]

To a majority of Commons members, Grattan had been rash and

---

43. Ibid., 1:50.
44. Ibid., 1:53–55. The vote given here is 133 to 99; in Grattan, *Memoirs*, 1:50, and the *Freeman's Journal*, 22 April 1780, it is listed as 136 to 97.

imprudent, impolitic in his timing and intemperate in his language, though not necessarily wrong in his basic assumption. Daly, whose views may well have been shared by many others, opposed the motion but also denied the right of the British Parliament to legislate for Ireland. He could see no point, however, in insulting British pride or incurring the wrath of Whitehall or Westminster. Ireland had just won an important trade concession and should be grateful and, above all, patient and prudent. Although he felt that way in 1780, he would not just two years later, and neither would an overwhelming majority of the others in Commons. Grattan had only lost a skirmish; he would win the larger battle because he was not the only M.P. concerned with defining and defending Irish constitutional rights.

Months before Grattan's speech, it had been rumored that Barry Yelverton was preparing to "dispute the validity" of the Declaratory Act of 1720. Furthermore, Poynings' Law again came under fire, in a different, more threatening way than in the past. The law had often been criticized for its application. It had rarely been condemned for being flawed from its inception; that, contended two 1780 pamphlets, was why it had been employed over the centuries to undermine the power of the Irish Parliament. Both emphasized that Poynings' Law had been passed by a "rump" parliament that was an extension of English will rather than a representative assembly of the Irish people. Both also noted that the law had been revised once and repealed at least twice, proving that it was neither perfect nor constitutionally sacred. They advised that it be reviewed; reading between the lines, they were calling for its repeal.[45]

Building on a 1557 modification of Poynings' Law, the Irish Parliament routinely passed the "heads" of a bill—in effect a bill—and then sent it through the lord lieutenant and Irish privy council to the British privy council for review. Bills brought before the British council stated "we pray it be enacted" instead of "be it enacted," which gave the Irish Parliament some initiative and at the same time seemed to preserve the sovereign power of the king in council. Thus bills often originated in the Irish Parliament, and the British "connived at the practice." The king,

---

45. *Plain Reasons for New-Modelling Poyning's Law, in Such a Manner as to Assert the Ancient Rights of the Two Houses of Parliament, without Entrenching on the King's Prerogative* (Dublin: William Hallhead, 1780); and *Sketches of the History of Poynings' Law, and of the Usage of Parliament in Ireland, In the Reign of the Tudors* (Dublin: S. Colbert, 1780). The tone of both of these is much more critical than that of *The Constitution of Ireland, and Poyning's Law Explained* (Dublin: G. Faulkner, 1770), sometimes attributed to Richard French, which takes the old approach that Poynings' Law had been a valuable reform measure that had been misapplied over the years. For the 26 April 1780 debate on Yelverton's motion, see the *Freeman's Journal*, 29 April 1780. Those who voted for (105) and against (130) Yelverton are listed in the 6 May 1780 issue.

his ministers, and the British Parliament "were willing to humour" the Irish Parliament "so long as it did not demand too much."[46] British leaders believed that they could be flexible without giving up their sovereignty. The king in council retained the right to veto or revise the "heads" of any bill sent over from Dublin. And any bill revised and returned to Dublin could not be altered there. The Irish Parliament could accept it, or reject it and try again the next session. In part this arrangement was a matter of legislative efficiency; in part it was also based on comity. Most of the time Whitehall and Westminster tried to avoid an adversarial relationship with the Irish Parliament. But to a growing number of Irish parliamentary Patriots, confrontation could no longer be evaded. Frustrated by the roles played in their legislative affairs by both the Irish and British privy councils, they concluded that the legislative rules had to be changed.

The pamphlets attacking Poynings' Law appeared, not coincidentally, at the same time Barry Yelverton finally made his move. He did not attack the Declaratory Act; instead, he took on Poynings' Law. Scarcely a week after Grattan's 19 April address, Yelverton tried unsuccessfully to carry the heads of a bill that would clarify the rights of the Irish Parliament to initiate legislation and partially repeal Poynings' Law. Commons was still not worried enough about its theoretical rights to go that far, though it was inching closer to the Yelverton view. Twice within a year the British government had given it a rebuff. It passed a sugar tariff that was reduced when it was sent to London for privy council approval; then it passed an annual mutiny bill that the privy council returned as a perpetual bill, empowering the king to maintain a standing army in Ireland at his discretion.

The perpetual mutiny bill was particularly insulting to some Irish M.P.s. In May 1780, Gervase Parker Bushe, another supporter of Yelverton's motion, had introduced the heads of an annual mutiny bill as, in effect, a test of Irish constitutional rights. If the Irish were entitled to the same rights as Englishmen and if the Irish Parliament were at all a sovereign body, Bushe reasoned, then Ireland should govern its own troops. Langrishe was opposed, but Grattan, Yelverton, and Hussey Burgh stood behind him. Grattan, referring to his own disappointment the month before, exclaimed that "the House of Commons may refuse to declare the rights of this country, but they cannot compel the people to be slaves." Fixing on control of the army to make the same point he had failed to carry before, Grattan warned that "if you give the King an

---

46. Edward and Annie G. Porritt, *Unreformed House of Commons*, 2 vols. (Cambridge: Cambridge University Press, 1903, 1909), 2:430.

army, and the Parliament of England the power of regulating that army, you are not a free Parliament nor a free people."[47]

Bushe's move backfired. His bill passed easily, but only after being amended, over his and Grattans's objections, by a pro-administration majority so that it could not be construed as a challenge to the Crown. When the British privy council revised it and returned it as a perpetual bill, Grattan and Bushe protested on both practical and constitutional grounds. It passed over their objections quite handily, garnering more votes than the original annual bill. It did so because Buckinghamshire, having long before abandoned his design to rule without patronage, sold peerages, doled out pensions, and added to the civil list to gain votes. As Maurice O'Connell has noted, "Dublin Castle played a clever game," and Buckinghamshire, stepping down as lord lieutenant at the end of the year, felt that he had gained more than he had lost.[48]

Buckinghamshire was replaced by the earl of Carlisle, who brought William Eden with him as chief secretary. Carlisle and Eden had failed in their reconciliatory mission to the American revolutionaries in 1778; they fully expected to be more successful in Ireland. Administration men like John Beresford, irked with Buckinghamshire, looked forward to the change. "This country is, at the moment, right-headed and kindly disposed," Chief Secretary Eden wrote with some relief, and would continue to be "if frankly and fairly used."[49] Eden was talented and adept at building Castle strength, and his well-known attachment to the free trade ideas of Adam Smith made him popular. Commenting on the opening of a new parliamentary session in October 1781, he wrote, with great satisfaction, "Our strength was so obvious, that we did not meet with anything tending even towards an attack."[50] Carlisle and Eden knew that Yelverton wanted to take up the issue of Poynings' Law again and that Grattan might return to his demand for a declaration of right. They hoped that these men in Commons and Charlemont in Lords, though in "determined opposition," could be kept from gathering a following.[51] The Castle liberally dispensed favors; "there was no pretense that government was above faction and corruption."[52] For a time Car-

47. Grattan, ed., *Speeches of Grattan*, 1:56–79, quotes from pp. 58 and 62, resp. Also see O'Brien, *Anglo-Irish Politics*, 34–37, for the mutiny bill, and passim for the Irish Patriots in general.
48. O'Connell, *Irish Politics*, 239.
49. Beresford, ed., *Correspondence of Beresford*, 1:161, William Eden to John Robinson, 21 March 1781.
50. Ibid., 1:174, letter from Eden to Robinson of 13 October 1781.
51. HMC, *The Manuscripts of the Earl of Carlisle* (London: Eyre and Spottiswoode, 1897), Carlisle to Lord Gower, 30 June 1781, 509–10.
52. Molloy, "Irish Executive and North Ministry," 106.

lisle succeeded, Eden reporting late in February 1782 that "our public situation here continues as prosperous & as promising as the general State of the Empire can possibly admit."[53]

And there lay much of their problem. The "State of the Empire" had deteriorated badly, marked by Cornwallis's disaster in Virginia and the complete breakdown of the North ministry. With the fall of North, Carlisle and Eden were finished. Carlisle's successor in March 1782, the duke of Portland, inherited problems that his predecessor had only kept at arm's length. Neither Grattan nor Yelverton had given up. During the last few months of Carlisle's administration they redoubled their efforts.

Yelverton intended to bring Poynings' Law up for debate in December 1781, but when news of Yorktown was received, he postponed that discussion to propose his resolution avowing loyalty to the king "and our most earnest wishes for the British empire." Grattan, Ogle, and others ready to back him on the question of Poynings' Law would have preferred that no such resolution be passed and objected to making any statement seeming to countenance the "madness" of a "ruinous" war.[54] Yelverton's resolution carried anyway. Perhaps hoping that he had won a measure of good will from the Castle and that he had proved, again, that he and other Patriots were not rebels or separatists, Yelverton returned to the question of Poynings' Law.

Yelverton found himself in competition with Henry Flood, back among the Patriot ranks after having been dismissed from office by Carlisle. Flood had not been a firm administration man for several years, and once ties were formally severed he returned to the opposition with a vengeance. He did not support Grattan's April 1780 declaration, but he did vote for Yelverton's motion to partially repeal Poynings' Law. Lacking Yelverton's tact and patience, Flood pushed too quickly and too hard, calling on 11 December for a formal review of Poynings' Law and outlining in great detail how it had been abused over the centuries and, through that abuse, how more and more illegitimate power had accrued to the Crown. He called for the Irish privy council to be removed altogether from the legislative process. His proposal was easily defeated (some powerful House members were also privy councillors). Yelverton, having learned his lesson when he and Grattan were blocked the year before, merely proposed a week later that the wording of bills be changed from "we pray it may be enacted" to "be it enacted," thereby

---

53. Letter of 24 February 1782 in Add. MS. 34, 418, fo. 333, Auckland Papers, vol. 6, BL.
54. *The Parliamentary Register: or, History of the Proceedings and Debates of the House of Commons of Ireland*, 17 vols. (Dublin: James Moore, 1782–1801), 1:125–34.

challenging Poynings' Law more obliquely.[55] Nonetheless the Castle was able to delay action on this bill and even managed to check Grattan the following February when he again attempted to push through a statement of Irish rights.

Grattan's 22 February 1782 speech retraced the ground covered two years before. Grattan had remained silent over most of that time, he explained, but could restrain himself no longer because the British Parliament "continued its tyrannical and unconstitutional assumptions." Once again critical, though not of his colleagues this time, he tried to employ more reason and less invective. Speaking "in a very rapid and animated manner," he repeated his assertions that the Irish were a "free" people living in a distinct kingdom with a sovereign parliament tied to England through "an imperial crown." More meticulous in his treatment of Irish history than he had been before, he cited statutes and court cases, and used Locke to counter Coke and Blackstone. After noting that history was on his side, he ultimately dismissed the relevance of historical precedent (as he had in April 1780) by asserting that his claims were for a "Birthright" based on "fundamental laws." He reminded Commons that the opportune moment had arrived because "Ireland is in strength, she had acquired that strength by the weakness of Britain, for Ireland was saved when America was lost." Not wanting to look too much like an opportunist, however, he styled his motion "an humble address" instead of the curt "declaration" he had pressed in 1780.

As before, Forbes, Ogle, and Hussey Burgh gave their support; Gervase Parker Bushe changed his 1780 position and joined them. Even so, Grattan's more moderate tone gained him little, and his motion was defeated by an even larger margin than the vote on the original declaration.[56] In this instance, it should be noted, Henry Flood, like Bushe, switched sides. He and Grattan temporarily renewed their old friendship and formed, for a few crucial months, an alliance that gathered strength as winter gave way to spring. Flood raised the issue again on 26 February and failed by nearly as large a division as Grattan four days earlier. His failure notwithstanding, virtually no one opposed him or Grattan on

---

55. Ibid., 1:153–54 for Flood (voted down 139 to 67, noted on 1:174); Yelverton on 1:180, 187.

56. Ibid., 1:266–69, gives the gist of Grattan's 22 February 1782 address. The Irish Parliamentary Debates, vol. 24, container 9, pp. 173–236, gives a much fuller version and notes Grattan's "animated manner" (173). Grattan, ed., *Speeches of Grattan*, 1:104–19, is purportedly the speech itself; quotes are from the *Parliamentary Register* versions. Also see the MS. copy of Irish Parliamentary Debates, minutes for 26 and 28 February 1782, vol. 25, container 10, pp. 174–75.

An austere and yet elegant Henry Flood, painter unknown. Courtesy of the Board of Trinity College, University of Dublin.

principle; the basic objection was still to timing and tone. Opponents voted for postponement, not outright rejection. Grattan and Flood, Yelverton and Hussey Burgh, would continue to chip away at the resistance. With the fall of North and the defeat of British arms in America, that resistance crumbled and fell.

Grattan and Yelverton would not let the subject drop. They returned to it repeatedly through March 1782, the same month that North was ousted and a new ministry formed under the marquess of Rockingham.[57] The Rockingham cabinet "agreed that the foundation of all true policy" on the issues raised by Grattan was "to win Irish goodwill," one historian has concluded.[58] Nonetheless, Rockingham and his new lord lieutenant, the duke of Portland, wanted Grattan and his followers in the House and Charlemont, with his in Lords, to be patient. They did not get what they wanted.

Grattan and Charlemont had enough of waiting. On 16 April 1782, the first day that Parliament met after Portland arrived, Grattan made his move and at long last succeeded. Confident that he would carry the day, Grattan avoided taking a critical tone, emphasizing instead the unity of the Irish people and ties of affection binding Ireland and Britain. "This country rightly governed," he proclaimed, "is connected with England, not by allegiance only, but liberty likewise."

> The two Nations naturally form a Constitutional Confederacy. The Crown is one great bond, but Magna Charta is a greater one: because we could get a King any where, but England is the only Nation, that can communicate to us a Great Charter. This makes England your natural connexion. This makes the King of England your natural King.[59]

---

57. See *Irish Parliamentary Debates*, 11 March 1782, vol. 26, container 10, pp. 35–36, for example.

58. J. Steven Watson, *Reign of George III, 1760–1815* (Oxford: Clarendon Press, 1960), 245.

59. *Irish Parliamentary Debates*, vol. 26, container 10, p. 102; pp. 86–124 for the entire speech. The most famous passage supposedly from this oration is: "Spirit of Swift! spirit of Molyneux! your genius has prevailed! Ireland is now a nation! in that character I hail her! and bowing to her august presence, I say, Esto perpetua!" included in Grattan, ed., *Speeches of Grattan*, 1:123. The Parliamentary Debates account, usually sensitive to dramatic flair and memorable phrases, does not include anything approximating this passage. Neither does the *Parliamentary Register*, 1:334–39; the *Freeman's Journal*, 18 April 1782; or the *Dublin Journal*, 20 April 1782. Chances are that this passage was added later, as were undoubtedly other parts of the speech—most notably an allusion to France that would have made sense only *after* 1789 (see Grattan, ed., *Speeches*, 127) and comments about the Volunteers deferring to their leaders, which Grattan had not made in other versions (see pp. 126–27). Building on the foundation laid by Richard Koebner (see note 41 supra) Gerard O'Brien, "The Grattan Mystique," *Eighteenth-Century Ireland* 1 (1986): 177–94, comments on this speech and the difficulty of using Grattan to define the Patriot tradition. Also see W. J. McCormack, "Vision and Revision in the Study of

Grattan's speech was almost but not quite free of recrimination. "To acknowledge the independence of America, & not acknowledge the freedom of Ireland, will be indeed the disgrace of England," he could not resist stating, knowing that the new ministry had just begun negotiating a peace with the Americans.[60] Grattan stipulated that the Irish Parliament be recognized as an independent body and that the House of Lords have its appellate rights restored, that the British Parliament abandon its claim to legislate for Ireland and repeal the Declaratory Act of 1720, that the Irish privy council be excluded from the legislative process and Poynings' Law be amended, and that the perpetual mutiny bill be repealed. Yelverton, who put aside his indirect assault on Poynings' Law to side with Grattan, joined in the chorus of support, and Grattan's motion passed without a dissenting voice.[61]

Spectators expecting this outcome jammed the House galleries. According to some accounts, they spontaneously broke into applause as the motion carried. Grattan stood center stage, celebrated by fellow M.P. George Ponsonby as "the father of the independence of this Country."[62] He had secured more than parliamentary independence, he and his more ardent supporters believed; he had saved the ancient constitution, the compact of rights and liberties tying Ireland to England in the twelfth century, with a new constitution that strengthened the imperial tie and guaranteed Irish freedom. Grattan led a procession to the Castle to deliver what was made a resolution by both houses of Parliament. Throngs of people reportedly lined the way, cheering wildly. Portland accepted the message, George III sent a friendly response the next month, the Irish Parliament replied in kind and reaffirmations of loyalty and attachment to the empire filled the air. A month and a half after Grattan made his

---

Eighteenth-Century Irish Parliamentary Rhetoric" in ibid, 2 (1987): 7–35, and O'Brien's retort in ibid. 3 (1988): 149–55. This does not mean, however, that Grattan did not think of himself as being in the mold of a Molyneux or a Swift—as his rewritten 16 April speech shows. His old friend Hercules Langrishe referred to Darcy and Molyneux during the 26 February debates (*Parliamentary Register*, 1:282), in the context of issues that Flood and Grattan raised (although Langrishe thought it best not to push for a resolution claiming what Parliament had already asserted back in 1641). Also see the account in Jonah Barrington, *Rise and Fall of the Irish Nation* (New York: Sadlier, 1885; orig. ed., 1833), 161–65, where Barrington claims to have been in the gallery to hear this "most luminous, brilliant, and effective oration ever delivered in the Irish parliament" (161); cf. James Anthony Froude, *The English in Ireland in the Eighteenth Century*, 3 vols. (London: Longmans, Green, 1872–74), 2:330–31, for a different view. Interestingly enough, *Esto Perpetuo* had appeared on the title page of *The Letters of Owen Roe O'Nial* in 1779.

60. Irish Parliamentary Debates, vol. 26, container 10, p. 106.
61. The vote was noted as nem. con. in both the *Parliamentary Register*, 1:334, and the *House of Commons Journal*, 10:335.
62. Irish Parliamentary Debates, vol. 26, container 10, p. 129.

speech, the Irish Commons, in gratitude for what he had done, voted him 50,000 pounds to buy an estate and build a mansion.

The euphoria was temporary, the appearance of unanimity deceptive. Divisions within the Irish Parliament and Irish society at large, like the different priorities of Ireland and Great Britain, could be masked for only so long. Portland and the Rockingham Whigs were annoyed that Grattan did not delay. "Every day convinces me not only of the impossibility of prevailing on this country to recede from any one of the claims set forth in the addresses, but of the danger of new ones being started," Rockingham complained to the earl of Shelburne.[63] The Rockinghamites and Pittite Whigs in the British Parliament, Edmund Burke and Charles James Fox included, did not want the Irish Parliament to insist on independence. They had urged the Irish to criticize the North ministry and they had encouraged the free trade movement in 1779; they had not expected Irish demands to increase rather than decrease after that, and they did not understand the role they played in furthering Irish ambitions. Trapped by their own political maneuvering as much as their sympathies for the Irish, they had little choice but to follow through and see to the repeal of the Declaratory Act of 1720. Poynings' Law was soon revised, as Yelverton had wanted, and the perpetual mutiny act was altered as well.

Grattan was satisfied; Flood was not. Flood insisted that repeal of the Declaratory Act did not mean that the British Parliament renounced its right to legislate for Ireland. "Nothing is relinquished, that is not renounced," he warned. He therefore wanted the British Parliament to pass a formal act of renunciation. Simple repeal, he contended, could be interpreted to mean that the British were voluntarily surrendering a right they had once enjoyed and could someday reassert. Grattan countered that the British would be affronted if the Irish Parliament demanded formal renunciation. At most he was willing to call for an Irish declaration of right and a resolution that constitutional issues should never again divide the two kingdoms. Both of his motions failed to pass. Still, Grattan managed to hold the majority on repeal alone, and Flood's repeated attempts to insist on renunciation failed.

The British Parliament did eventually pass an act of renunciation early in 1783, but by then Grattan and Flood were no longer friends. They sniped at each other over renunciation and traded malicious insults during debates on another question in October 1783. Grattan was especially caustic, denouncing Flood as "venal" and "corrupt" for having

---

63. Portland to the earl of Shelburne, 4 May 1782, in Edmund Fitzmaurice, *The Life of William, Earl of Shelburne*, 3 vols. (London: Macmillan, 1875–76), 3:146.

Henry Grattan as he appeared in the Irish House of Commons, 16 April 1782, in his Volunteer uniform of a red coat faced in blue, with a white waistcoat. By Nicholas Kenny. Courtesy of the Board of Trinity College, University of Dublin.

taken office under Harcourt and, as a member of the administration, for having endorsed the sending of troops to "butcher" Americans.[64] When Grattan refused to apologize, Flood challenged him to a duel. Flood had already killed one man in this fashion earlier in his career. During friendlier times, he once played Macbeth to Grattan's Macduff in an informal bit of acting; he had no intention of doing that role again. Sheriffs were on hand to stop them, no shots were fired, no blood was shed, but with their falling out, Grattan and Flood exposed at last the divisions among Irish Patriots that had lain hidden beneath the surface during the halcyon days of the spring of 1782.[65]

The Irish Patriots were badly disorganized and had been ever since the controversy over renunciation. Yelverton, Ogle, and Hussey Burgh stood by Grattan through it all, as did many others. Grattan's friend and fellow Monk the earl of Mornington fumed that Flood was a "very shrewd and wicked politician; and for the peace of both countries I wish he was gagged."[66] As men like Mornington saw it, Flood had become jealous of Grattan and adopted renunciation in a fit of pique. Others felt that Flood had logic on his side, particularly after one erratic member of the British Lords asserted the legislative supremacy of his parliament, and Lord Chief Justice Mansfield continued to hear a case on appeal from Ireland that had been brought forward before repeal of the Declaratory Act.

The earl of Charlemont was probably the most pained of all by the break in Patriot ranks. Patron to both Grattan and Flood, he counted Flood among his dearest friends. When his son drowned in 1775 he would have offered the borough seat that death left vacant to Flood if Flood had not joined Harcourt's administration. With Flood's defection he turned to Grattan and chided Flood, "You can not *serve God and*

---

64. See the accounts in the Irish Parliamentary Debates, vol. 29, container 11, pp. 22–27, 39–51, for Grattan's attack, and pp. 27–35, 53–61, for Flood's rejoinder; and the *Parliamentary Register*, 2:39–42, 61–70. For potential confusion because of the wording of the repeal and renunciation acts, see my comments in chap. 3, n. 26.

65. Macduff and Macbeth in Grattan, *Memoirs*, 1:144–45; and ibid., 3:98–101, a letter from General John Burgoyne to Charles James Fox, 31 October 1783, for the narrowly averted duel.

66. Mornington to W. W. Grenville, 12 July 1782, in HMC, *The Manuscripts of J. B. Fortescue, Esq.*, 10 vols. (London: Eyre and Spottiswoode, 1892–1927), 1:163. Mornington was convinced that Mansfield's actions showed that the issue of appellate jurisdiction would have arisen, even with formal renunciation. See his letters to Grattan of 9 December 1782, 22 and 24 January 1783, in "Letters relating to Irish Affairs, 1782–1837," Add. MS. 38103, BL. In fact, Grattan and Yelverton, although opposed to renunciation as Flood proposed it, would have been happy to see the British House of Lords formally renounce any appellate power over Ireland—and so they said in letters to Charles James Fox of 31 December 1782 and 9 January 1783, resp., in the Charles James Fox Papers XIV, Fos. 145 and 149, MS. 47582, BL.

A 1783 English broadside lampooning Grattan and Flood with their own words and ridiculing the notion that these men were truly Irish "Patriots." Courtesy of the British Museum.

Mammon." He was overjoyed when Flood rejoined the Patriots and crestfallen when Flood made an issue of renunciation, dividing the Patriots and the public. Initially supporting Grattan's view on the satisfactoriness of simple repeal, he came to have second thoughts by the end of 1782 and was horrified by Grattan's denunciation of Flood in October 1783.[67] His inability to prevent their falling out was matched only by his anguish at seeing the fragile unity of the Patriots broken.

In the long run, Flood's reputation suffered more than Grattan's, although Flood enjoyed some popularity for having championed renunciation and even more for his role in promoting parliamentary reform in 1783. He stayed in the Irish Commons until 1790. He also finally secured a seat in the British Parliament in 1783, feeling, perhaps, as one fawning admirer told him, that the Irish Parliament was too small for his talents.[68] Flood was true to form, having sought a seat in Westminster since the beginning of his career. That and his willingness to accept office under Harcourt has marked him in the eyes of some as an ambitious opportunist. As such he becomes an example of what has been taken to be the corruptibility of most Irish M.P.s. Indeed, one of the most familiar anecdotes about the Irish Parliament concerns the voracious appetite for preferment of one of its leading members, John Hely-Hutchinson. Supposedly George III saw Hely-Hutchinson at a levee and asked Lord North who he was. North replied "That is a man on whom, if your Majesty were pleased to bestow England and Ireland, he would ask for the Isle of Man as a potato garden."[69]

The rift between Grattan and Flood was undeniably disastrous to all concerned, inside the Irish Parliament and out.[70] "There does not now remain one national object of sufficient importance to unite men in the same pursuit," lamented Charles Francis Sheridan just two years after

---

67. Charlemont to Flood, 13 April 1775, for quote; and Charlemont to Flood, 28 June 1782 and 9 November 1783, for later sentiments, in the Flood Correspondence, BL.

68. Daniel Webb to Henry Flood, 7 November 1783, Flood Correspondence, BL.

69. Taken from J. T. Ball, *Historical Review of the Legislative Systems Operative in Ireland* (Dublin: Hodges, Figgis, 1889), note AA, p. 278.

70. Teresa M. O'Connor, "The Conflict Between Flood and Grattan, 1782–3," in Cronne, et al., eds., Essays in British and Irish History, 169–84. Also see David Dickson, "Henry Flood (l732–91) and the Eighteenth-Century Irish Patriots," in Ciaran Brady, ed., *Worsted in the Game: Losers in Irish History* (Dublin: Lilliput, 1989), 97–108. Flood went on to a frustrating career in the British Parliament and was not able to win a seat in the Irish Parliament after 1790. He died in 1791. He was not unique in sitting in the British and Irish parliaments simultaneously—so did Thomas Conolly earlier in his career, and others. By then Flood and Grattan had patched up some of their differences. Grattan even defended Flood's reputation in *An Answer to a Pamphlet, entitled, The Speech of the Earl of Clare, on the Subject of a Legislative Union between Great Britain and Ireland* (London: G. G. and J. Robinson, 1800), 37–38.

Grattan's triumph. Even when united, he complained, Irish politicians had "made a virtue of necessity" and were only roused to action because of "the spirit of the people."[71] With repeal of the Declaratory Act, they reverted to their old faction-ridden ways.

There was undeniably a fair amount of greed and corruption in Irish politics, much of it the result of the Castle's need to build support through patronage and buying off the opposition. Buckinghamshire apparently persuaded Frederick Jebb, author of the "Guatimozin" letters and a Monk of St. Patrick, to switch from administration critic to Castle defender. Carlisle was even more successful; he undercut the *Freeman's Journal*—which had prided itself as "a literary field of battle"—and moved it away from its traditional anti-administration editorial stand.[72]

The Irish Parliament should not simply be dismissed as a hopelessly corrupt body, however. Grattan was not, as J. A. Froude argued, the one exception proving the rule. To be ambitious was not necessarily to be corrupt. The Patriots of 1782 split rather quickly, but that should not be surprising in an age when shifting alliances rather than modern parties dominated politics. Even a small group like the Monks of St. Patrick lacked cohesiveness. The Monks came together with the free trade controversy and drifted apart after that. They might have continued to assemble through 1785 or possibly even later; if they did it was for socializing only. Politically they divided much earlier.

Members Henry Grattan and Denis Daly were intimate friends; still, they did not agree on every issue. Daly opposed Grattan's April 1780 motion for a declaration of right and he disagreed with Grattan over the need for parliamentary reform. Grattan was very close to Yelverton and Hussey Burgh, yet they sought office while he made it a point of honor not to do so himself. Yelverton became attorney general under Portland in 1782 and the next year succeeded Hussey Burgh in the post of chief baron of the exchequer after Hussey Burgh died of a fever. Before he died Hussey Burgh had importuned two successive lord lieutenants,

---

71. Sheridan to his brother, Richard Brinsley Sheridan, 10 March 1784, in Thomas Moore, *Memoirs of the Life and Times of the Right Honourable Richard Brinsley Sheridan.* 2 vols. (London: Longman, Rees, Orme, Brown, and Green, 1876), 1:410–11.

72. Jebb in Grattan, *Memoirs,* 2:174; *Freeman's Journal* boast on 5 February 1780; and administrative influence over the paper in a note from Chief Secretary Richard Heron to William Eden of 9 January 1781 in Add. MS. 34,417, fo. 293, Auckland Papers, vol. 6, BL. Jebb was once thought to have been the author of *Considerations Submitted to the People of Ireland* (Dublin: W. Wilson, 1781), which was written as a rebuttal to *Observations on the Mutiny Bill* (Dublin: W. Wilson, 1781), attributed to Henry Grattan. *Considerations* (on the copy at the NLI) is now ascribed to William Eden, noted as "wrongly ascribed to F. Jebb." Yet would Eden have called himself "an Irishman," as the author of the pamphlet does, so soon after arriving in the country? Even if Jebb was not author of *Considerations,* he was by 1781 an administration man.

Earl Temple and the earl of Northington, for advancement to the Irish peerage.[73] Although Hussey Burgh did not fulfill his dream of sitting in Lords, Yelverton did, being created Baron Avonmore in 1795.

Charles Francis Sheridan's political wanderings are even more intriguing. Despite his 1779 assault on British parliamentary sovereignty, Sheridan only halfheartedly supported repeal of the Declaratory Act, he opposed Grattan on the need for a declaration of right, and he argued against repeal of Poynings' Law, perhaps because he too sought office.[74] In 1785 Sheridan, by then a secretary in the administration, threw his support behind Pitt's commercial resolution, an indication of his gradual drift toward the Castle and away from old associates like Grattan and Forbes.

Longtime opposition leader George Ogle supported the Northington administration in 1784.[75] Charlemont and Grattan divided at the same time, Grattan wanting to befriend Northington, Charlemont wanting to keep his distance. They also differed on the issue of Catholic emancipation, with Grattan being far more sympathetic to Catholic ambitions than either the earl or Ogle.

Grattan himself was not always in opposition; he tried to work with Portland and Northington, and in 1795 he lined up behind the new lord lieutenant, Earl Fitzwilliam. He nevertheless showed a streak of vanity and obstinacy. With a will likened to "the bow of Ulysses," Grattan's very devotion to his cause of parliamentary independence was a blindspot.[76] As Flood reminded Grattan in their heated 1783 exchange, early in his career, before he took a seat in Commons, Grattan had called the Irish Parliament a "sink of prostitution." Some years later he concluded that "an active perseverance is beyond the spirit of our parliament or people."[77] The Irish Parliament had not changed much when, within a

---

73. For Hussey Burgh's attempts at advancement to the peerage, see the letter from the marquis of Buckingham to Thomas Townshend of 15 November 1782 in Add. MS. 40,1777, Buckingham Letter Book, vol. I, appendix, p. 15, BL; and the Hussey Burgh Papers, Correspondence 109–23, TCD, undated letter from Hussey Burgh to Earl Temple, and one of September 1783; and HMC, *Fortescue*, 1:174, 176, 177.

74. Sheridan was apparently the author of *A Review of the Three Great National Questions, Relative to a Declaration of Right, Poynings' Law, and the Mutiny Bill* (Dublin: M. Mills, 1781). If Sheridan was the author, he was straining to keep from reversing his own 1779 arguments in his critique of Blackstone. The anonymous author of *An Answer* (Dublin: John Cash, 1782) to *A Review* was certain that Sheridan had written the tract. Sheridan did favor repeal of the Declaratory Act—see his letter to his brother Richard of 27 March 1782 in Grattan, *Memoirs*, 2:214–15.

75. Northington to Lord Sydney, 25 January 1784, in the Northington Letter-Book, Add. MS. 38,716, BL.

76. Falkland, *Review of the Principal Characters*, 190.

77. "Sink of prostitution" in Grattan, *Memoirs*, 1:122, a letter of 25 February 1768;

decade, Grattan became its foremost defender. Of course Grattan defended the idea of an independent parliament, not Parliament as it was. He joined those pushing for its improvement through reform, yet he never seemed to understand the workings of what has come to be remembered, ironically, as "Grattan's Parliament."

That Parliament was not created with the unanimity Grattan would have preferred. Grattan later complained that he had had to carry "the Lords upon my back," because of reluctance among them to press for parliamentary independence. Even in Commons, his motion of 16 April 1782 carried *nemine contradicente*: unopposed, not unanimously. Some M.P.s might have been hostile but were afraid to vote against Grattan and risk alienation. Perhaps they sat in a stony if conspicuous silence. Others might have stayed away in anticipation of Grattan's motion carrying. One House member on the verge of objecting was intimidated into passivity by Grattan's vocal backers.[78] John Fitzgibbon spoke in support, yet he did so grudgingly, and in 1799 he led the advocates of parliamentary union. Moreover, Fitzgibbon's motion—that Portland's predecessor, the duke of Carlisle, be thanked for his service—passed over Grattan's objection and was added to the resolution that had been amended to carry Grattan's demand. Within a matter of minutes, Grattan went from leading the House to being outvoted, a portent of what would follow. Barry Yelverton later claimed that he would have supported a union in 1782 if someone had presented a workable plan; so too did Thomas Conolly. The duke of Portland, lord lieutenant when parliamentary independence was achieved, might well have tried to propose one if he had had the time.[79]

Portland tried to strengthen his hand by courting leading Irish Patriots and tying them more closely to the Whigs at Westminster. His modest achievements were all but undone when he returned to England. Northington tried unsuccessfully to pick up the pieces during his lord lieutenancy. The Irish Patriots did not make good administration men.

---

and failure of the people and Parliament in ibid., 2:260, letter to Robert Day, 27 February 1772.

78. Chief Secretary Richard Fitzpatrick complained to Charles James Fox about how the vote carried, in a letter the next day, printed in Lord John Russell, *Memoirs and Correspondence of Charles James Fox*, 4 vols. (London, Richard Bently, 1853–54), 1:397. The M.P. intimidated into silence is mentioned in Irish Parliamentary Debates, vol. 26, container 10, p. 143.

79. For Grattan on Lords see Grattan, *Memoirs*, 2:254–55; for Portland see 2:284–99. An Irishman had apparently written a pro-union tract, *Renovation without Violence Yet Possible* (Dublin: William Hallhead, 1779), which recommended that all parts of the British empire—India, the East Indies, Ireland, and the American colonies—be allowed to send members to the British Commons and have peers sitting in Lords.

They found it nearly impossible to answer popular demands they had championed and upon which their reputation rested and simultaneously to satisfy the expectations of British Whigs looking for a compliant, cooperative Ireland. Their different priorities remained unchanged. Nonetheless, Yelverton's later comments about the "Constitution of 1782" are a reminder that Irish Patriots searched for a way to reconcile their differences with Britain and protect their interests *within* the empire. To the frustration and confusion of British M.P.s, they were neither dependable allies nor implacable foes.[80]

What the Irish Patriots achieved and what they thought they achieved are quite different. W. E. H. Lecky echoed the most enthusiastic responses to parliamentary independence when he wrote many years later that "the whole Constitution of Ireland was changed, and a great revolution was accomplished." J. C. Beckett's comment, that the "so-called 'Constitution of 1782'" was "at best a ramshackle piece of work," is indicative of what more skeptical observers at the time and most scholars since have concluded.[81] Repeal of the Declaratory Act and formal renunciation had redefined—or in Irish nationalist eyes simply made explicit and constitutionally correct—the relationship between the British and Irish parliaments, not the British and Irish people. The two "kingdoms" were still tied through the "imperial" Crown, and the king still appointed the lord lieutenant. Who would be lord lieutenant was determined by politics within the British Parliament governing the formation of new ministries. The lord lieutenant continued to appoint the chief

---

80. See Charles Francis Sheridan's explanation to his brother Richard of why Irish politicians could not be an extension of British parliamentary parties, in Moore, *Memoirs,* 1:409–17, a letter of 10 March 1784.

81. William Edward Hartpole Lecky, *A History of Ireland in the Eighteenth Century,* 5 vols. (London: Longmans, Green, 1913–16; orig. ed., 1892), 2:317; J. C. Beckett, *The Anglo-Irish Tradition* (London: Faber and Faber, 1976), 50; and Peter Jupp, "Historical Revision: XVII Earl Temple's Viceroyalty and the Renunciation Question, 1782–3," *Irish Historical Studies* 17 (September 1971): 499–520, which takes issue with Lecky's view that renunciation was the "coping-stone" of the Irish "Constitution." Jupp argues that the British act was worded very carefully to be a recognition of Irish rights rather than a renunciation or repudiation of everything that had gone before. For the views that free trade in 1779 and, more importantly, parliamentary independence ushered in an all-too-brief period of prosperity, see George O'Brien, *The Economic History of Ireland in the Eighteenth Century* (Dublin: Mansel and Company, 1918). For the revisionist view, see L. M. Cullen, *An Economic History of Ireland since 1660* (London: B. T. Batsford, 1972). For other comments see J. C. Beckett, *The Making of Modern Ireland* (New York; Alfred A. Knopf, 1969), 227–32; R. R. Palmer, *The Age of the Democratic Revolution* (Princeton: Princeton University Press, 1959, 1964), 1: 292–94; Joseph Lee, "Grattan's Parliament" in Brian Farrell, ed., *The Irish Parliamentary Tradition* (Dublin: Gill and Macmillan, 1973), 149–59; and R. Coupland, *The American Revolution and the British Empire* (London: Longmans, Green, 1730), 140–46.

officers of the Irish government. He dispensed patronage by creating, with the king's permission, new peers and awarding pensions and places. No act passing the Irish Parliament became law unless the king signed it; the king, in turn, consulted his privy council before giving the royal assent. That assent had not been refused for over seventy years, even to acts passed at Westminster, yet its possible refusal still posed a theoretical problem. Simply by holding onto bills passed in Dublin and delaying their return, the British privy council could impede the progress of legislation through the Irish Parliament.

Smooth relations continued to depend on trust and the belief that formal ties were mutually beneficial. That trust was soon broken. Ireland's economy only slowly increased its vitality, and the small gains it made could be more fairly attributed to the end of war than to any change brought by parliamentary independence. Bad weather and poor harvests from 1782 to 1784, with the attendant economic dislocations, brought social unrest and popular agitation. Some Irish leaders continued to be suspicious of the British, and some British leaders continued to feel that the Irish were too provincial in perspective and ungrateful for the benefits they enjoyed as members of empire.

Belief that "free" trade and an "independent" parliament had been won was severely shaken in 1785 in a new commercial controversy. Ireland's status as a trading partner with Britain, its ability to demand free access to imperial markets as a right or to request access as a privilege, its obligation—or not—to pass prohibitory duties similar to those passed at Westminster for trade outside the empire, were still not defined. Lord Lieutenant Northington had been instructed two years before that he should "prevent, as much as possible, those fresh Demands, and fresh Projects of Trade, which the Irish are continually forming to the Prejudice of this Country." He managed to mollify Irish leaders with some minor concessions. His successor, the high living and hard drinking duke of Rutland, could not silence the disaffected. Irish manufacturers wanted protection. Pitt's ministry seemed to be amenable and sent over a proposal to equalize duties and remove prohibitions. The Irish Parliament accepted most of Pitt's outline and amended what it did not like, but by the time that Pitt received a response, his government had come under intense pressure at home from manufacturers and political opponents. He abandoned his original proposal for one more acceptable to protesting English commercial interests, one that his political adversaries could not block. Grattan led the way in condemning Pitt's change of heart. Crowds once again roamed Dublin, the Irish Parliament split,

Rutland's administration shook, and there was much talk of constitutional as well as commercial grievances.[82] Meeting resitance from an unusually strong opposition led by Grattan, the Irish administration withdrew the proposed bill and Pitt turned his attention away from Ireland for the time being.

For all the many changes that had come in British-Irish relations, the most troublesome constitutional and political problem remained: *imperium in imperio*. Thomas Pownall had noted the dangers of this condition a full decade earlier. Thomas Conolly, no deep thinker, claimed—in 1799, conveniently—to have known this and to have been reluctant in backing Grattan in 1782 as a result. Apparently he had let the enthusiasm of the moment overpower his better judgment. For whatever reasons, he, like Yelverton, did not call attention to the problem of having two "sovereign" legislatures in 1782. More likely they had not seen as clearly as they later claimed.

Interestingly enough, in the early 1770s Pownall had held as a solution to the British-American conundrum a relationship like that of Britain and Ireland, or the different arrangement linking England and Scotland.[83] But Americans had been even less interested in a parliamentary union than were the Irish. They had no desire to follow Scotland's example, and becoming more like Ireland would not have helped either, as any Irish Patriot could have told his American counterpart. Pownall's solution was not a solution at all, especially for an Ireland whose interests were quite distinct from those of Britain. Consequently, the arguments used by Pitt's supporters to carry the commercial resolution of 1785 in Britain—emphasizing that the Irish were not being given too much—were the very arguments that Irish critics pointed to as proof of Pitt's insensitivity and insincerity.

Francis Dobbs's *History*, rushed into print soon after Grattan's April

---

82. See North's instructions to Lord Lieutenant Northington of 3 November 1783, Northington Letter-Book, Add. MS. 38,716, BL, where North, once again heading a ministry (in a coalition with Charles James Fox), sounds very much like he did when dealing with Buckinghamshire in 1779, in the aftermath of the free trade crisis. In that same letter he also directed "that the treaties of Peace ought by no means to be laid before the Parliament of Ireland. If the King is to take the Advice of the Irish Parliament in matters relating to War and Peace, and foreign States, the utmost Confusion must be the Consequence." This is yet another illustration of the problematic nature of the British-Irish imperial tie. For the 1785 commercial crisis, see *The Present Politics of Ireland* (London: John Stockdale, 1786), which includes a letter from John Hely-Hutchinson supporting Pitt's twenty resolutions; for Hely-Hutchinson, at least, the 1785 crisis was not a repeat of what had happened in 1779, when he wrote his critical pamphlet. Also see the discussion in O'Brien, *Anglo-Irish Politics*, 63–84.

83. Thomas Pownall, *The Administration of the British Colonies*, 5th ed. (London: J. Walter, 1774), 2:82. For Conolly, see the 1799 debates in chap. 7.

1782 motion passed, rhapsodized that Ireland had been "emancipated—a bloodless Revolution took place, and we became united with our former tyrant, by the sacred bond of *Freedom*."[84] Dobbs's panegyric was unconvincing. As Dobbs well knew, British-Irish relations were imperfect and Irish society was still divided. British leaders might have worried at the qualified loyalty of Grattan as well as Dobbs, since both professed that their attachment to Britain was second "only" to their love of liberty. In part Dobbs wrote to close gaps that he feared would widen, not so much between Britain and Ireland but between contending groups within Ireland itself. Dobbs followed Grattan in feeling that formal renunciation by the British Parliament was unnecessary. The growing public clamor against simple repeal disturbed him. Parliament was being inundated with calls for renunciation from the Volunteers—Hussey Burgh's "dragon teeth" that had sprung up as "armed men." The Volunteers styled themselves as the true representatives of popular will and the primary defenders of the public interest.

One pamphleteer had attempted to warn Grattan and the Patriots in 1781 against pushing for change and appealing to the people for support. The Volunteers were nowhere mentioned by name, though he obviously had them in mind. He argued that politicians were foolish to cater to the people in an attempt to carry through their plans. The people would never be satisfied, and they would add their own demands to the list of changes the Patriots wanted, bringing "Incessant tumults and civil broils." He urged them to "yield not" to the "clamour" of the people; if they did, the people "will be again tumultuous with additional force, and cease not 'till they abrogate every law displeasing to their factious leaders."[85] In essence he warned that the Patriots were opening the Pandora's box of democratic politics. To him the Volunteers were the embodiment of a new and dangerous form of republicanism.

The Volunteers sprouted spontaneously in 1778. Back in 1770 Townshend had wanted to provide for a Protestant militia to check rural unrest marked by the depredations of the Whiteboys. Nothing much was done during his viceroyalty. Harcourt, Townshend's successor, authorized the temporary forming of independent companies to deal with localized disturbances. After the additional four thousand troops were sent from Ireland in 1775 for service in America, the Irish establishment

---

84. Dobbs, *History*, from a message "To the Public"; also see the over-optimistic letter from George Rawson to Thomas Townshend of 30 May 1783 in the Sydney Papers, MS. 52, vol. II, packet K, NLI.

85. *An Essay on the Act of Poynings, and the Present Mode of Appeal* (Dublin: William Hallhead, 1781), 15 and 16, resp.

was reduced to just over five thousand regulars fit for duty. Anticipating passage of a militia law in 1776, Harcourt toyed with the idea of allowing the gentry to recruit new companies. Once he learned that Whitehall opposed the passage of a militia act and that the Whiteboy disturbances had trailed off, he forbade "the assembling of any Bodies of Men, and the practice instantly died away, with the Necessity that produced it."[86]

With the fear of a French invasion in 1778, new companies again formed, without waiting for authorization from Lord Lieutenant Buckinghamshire, Harcourt's replacement. Whitehall still opposed formally organizing a militia in Ireland, so Buckinghamshire did not object to the Volunteers, at least initially. On the contrary, he eventually allowed some companies to equip themselves from government stocks.[87] Leading gentlemen had traditionally raised independent companies, and sometimes regiments, which were then incorporated into the regular military. In this system, government benefited by obtaining troops to fill its needs, and the wealthy men who organized them obtained commissions or the power to recommend others in their stead. When Volunteer companies began forming in Ulster, those involved could claim that they were not doing anything illegal; rather, they were providing for the equivalent of a national militia. By 1779 there were some fifteen thousand enrolled in Volunteer companies around the island. By the summer of 1780 the total had jumped to sixty thousand, with many companies organized into regiments. They showed no sign of disbanding, even after threat of a French invasion had passed. Carlisle, Buckinghamshire's successor in 1781, saw no alternative but to accept their service, however reluctantly.[88]

He was reluctant because by the time he arrived the Volunteers had been thoroughly politicized. The Volunteers grew in numbers and strength with the free trade movement in 1779. They made it clear that they concurred in the need for commercial relief and that they supported

---

86. Harcourt Papers, vol. II (MS. 94), 152–53, Gilbert Library, Dublin City Library; and the account in Thomas Francis Moriarty, "The Harcourt Viceroyalty in Ireland, 1772–1777" (Ph. D. dissertation, University of Notre Dame, 1963), 391–98.

87. Buckinghamshire to George Germain, 25 March 1778, Heron Papers, MS. 13,036, NLI; also see Buckinghamshire to Lord North, 30 April 1778, in ibid.

88. For overviews of the rise of the Volunteers, see Daniel H. Smyth, "The Volunteer Movement in Ulster: Background and Development, 1784–5" (Ph.D. dissertation, Queen's University of Belfast, 1974); R. B. McDowell, "Parliamentary Independence, 1782–9," in Moody and Vaughan, eds., *New History of Ireland*, 4:265–88; and idem, *Ireland in the Age of Imperialism and Revolution, 1760–1801* (Oxford: Clarendon Press, 1979), 239–326. For British concurrence because of the lack of alternatives, see George Germain to Edmund Sexton Pery, 15 July 1779, in HMC, *Eighth Report*, Part I, 201; and North to Pery on 3 August 1779, in ibid., Part I, 201–2; also see Carlisle to Hillsborough, 8 September 1781 in HMC, *Manuscripts of Carlisle*, 517.

non-importation. They helped form the non-importation associations that mushroomed in 1779 and also organized committees of correspondence—imitating American protestors of a few years before. One alarmist warned William Knox in October 1779 that "the malcontents of this kingdom, who make almost the whole, are not to be wrought upon by any reasonings." He was convinced that the Volunteers were stirring up trouble for the empire. "Under a pretence of preparing to repell an invasion on this island, all sorts of Protestants, but the dissenters most warmly," he complained, "have taken up arms, which they now threaten to employ against England."[89] He exaggerated their anti-British sentiments, albeit he was right in noting that they were aware of their political as well as their military power and that they intended to use that power to improve Ireland's place in the empire.

When members of the Commons carried their free trade resolution to the Castle in 1779, the crowds they passed through included Volunteer companies drawn up in formal review. Thomas Conolly's motion in the House that the Volunteers be thanked for their "spirited exertions" on behalf of the country passed unanimously, because no one, not even administration men, dared oppose it.[90] Even so, at that point most members of Commons did not grumble that they were being tyrannized by the Volunteers. Many of them—Grattan and Flood included—were officers in Volunteer companies. The duke of Leinster, ranking member of the Irish peerage, commanded the Dublin companies in 1779 and by 1782 was a "general." The earl of Charlemont was commander-in-chief. Through 1782, in fact, the ruling gentry dominated the Volunteers. The Volunteers had been politicized in part by gentry and parliamentary leaders wanting to use them to force the issue of parliamentary independence. For example, Grattan was colonel of the Dublin Independent Volunteers. Many of the men in that company were leaders in city politics, and they pushed through a resolution endorsed by the freemen, freeholders, gentlemen, and clergy of Dublin:

that no parliament had, has, or of right out to have any power or authority whatsoever in this realm, except the parliament of Ireland; that no statute has the force of law in this kingdom, except enacted by the king, with the consent of the parliament of Ireland: and we are convinced that this principle is indispensable necessary to preserve a connection between Great-Britain and Ireland.[91]

---

89. HMC, *Report on MSS. in Various Collections*, 6:447, letter from Dr. Phillip Skelton of 30 October 1779.
90. Grattan, *Memoirs*, 1:389.
91. *Hibernian Magazine*, 10 March 1780: 174. Also see "A Native of IRELAND,

This resolution passed in February 1780, well before Grattan made his first formal plea in Commons for a declaration of right and simultaneously with Grattan's and Yelverton's early moves in that direction. Indeed, by the time Grattan spoke, other Volunteer companies had passed similar resolutions, as had voters in some counties, many of whom, no doubt, were also Volunteers.

Delegates from one hundred forty-three Ulster Volunteer companies assembled at a grand convention in Dungannon on 15 February 1782. Grattan and Flood actually wrote several of the key resolutions that passed there after they were introduced by representative Francis Dobbs, who acted at their behest. Grattan wrote the resolution stating "that a claim of any body of men, other than the King, Lords and Commons of *Ireland,* to make laws to bind this kingdom, is unconstitutional, illegal, and a grievance." It passed unanimously. Flood wrote the resolution "That the powers exercised by the Privy Councils of both kingdoms, under, or under colour, or pretence of, the law of Poynings', are unconstitutional, and a grievance."[92] It passed with only one dissenting voice. Resolutions condemning the perpetual mutiny bill, calling for greater judicial independence, and claiming more trade rights than had been granted in 1779 by the British Parliament also passed. Committees saw to it that the resolutions were communicated to Volunteer corps throughout the country and to the members of Parliament, some of whom were present at Dungannon as "representatives" from Volunteer companies. By the time that Grattan rose in Commons on 16 April to call again for a declaration of right, those other units had responded. He had at his back the full force of the Volunteers, and he was prepared to use the implicit threat they posed to carry his motion.[93]

---

and a Lover of the BRITISH EMPIRE," *The Usurpations of England the Chief Source of the Miseries of Ireland* (Dublin: R. Burton, 1780), for one example of the rising criticism of Britain and agitation for basic change. The author contended that the Irish could not prosper "until we are emancipated from British authority" (27), yet he was not calling for complete independence; like so many others, he was convinced that parliamentary independence could be a panacea for their ills. Also see the resolution passed by over two hundred freeholders of County Galway in the *Freeman's Journal,* 18 April 1780, which called for a repeal of the Declaratory Act and restoration of Ireland's "constitution" to "its pristine vigour."

92. Henry Grattan, ed., *Miscellaneous Works of the Right Honourable Henry Grattan* (London: Longman, Hurst, Rees, Orme, and Brown, 1822), 170–72, for the Dungannon resolutions; idem, *Memoirs,* 2:205–6, for authorship.

93. According to Robert Day, one of Grattan's close friends, Grattan had not ruled out use of the Volunteers to carry his point by force if the Rockingham ministry proved too unreceptive; see Grattan, *Memoirs,* 2:272. For resolutions passed by various Volunteer units endorsing Grattan's April 1780 position, see ibid., 2:102–3, 130–31, 147–50; and the letters of thanks in Grattan, ed., *Miscellaneous Works,* 144–61. See ibid., 173–244, for the letters of support and thanks after the 16 April 1782 speech and vote.

He did not have to go that far. Whether out of fear, confusion, or genuine commitment, both houses of Parliament gave their concurrence. To many members of the Volunteers, Grattan's success was theirs as well. They had supported him when the majority of his colleagues in Commons did not. They thanked him for his April 1780 stand and over the following two years added their voices to his in renewing the motion for a declaration of right.

Like the members of Parliament, the Volunteers were torn over the issue of simple repeal versus formal renunciation. Most seemed to support simple repeal initially but shifted as Flood pressed his arguments and Englishmen like Mansfield aggravated their insecurities. The Lawyers Corps of Volunteers voted overwhelmingly in November 1782 that repeal was not enough and called on the British Parliament to pass an act of renunciation. Grattan's own company, the Dublin Independent Volunteers, followed the lead of the lawyers and changed its position. Saddened by this turn of events, Grattan resigned his colonelcy. Flood, his one-time second in command, could at last feel vindicated. Just months before a national hero, Grattan now had to endure growing criticism. He and Yelverton, who continued to back Grattan's stand on simple repeal, were criticized in the press, one writer concluding that they were "utterly indifferent about giving Ireland a security of her liberties worthy of her cause."[94]

Grattan tried not to condemn the Volunteers for their part in his loss of face. He was nonetheless ambivalent about their political role, not only because they claimed so much of the credit for what was done in 1779 and 1782, but because their agenda did not end with the achievement of parliamentary independence. Denis Daly wrote Grattan in December 1782 that the parliamentary opposition had enjoyed "the benefits of having armed the people, and now I hope we shall avoid the inconveniences of it."[95] Unfortunately for Daly, it was already too late. The Volunteers had begun agitating for parliamentary reform, and they were less willing to defer to opposition leaders in Commons. Although Grattan did not oppose reform, he did object to the biting criticism aimed at Parliament, criticism not so different from his own in his preparliamentary days. In addition to calling for "free trade" and, later,

94. *An Address to the Right Honourable Henry Grattan, Esq. by the Independent Dublin Volunteers* (London: J. Debrett, 1782), 12; included in Irish Volunteers, MS. 212, Gilbert Library, Dublin City Library, with the report of the Lawyers Corps that passed 77 to 21, on 20 November 1782, and the Independent Volunteers resolution of December 1. See Grattan, *Memoirs*, 2:305, for the 18 June 1782 resolution of the Volunteer national committee that simple repeal was enough.
95. Daly to Grattan, 15 December 1782, in Grattan, *Memoirs*, 3:17.

repeal of the Declaratory Act and recognition of parliamentary independence, many Volunteer companies had also pledged not to support M.P.s who stood opposed. Without necessarily saying as much, they were coming to treat M.P.s as "trustees" of the people, resurrecting arguments and reflecting attitudes once associated with Charles Lucas.

Members of the opposition in the British Parliment had been disappointed in 1779 when the Irish free trade movement expanded to become a drive for parliamentary independence. Wanting the former, they dreaded the latter. So too with Irish politicians in 1782 who celebrated parliamentary independence and resisted efforts from without to alter the internal workings of Parliament. Given their reluctance to broaden the electorate or do more than pay lip service to popular sovereignty, they were powerless to stop the drive for reform and their precipitous fall from public grace.

Grattan was appalled, yet he should not have been surprised. From 1779 to 1782 he and other leaders of the opposition in Commons had played to the Protestant electorate in their campaign to secure Ireland's constitutional rights. So too had pamphleteers like Frederick Jebb and Joseph Pollock. "Every citizen," wrote Jebb as Guatimozin, has the right "to expound the constitution"; in general, Joseph Pollock wrote as Owen Roe O'Nial, "we cannot expect politicians to be either generous or just," so it was time for the people to rise "with the energy of soul and body."[96] Grattan went out of his way during his 16 April 1782 speech to defend the Volunteers, characterizing their meeting at Dungannon as rivaling that at Runnymede, a convention that was extralegal but justifiable because its intent was to defend the constitutional liberties of Ireland. "Have not the constituents a right to inform their representatives?" he asked.[97] By his question, Grattan, no less than Pollock and Jebb, had given the "people" political life. A careless farmer in the field of democratic politics, he was about to reap what he had sown.

96. [Jebb], *Guatimozin*, Letter II, 6; [Pollock], *Owen Roe O'Nial*, 7 and 3, resp.
97. *Parliamentary Register,* 1:336. The Runnymede allusion was recorded in the Irish Parliamentary Debates, vol. 26, container 10, pp. 95–96. "I say the Constitution of this Country gives every Elector a share in it . . . ," Grattan also contended.

CHAPTER 5

The Limits of Democratic Reform

Rouse then, Hibernians, rouse each latent flame;
Stand firm, resolv'd, all tyranny disclaim:
Force base usurpers to restore your right,
And teach those men who've dar'd your voice to slight,
That if they dare refuse your just demands,
You have the means of freedom in your hands;
Arm'd to promote your injur'd country's good,
And in her cause prepar'd to spill your blood.
                                    Volunteer Journal, 1784[1]

William Blackstone's conclusion that Ireland was a dependent kingdom subordinate to the British Parliament had not won him many friends across the Irish Sea. Charles Sheridan took Blackstone to task in a pamphlet; Henry Grattan slashed at him in the Irish House of Commons. Blackstone's ideas about the relationship of a member of Parliament to his constituents also stirred up controversy, in England as well as Ireland. "Every member, though chosen by one particular district, when elected and returned serves for the whole realm," wrote Blackstone. "Therefore he is not bound . . . to consult with, or take the advice, of his constituents upon any particular point, unless he himself thinks it proper or prudent so to do."[2]

Blackstone described assumptions governing behavior in the British House of Commons when he wrote those lines. Many British M.P.s shared his view, as did most members of the Irish Commons when they

---

   1. As taken from Georges-Denis Zimmermann, *Songs of Irish Rebellion* (Hatboro, Pa.: Folklore Associates, 1967), 36–37.
   2. William Blackstone, *Commentaries on the Laws of England*, 4 vols. (Chicago: University of Chicago Press, 1979; facsimile of the orig. 1765–69 ed.), Book One, chap. 2, in I:155.

pondered the tie between elector and elected in their own land. Undoubtedly some Irish leaders who did not accept Blackstone's conclusion that Ireland was a subordinate kingdom found nothing objectionable in his ideas about representation. Nonetheless, the notion that a member of commons was not bound by the wishes of his constituents, like the notion that most citizens were "virtually" even if not actually represented in Parliament, was challenged on both sides of the Irish Sea during the American Revolutionary era.

The move for parliamentary reform in England accelerated with the Wilkite agitation and Middlesex election controversies in the late 1760s, and by 1780 had spread to Yorkshire with formation of The Association there. English "radicals" were not intent on a revolution to overturn the system. Rather, they considered themselves reformers out to improve government and restore the lost ideals of the Glorious Revolution. Some would push for triennial parliaments, others for annual parliaments; some wanted to increase county representation and decrease that of "corrupt" boroughs; some wanted M.P.s to be treated as delegates bound by the will of their constituents, others would have been content with "independent" men; many were convinced that the power of the Crown had to be curtailed and that greater economy had to be brought into government, but hardly any talked of creating a republic. Reformers in England simply wanted to eliminate the grosser inequities of public life and make Crown and Parliament more responsive. They hoped to do something about a House of Commons whose membership was not based effectively on population, landholding, or overall wealth, but they were not consciously moving toward the more modern democratic notion of one man, one vote, nor had they any ambitions of eliminating the House of Lords or dethroning the king.[3]

The American crisis of the 1760s and early 1770s added fuel to the political fires in Middlesex; the subsequent American war helped to ig-

3. See George Stead Veitch, *The Genesis of Parliamentary Reform*, 2d ed. (Hamden: Archon Books, 1965; orig. ed., 1913); Ian Christie, *Wilkes, Wyvill and Reform* (London: Macmillan, 1962); idem, "The Wilkites and the General Election of 1774" and "The Yorkshire Association, 1780–4," in *Myth and Reality in Late Eighteenth-Century British Politics and Other Papers* (Berkeley: University of California Press, 1970), 244–60 and 261–83, resp.; Eugene Charlton Black, *The Association* (Cambridge: Harvard University Press, 1963); John Brewer, "English Radicalism in the Age of George III," in J. G. A. Pocock, ed., *Three British Revolutions: 1641, 1688, 1776* (Princeton: Princeton University Press, 1980), 323–67; Colin Bonwick, *English Radicals and the American Revolution* (Chapel Hill: University of North Carolina Press, 1977); R. R. Palmer, *The Age of the Democratic Revolution*, 2 vols. (Princeton: Princeton University Press, 1959, 1964), 1:295–300; John Cannon, *Parliamentary Reform, 1640–1832* (Cambridge; Cambridge University Press, 1973); and Edward and Annie G. Porritt, *The Unreformed House of Commons*, 2 vols. (Cambridge: Cambridge University Press, 1903, 1909), 2:185–529.

nite the Yorkshire movement in 1779–80. If English reformers did not draw much inspiration from Irish affairs, Irish reformers nevertheless drew inspiration from them. The Irish opposition press followed John Wilkes's early career closely and sympathetically, and by the outbreak of the American war, news about Wilkes and comments about the corrupt state of British politics were fairly common. Just days after Irish papers reported that freeholders in Middlesex had agreed that M.P.s should be bound by the will of their constituents, the freemen of Derry, not coincidentally, resolved that "it is the inherent Right of Electors, at all Times, to instruct their Representatives, with Regard to their Conduct in Parliament and that [as] such their Instructions should be adhered to."[4]

From its inception the Irish Parliament had been patterned after the one in Westminster; it consequently suffered from some of the same problems, and Irish reformers in the 1780s sought some of the same solutions their English counterparts sought. They concentrated on the House of Commons, supposedly the democratic arm of mixed and balanced government. Of the 300 members in the Irish Commons, 64 were elected to sit for the 32 counties (2 from each), 2 sat for Trinity College, Dublin, and the remaining 234 were returned from 117 boroughs in rural areas, towns, and cities. From that total fewer than a fifth—between fifty and sixty—really stood for open elections where the outcome could be in doubt until the freemen or "burgesses" voted. The vast majority held seats controlled by patrons, some of whom sat in Lords, some of whom were members of Commons, and a few of whom were absentees in England. As with the British Commons, there were almost no general residency requirements for Irish boroughs, either for electors or for candidates for office. In rural boroughs it was not uncommon to have only twelve or thirteen freemen who were designated as burgesses. They alone had the right to vote, and they could be nonresidents who voted for two other nonresidents to represent them. Towns and cities determined the number of eligible voters by their charters and could use those charters or acts of incorporation as a way of controlling and keeping small the number of electors.

Calculating how many Irishmen could vote is as difficult as counting how many actually exercised their franchise. Statistics gathered in 1783 to determine the total population by county, borough, and town are

---

4. *Freeman's Journal*, 10 October 1775; for other examples of how the Irish press followed Wilkes's career see ibid., 6 April 1776; and the *Hibernian Magazine*, 4 (April 1774): 199–204. George Rudé discussed Wilkes and the movement associated with him in *Wilkes and Liberty* (Oxford: Clarendon Press, 1962).

imperfect and imprecise. The same is true for the number of freemen listed on voting rolls, showing that little value was placed on holding the franchise simply for the privilege of having it. The number of forty-shilling freeholders eligible to participate in county elections varied dramatically, from an apparent high of one for each twelve or so inhabitants of County Fermanagh to a low of one freeman for every 235 residents in County Galway. Only Protestants could qualify as freemen, so there tended to be a higher ratio of freemen to general population in northern and eastern counties than in those to the south and west. County electors were expected to live within county boundaries; county M.P.s were not.

Disabilities against Dissenters were not removed until 1780. Dissenters then became eligible to vote as freemen in county elections, but in most boroughs they, like other Protestants, also had to be accepted as "burgesses" to vote. Some towns like Athlone and Drogheda had sizeable numbers of voting freemen; others like Kilkenny and Castlebar did not. Fewer than 600 were eligible to vote in Galway, a town of over 12,000. That was a higher ratio by far than the 4000 or so eligible to vote in the city of Dublin, with its 150,000. Despite reforms introduced after Lucas's agitation, Dublin's politics were hardly democratic. Trinity College was in some sense the best-represented of any real constituency, with two M.P.s for fewer than one hundred scholars and fellows. Scholars were even exempt from the age requirement (twenty-one years) that bound voters in virtually every other parliamentary district.

Decidedly smaller numbers held the franchise in most rural parliamentary boroughs. A few boroughs—like Harristown in County Kildare, under the patronage of the duke of Leinster—had no residents whatsoever. Among the most "venal and corrupt" were the neighboring boroughs of Bannow, Clonmines, and Fethard in County Wexford. The thirteen men eligible to vote as burgessess in Fethard were also the only men eligible to vote in the other two boroughs. Thus thirteen men, who were in turn under the influence of a patron, the earl of Ely, returned six M.P.s to Commons. These boroughs were not unusual in being dominated by a patron or in having burgesses eligible to vote who were also nonresidents. Charlemont, it should be recalled, was patron of his own borough, just as the earl of Arran was for the borough of Donegal. The earl of Mornington was patron for the town borough of Trim, and Denis Daly acted more or less as patron for the town of Galway, despite its size.[5] Charlemont, Arran, Mornington, and Daly considered their pa-

---

5. Technically there were differences among the eleven "potwalloper" boroughs, the

The Limits of Democratic Reform 157

tronage to be a sign of political health rather than decline, because they fostered "independent" candidates, "Patriots" of the opposition like Grattan and Flood, who otherwise might not have found a seat in Commons. They certainly did not see their patronage as being the same as that of a bishop of Clogher or someone else who used borough control for advancing their own power or wealth.

Whether they sided with the opposition or lined up as firm administration men, members of the Irish Parliament were part of a ruling elite. Some came from old, distinguished families, leaders for generations. Many members of Commons were the sons, the younger brothers, the nephews and protégés of peers sitting in the House of Lords. Together they constituted the most powerful element of the aristocratic elite that dominated Ireland. For example, through much of the 1780s, while the duke of Leinster sat in Lords, three of his brothers held seats in Commons: Charles for County Kildare, Henry for the borough of Kildare, and Edward for Athy, another Kildare borough. These four FitzGeralds were thereby enabled to protect family interests and insure the primacy of Carton, the vast Kildare estate that symbolized their power. There were also men in Parliament from more humble origins—Henry Flood and Barry Yelverton being two notable examples, but once they became members of the aristocratic club they had a vested interest in protecting it.

Up through the 1740s and the days of Charles Lucas, the electorate did not expect parliamentary politics to be any different from what they were, and occasional objections raised then were not pressed vigorously. Protestant electors, into the 1770s, usually deferred to the will of their

---

seven "manor" boroughs, and the remaining "corporate" boroughs. "Manor" boroughs might have been the easiest for patrons to control, while "potwallopers" lacked patrons and were therefore, in theory, more open; but even potwallopers tended to return the same powerful men over and over—such as Hercules Langrishe for Knocktopher. See Henry Grattan, *Memoirs of the Life and Times of the Rt. Hon. Henry Grattan*, 5 vols. (London: Henry Colburn, 1849), 3:472–87 (appendix) for a list compiled in 1783 showing estimates of total population and voters for all of the counties and boroughs, and comments on "corruption." According to this list Dublin had three hundred thousand residents, a total that, based on Arthur Young and Philip Luckombe's estimates, should be cut in half. Sir John Newport, *The State of the Borough Representation of Ireland in 1783 and 1800* (London: J. Rockwell, 1832), 1–28, includes a somewhat briefer list. Newport was a member of the committee at the Volunteer convention in 1783 that assembled the information used for both lists. Also see the *Freeman's Journal*, 5 July through 8 September 1774, listing all of the M.P.s and their political tendencies at that time (one hundred sixty "courtiers," eighty-four "patriots," fifty-three "doubtful," and three vacant seats). Edith Johnston, *Great Britain and Ireland: 1760–1800*, (Edinburgh: Oliver and Boyd, 1963), appendix B, pp. 321–30, includes Johnston's composite sketch of borough affiliations from 1760 to 1800. Over this period, by her calculations, only thirteen of one hundred seventeen boroughs were not controlled by a patron or single interest.

social betters and accepted the leadership of the few. Thus Thomas Conolly continued to sit for the borough of Londonderry long after he had moved his residence from the old family home there to the larger estate at Castletown in Kildare. Residence in the district he represented was neither required nor expected. Likewise, in 1776 Barry Yelverton was elected to sit for the borough of Donegal (in County Donegal) and the towns of Belfast and Carrickfergus in County Antrim.[6] Not only were these three distinct constituencies, they were located in two different counties, and Yelverton did not live in either one. He could sit for only one—he chose Carrickfergus—but the fact that he was elected in all three is a commentary on the expectations of the voters as well as the attitudes of M.P.s.

The number of peers in the House of Lords increased dramatically during the latter part of the eighteenth century. All were, of course, Protestants, except for a handful of Catholics who did not actually take their seats because they were unwilling to repeat the oath of supremacy. There were twenty-two "lords spiritual" (four archbishops and eighteen bishops) throughout the century. The number of "lords temporal" jumped from just over one hundred in 1700 to better than twice that number at the end of the century. George III awarded peerages in both Britain and Ireland as favors to friends and to build alliances in what was a generally accepted, virtually unavoidable way of practicing politics. In Ireland the Crown had few other options and an even greater need because of Ireland's peculiar status in the empire. Some of those peerages went to Englishmen who had no intention of crossing St. George's Channel to become involved in Irish affairs; "spiritual" peers were often Englishmen (including all of the archbishops), but most of them did reside in Ireland at least part of the year. So did many of the Irish-born peers who owed their elevation to George III.

The House of Lords increased more in size than in power during the eighteenth century. Commons, on the other hand, grew no larger in size after 1692, but it became much more powerful and ambitious. Lords was crippled by the fact that so many of its members were absentees or men with little political interest, and because it had been stripped of its

---

6. For Yelverton, see the *Journal of the House of Commons of the Kingdom of Ireland*, 20 vols. (Dublin: George Grierson, 1796–1802), 9:291–92. Also see the brief overview by J. L. McCracken, *The Irish Parliament in the Eighteenth Century* (Dundalk: Dundalgan Press, 1971); Edith Johnson's much more involved *Great Britain and Ireland*; and two essays by A. P. W. Malcomson: "Election Politics in the Borough of Antrim, 1750–1800," *Irish Historical Studies* 17 (March 1970): 32–57, and "The Parliamentary Traffic of This Country," in T. Bartlett and D. Hayton, eds., *Penal Era and Golden Age*, (Belfast: Ulster Historical Foundation, 1979), 137–61.

Parliamentary constituencies by county and borough, 1692–1800. Boroughs represented at Westminster with the Act of Union are underlined.

appellate jurisdiction under the Declaratory Act. There were no modern political parties in Ireland—nor were there in Britain, for that matter; instead, there were factions in both houses organized around great families and controversial issues. Emphasis on oratory notwithstanding, Irish politicians engaged in cloakroom politics, and many votes were virtually decided before debate began. If there were times when it was difficult to muster the forty M.P.s necessary to form a quorum and conduct business in Commons, there were other times when well over two hundred attended. Whenever a question was raised about parliamentary prerogative, especially when it involved the relationship of Parliament to the lord lieutenant, the turnout could be large and debate heated.

Disputes that raged within Parliament House sometimes spilled over to involve the public. Proceedings of the House of Lords were closed to public view, but visitors listened in on Commons from the gallery. Votes in Commons had been published since 1692, often on the day they occurred. Although names of M.P.s were rarely included and votes were recorded only by numerical totals, issues were brought to public notice. By the time of the American Revolution, newspapers like the *Freeman's Journal* and *Hibernian Journal* routinely printed summaries of debates in Commons where individuals, their views, and their political loyalties were identified. M.P.s in Commons often reviewed and debated election returns, with rival factions dividing over the seating of new members. Those sensitive to Castle efforts to build strength through patronage put their complaints on a higher level, arguing that the administration was corrupting Commons and depriving the people of their constitutional right to representation. "I wish to have the House full, but full of the Members whom the people chose," complained Denis Daly in 1777. "The publick have a right to be represented. The publick have a right to the privileges of Parliament," echoed Barry Yelverton not long after.[7]

No member of Commons would have had the temerity to deny that he was in some sense a representative of the people. There was, however, some confusion as to who, exactly, the "people" were and how much Commons was expected to bend to their will. Lords and Commons together might have constituted a legislative elite, but they had never been so detached from public life that they were immune to popular pressure. Members of Commons added to that pressure, perhaps without fully

---

7. Parliament, House of Commons Debates, 1776–1789, Library of Congress MS. 16,363.1, vol. 1, container 4, p. 80 for Daly and p. 260 for Yelverton. See J. R. Pole, *The Gift of Government* (Athens: University of Georgia Press, 1983), 87–116, for a discussion of how the British House of Commons only gradually opened its debates to public scrutiny during the eighteenth century.

understanding that in their efforts to gain power they also had to give some away. As a case in point candidates for a seat in Commons often wrote newspaper notices like the following in 1759:

> As there is a Vacancy in Parliament, by the Death of my Father Robert Handcock, esq; your late worthy Representative, and also a Burgessship in said Borough, I am encouraged, by my Friends, to offer myself a Candidate for both: and if I have the Honour of being elected, I shall always make it my Study to merit, by my further Conduct, the Confidence you are pleased to repose in me, who am, Gentlemen, your most obedient humble Servant,
>
> WM. HANDCOCK[8]

Handcock won his election and conscientiously ran another notice, dutifully thanking the voters in the borough of Athlone for giving their support, noting that "The Trust repos'd in him he hopes ever to discharge with Candour and Integrity."[9]

Handcock's original notice had been only one of fifteen printed in the *Dublin Journal* for that date, and it was very similar in tone and content to the other fourteen, which had been written by county as well as borough candidates, by men already sitting in Commons as well as prospective M.P.s. Handcock's appeal reflected both the aristocratic and the democratic sides to Irish parliamentary politics. It was aristocratic to the extent that Handcock, although not a resident of Athlone and perhaps not very well known by the electors there, was son of the man who had represented them and owned land in the borough. He expected his name and his family's prominence to offset his being a nonresident. The notice was democractic to the extent that it was written at all, that Handcock wrote it as a supplicant, and that he promised to honor the "Trust respos'd in him." He had not, however, expressly bound himself to vote as instructed nor had he characterized himself as a mere delegate of the electors with no will of his own.

In a more deferential age, men like Handcock could have employed the language of democratic politics without suffering the consequences. Difficulties came because the system of deference had begun to erode. Agitators for parliamentary reform during the American Revolutionary era built on what Patriots in the Irish Parliament and popular leaders like Charles Lucas had done two decades before. If the system of deference had only begun to erode in the 1750s, it was being thoroughly undermined in the 1770s.

There is no single cause, no simple explanation, for this phenomenon.

8. *Dublin Journal*, 9 October 1759.
9. Ibid., 20 November 1759.

The challenge to empire posed by rebellious Americans was one source of inspiration to the Irish and therefore one cause of the threat to deferential politics; so too was the Wilkite agitation in and around London at the same time. Other reasons can be traced to purely Irish concerns: to the problems stemming from Ireland's place in the empire, to the schizophrenic identity of the Anglo-Irish elite, and to the inherent contradictions of a political system that was aristocratic, even oligarchic, but not entirely isolated from democratic impulses. Add to all of this a constitutional tradition built on the foundation of a "kingdom," a nation of "free people."

And yet the democratic impulse was not very strong for most of the eighteenth century. For example, with the approach of parliamentary elections, the *Freeman's Journal* in November 1774 called on all those planning to stand for a seat in Commons to take an oath that they would not accept bribes, that they would vote according to their best judgment, and also that:

when instructed by my constituents, in publick, in general assembly the Sheriff convened, I will deem it my duty, to conform to, and be guided by said instructions, even tho' I should, in private opinion, possibly dissent therefrom, acknowledging myself whilst in parliament, to be merely the representative of my constituents.[10]

Few if any members of Commons would have been willing to take such an oath unless they were desperate to win their seat. At this point, few borough or county electors expected them to do so. A group of freemen in County Londonderry that tried to oust Thomas Conolly and Edward Cary for going against them failed in their bid just a few months before the *Freeman's Journal* made its recommendation.

Agitation for parliamentary reform, like insistence that M.P.s were bound to follow the instructions of their constituents, did not come in a rush. Before the 1780s it was more common for habitually absent members or lock-step administration men to be criticized than the institution of Parliament itself. Readers of the *Freeman's Journal* or Walker's *Hibernian Magazine* might have expected more of their M.P.s in 1774 than they had even a decade before; even so, their criticisms and dissatisfactions with the system were still fairly muted by the standards of what would come.[11] The call printed in the *Freeman's Journal* in November 1774 was just slightly ahead of its time.

10. *Freeman's Journal*, 29 November 1774.
11. Ibid., 21 June 1774, for Conolly and Cary, who were returned to their seats and sat when a new Parliament opened in October 1775. See ibid., 8 January 1774 and 30

That call would be taken up by the Volunteers in 1779. By then they had been catered to by the parliamentary opposition and their claims to being the equivalent of a national militia had been acquiesced in by Lord Lieutenant Buckinghamshire. They elected their own officers, they formed companies and combined them into regiments and corps, they armed themselves and adopted their own uniform colors, they marched and drilled and fought sham battles.[12] On muster days they heard sermons proclaiming the right of the people to take up arms in self-defense. Their virtues were extolled, and they were urged to be vigilant because, as William Steel Dickson preached to the Echlinville Volunteers in March 1779, "the Safety of a Nation must ever depend on the Spirit of the People."[13] Already considering themselves the defenders of public safety, they were fast coming to see themselves as the embodiment of popular will.

Buckinghamshire's inability to control the Volunteers worried the men around him. Volunteers were "under no restraint of Government, having principles of independence within themselves," complained John Beresford, "and being headed by men in general adverse to Government, and who take pains to instil into them their own doctrines."[14] By October 1779, Attorney General John Scott had joined Beresford in urging London to recall the lord lieutenant and replace him with someone better able to wield power.

Beresford and Scott looked on with chagrin the next month when

---

June 1774, for the examples of constituent pressure, and the general comments of Theresa Margaret O'Connor, "The More Immediate Effects of the American Revolution on Ireland, 1775–1785" (M.A. thesis, Queen's University of Belfast, 1938), 84–85, and R. B. McDowell, *Irish Public Opinion 1750–1800* (London: Faber and Faber, 1944), 84. For an even better example of constituents instructing their M.P.s, see the resolution passed by County Galway freeholders printed in the *Freeman's Journal,* 18 April 1780. Before the 1780s, voters were more often urged to elect independent men and to admonish M.P.s rather than instruct them; see, for example, the *Freeman's Journal,* 12 August 1775 and 9 July 1776, and the *Hibernian Magazine* 5 (December 1775): 767–74. Calls for a more representative parliament were quite common by the mid-1770s—such as one in the *Hibernian Journal,* 9 February 1774.

12. See the duke of Leinster's orders to the Dublin Volunteers of 9 April 1780, in Irish Volunteers, MS. 212, Gilbert Library, for one of the better examples of a large-scale drill and mock battle.

13. William Steel Dickson, *A Sermon, on the Propriety and Advantage of Acquiring the Knowledge and Use of Arms, In Times of public Danger* (Belfast: James Magee, 1779), 11. Also see "A Cork Associate," *A Defense of the Armed Societies of Ireland, with Respect to Their Legality* (Cork: Robert Doblyn, 1779), which discusses the Volunteers in their military, not political, role.

14. William Beresford, ed., *The Correspondence of the Right Hon. John Beresford,* 2 vols. (London: Woodfall and Kinder, 1854), 1:58, letter to John Robinson of 13 October 1779. Also see Attorney General John Scott's letter to Robinson of 13 April 1779 in ibid., 1:39.

Volunteers effectively took over the traditional November 4 celebration of the Glorious Revolution. In previous years the lord lieutenant, lord chancellor and various members of the administration, joined by the lord mayor of Dublin and other civic officials, had proceeded from the Castle down Dame Street to College Green, then to St. Stephen's Green, back to College Green, thrice around the statue of William III opposite it, and finally back to the Castle. As the procession made its way crowds cheered, bells rang, cannons boomed, and the regulars fired their muskets in volley. Volunteers rather than the lord lieutenant began the 1779 observance, starting their own procession from St. Stephen's Green that wound by a longer route to College Green and ended at William III's statue. The duke of Leinster was in command; Henry Grattan and Henry Flood marched with their company; so too did numerous other members of Parliament, including John Fitzgibbon. Placards had been placed on all four sides of the base of William's statue, reading: The Loyal Volunteers; The relief of Ireland; A Glorious Revolution; and, on the north side facing Parliament House, the more threatening "A Free Trade or Else." Only after the Volunteers had drawn up in formation, some one thousand strong in an assortment of uniforms denoting the various companies, did Buckinghamshire pass by with his procession. The Volunteers cheered his arrival and fired volleys to salute him, but the significance of the occasion could not have been lost on him or the Volunteers.[15]

Buckinghamshire thought that "there are some companies whose principles are determinedly republican," this despite their profession of loyalty and the presence among them of peers like Leinster. "It concerns me to hear from every quarter," he wrote, that the rank and file of Volunteers were becoming "so independent of their ostensible leaders."[16] The Volunteers had not aimed any direct threats at the government, it was true, and they would have nothing to do with the rioting that broke out in mid-November during the free trade controversy. If anything, they would try to restore order. Still, Buckinghamshire, too late for his own fortunes, finally saw what had worried the Beresfords and Scotts months before. The Volunteers were not lawless rabble; the ranks of Dublin's companies were filled with artisans and merchants, most of them freemen of the city. Volunteer companies from the countryside were equally respectable. They drew from the yeoman farmers who were predomi-

15. Ibid., 1:73–75, Beresford to Robinson, 5 November 1779.
16. Historical Manuscripts Commission, *Report on the Manuscripts of the Marquis of Lothian* (London: Eyre and Spottiswoode, 1905), 358, letter to George Germain of 24 October 1779.

nantly freemen and almost exclusively Protestant. Yet they posed a threat to established government, because they had taken on a political as well as a military identity.

Those members of the parliamentary opposition who had benefited from the rise of the Volunteers were even slower to see the implications of the movement. They became anxious once they did. Grattan said nothing in public, but in private he told John Forbes that he did not want the Volunteers to meet again after their first assembly at Dungannon in February 1782. The earl of Charlemont, despite his having been elected titular commander-in-chief of the Volunteers nearly two years before, agreed with Grattan that Volunteers should leave popular politics to members of Parliament. He had not wanted the Ulster Volunteers to send a delegation to the king to reaffirm their loyalty and express thanks for repeal of the Declaratory Act; they went ahead anyway. He was even more disturbed by divisions produced in the subsequent debate over renunciation.[17]

Charlemont and Grattan suffered the consequences in 1782 of what they had helped give form to several years earlier. Charlemont knew before he became commander-in-chief that the Volunteers were politicized. He had even acknowledged that Volunteers could be the key to securing what Grattan had failed to obtain from Parliament in April 1780. Through the Volunteers, he wrote to Francis Dobbs the following July, "our Rights will be ascertained and established."[18] In condemning the perpetual mutiny bill in 1781, Grattan charged that the Irish Parliament had not protected Ireland's constitutional rights. It had allowed Britain to usurp power and, if Ireland was to avoid being trampled as Britain had trampled the American colonies, then the people were right to keep their "armed associations." Lashing out at his colleagues in Commons he contended, "that parliaments are neither eternal nor omnipotent; their powers are not original, but delegated, and their delegation is to act within the frame of the constitution, not to alter, still less to destroy it." The people "form and may reform parliament." Commons was obliged to exercise rather than alienate popular power, because it was entrusted with protection of the public will.[19] In saying this Grattan

---

17. Grattan to Forbes, undated letter sometime in 1782, in Forbes Letters, MS. 10,713, National Library of Ireland; Charlemont to Rockingham of June 1782 in Francis Hardy, *Memoirs of the Political and Private Life of James Caulfield, Earl of Charlemont*, 2 vols. (London: T. Cadell, 1810), 2:40–43.

18. Charlemont to Dobbs, 15 July 1780, in the Dobbs Letters, 1777–1801, MS. 2251, NLI.

19. [Henry Grattan], *Observations on the Mutiny Bill* (Dublin: W. Wilson, 1781), quotes from pp. 30 and 75, resp.

reaffirmed arguments he made during the debates over free trade in 1779. Indeed, he had gone so far then as to characterize M.P.s as "trustees" of the people:

I consider a member of parliament to be a trustee, the delegate of his constituents; their instructions he is to a certain degree as much bound to respect as the servants of the crown are royal authority; and if the member deviates from the intentions of his constituents they are authorized to associate against him for the purpose of reprobating his proceedings. The greatest events have been produced by the interposition of the people; it has proved the great basis on which constitutional measures have depended.[20]

Grattan might have come to regret his Lucas-like talk of "trustees" and "delegates," but his use of the terms from 1779 to 1782 and his frustrations with Parliament were perfectly natural. He indulged in rhetorical excess when he compared the Dungannon Convention of February 1782 with the events at Runnymede, but that too makes sense, given his excitement at the moment. What came to disturb Grattan, and what he never fully understood, was that the "people" were not his creation, nor were they always at his side. His own criticisms are proof that he knew an unresponsive Irish Commons was not really the seat of popular power. Once Commons became more responsive, Grattan felt that the people should accept the leadership of its members. Grattan wanted to pick and choose when the people should be deferential and when they could be more demanding. Just as in the 1760s Charlemont had thought that Lucas could be managed, twenty years later Grattan thought that the Volunteers could be manipulated by parliamentary Patriots.[21] But he could not play the Volunteer trump without running risks. It was one thing for a member of Parliament to consider himself a delegate; it was quite another to be labeled that by an outsider. Unfortunately for Grattan and Charlemont and others who dabbled in democratic politics, the people might want to lead when the elite expected them to follow. That the Volunteers had organized at all proved that the "people" would not always wait. Many of the gentry and parliamentary leaders who became involved with the Volunteers did so reluctantly. Grattan had not been

20. Henry Grattan, Jr., ed., *The Speeches of the Right Honourable Henry Grattan*, 4 vols. (London: Longman, Hurst, Rees, Orme, and Brown, 1822), 1:26. Also see Grattan and Yelverton's remarks on 26 April 1780 in Commons in the Parliamentary Debates, vol. 22, container 8, pp. 229–30 and 127, resp.

21. For example, Grattan wrote Charles James Fox a long letter two days after his 1782 victory in Commons. Although adopting a conciliatory, hopeful tone, he pointed out that "we have not gone to the Castle with the Volunteers as in 1779"—as if to say that the British were lucky; the Patriots had kept their hound on its leash. Grattan to Fox, 18 April 1782, Charles James Fox Papers, X, Fo. 95, MS. 47568 BL.

James Caulfield, the earl of Charlemont, by William Cuming: borough patron and friend of Patriot politicians; champion of parliamentary reform and opponent of Catholic emancipation.
Courtesy of the National Gallery of Ireland.

as reluctant as some, but then he probably had more illusions about his ability to channel Volunteer energies.

Volunteers called for an extra-parliamentary national convention long before the Dungannon meeting of February 1782. One scheme for a "Constitutional Association" in 1780 made the same proposals that Grattan and Yelverton could not yet carry in Commons: a clear statement of parliamentary independence, review of Poynings' Law, reduction of placemen and pensioners, and independent M.P.s elected by honest voters.[22] These were more or less the resolutions passed at Dungannon nearly two years later, not by a "Constitutional Association" but by a group that saw itself as performing the same role. Although Grattan and Flood drafted some of the resolutions passed at Dungannon, they had no hand in writing the "address" to the "minority in both houses of parliament" appended to those resolutions:

WE thank you for your noble and spirited, though hitherto ineffectual efforts in defence of the great constitutional and commercial rights of your country. Go on. The almost unanimous voice of the people must prevail. We know our duty to our sovereign and are loyal; we know our duty to ourselves and are resolved to be free. We seek for our rights and no more than our rights, and, in so just a pursuit, we should doubt the being of a Providence, if we doubted of success.[23]

The message here is a bit confusing, a mixture of modesty and assertiveness. In professing to be loyal while at the same time insisting on what they took to be their constitutional rights, the Dungannon delegates were being no more confused or contradictory than Grattan had been when he stated that members of Commons were trustees bound "to a certain degree" to obey instructions. Similarly, Grattan was deluged with congratulatory messages from dozens of Volunteer units after his April 1782 triumph in Commons. Most were very deferential in tone, thanking Grattan for his leadership and treating the victory as primarily his. Others, however, gave the impression that Volunteers had led and that members of Parliament, Grattan included, had followed. The Volunteers "have declared the rights of Ireland," wrote the Eyrecourt Buffs; although most units referred to Grattan as their "political saviour," the Cavan Independent Volunteers reserved that distinction for themselves and their fellows in arms.[24]

22. *A Scheme for a Constitutional Association* (Dublin: William Hallhead, 1780); also see Maurice O'Connell, *Irish Politics and Social Change in the Age of the American Revolution* (Philadelphia: University of Pennsylvania Press, 1965), 178–83.
23. Reprinted in William Crawford, *A History of Ireland*, 2 vols. (Strabane: John Bellew, 1783), 2:359–60.
24. Henry Grattan, Jr., ed., *Miscellaneous Works of the Right Honourable Henry*

Grattan no less than Charlemont had become involved in activities leading to unintended consequences, and they were not alone. When the Lawyers Volunteer Corps resolved in February 1782 that members of Commons "derive their power *solely* from the people," it tried to undercut Grattan's opponents, not to reduce M.P.s to the status of trustees and delegates. Charles Francis Sheridan had comparable objectives in his critique of Blackstone's *Commentaries,* when he denied that the British "had an indubitable right, whenever they thought proper, to *take from* the people, what an act of Parliament itself acknowledges the People have an indubitable right to *keep*."[25] This was the same Sheridan who had acclaimed the Volunteers as an "Army of Freemen" and then afterward denied the need for parliamentary reform and resented the Volunteers' intrusion into parliamentary affairs.[26]

Charlemont later lamented that with the Volunteers' rising political ambitions "a spirit was raised which nothing could quell, a spirit more formidable as it was temperate."[27] He and Grattan and Sheridan had encouraged the discussion of first principles and with it a re-evaluation of the relationship between governor and governed. Most Volunteers remained "temperate" in never ceasing to profess their loyalty to the Crown and their desire to restore the constitution rather than introduce constitutional innovations. When they ventured from that course, they lost their cohesion—as would be seen with the attempt by some Volunteers to hasten Catholic relief. Charlemont, however, felt that they ceased to be "temperate" when they tried to impose their will on Parliament. Once flattered to be named their commander-in-chief, he continued his association with them so that he could preserve an element of moderation, which he feared they would lose without him. He was not being disingenuous when he described himself as "more of a commoner than a peer" in his sentiments.[28] He responded to what he de-

---

Grattan (London: Longman, Hurst, Rees, Orme, and Brown, 1822), 173–242 (appendix) for messages to Grattan and his responses; Eyrecourt Buffs on p. 173, Cavan Independent Volunteers on p. 199.

25. Lawyers Corps cited in George Barnes, *The Rights of the Imperial Crown of Ireland Asserted and Maintained, Against Edward Cooke, Esq.*, 3d ed. (Dublin, 1803; orig. ed., 1799), 66; Sheridan, *Observations on the Doctrine Laid Down by Sir William Blackstone respecting the Extent of Power of the British Parliament, particularly in relation to Ireland* (Dublin: The Company of Booksellers, 1779), 9.

26. For the Volunteers as an "Army of Freemen" see [Sheridan], *A Review of the Three Great National Questions, Relative to a Declaration of Right, Poynings' Law, and the Mutiny Bill* (Dublin: M. Mills, 1781), 20; and for Sheridan's views in general see James J. Kelly, "The Irish Parliamentary Reform Movement: The Administration and Popular Politics, 1783–5" (M.A. thesis, University College, Dublin, 1981), 111–12. Also see n. 77 for this chapter.

27. HMC, *Charlemont,* 1:51.

28. HMC, *The Manuscripts of the Earl of Buckinghamshire, the Earl of Lindsey, the*

termined was public need, and in 1783 he (seemingly) surrendered control of his borough as a symbolic gesture of his commitment to parliamentary reform. Still, he was never comfortable with extra-parliamentary politics, and he was no republican enthusiast. Before, and even after, he supposedly gave up his borough, he thought nothing of holding its M.P.s to his views.

M.P.s had always been expected to please their constituents, whether those constituents were patrons like Charlemont and Leinster or the freemen of Dublin. Constituent pressure in an aristocratic system flowed from top to bottom; in a more democratic arrangement, pressure would flow in the opposite direction. To some extent the Volunteers did question traditional notions of constituent power. As importantly, they challenged notions of size, asking how many members of the political compact—theoretically all freemen—could be active participants in government. And Volunteers were no different from a growing number of electors and freemen at large who had begun to assert their views more forcefully. By November 1781, in fact, voters in counties Down, Leitrim, and Dublin had all passed resolutions stating their right to instruct "their respective delegates in all constitutional points."[29] Without doubt, many of these electors and freemen were also Volunteers.

With the Volunteers' rising political ambitions, there were greater opportunities for men outside Parliament to have their voices heard, men like Francis Dobbs and William Drennan. Both were less prominent than Grattan and other parliamentary leaders, yet their rise does not mark a class division or the conscious pursuit of radical politics. Dobbs was son of a minister in County Armagh and nephew to Arthur Dobbs, onetime governor of North Carolina. He attended Trinty College, Dublin, spent a term or two at one of the Inns of Court, and by 1773 had been admitted to the Irish Bar. Drennan, like Dobbs an Ulster man (he was from Belfast) and Presbyterian minister's son, studied at Glasgow before obtaining his medical degree at Edinburgh. While at Edinburgh he rubbed shoulders with David Hume and was the student of Dugald Stewart, a luminary in what is now styled the "Scottish Enlightenment." Their beginnings, then, were no more humble than Grattan's and considerably more advantaged than Yelverton's.

Earl of Onslow, Lord Emly, Theodore J. Hare, Esq., and James Rand, M. P. (London: Eyre and Spottiswoode, 1895), 197, Charlemont to Edmund Sexton Pery, 21 August 1789.

29. *Hibernian Magazine*, 11 (November 1781):615; also see the comments of R. B. McDowell, *Ireland in the Age of Imperialism and Revolution, 1760–1801* (Oxford: Clarendon Press, 1979), 293–94; and the *Dublin Journal*, 12 February 1778, for an earlier example of freeholders instructing their M.P.s.

Francis Dobbs: barrister and M.P., advocate of parliamentary reform and borderline republican, by ——— Wilson. Courtesy of the National Library of Ireland.

Dobbs and Drennan were more notable as penmen than as orators and organizers, and in their writings they did not flinch at criticizing the Irish Parliament for its failings, as well as the British government for its intrusiveness and its treatment of Ireland as an inferior partner in empire. Both were more comfortable with extra-parliamentary politics than were Grattan and Charlemont, though both tried to keep ties with the parliamentary opposition. Drennan never sat in Commons; Dobbs sat for a short while as an M.P. for Charlemont's old borough, from 1797 until the Act of Union. Drennan was somewhat more liberal in his ideas than Dobbs, becoming one of the leaders of the United Irishmen in the 1790s. Even if convinced as early as 1785 that separation from Britain would be better for Irish interests, he was never enthusiastic about fighting a war of independence to force the issue. He and Dobbs felt that the Irish Parliament was too unresponsive to the public will; yet neither was entirely comfortable with the idea of Catholic equality, and neither championed universal manhood suffrage for Protestants. They and other leaders of the more progressive element of the Volunteers were thus not set in constant opposition to the Grattans and Charlemonts, who were also Volunteers. They were less leery of the Volunteers as a political pressure group and they possessed certain republican notions that Grattan and his group did not, but they were not democrats; Dobbs was in some ways hardly even a republican. They claimed that they were saving the constitution, that they were using liberal means to achieve a conservative end, and that they were mobilizing the people to restore and preserve order, not to subvert it.

Dobbs and Drennan did not formally break with the parliamentary opposition, although they stressed popular power and the rights of the Volunteers much more stridently than did any member of Commons. Drennan characterized the forming of the Volunteers as "a revolution founded on the broad base of the people";[30] like Drennan, Dobbs wrote that the Volunteers, not Parliament, had secured the "Constitution of 1782." "It was easily seen that the voice of an armed, and now an united People, must be heard," claimed Dobbs, "a prostituted Parliament could no longer support the Government that had seduced it." It was the Volunteers who "redeemed" their "native land."[31]

30. [William Drennan], *A Letter to Edmund Burke, Esq.* (Dublin: William Hallhead, 1780), 18; and Colin P. Hill, "William Drennan and the Radical Movement for Parliamentary Reform, 1779–1794," 2 vols. (M.Litt. thesis, Trinity College, University of Dublin, 1967), for Drennan's career as a "radical publicist and popularizer of ideas, rather than an originator of a liberal philosophy" (1:32). Also see A. T. Q. Stewart, *A Deeper Silence: The Hidden Origins of the United Irishmen* (London: Faber and Faber, 1992), which has a great deal on Drennan.

31. Dobbs, *A History of Irish Affairs from the 12th of October, 1799, to the 15th of*

The Limits of Democratic Reform 173

Although both men celebrated the accomplishment of parliamentary independence, neither wanted to stop there. They pressed for parliamentary reform, and they agreed that Volunteers should lead the way. Parliament could not be trusted to reform itself; the "people" had to take charge. On 16 April 1782, the day that Grattan made his most famous address in Commons, Dobbs had been urged by a Belfast friend that "*now* is the very time" when an assembly should be held in Dublin, called by the Volunteers to force the Irish Parliament to do what Grattan, unbeknownst to Dobbs's friend, was at that moment doing.[32]

Dobbs's correspondent was one of many Volunteers not satisfied with passing resolutions and then waiting for Parliament to act—as had happened at the Dungannon meeting of February 1782. If Grattan had not finally carried his motion, it is very possible that something like a national Volunteers convention would have been held in 1782, a full year before the eventual gathering in Dublin at the Rotunda. Instead of Grattan using the threat of the Volunteers against administration men in Commons, Volunteers might have made the threat themselves and aimed it at all members of Parliament, Grattan included.

Before the year was out, the Volunteers of Dublin served notice that there was unfinished business left for them to complete:

THE Volunteer Army has indeed in a short Period, effected Wonders, they demanded and obtained the Freedom of our Commerce, they vindicated and established the legislative Supremacy of our Parliament, they have emancipated their Country from the galling Yoke of foreign Subjugation, but they have not restored the Vigour of the Constitution, they have not expelled the corroding Poison of domestick Corruption, their Rise and Progress executed the former, their permanent Establishment may in Time effectuate the latter.[33]

As these Volunteers saw it, they, not Parliament and not Grattan, who was simply one M.P., had delivered the country. By then advocates of formal renunciation they were convinced that the British could not be trusted to protect Irish interests. They expressed grudging respect for Lord Lieutenant Temple, who at least was not as rapacious as his predecessors. Issuing a warning to him and to the Irish Parliament, however, they made it clear that they would not accept any militia act designed to replace them. They characterized themselves as dedicated defenders

---

September, 1782, the Day of Lord Temple's Arrival (Dublin: M. Mills, 1782), 67; also see Dobbs's *Thoughts on Volunteers* (Dublin: M. Mills, 1781), 6.

32. Robert Thomson to Francis Dobbs, 16 April 1782, in the Dobbs Letters, MS. 2251, NLI.

33. From p. 1 of the resolution by the Volunteer Corps for the city and county of Dublin in the Irish Volunteers, MS. 212, Gilbert Library.

of the constitution; therefore it was necessary for them to be politically active and exercise moral suasion. "The Volunteers may be Enemies to the Government, and yet Friends to the Constitution," they declared; "their Love of the one may be the Cause and the Foundation of their Hatred of the other."[34] They could make these pronouncements without feeling they were radicals, because they were working toward a conservative goal: restoration of constitutional government and "redemption," as Grattan said in Commons, of the Irish nation. They could likewise support a national convention that sought to draft legislation and push it through the Irish Parliament.

The move toward a national convention was gradual yet inexorable. The Dungannon meeting of February 1782 pointed the way. Other Volunteer groups met to endorse resolutions passed there and in some cases to add some of their own. Delegates from fifty-nine Connacht units met in March to approve the Dungannon measures and added that because "the virtue of the people is the most effectual cheque to the venality of the representative," they would not elect anyone to Commons who would not obey their instructions.[35] Volunteers in all four provinces had formed committees of correspondence to keep apprised of each other's activities, and the Dungannon group was careful to resolve in February 1782 that it would meet again.

The second meeting of Ulster Volunteers opened at Dungannon on 8 September 1783. It seems only right that these men should assemble to discuss parliamentary reform in a town that was itself a rotten borough, an example of the inadequacies of the existing electoral system. Nearly five hundred delegates elected to represent some twenty thousand Volunteers turned out, all of them expected, if not formally bound, to follow the instructions of their comrades in arms. This included the fifteen M.P.s arriving as delegates.

Resolutions reaffirming that freedom was the indefeasible right of all Irishmen and that the Irish were free only if they were governed by their own consent passed unanimously, as did resolutions that the Irish Parliament was not representative, that the people had a right to correct parliamentary abuses and that they were calling for a "renovation" rather than an "innovation" of the constitution.[36]

34. Ibid.
35. *Hibernian Magazine* 12 (March 1782): 167–68; also see ibid., 12 (April 1782): 221, for a resolution by the Ulster Volunteers on 6 April 1782 that does not go quite as far, admonishing electors to "vote only for men whose past conduct in parliament you and the nation approve, and for such others as will solemnly pledge themselves to support the measure you and the nation approve." Also see Kelly, "Irish Parliamentary Reform," 25–30.
36. *Hibernian Magazine* 13 (September 1783): 499–502.

The Limits of Democratic Reform 175

Francis Dobbs, though not a delegate, tried to introduce his "universal" reform and new "Code of Laws" that included a brief, written constitution. Dobbs's reform was fairly radical in proposing elimination of borough representation in Commons, moving instead to representation by county only. Each county would have its percentage of the three hundred members determined by the number of homes with two hearths, and all men—Protestant or Catholic—who could pay the hearth tax would be eligible to vote. Furthermore, all placemen and pensioners would of necessity be eliminated under this scheme, and parliamentary elections would take place at least once every three years. The people could nominate their own candidates for a seat in Commons, provided an insufficient group "either in number or character" presented themselves to the sheriff as candidates. Dobbs even fixed the salaries of government officers, from lord lieutenant down to local officials like sheriffs, with most posts to be held during good behavior. Finally, Volunteers were to be recognized as the national militia and organized in military districts corresponding to parliamentary districts, and many strictures were to be removed from the Catholics.

Nonetheless, Dobbs's "universal" reform did not give Catholics the right to sit in Parliament, even if it granted them the right to vote, and Dobbs did not eliminate the king's annual salary, even if he eliminated most of the royal patronage. The king was still to call Parliament and he could still prorogue it at his pleasure. Dobbs in no way altered the basic arrangement of mixed government, keeping king, Lords, and Commons intact. In short, Dobbs was no republican visionary; he wanted reform, not revolution. Dobbs had once written a play called *The Patriot King* as a way of building nationalistic pride, yet the more he became involved in politics, the more concerned he was that constitutional nationalism not bring with it a lapse into democratic excess. "The Volunteers have been saviours, but it is also in their power to be the destroyers of their country," he warned. At that point it seems that Dobb's warning was unnecessary. That his proposal had no chance of passing testifies to the moderate tendencies of this extra-parliamentary group.[37]

The Dungannon delegates called for a Grand National Convention to assemble at the Royal Exchange in Dublin on 10 November. Volun-

---

37. Quote from Dobbs, *History,* 151; proposed reform in Francis Dobbs, *The True Principles of Government, applied to the Irish Consititution in A Code of Laws* (Dublin: J. Chambers, 1783). Dobbs's play *The Patriot King: or Irish Chief. A Tragedy* (London: J. Bew, 1774), enjoyed a brief run in Dublin's Smock Alley Theatre in 1773. It was altered somewhat before Dobbs had it published.

teers in the other three provinces reaffirmed most of the Dugannon resolutions and supported the call for a national convention. Delegates from the Leinster Volunteers had met in the Royal Exchange in October and determined that "the present state of the representation of the people of this kingdom requires to be reformed" because the constitution could not be returned to "its original purity" without "a more equal representaton of the people in Parliament."[38] One of the delegates, Peter Burrowes, moved that an explicit resolution calling for the Catholic franchise be included. When other delegates rose to object, it was decided to postpone consideration of that question until the larger group met.[39]

The site of the national meeting was changed from the Royal Exchange to the Rotunda, which could better accommodate the one hundred ninety or so delegates expected to attend. The earl of Charlemont presided and five other peers attended. Henry Flood, John Forbes, Edward Newenham, George Ogle, and fifty-five other members of Commons were elected as delegates, though some undoubtedly did not participate.[40]

Desultory meetings dragged on from 10 November to 2 December. As it turned out, the delegates had difficulty agreeing on anything beyond the fact that they wanted some sort of parliamentary reform. There were those wanting to assist Catholics. Ever since the first Dungannon

---

38. *Hibernian Magazine* 13 (October 1783): 558. For a sympathetic look at the Volunteers and the defense by some of them of Catholic rights, see Patrick Rogers, *The Irish Volunteers and Catholic Emancipation* (London: Burns, Oates and Washbourne, 1934).

39. *The History of the Proceedings and Debates of the Volunteer Delegates of Ireland, on the Subject of a Parliamentary Reform* (Dublin: W. Porter, 1784), 19–23, for Burrowes and the Catholic issue.

40. Ibid., for the Grand National Convention; and Kelly, "Irish Parliamentary Reform," appendix, 338–42, for a list of the M.P.s elected to attend the 1784 and 1785 conventions as well as the first assembly in 1783. Also see Grattan, Memoirs, 3:472–87 (appendix) for the six who surrendered borough control, though in Flood's case, it must be noted, Flood was giving up his claim to the right of control, not control itself—that he had already lost. Even though Charlemont supposedly gave up control of his borough, he still dominated the selection of M.P.s there. In fact, he offered a seat to Richard Sheridan in 1790 and said nothing about having consulted the electors first. And, as with M.P.s in earlier years, it was clear that he expected Sheridan to share his "Whig" view (see Hardy, *Charlemont*, 2:318–20). Furthermore, a couple of the others did not have full control of the boroughs whose "control" they gave up. Sir Vesey Colclough, another of the six, was charged with election fraud for trying to get a candidate elected, interestingly enough, in November 1783, when he had forsworn such things—see *House of Commons Journal*, 11:239. Thus it is difficult to know exactly what these six men did beyond taking a symbolic stand. For the convention see the very opinionated account in Jonah Barrington, *The Rise and Fall of the Irish Nation* (New York: D. & J. Sadlier, 1885; orig. ed., 1833), 276–304, and the more balanced assessments in Kelly, "Irish Parliamentary Reform," 81–106, and R. B. McDowell, "Parliamentary Independence," in T. W. Moody and W. E. Vaughan, eds., *A New History of Ireland*, vol. 4 (Oxford: Clarendon Press, 1986), 265–75.

meeting in February 1782, some of them had been urging relaxation of the penal laws and a resolution supporting freedom of conscience. Others, as at the Leinster meeting the month before, preferred to defer the Catholic question, despite the fact that Catholics had for several years been joining a few Volunteer companies. George Ogle, who seemed to be concerned primarily with keeping the proceedings restrained, turned the issue of delegates being bound by their electors to his advantage by arguing that he had no instructions to discuss the Catholic matter. Charlemont, Flood, and four others ostensibly gave up control of boroughs they had dominated as patrons, but Flood, and more particularly Charlemont, concentrated on not doing anything that would offend or threaten Parliament. And Flood had not changed his ideas about the relationship between M.P.s and their constituents. He would soon be preoccupied with buying himself a seat in the British Parliament, and he did not seem to be overly worried about representing his English constituents.[41]

That the Grand National Convention met at all was offensive enough to many M.P.s. Those not offended by the meeting itself could have been put off by the behavior of some delegates, most conspicuously that of the bishop of Derry. Earl of Bristol as well as Church of Ireland prelate, the bishop of Derry was bombastic and eccentric. Outspoken advocate of easing Catholic restrictions and self-styled populist, he expected to dominate the proceedings, and he glowered when Charlemont, not he, took the chair. He had arrived in Dublin in great finery: dressed in purple, transported to the Rotunda in a six-horse carriage driven by liveried servants and escorted by his own little group of dragoons. He even stopped at Parliament House on his way to the Rotunda to give M.P.s a chance to come outside and pay their respects. He made a great spectacle of himself while in Dublin but left before the convention closed, frustrated that neither his personal ambitions nor his reform plans had been satisfied. He was a strange and rather unconvincing spokesman for the people.

The bishop was not alone in being disappointed at how little was accomplished. Still, if the proposed changes were not sweeping, they were hardly inconsequential. After much haggling and some decisive maneuvering by Flood, the delegates with stamina to remain approved resolutions calling for triennial parliaments, revised borough boundaries,

---

41. See the letters from the duke of Chandos to Flood of 13 and 22 April 1784, and Flood to Chandos of 10 and 15 April 1784, in the Flood Correspondence, Add. MS. 22,930, BL. Flood's attitudes had not changed much since he first sought a seat in the British Parliament. See his letter in ibid. of 9 February 1769 to Frederick Campbell.

elimination of placemen and pensioners, residency requirements for all voters, extension of the franchise to all Protestant freeholders satisfying the residency requirement, and an oath to be sworn by all members of Commons that they had not sold their vote to obtain their seat. They were not by this oath obligated to follow instructions or to consider themselves "trustees" of the people. A residency requirement for M.P.s themselves was not even considered, the Catholic question was postponed, and no clear procedures for eliminating rotten boroughs or establishing freemanship were passed.[42]

Those parliamentary leaders not involved with the various conventions that began at Dungannon and culminated in the national convention in Dublin had watched developments very closely. Administration men adamantly opposed giving in to external pressure. Whitehall advised the earl of Northington, a relatively new and inexperienced lord lieutenant, to keep a tight rein on Parliament and, if necessary, to arrest members of the national convention if they became too dangerous. "The Military will be at your Command, and you may use it in Defence of the Peoples' Rights, secure the Ringleaders, issue a special Commission & bring them to immediate Trial and Punishment," counseled the duke of Portland.[43] Northington did not have to go so far, because the delegates avoided making threats, they were not out to revolutionize Irish politics, and they had little support among members of the parliamentary opposition, who heretofore had been friendly to the Volunteers. "There can be little room for Apprehension," Northington had already assured Lord North, given the disposition of Parliament. Northington was astute enough to court Grattan as well as Yelverton, and to promote Irish manufactures, as well as annual over biennial parliamentary sessions.[44]

The earl of Mornington, normally a leader of the opposition in the House of Lords, refused to have anything to do with the Volunteers and declined to attend the national convention, despite his election as a delegate. His friend Grattan, he was confident, was "against the whole business."[45] George Ogle, he claimed, afterward "wished to God" he

---

42. Resolutions in Grattan, *Memoirs*, 3:143–46.
43. Portland to Northington, 18 October 1783, Northington Letter-Book, Add. MS. 38,716, BL.
44. Northington to North, 23 September 1783, in ibid; also see Northington to Charles James Fox, 17 November 1783, in ibid., where Northington again expresses his confidence that government had nothing to fear from the convention.
45. Mornington to W. W. Grenville, 15 September 1783, in HMC, *The Manuscripts of J. B. Fortescue*, 10 vols. (London: Eyre and Spottiswoode, 1892–1927), 1:221.

had not taken part in the proceedings at the Rotunda. Ogle and others were "embarrassed beyond imagination" because "they find their characters of no consideration in the Convention which, like death, levels all distinctions."⁴⁶ Although he sat as president of the convention, Charlemont thought that the activities of the Volunteers had become "exceptionable, impudent and dangerous." He feared that their agitating would produce "civil contention." As nominal commander-in-chief he agreed to preside over the national convention, but he confessed that he stayed involved only to act as a moderating force, as did William Brownlow and other M.P.s who were also delegates. "As a true friend to liberty I abhor democracy," Charlemont later wrote; the Volunteers, he worried, were dragging the country down the road to democracy by setting themselves up as a rival source of popular power.⁴⁷

Privately Grattan may have felt as Mornington said; publicly he did not condemn the national convention and neither did Ogle. Perhaps, as Portland observed to Northington, because Grattan rose to power as a popular figure, a tribune of the people, he was trapped, his popularity proving to be a liability. Nevertheless, Grattan did not oppose reform, so he supported Edward Newenham's motion in Commons on 29 November that Parliament pass a bill "for the more equal representation of the people." This was not the first time Newenham had introduced such a motion. What made this one different is that Newenham was at the same moment a delegate to the Rotunda convention. On this day he wore his Volunteer uniform in Commons, as did Henry Flood, who seconded the motion and explained and defended what had been done by the conventioneers. Flood then formally introduced a reform bill, thereby linking his actions at the Rotunda with parliamentary business.

Although barely a month had passed since they had exchanged insults on the floor of Commons and come close to dueling, Grattan sided with Flood. Yelverton and Daly, Grattan's brother-in-law Gervase Parker Bushe, and his longtime friend Hercules Langrishe did not. According to Francis Hardy, who voted with Grattan on the issue, the debate was heated. "If ever a popular assembly wore the appearance of a wild and tumultuous ocean, it was on this occasion," he would reminisce.⁴⁸ Grattan argued that Commons should look beyond the source of the bill

46. Mornington to Grenville, 23 November 1783, in ibid., 1:224–25.
47. HMC, *Charlemont*, 1:136. For similar fears of extraparliamentary political agitation, see the essay of "Junius Hibernicus," *Freeman's Journal*, 28 February 1782.
48. Quote from Hardy, *Charlemont*, 2:136; Newenham's motion on 11 June 1782 is in the Irish Parliamentary Debates, vol. 28, container 11, p. 11, and for November 1783 on p. 172.

being presented. "I am glad to investigate the subject, let it come from what quarter it may."[49] His oldest friends and closest associates did not agree, even if many of his onetime colleagues in the old Monks of St. Patrick did.

Yelverton joined Langrishe in resenting reform being thrust at Parliament from an "armed assembly" on the tip of a "bayonet." Daly denounced Flood as a "turbulent demagogue" and warned that the Volunteers were "advancing to anarchy and destruction."[50] William Molyneux, namesake of his more famous relative, and a few others tried, like Flood and Grattan and even Ogle and Brownlow, to argue that the need for reform should take priority over the source of the motion. They were out of step with the majority. Although few denied that reform was desirable, most concluded that the Volunteers, knowingly or not, were subverting the very constitution they professed to be upholding by attempting to coerce Parliament. The House refused overwhelmingly to receive Flood's bill. Moreover, a very solid majority thought it necessary to declare "that the House will maintain its just rights and privileges against all incroachments whatsoever."[51] The Volunteer uniform, once a badge of pride to so many M.P.s and worn by Grattan when he made his April 1780 motion for a declaration of right, had taken on a new symbolism to men like Yelverton, who had donned it in years past but would no more.

---

49. Grattan, ed., *Speeches*, 1:194.
50. *The Parliamentary Register: or, History of the Proceedings and Debates of the House of Commons of Ireland*, 17 vols. (Dublin: James Moore, 1782–1801), 2:264, for Daly; pp. 225–264 for a summary of the debate; also see Mornington to Grenville, 30 November 1783, in HMC, *Fortescue*, 1:225.
51. The difficulty of knowing the vote after the debate reflects the larger difficulty of documenting much of what went on during this period in Irish history. The *House of Commons Journal*, 11:144, gives the vote as 77 to 157 in favor of receiving Flood's bill, and 150 to 68 in favor of making the statement about the rights of Commons; the *Parliamentary Register*, 2:264, gives the votes as 49 to 158, and 150 to 68, resp.; Grattan's *Memoirs*, 3:150, lists the votes as 77 to 150, and 150 to 60. In the latter case, the names of those voting for and against the first motion (receiving Flood's bill) are listed. There are 81 names instead of 77 in the "for" category, and 174 rather than 150 "against." Thus, not only are there differences among accounts, but discrepancies within the one that is most detailed. (In the Grattan account, 11 members of the Monks of St. Patrick were listed as "for" and 7 "against.") Also see Johnston, *Great Britain and Ireland*, appendix D, 391–401, which includes the vote on Flood's November 29 motion as reported in the *Belfast Newsletter*, 2–5 December 1783. According to the list there, 41 county M.P.s were in favor, 14 were against, and 9 were absent. All of the M.P.s from boroughs controlled by the most powerful patrons (Leinster, Shannon, Ely) were opposed. Votes like this help to explain why some felt that county M.P.s were more responsive than those in boroughs and that county representation should therefore be increased and borough representation decreased.

The Limits of Democratic Reform 181

Northington stepped down as lord lieutenant in February 1784, following the collapse of the Fox-North coalition ministry. Parliament hardly paused in its business to welcome the duke of Rutland as his replacement, and the reform question came up again. Armed with petitions that called for action and were signed by freeholders in twenty-six of the thirty-two counties, Flood reopened the debate in March. Opponents to reform produced a smaller number of petitions from freeholders professing to be content to leave well enough alone. Brownlow, Newenham, Curran, and Grattan again lent Flood their support, Grattan repeating his contention that reform would be a "renovation" rather than an "innovation" in the constitution. Grattan's friend Thomas Conolly had reportedly been "violent in his indignation against the Bishop of Derry and against Reform in Parliament."[52] He no doubt voted against reform again, as almost certainly did Denis Daly and other Patriots who had taken anti-administration stands before the "Constitution" of 1782. The champions of reform did pick up a few votes, though not nearly enough to overturn the majority held by their opponents, who either professed to be friendly to the idea of reform but not in the guise it took in Flood's bill (as Gervase Parker Bushe argued) or (like John Monck Mason) rejected the need to alter borough representation, arguing, in effect, that all Irishmen were virtually represented in Parliament.[53]

Stymied in Commons, reformers outside Parliament continued to agitate. In June the freemen of Dublin asserted the right of the people to participate directly in the legislative process. They claimed "their just, inherent and unalienable privilege to *correct abuses* in the representation whenever such abuses shall have so increased as to deprive them of their constitutional share in their own government." Despite the aggressive talk, little was accomplished. A second national congress called by Dublin Volunteers in October 1784 fizzled and fell flat. Only thirteen counties and six towns nominated delegates. Fewer than one hundred men attended where three hundred had been expected. The convention disbanded after only two days and the passage of two very bland, very general resolutions. A third meeting, again in Dublin, took place in Jan-

---

52. From a characterization of Conolly in a list ca. 1784, noting M.P.s and their disposition toward the administration, reproduced in Edith M. Johnston, "Members of the Irish Parliament, 1784–7," *Proceedings of the Royal Irish Academy* 71, sect. C (1971): 139–247; quote from 176.

53. *Parliamentary Register*, 2:388–93, 402, 412–14, for petitions; 3:13–85, for debate and vote; and Grattan, ed., *Speeches*, 1:199, for Grattan statement. The vote was 159 against and 85 for Flood's motion.

uary 1785. Better attended, it nevertheless accomplished almost nothing. As James J. Kelly has noted, by then the Volunteer movement had lost its momentum and perhaps even its political soul.[54]

Grattan supported Flood in 1783 and 1784, and he may have stressed the *need* for reform rather than its *source* at that time, but by 1785 he was thoroughly disillusioned with the Volunteers. He even differentiated between the "good" and "true" Volunteers of the years before the Dungannon meeting of February 1782 and the more aggressive, disruptive Volunteers who rose up afterward. As he saw it, the Volunteers had overstepped themselves and deserved their fate. "It is said that they rescued the constitution, that they forced Parliament to assert its rights, and therefore Parliament should surrender the constitution into their hands," he pronounced in his post-mortem shortly after the failure of the third national congress. "But it is a mistake to say they forced Parliament," he corrected; "they stood at the back of Parliament, and supported its authority; and when they acted thus with Parliament they acted to their own glory; but when they attempted to dictate, they became nothing."[55]

He and other M.P.s who had once been Volunteers supported an administration-sponsored move to pass a new militia act and embarrass the Volunteers into disbanding. Onetime Volunteer colonel Luke Gardiner wrote a House resolution in February 1785 that more or less told the Volunteers to go home. The resolution, which passed overwhelmingly despite the objections of Henry Flood, thanked the Volunteers for performing their military role loyally, said nothing about their push for commercial relief or support of parliamentary independence, and closed by approving "the Conduct of those who, since the Conclusion of the War, have retired to cultivate the Blessings of Peace."[56]

The Volunteers were not without their supporters in Parliament, however. Not all of the M.P.s attending the congresses had been there to disrupt the proceedings or prevent the passage of significant resolutions, and not all were as aloof as Grattan had become by 1785. William Todd Jones, M.P. for Lisburn, published a letter to his constituents in which he stated that it was his duty (and by implication that of colleagues) to vote "in full conformity to your instructions" and to fulfill

54. Freemen of Dublin in Kelly, "Irish Parliamentary Reform," 205; and 285–91 for general account. Also see Grattan, *Memoirs*, 3:204–8.
55. Grattan, ed., *Speeches*, 1:218; account of proceedings in Kelly, "Irish Parliamentary Reform," 311–17, 324–25.
56. *House of Commons Journal*, 11:354, 18 February 1785; also the debates in the *Parliamentary Register*, 4:262–97. The resolution carried, 179 to 57.

his "trust" to speak in Commons "only with your mouth."[57] A handful of others had said much the same during the November 1783 and March 1784 debates. They accepted their status as "trustees" and "delegates" bound by the will of their constituents. Even if they remained a distinct minority in Commons, they had won a few county and borough seats in the general election of 1783.

Older newspapers like the *Hibernian Journal* and *Freeman's Journal* were lukewarm in their support of reform, but newer, more liberal papers like the *Dublin Evening Post* and *Volunteer Journal* were enthusiastically behind the reformers. So too were numerous pamphleteers. "Neither servile nor licentious," wrote one, "the *people* may now acquire their *just rank* in the government, and by recurring to the *true principles* of the constitution, mark out the proper limits of their *freedom,* and restore the *long lost ballance* of power betweens the *governors* and the *governed.*"[58]

Furthermore, English reformers encouraged their Irish counterparts. As early as 1780 John Cartwright had urged Francis Dobbs to use the Volunteers to push reform rather than trust Parliament to reform itself.[59] Volunteer leaders like Dobbs and William Drennan kept up their correspondence with Cartwright and other leaders like Christopher Wyvill and John Jebb. A few English reformers watched Irish affairs with great concern as well as interest, feeling that the success of their own movement in part hinged on what happened in Ireland. Jebb determined that "our fate will in a great measure depend upon" the Dungannon Convention scheduled to take place in September 1783.[60] If, Jebb counseled Dobbs, the delegates there carried out their task, "unborn generations will have reason to look" to the Dungannon meeting "as the Era of the establishment of true freedom."[61]

Jebb's own ideas had changed; he was more radical than he had been just three or four years before. In 1779 he had felt that M.P.s should be able to vote their consciences, even when they disagreed with their constituents. By 1783 he had decided that M.P.s in the British and Irish parliaments should resign their seats if they could not vote as instructed. He also became completely disenchanted with borough representation

---

57. W. T. Jones, Esq., *A Letter to the Electors of the Borough of Lisburn* (Cork: W. Flyn, 1784), 3.
58. W. W. Seward, *The Rights of the People Asserted and the Necessity of a More Equal Representation in Parliament Stated and Proved* (Dublin: P. Byrne, 1783), 7.
59. Cartwright to Dobbs, 12 January 1780, Dobbs Letters, MS. 2251, NLI.
60. Jebb to John Forbes, 15 August 1783, Forbes Letters, MS. 10,713, NLI.
61. Jebb to Dobbs, 15 August 1783, Dobbs Letters, MS. 2251, NLI.

and was an advocate of annual parliamentary elections in Britain as well as Ireland. He went so far as to call for "universal suffrage" for all Irish males, Catholics included, "not disqualified by mental imbecility or criminal conduct."[62] With advice like this to draw on, the Volunteers could well feel that what they advocated was not radical or revolutionary.

Nonetheless, what they intended was far too radical for their critics. There were those, of course, who denounced the whole idea that reform was necessary or that, if it was, it could come from outside Parliament. Some Irish reformers pointed to the American example to show that the "people" could be trusted; others countered that the United States was teetering on the edge of insolvency and anarchy, a new nation with a grim future.[63] Still others attacked the very notion that the "people" were entitled to political rights or that any freedoms could exist outside of society and those recognized by government. "Weak men," complained one of Charlemont's friends, "are led away by some abstract ideas of what they call the common rights of mankind." Such thinking was nonsense, he believed, because "the most perfect state of civil society implies that certain natural rights must be surrendered for acquired rights."[64] Even those professing to be sympathetic to the idea of reform recommended that Parliament be allowed to lead the way. If the reformers refused, there would be a negative reaction to their meddling. "For, as most Men love and venerate established Constitutions, they will think it safer to dwell in the old Mansion, though out of Repair," one author advised, "than hazard pulling the Building down over their Heads by modern fanciful Improvements."[65]

English reformers were even less popular in Westminster than the Volunteers were in the Irish Parliament. Talk of M.P.s as trustees or delegates proved worrisome; the "doctrine of instruction" was, as J. R. Pole noted, odious to most British politicians.[66] Rockingham favored economic reform and Edmund Burke's bill to reduce placemen and pen-

---

62. John Jebb, *Letters Addressed to the Volunteers of Ireland, on the Subject of a Parliamentary Reform* (London: W. Richardson, 1784), 10.

63. *A Reform of the Irish House of Commons Considered* (Dublin: Henry Watts, 1783), 18–19.

64. William Campbell to Charlemont, 9 October 1984, in HMC, *Charlemont* 2:7–8.

65. *An Address to the Dungannon and Leinster Volunteer Delegates on the Matter of Parliamentary Reform* (Dublin: R. Moncriefe, 1783), 27.

66. J. R. Pole, *Political Representation in England & the Origins of the American Revolution* (London: Macmillan and Co., 1966), 412, 419, 441, and 541–52, on a "fallacy" in the theory. See chap. 2, n. 37, for Derek Hirst's study of the modest beginning of "instruction" during the 1640s in England.

sioners, but he did not favor the type of sweeping political changes championed by the Yorkshire Association or writers like John Jebb. Charles James Fox seemed to be friendly to reform before he formed his coalition ministry with Lord North. And yet, once in power, his government showed a "general anti-reform tendency."[67] When William Pitt the younger moved in May 1783 to add one hundred county and city seats and gradually to reduce the number of borough M.P.s, his motion was defeated roundly. As head of his own ministry, Pitt tried again two years later and lost by almost as wide a margin. He therefore "put aside thoughts of parliamentary reform as too partisan for the present."[68]

Pitt stayed on as chief minister. His seeming abandonment of the cause did not endear him to Irish reformers, just as his handling of commercial relief alienated Henry Grattan and other leaders in the Irish Parliament. Although early on Pitt had supposed that political reform would have to come in Ireland as well as Britain, and "the sooner the better," eventually his Irish policy was similar to that of his predecessors.[69] Charles James Fox had been very firm in telling Northington to resist any attempt by the Volunteers to impose their will.[70] Northington's successor, the duke of Rutland, received the same instructions from Pitt. Parliamentary reform would be "so ruinous to the prosperity of Ireland, that I cannot doubt of the good sense of the Parliament on this occasion, or of their disposition to reject so crude and undigested a proposal," Lord Sydney, the home secretary, wrote to Rutland.[71] Rutland did not need to be convinced. Seeing firsthand the divisions in the Irish Parliament and the Volunteers' inclinations, he had already advised Pitt that "Government cannot embark in the measure without the risk of absolute ruin."[72] Pitt, whose commitment to Irish parliamentary re-

67. Christie, *Wilkes, Wyvill and Reform,* 179.
68. Watson, *Reign of George III,* 278; general account in Christie, *Wilkes, Wyvill and Reform,* 185–221; and the views of Grattan's son of what this all meant for Ireland in Grattan, *Memoirs,* 3:102–3; and John Jebb to John Forbes, 22 November 1785, Forbes Letters, MS. 10,713, NLI.
69. Pitt to Rutland, 4 December 1784, in the *Correspondence between the Right Hon. William Pitt and Charles Duke of Rutland, Lord Lieutenant of Ireland, 1781–1787* (London: A. Spottiswoode, 1842), 47.
70. See Fox's letter to John Burgoyne of 7 November 1783 in Kelly, "Irish Parliamentary Reform," 72; and Fox to Northington, 1 November 1783, in Grattan, *Memoirs,* 3:106–12.
71. HMC, *The Manuscripts of His Grace the Duke of Rutland,* 4 vols. (London: Eyre and Spottiswoode, 1888–1905), 3:79, Sydney to Rutland, 9 March 1784. Also see the note for a meeting on 10 January 1785 in the Sydney Papers, vol. II, packet P, MS. 52, NLI, where the leaders of Pitt's cabinet made it clear that they were opposed to reform, at least for the time being.
72. HMC, *Rutland,* 3:148, Rutland to Pitt, 14 November 1784; and Rutland to Sydney, 18 September 1785, ibid., 3:242, on the failure of "the instruments of faction" to stir up the country.

form had never been as strong as his desire to reform Westminster, joined Rutland in feeling relieved that the Volunteers were losing their political potency and that Flood's reform bill did not carry in 1785, just as it had failed the preceding two years.

The Irish Commons occasionally received petitions during the closing months of 1784 and first part of 1785 urging it not to put aside reform. Most of those petitions were very moderate in tone, written by freeholders in various counties who were careful to pledge their attachment to the constitution, the empire, and the existing forms of government. The freeholders of County Cork expressed their desire to "lessen aristocratic influence" in Commons and restore balance to the constitution, yet they avoided making their petition read like a demand. Frustrated M.P.s could be harsher. William Brownlow rebuked his colleagues because they lacked "virtue enough to reform" the defects in their House. While most M.P.s probably did not share Hercules Langrishe's view that Flood wanted to eliminate "evils that do not exist," they voted down John Forbes's pension bill as well as Flood's measure.

Indeed, the only bill that passed Parliament in 1785 touching on reform was limited to improving procedures for registering freemen. It did not require boroughs to increase the number of voting burgesses or oblige M.P.s to become residents. First suspended, then amended, and finally enlarged, this modest law was not effective for another decade.[73] Moreover, the "reform" that resulted in annual parliamentary sessions beginning in 1784 had been agreed to by Whitehall only as a way of better managing the Irish House of Commons. As the earl of Northington, lord lieutenant at the time, observed, more frequent sittings would enable him and his successors to "marshall the phalanx" of government men.[74] Therefore what might have appeared to Grattan as a concession to Irish needs or rights was viewed from an entirely different perspective by his political opponents.

Ireland remained almost as unchanged by its reform movement of the 1780s as England had been by its reform groups, though in Ireland, because of the Volunteers, the reform impulse had been momentarily

---

73. County Cork petition in *House of Commons Journal*, 11:416; others in ibid., 11:249, 270. For Brownlow and Langrishe see *Parliamentary Register*, 5:189, during the 12 May 1785 debates over Flood's reform bill, which was defeated on the first reading, 112 to 60. See ibid., 5:188–96 for the debate summary. For the freemen registry law, see *The Statutes at Large*, 20 vols.(Dublin: George Grierson, 1786–1801), 13:361–67 (25 George III c. 52), and the extensive revisions in 1795 in ibid., 17:536–69 (35 George III c. 29).

74. See Northington's long letter to Charles James Fox of 17 November 1783 in the Northington Letter Book, Add. MS. 38,716 BL.

stronger. Pitt probably realized that he and the Irish government were lucky that there were no clashes between regular troops and Volunteers. The Irish public traditionally disliked having regulars about, and there had been a few near-misses where Volunteers and regulars crossed paths and almost crossed swords, but no blood was shed.[75] It was only natural that some Volunteers, who by far outnumbered the regulars, even in Dublin, would want to test their strength. Despite this, there is no evidence that any military confrontation was ever intended; there might have been some jostling and name-calling, but little else.

Alarmists warned Dublin Castle and Whitehall that something more was brewing, that the Irish were about to follow the Americans in rising up and asserting their independence, with Volunteers leading the way. They could not separate mob activity—an old Dublin tradition—and the recurrence of Whiteboy disturbances in the countryside from the Volunteer movement. Occasionally crowds would mill about College Green; in April 1784 a mob burst into the Commons chambers looking for, and threatening the lives of, any M.P.s they felt stood in the way of commercial relief. An anonymous correspondent told the king that "the people at large" would not be satisfied with a reformed Parliament or protective duties; they "now think and openly talk of nothing but absolute Independence, and an entire separation from Great Britain."[76] Just two months later, in August 1784, Lord Lieutenant Northington was advised that the more middling people had developed a taste for power, that Catholics and Presbyterians were joining together and felt "a Silly pride as *Irishmen*." They had combined in the Volunteers and, not content to have an independent parliament, they planned "to awe Great Britain into acquiescence in all their measures, and Bully the rest of the World to take their Manufactures whether they chuse it or not."[77]

---

75. For one narrowly avoided incident between regulars and the Volunteers, see Beresford, ed., *Correspondence of Beresford*, 1:125, John Blaquiere to John Beresford, 23 February 1780; for an altercation between civilians and regulars, see the *Dublin Journal*, 10 March 1778.

76. From an unsigned letter to the king dated 5 June 1784, from Dublin, in the Sydney Papers, vol. 2, packet O, MS. 52, NLI. As Kelly, "Irish Parliamentary Reform," 221–35, pointed out, alarmists were not ignored; indeed, "The Castle were permitting the evident similarity of Ireland in the early 1780s with America in the 1770s to determine their thinking" (231). See Mornington to Grenville, 23 November 1783, HMC, *Fortescue*, 1:223–24, and Rutland to Sydney, 8 April 1784, in HMC, *Rutland*, 3:86, for worries about mob violence; and John Beresford to John Robinson, 11 April 1784, in Beresford, ed., *Corres. of Beresford*, 1:253–56, for an example of alarmist thinking.

77. From a long report submitted by a Mr. Sheridan—probably Charles Francis Sheridan—to Northington dated August 1784 in the Bolton Papers, MS. 16,350, NLI. If the author was in fact Charles Sheridan, this report illustrates how estranged he was from the Volunteers by this time (or, like Grattan, he distinguished between the good and "true" Volunteers of 1782 and the later perversion of them).

Those suspecting that the Volunteers had mischief in mind could have read William Drennan's 1784 *Letters of Orellana* and easily believed the worst. Drennan admired Joseph Pollock's 1779 "Owen Roe O'Nial" series and styled himself "an Irish Helot" in imitation of Pollock's Briton-Irish, Spartan-Helot analogy. Drennan nevertheless far outstripped Pollock in his criticisms of British and Irish leaders, and in his urging the people to rise in protest. Disappointed at the poor attendance that crippled the second Volunteer congress in October 1784, he greeted his readers as "Fellow Slaves." There were only two conditions of life, he preached: slavery and freedom. The Irish were slaves and deserved to remain so if they did not press their rights more vigorously.

Drennan's arguments also displayed his ambivalence. He did not explicitly urge the people to resort to force; on the contrary. Yet he implied that force would be their only recourse if government continued to be unresponsive. He claimed that he only wanted to improve the existing system, yet he was bitter in his condemnations of the mixed arrangement of king, Lords, and Commons. He conflated natural rights with rights held under the British constitution, implying that the former, which the Irish had been denied, took precedence over the latter. He condemned William Pitt as an opportunist with no real concern for Irish freedoms, and he even needled Grattan for losing his zeal in the cause. "Free Trade" and an "Independent Constitution," scoffed Drennan, are "two of the greatest CURSES, I am free to say, that ever can befall a country, unless they be crowned, and that speedily too, with Parliamentary Reform."[78]

The administration regarded Drennan as a bull in a political china shop. His ideas were those of the Volunteer movement pushed to their logical extreme. Fortunately for the Castle, few were willing to go that far. Although the Volunteers had been politicized early and eagerly, many of the Volunteers themselves were reluctant to press too hard, to insist on too much. Some did not want to "instruct" M.P.s and dictate terms to Parliament, just as some preferred to avoid criticizing leaders like Grattan and those among the opposition in the British Parliament

78. [William Drennan], *Letters of Orellana, an Irish Helot, to the Seven Northern Counties, not represented in the National Assembly of Delegates, held at Dublin, October, 1784, for obtaining a more Equal Representation of the People in the Parliament of Ireland* (Dublin: J. Chambers and T. Heery, 1785). The language, of course, was more inflammmatory than most, but the basic message was not different from more moderate assertions; for example, that of the Clanricarde Volunteers in their resolution of thanks to Henry Grattan in 1782 when they stated that "though they would die in defence of *British honour*, they would first live or perish in support of *Irish freedom*" (in Grattan, ed., *Misc. Works*, 229). Thus their loyalty to Britain was qualified; Ireland came first, as Grattan himself had said in Commons.

who appeared to be friendly.[79] And some might have been swayed by critics who pointed out that parliamentary borough seats had been held by the most independent members of Commons, the very men who had defended their rights. What would happen to the Henry Grattans, they asked, if boroughs were changed too much or eliminated altogether? One tract supposedly written to show the corruption of borough politics and the need for more county representation actually proved just the opposite: county M.P.s were often less independent than those sitting for boroughs.[80]

Critics of reform probably agreed that it was too fanciful to think that all men, even if they held property, should have a right to vote or, beyond that, sit in Commons. Even Drennan had his democratic limits. In *Orellana* he wrote as a champion of the "people," yet he was for gradual, not immediate, Catholic emancipation, and he did not think that Catholics were ready to be allowed back into the Irish Parliament. Leading Catholics were not ready to insist on a complete restoration of rights anyway: for instance, Charles O'Conor did not approve "of the Intemperance of some modern Writers, on our modern political Questions."[81]

Notwithstanding this criticism, O'Conor, for thirty years a defender of the good name of Irish Catholics, must have been heartened to see that some Irish Protestants had seemingly lost their fear of "Papists." Grattan, Daly, Bushe, Ogle, and Langrishe all supported the 1782 reforms allowing Catholics more freedom to own and rent land, and to meet as religious bodies. In his foreword to the 1786 edition of John Curry's history of Ireland, first published over a decade before, O'Conor conceded that Molyneux and Swift had been "great patriots," but they lived during an age when religious prejudices were pronounced, so pronounced that they were not free of prejudice themselves. Now, he hoped,

---

79. See McDowell, "Colonial Nationalism," in Moody and Vaughan, eds., *New History of Ireland*, 4:228–29; and Hill, "William Drennan," 1:34–35, for the reluctance of some Volunteers to become politicized. Also see the case of Richard Wilson, who was forced to resign from the County Dublin Light Dragoons because he was politically out of step with the majority (Irish Volunteers, MS. 212, Gilbert Library).

80. Falkland, *Parliamentary Representation: Being a Political and Critical Review of all the Counties, Cities, and Boroughs of the Kingdom of Ireland, with Regard to the State of their Representation* (Dublin, 1790), usually attributed to the same John Robert Scott who wrote *Principal Characters* (see chap. 4, n. 6). Also see Grattan, *Memoirs*, 3:340, for an illustration of how Grattan continued to hunt for boroughs where he could win a seat. He assumed that the people would accept him, whether he was a resident or not. His behavior did not seem to bother electors, even as late as 1790, when he switched from Charlemont's borough to one of the seats for Dublin city.

81. O'Conor to Charles Vallancey, 13 October 1784, Bolton Papers, MS. 16,350, NLI.

things would be different; there truly could be one Irish society, one Irish identity.[82] Others shared his hopes.

Volunteer and M.P. William Todd Jones was convinced that Protestants had nothing to fear from Catholics. He contended that Catholics had contributed their share to the defense of Irish freedoms, citing with approval the petition to Charles I from Catholic Confederates in 1643 and demands made by the "Patriot" Parliament in 1689. Catholics were not servile and subversive. He believed that Catholic property owners should be as entitled to vote as Protestant freemen.[83]

Jones had his sentiments published, but they did not enjoy the circulation achieved by William Crawford's two-volume history of Ireland published in 1783. Crawford, chaplain for the First Tyrone Volunteer Regiment, dedicated his tome to the earl of Charlemont and wrote it as a series of "letters." He lauded Molyneux's *Case* and Swift's "Drapier" and emphasized the rights to which Ireland had been entitled since the time of Henry II. He was more strident than Molyneux (though not more strident than Swift). He condemned Henry's invasion as an "unjust" act fortunately followed by a voluntary compact between Henry and most of the Irish lords. Even then, the English had behaved cruelly by imposing Poynings' Law as "an instrument of despotism," and later by adding the utterly unconstitutional Declaratory Act.[84] In passing a Woolens Act, the British Parliament had treated the Irish as "slaves" without "honor, without laws and constitution."[85] Crawford celebrated the Volunteers as a "gallant band of patriots," the true champions of Irish rights, but he did not thereby impugn the Irish Parliament. He also tried to be evenhanded when dealing with the repeal-renunciation controversy. He did not mention Darcy's *Argument* or the Patriot Parliament of 1689, although he cited approvingly the 1644 "Declaration." Moreover, he commented favorably on the Catholic Confederates of the 1640s and gave them a place within the Irish constitutional nationalist tradition.[86] He depicted the divisions separating Protestants from Catholics as tragic and "hostile to the benevolent spirit of the Gospel," and he called for a restoration of Catholic civil and religious liberties.[87]

82. O'Conor in John Curry, *An Historical and Critical Review of the Civil Wars of Ireland*, 2 vols. (Dublin: Luke White, 1786; orig. ed., 1775), 1:iv.
83. Jones, *Letter to the Electors*, 16–24.
84. Crawford, *History*, 2:26, for Henry II's "unjust invasion"; 1:110–123, for the extension of rights by Henry II, including the right to an independent parliament; 2:11 for Poynings' Law; and 2:273, 281, for the Declaratory Act.
85. Ibid., 2:242.
86. Ibid., 2:340, for Volunteers as "gallant" patriots; 2:53–54, for Catholic Confederates.
87. Ibid., 2:37; also see 1:vii–viii.

The Limits of Democratic Reform 191

Over one thousand subscribers were listed in Crawford's *History*, and they included most leaders in the Irish Parliament, administration men as well as members of the opposition.[88] The subscribers did not necessarily share the author's views, however. Crawford might have been too harsh in his criticism of Britain for some readers. His friendly view of Charles Lucas might not have been popular with others. He was vague in saying what he meant by a restoration of Catholic rights. That he brought those "rights" up at all could have been disturbing enough to Charlemont, who was Crawford's patron but no advocate of Catholic political participation.

Others were friendlier to the Catholics than Charlemont was, but their tolerance was not based on real acceptance. The idea that Catholicism would eventually lose its appeal and fade as a social force was hard for some to shake. Peter Burrowes' recommendations to ease Catholic restrictions came nearly fifty years after those of George Berkeley and Samuel Madden, yet the underlying assumption was the same: a liberal policy would lift the Catholic sense of persecution and pave the way for a unified, *Protestant,* Ireland. Catholics owning property could vote, they could even hold office, Burrowes believed, because toleration would all but eliminate religious divisions.[89]

Therefore, not only were most Protestants delaying Catholic equality for the present and making the Catholic future unsure, they were still denying Catholics a legitimate part in the past. The footdragging of Volunteers and the parliamentary opposition, no matter how understandable given the times, made the achievement of a true sense of Irish unity difficult for the next generation. O'Conor's dream that there would be one Irish society and one Irish identity was not soon to be fulfilled. When Catholics eventually did gain equality, they were naturally tempted to

---

88. The list of subscribers included about a dozen of the Monks of St. Patrick (notably Ogle, Yelverton, Hussey Burgh, Newenham, Pollock, and of course Charlemont). Henry Flood and Francis Dobbs were also listed; Grattan was one of the few opposition leaders who was not. Sir John Blaquiere and John Beresford were also subscribers, which seems somewhat odd, given their defensiveness about the British tie. This was history as polemic; at the same time, Crawford did go back to the sources in some cases, and his views were better supported than were those of Thomas Leland a decade earlier. J. C. Beckett is no doubt right in noting that Irish historical writing during this period was not overly accomplished, but at least Crawford, whom Beckett does not mention, showed an ability to escape some prejudices that Leland could not. For Beckett see his "Introduction: Eighteenth-Century Ireland," in Moody and Vaughan, eds., *New History of Ireland*, 4:lx–lxv.

89. [Peter Burrowes], *Plain Arguments in Defence of the People's Absolute Dominion over the Constitution. In Which the Question of Roman Catholic Enfranchisement is Fully Considered* (Dublin: Thomas Webb, 1784); rebutted in [John Johnson], *Strictures on a Late Pamphlet entitled Plain Arguments, &c.* (Dublin: P. Byrne, 1784).

rewrite Irish history and turn the tables on the Anglo-Irish Protestant elite. Protestant delay of the inevitable not only jeopardized the place of Protestants in the Ireland of the future, it rendered precarious their place in the eventual national historical memory.

The Volunteers were no more capable of speaking with one voice than were members of the parliamentary opposition. They divided among themselves, not as dramatically as Flood and Grattan had split Commons in 1782, but the divisions were real and damaging enough. Francis Dobbs was more or less chased out for having accepted a commission in the "Fencibles," an administration-sponsored alternative to the Volunteers. Joseph Pollock struck more radical leaders like James Napper Tandy as being too weak and equivocating.

Tandy was part of a distinct minority, however. Few—very few—Volunteers ever wanted to force change at gunpoint, as a young Archibald Hamilton Rowan had recommended to a most unsympathetic Charlemont.[90] Fewer still condemned as beyond salvage the system of mixed government under which they had been raised or the imperial tie with Britain that caused them such frustration. The Volunteers had a middle class core and volunteering broadened the political horizons of men heretofore on the fringe of public life. Yet the Volunteers as a whole never turned on the landed aristocracy and they retained a certain amount of deference to the old elite.

Furthermore, parliamentary reform generated a great deal of interest, yet not as much as parliamentary independence or commercial relief. The leaders of Parliament claimed that they had secured their independence themselves and that they had led the fight for Irish trading rights. Some Volunteers disagreed with that view, but most would not break completely with Parliament over the question of who deserved the most credit for change. Besides, since some M.P.s were involved in volunteering even through the disappointing days of 1784 and 1785, there was never a time when M.P.s and Volunteers were completely distinct, rival groups.[91]

For every Drennan posing as a "Helot," there were other pamphleteers urging moderation and reaffirmation of imperial ties.[92] Still, it was

---

90. William H. Drummond, ed., *The Autobiography of Archibald Hamilton Rowan* (Shannon: Irish University Press, 1972; orig. ed., 1840), 117.

91. See Smyth, "The Volunteer Movement in Ulster: Background and Development, 1784-5" (Ph.D. dissertation, Queen's University of Belfast, 1974), 2–23, 154–79; and idem, "The Volunteers and Parliament, 1779–1784," in Bartlett and Hayton, eds., *Penal Era and Golden Age*, 113–36; and Kelly, "Irish Parliamentary Reform," 129–30, 239–40.

92. Rev. William Butler Odell's *Impartial Thoughts on Party and Parliamentary Re-*

The Limits of Democratic Reform 193

the extremists who probably caused the biggest stir among Irish M.P.s and worried British observers. The most radical had made oblique calls for revolution, for a political uprising against the "aristocratic" and "unresponsive" Irish Parliament, and a more insistent assertion of constitutional rights in the face of continued British interventionism. The *Volunteer Journal* made it policy to publish threatening pieces and hints that Ireland would some day go the way of the American colonies. Even in more moderate tracts, talk of popular sovereignty was uneasily juxtaposed with talk of the three estates in society represented by king, Lords, and Commons in government. Numerous writers concluded that the Irish Commons did not really represent the people; almost as many argued that the people were not simply one "estate" among three, because all power derived from them. The threat that they would leave behind their old allegiances and insist on something different, something more democratic, was there for fearful aristocrats to see. Yet pamphleteers wrote without seeing that, philosophically, they were republicans if not populists, so inbred were older notions of political society.

To some critical observers, even the moderates were radical; in a sense they were, though they hardly realized that fact. By the second year of his lord lieutenancy, the duke of Rutland had begun to doubt if affairs could continue as they were without some sort of eruption. On a December 1785 trip to Cork, he did not stop in Kilkenny because the residents there had warned him that they would not turn out to pay their respects. Smuggling was rampant nationwide; Whiteboys were active again in the south and west; the French, Rutland was told, had sent spies to stir up trouble; agitation for political reform and commercial relief had been put aside only temporarily.[93] More than a year earlier, Rutland

---

form (Limerick: Edward Flin, 1784) is one of the better examples of a carefully argued, moderate stance. But even many moderate pamphleteers, because they argued that reform was needed and that the people were the basis of all legitimate power, could have a more radical, even revolutionary, side to their arguments. See, for example, Andrew Doria, *A Letter to the Volunteers upon the Subject of a Parliamentary Reform* (Dublin: D. Graisberry, 1784), and Memmius, *The Voice of the People in a Letter to the Secretary of his Grace the Duke of Rutland* (Dublin: P. Byrne, 1784), both of which accept the notion that there were three estates in society but, at the same time, assert that people were the source of all legitimate power and had the right to rise up against bad government. Gracchus, *The History of the Last Sessions of Parliament, Addressed to the Right Hon. The Earl of Charlemont* (Dublin: T. Henshall, 1784), and *An Utilist to the Aggregate Body of the Irish Nation* (Dublin: J. M. Davis, 1784), had more in common with Dobbs and Drennan.

93. Rutland to Sydney, 6 December 1785, in HMC, *Rutland*, 3:264–66; also see ibid., 3:284–85, Rutland to Sydney, 27 February 1786; and Maurice J. Bric, "Priests, Parsons and Politics: The Rightboy Protest in County Cork, 1785–88," in C. H. E. Philpin, ed., *Nationalism and Popular Protest in Ireland* (Cambridge: Cambridge University Press, 1987), 163–90.

had complained to Pitt that government was "precarious" because Volunteers were pressuring Parliament into "wild and visionary schemes." Were "I to indulge a distant speculation," he ventured, "I should say that without *an union* Ireland will not be connected with Great Britain in twenty years longer."[94] To Pitt, Rutland's suggestion made perfect sense. Parliamentary union would eventually become his solution to the Irish problem.

Unhappy with Pitt's attempt at commercial relief, Grattan felt betrayed when Pitt later pressed for union. He and the other leaders of "Grattan's Parliament" in 1782 had managed to make their nationalist claims without consciously embracing revolutionary ideology. Most Volunteers, too, had styled themselves as defenders of ancient rights, reformers with the conservative goal of "renovating" the constitution rather than radicals out to "innovate." Catholics had hoped that restoration of their rights would come as part of the "renovation." Ultimately the Volunteers did not officially endorse the franchise, much less officeholding for Catholics. By 1785 and their political collapse they had barely progressed beyond their vague resolutions at Dungannon in February 1782, when the Ulstermen tentatively extended their hand in friendship.

During the 1790s it would be more difficult than ever for Catholics as well as Protestants to be nationalists defending Irish constitutional rights in the empire without turning into revolutionaries advocating independence. Some like James Napper Tandy and Theobald Wolfe Tone gave in to the revolutionary impulse. They were frustrated nonetheless. So was Henry Grattan, who clung to his ideal of an independent Irish Parliament under a restored constitution, and tried to continue being a nationalist even as he rejected revolution.

94. Rutland to Pitt, 16 June 1784, in *Correspondence between Pitt and Rutland*, 17.

CHAPTER 6

An End to "Independence"

Oh, vanished Hope! oh, transient boast!
Oh, country gained but to be lost!
Gained by a nation, raised, inspired,
By eloquence and virtue fired,
By transatlantic glory stung,
By Grattan's energetic tongue,
By Parliament that felt its trust
By Britain—terrified and just.
Lost—by thy chosen children sold;
And conquered—not by steel, but gold;
  William Drennan, 1802[1]

Aristotle outlined in his *Politics* what he thought were the three basic or "true" forms of government: monarchy, aristocracy, and democracy. If unchecked, each could devolve into a perversion of its original. The perverted form of monarchy was tyranny; for aristocracy the perversion was oligarchy; for democracy it was the devolution into anarchy. Most Irish political thinkers in the late eighteenth-century accepted Aristotle's basic theory, and a fair number of them believed that a twisted, perverted form of government was taking shape in their own land.

Leaders of the Anglo-Irish Protestant Ascendancy, disturbed by the Volunteer movement of the 1780s, were even more appalled by the United Irishmen in the 1790s. Some, perhaps remembering their Aristotle, thought that they were being plunged into anarchy, the abyss of majoritarian tyranny. The United Irishmen, like the Volunteers before them, saw themselves as the embodiment of popular will and as true

---

1. From "Independence," a passage in the longer poem "Glendalough," from R. R. Madden, ed., *Literary Remains of the United Irishmen of 1798* (Dublin: James Duffy and Sons, 1887), 42.

representatives of the people. They were convinced that the Anglo-Irish aristocracy had degenerated into an oligarchy. At the same time, the Anglo-Irish elite did not close ranks in the face of this challenge from below, seemingly illustrating Aristotle's contention that "in oligarchies there is the double danger of the oligarchs falling out among themselves and also with the people."[2] By the 1790s, the divisions splitting Irish society—divisions that followed ideological and ethnic as well as class and religious lines—were dangerously wide.

George Nugent-Temple-Grenville, marquess of Buckingham, had returned as lord lieutenant in 1787 to replace the deceased Rutland. As Earl Temple he had already served once in that post and hoped that his second Irish stay would be uneventful. At first it looked as though he would get his wish. The Volunteers had been discredited, Parliament had ceased to be agitated over the question of reform, Catholics were quiet and seemingly content for the moment, and strife over Pitt's commercial scheme had ended with Irish acceptance of compromise legislation first passed at Westminster. Rutland's administration had closed with a law and order emphasis, which was reflected in a new police act in 1786 and laws that were passed the next year to prevent "tumultuous risings," bring greater peace to the counties, and assist in collecting tithes. "I hope and believe the reign of the devil is almost finished," wrote one administration supporter.[3]

The quiet did not last. Buckingham arrived during a lull; by the time he left he had been almost deafened by the renewed political din. The clamor grew loudest during the regency crisis of 1788–89. In November 1788, a chronically ill George III lapsed into another period of mental instability. The British Parliament was more or less united in making his son, the Prince of Wales, regent in the interim, but there was a split over how much power the prince should be entitled to wield. Pitt's ministry wanted to keep his authority circumscribed; the opposition led by the duke of Portland wanted to give him full regal authority to act in his father's stead, but they could not carry the point. Portland had hoped that the prince, with full regal power, would sack Pitt and call for a new ministry to be formed.

---

2. Aristotle, *Politics*, from Richard McKeon, ed., *The Basic Works of Aristotle* (New York: Random House, 1941), 1186 (Book III, chap. 7), 1244–46 (Book V, chap. 7); quote from p. 1234 (Book V, chap. 1). I have taken the liberty of substituting "democracy" for "constitutional" and "anarchy" for "democracy" in order to simplify matters.

3. Edward Tighe to the earl of Buckinghamshire, 21 February 1787, in Historical Manuscripts Commission, *Report on the Manuscripts of the Marquis of Lothian* (London: Eyre and Spottiswoode, 1905), 432. Also see Francis Hardy, *Memoirs of the Political and Private Life of James Caulfield, Earl of Charlemont*, 2 vols. (London: T. Cadell, 1810), 2:163–65.

Never completely detached from British politics, the Irish Parliament was caught up in the competitive swirl. It mixed in the age-old Hanoverian disputes between father and son, and the jockeying for power between supporters of the king and his ministry, and an ambitious opposition. Naturally, Buckingham wanted the Irish Parliament to stay in line with the ministry. Not too surprisingly, Grattan, Yelverton, Forbes, and others jealous of Irish parliamentary prerogatives and tied (albeit loosely) to the British parliamentary opposition objected. They also disliked Buckingham and perhaps thought that the prince as regent would appoint a new lord lieutenant or at least force Pitt to recall Buckingham.

Soon after a new parliamentary session opened in February 1789, Grattan rose, warned against a "servile" imitation of the British Parliament, and urged that the Prince of Wales be recognized as regent "invested with the full regal power." To Buckingham's dismay a majority in both houses concurred with Grattan. When Buckingham refused to communicate its resolution recognizing the regency to the Prince of Wales, Parliament went ahead; members of each house (Leinster and Charlemont for Lords, Thomas Conolly and three others for Commons) hastened to deliver the resolutions personally.

Those resolutions were worded very carefully, showing that Grattan and those siding with him had constitutional as well as political considerations in mind. "No man, I hope, will presume to affirm," stressed Grattan, that a regent "made by English statute, has any authority in this kingdom, unless he shall be also made regent in Ireland by the consent and advice of the Lords Spiritual and Temporal, and the Commons of Ireland."[4] In Grattan's view, the regency issue was connected to Irish parliamentary independence and the "Constitution of 1782." Charles Francis Sheridan, once again a defender of Irish rights, echoed Grattan

4. Henry Grattan, Jr., ed., *The Speeches of the Right Honourable Henry Grattan,* 4 vols. (London: Longman, Hurst, Rees, Orme, and Brown, 1822), 2:126–27; also *The Parliamentary Register: or, History of the Proceedings and Debates of the House of Commons of Ireland,* 17 vols. (Dublin: James Moore, 1782–1801), 9:1–26, 33–84 and 119–55, for debates; *Journals of the House of Commons of the Kingdom of Ireland,* 20 vols. (Dublin: George Grierson, 1796–1802), 13:10–11, 12–13, 20; *Journal of the House of Lords of the Kingdom of Ireland,* 8 vols. (Dublin: William Sleater, 1779–1800), 5:233–35, 237–39; David R. Schweitzer, "The Prince of Wales, The Whigs and Irish Politics, 1784–1789," *Eire-Ireland* 21 (Fall 1986): 71–89; Denis Kennedy, "The Irish Whigs and the Regency Crisis in Ireland, 1788–1789," *Eire-Ireland* 18 (Fall 1983): 54–70; idem, "The Irish Whigs, 1789 to 1793" (Ph.D. dissertation, University of Toronto, 1971); and Gerard O'Brien, *Anglo-Irish Politics in the Age of Grattan and Pitt,* (Dublin: Irish Academic Press, 1987), 117–22, 135–45. For the mixing of British and Irish politics, with the concomitant confusion of constitutional issues, see J. C. Beckett, "Anglo-Irish Constitutional Relations in the Late Eighteenth Century," reprinted in Beckett's *Confrontations: Studies in Irish History* (Totowa, N.J.: Rowman and Littlefield, 1972), 123–41.

in contending that the regency was "a question not of English government, but of Irish constitution," of whether "the independent and supreme legislature of Ireland" had the right to judge for itself. To some, Buckingham had compounded the problem. Furious at his refusal to pass along the resolutions, William Todd Jones accused the lord lieutenant of raising "a question of national independence and external legislation."[5]

To all of these men, the constitutional crisis was very real. Technically no bill could be binding in Ireland or Britain until it had been stamped by the Great Seal. Without complete regal power, the Prince of Wales could not give the royal assent and sign bills into law. At Grattan and William Ponsonby's urging, the Irish Parliament seized the initiative and recognized the Prince of Wales as regent endowed with regal power, knowing full well that the British Parliament had not. Although Grattan denied the accusation, the Irish Parliament had acted as kingmaker. That the two parliaments settled on the same regent masked that fact. Barry Yelverton (and no doubt other Irish leaders) believed that if the British Parliament had chosen someone other than the prince to act as regent, Ireland would not have been bound by that action. "The crown of Ireland is . . . united to the *imperial* crown of Great Britain, and not to the government of Great Britain whatever that government may be," Yelverton decided.[6] The prince and only the prince could be regent.

The immediate crisis was averted when George III regained his senses and resumed the throne. The prince did not have to act, and a slightly embarrassed group of Irish M.P.s and peers delivered their resolutions and returned home. Nevertheless, an important constitutional issue had been raised, and the political infighting caused deep resentments, in England as well as Ireland. Irish opposition leaders had indirectly threatened the sovereignty of the British Parliament and confused the connection between Crown and Parliament by questioning who could be regent and what powers that regent could rightfully exercise. They had invited the Prince of Wales to act as king in Ireland even though he did not have clear authority to sit on the throne in Britain. If Yelverton's ideas were at all representative, they reserved for themselves, as members of the Irish Parliament, the right to recognize claims to the Crown. Yelverton was hardly original in seeing a distinction between the "imperial" Crown and the Crown of Great Britain. The Irish Parliament

---

5. Sheridan in *Parliamentary Register*, 9:42; Jones in ibid., 9:120.
6. Yelverton to John Forbes, 6 December 1788, in John Forbes. Letters. MS. 10,713, National Library of Ireland.

An End to "Independence" 199

had done so in 1640, as had Sir William Domvile in 1660 and William Molyneux thirty-eight years after that. All interpreted "imperial" in a way not intended when Henry VIII first used it in 1541.

Debate over giving the prince full power as regent, followed by debate over whether Parliament could or should transmit its resolutions to the prince over Buckingham's objections, forced Grattan, Ponsonby, Yelverton, and the rest to argue points of constitutional law even more intricate than those they had addressed in 1782. Some of their opponents contended that they had no right to interfere in the affairs of the royal family and, in the matter of Buckingham's refusal, the prerogatives of the Irish executive. Knowing the tenuousness of his and Grattan's position, Sheridan led in countering that the Irish Parliament could invite the prince to act as regent but could not pass an act officially naming him to the office; to do so would be to empower him to take the throne, which would be unconstitutional. But because of the constitutional "irregularity" brought by the king's incapacity and the political necessity of having a regent, Sheridan concluded, they had no choice but to extend the invitation. They were not conferring power; rather, they were recognizing a right, which he had to claim for himself.[7]

Critics were unpersuaded but outnumbered, and political necessity overrode their constitutional objections. Nonetheless, even though the invitation to the prince passed without a division, Attorney-General John Fitzgibbon refused to go along with the "criminal rashness" of bypassing Buckingham to approach the prince. Meanwhile, in London, William Pitt was distressed by Irish political infighting over the regency question. Moreover Pitt, who had already been urged by Portland to seek a parliamentary union, may have had his own desire for union reinforced by the convoluted constitutional arguments of Sheridan and Grattan.

Buckingham's chief secretary warned Pitt's ministry that a "spirit of jealousy & discontent" had been set loose.[8] Grattan and likeminded M.P.s had met at Charlemont's house to plan their strategy before Parliament even convened. When Buckingham let it be known that anyone holding an office who went against him could lose it, many of these same men, some fifty-six peers and members of Commons, agreed that they would view dismissal from office because of a vote in favor of a full regency "as a reprobation of our constitutional conduct, and an attack upon public principle, and the independence of Parliament; and that any

---

7. *Parliamentary Register*, 9:42–43.
8. Alleyne Fitzherbert to Lord Sydney, 23 November 1788, Sydney Papers, vol. 1, packet G, MS. 51, NLI.

administration taking, or persevering in any such steps, is not entitled to our confidence, and shall not receive our support."⁹

In effect, they threw the gauntlet at Buckingham's feet. Buckingham took it up. He dismissed the duke of Leinster and earl of Shannon from their posts; likewise the Ponsonbys, Charles Francis Sheridan, Gervase Parker Bushe, and several other officeholders in opposition. John Fitzgibbon, who sided with Buckingham, was named lord chancellor and elevated to the peerage. Other administration backers received pensions or posts, and some peers were advanced.

Observers at the time and historians since have seen the regency crisis as a turning point in the history of Grattan's Parliament. As one Fitzgibbon biographer concluded, the personal animosities provoked during the controversy might have "poisoned" Irish politics, fatally dividing Parliament against itself and raising the suspicions and resentment of Whitehall and the majority at Westminster.¹⁰ Fitzgibbon and Grattan, for example, became inveterate political enemies, and their rivalry was not unique. John Philpot Curran's animosity toward Fitzgibbon nearly outstripped that of Grattan. Yet even if the regency issue drove Grattan and Curran and a large group into pointed opposition, it did not reveal to Grattan the fallacy of his thinking that the Irish Parliament was truly independent.

Grattan used the regency crisis as the focal point of his grievances against Buckingham, whom he disparaged as a "jobber," but he had already distanced himself from the administration. After carrying his point about the regency, he joined with Charlemont and forty-six others, thirteen of whom had been Monks of St. Patrick, to form the Whig Club in June 1789. Within a year their numbers had more than doubled. The "Whigs" made it clear that their dissatisfactions reached far beyond the regency question. They reaffirmed their loyalty to the "House of Brunswick" and their attachment to Britain, yet they complained that the "undue influence of the Crown over both Houses of Parliament has been of late, beyond all example, increased"; they lambasted Buckingham "for his ill-advised, unwarranted, and unconstitutional conduct." They denounced Buckingham's policies, especially his disbursement of places and pensions, and his raising of salaries to enhance "the parliamentary

---

9. Henry Grattan, Jr., *Memoirs of the Life and Times of the Rt. Hon. Henry Grattan*, 5 vols. (London: Henry Colburn, 1889). 3:383. Of the fifty-six, ten had been Monks of St. Patrick and thirty-one would join the Whig Club. Also see Hardy, *Charlemont*, 2:171–72 (Hardy had been a Monk; he would also join the Whig Club).

10. Robert Edward Burns, "The Rise of John Fitzgibbon: A Study of Anglo-Irish Politics During the Age of the American Revolution" (Ph.D. dissertation, Harvard University, 1960), Summary, p. 5.

influence of the minister"—meaning William Pitt—"at the expence of the nation." Club members resolved that "the great object of this society is the constitution of the realm, as settled by the revolution in Great Britain and Ireland in 1688, and re-established in 1782."[11]

They repeated the assertion, made in the regency debates and for the seven years preceding, that the adjustment in 1782 had been not a political settlement but a recognition of constitutional right; further, it had itself become part of their reified constitution. If members of the Whig Club were not disingenuous in swearing loyalty to the king and fondness for the empire, they were unrealistic to think that history and logic were on their side. They emphasized the distinction between the "imperial" Crown and the British Crown and their reasons for acting as they did on the regency question. They did not convince anyone who was not already like-minded, and they did not always agree among themselves. They referred to themselves as a society rather than a party, not simply because they wanted to avoid being associated with faction, but also because they were not a tightly organized body with a legislative program in mind. Although they might have concurred on higher constitutional questions, they did not necessarily agree on how to act politically. They were initially more cohesive than the old Monks of St. Patrick had been, yet they accomplished, if anything, less rather than more and they did not last as long. They might, as Grattan stated later, have been solidly against undue Crown influence and any move toward legislative union, and they might have supported parliamentary reform if it came from within, yet they were, as another member confessed, a "more miscellaneous group than could have been wished."[12]

They did rally behind fellow Whig John Forbes, who in March 1789 renewed his quest begun a few years earlier for passage of a pension and place bill. With more than one hundred placemen and pensioners in Commons, Forbes contended that Parliament was too susceptible to administration control. The House approved the bill, only to have it defeated in Lords.[13] Forbes altered his bill to make it apply to pensions only; Grattan took up the issue of placemen in a separate bill. The ad-

---

11. From the resolutions and declarations of the Whig Club, 16 August 1789, in Henry Grattan, Jr., ed., *Miscellaneous Works of the Right Honourable Henry Grattan* (London: Hurst, Rees, Orme, and Brown, 1822), 266–69. Also see Kennedy, "The Irish Whigs, 1789 to 1793," 284; Grattan, *Memoirs*, 3:428–30; and the sneering comments in James Anthony Froude, *The English in Ireland in the Eighteenth Century*, 3 vols. (London: Longmans, Green, and Co., 1872–74), 2:519–20. Thirteen of the original forty-eight Whigs had been Monks of St. Patrick (including Grattan, Charlemont, Yelverton, Curran, and John Forbes).

12. Hardy, *Charlemont*, 2:206.

13. *Parliamentary Register*, 9:274–76, 312; *House of Lords Journal*, 6:274.

ministration mobilized its support, and neither bill made much headway during the next four years. Grattan's call for an investigation into the sale of peerages and seats in Commons fared no better. By 1792 Grattan had become so frustrated that he lashed out:

> It is now ten years since you recovered your constitution, and three since, in the opinion of some, you have lost it.... The people of Ireland would not consent to be governed by the British parliament; an expedient was devised—let the Irish Parliament govern the people of Ireland, and Britain govern the Irish Parliament.[14]

He was no less critical a year later in urging passage of a reform bill introduced by William Ponsonby:

> The people have not the blessings of the constitution; they are not represented; they are deprived of that great and invaluable blessing, supposed to be possessed by the electors of this kingdom, the blessing of being represented; and, accordingly, we find the House of Commons the organ of a will other than that of the people—the will of the minister, the will of the viceroy, the will of the secretary, but not the will of the people.[15]

Grattan's harangue notwithstanding, Ponsonby's bill went down to defeat, as it did the next year, when Ponsonby tried again. All that was accomplished in 1793, indeed, all that was accomplished before the Act of Union in 1800, was the nominal exclusion from Commons of pensioners and placemen who held their posts for profit. Revenue officers appointed by the administration were barred from sitting under this law, but treasurers and officers in the military were not. Furthermore, although anyone holding a post worth two hundred pounds per annum had to resign his seat, he could be re-elected if the voters wanted him back.[16] Since almost nothing had been done to reform borough representation, it was highly unlikely that placemen of this type would be defeated simply because they held government posts. Ponsonby's proposal—to bring a modicum of reform by giving each county three M.P.s, three each for the cities of Dublin and Cork, and more precise definition of borough electoral boundaries and residency requirements—never came close to passing.[17]

---

14. *Parliamentary Register*, 12:5; and the fuller (later revised?) version in Grattan, ed., *Speeches*, 2:340–58.
15. *Parliamentary Register*, 13:53; Grattan, ed., *Speeches*, 3:18–22.
16. *The Statutes at Large*, 20 vols. (Dublin: George Grierson, 1786–1801), 16:911–13 (33 George III c. 41).
17. Ponsonby in *Parliamentary Register*, 14:62–68; and the retort in *Sir H. Lan-*

More significant than the 1793 law regulating placemen and pensioners in Commons was the restoration of the parliamentary franchise to Catholics that same year. This law extended the relief begun in 1778 and 1782, removing the last restrictions on property ownership as well as granting Catholics the same rights as electors that were enjoyed by Protestants. Catholics could vote without taking the oath of allegiance and abjuration (but if they wanted to attend Trinity College they were not exempt from the oath). Those holding substantial freeholds (one hundred pounds) or owning significant amounts of personal property (one thousand pounds) also had the right to carry firearms. The practice of law had been reopened to Catholics the year before. However, Catholics were barred from acting as king's counsel, they were kept from holding any post in the administration, and they were still excluded from sitting in either house of parliament. In 1795 the Irish government authorized Catholics to endow their own college; nevertheless, the trustees appointed to supervise this proposed college were all Protestants and they controlled virtually everything connected with the new school.[18]

Grattan approved of what was done for the Catholics, even if he was disappointed that Parliament resisted reform from within. Ireland was still divided and conditions there fell far short of his idealized vision in 1782. Advocating Catholic relief that year, he had asked "whether we shall be a *Protestant settlement* or an IRISH NATION?" Anticipating passage of a relief bill, he proclaimed, "We are no longer a Protestant party oppressing the Catholick party. We are no longer a Catholick party without privileges, or the hope of privileges; but we are an united land, manifesting ourselves to the world in every single instance of glory."[19] So had he claimed, or at least so had he hoped, on the day he carried his motion for a recognition of parliamentary independence. He envisioned that recognition as the first step in a march toward greater unity and freedom. Parliamentary independence could be the means to an end, that end being a reciprocal empire and a prosperous, peaceful Ireland, secure in the protection of its constitutional rights. Yet, a decade

---

grishe's Celebrated Speech in the Irish House of Commons, Tuesday, March 4, 1794, on the motion of Mr. Ponsonby for a Parliamentary Reform (Edinburgh: J.& J. Fairbairn, 1794), where Langrishe made the same basic objections that he had made the previous July (which had also been published). Both show Langrishe's aversion to democracy, the French Revolution, and constitutional "innovation."

18. See the *Statutes at Large*, 16:685–92 (32 George III c. 21), for the Catholic relief act of 1793.

19. Parliament, House of Commons Debates, 1776–1789. Library of Congress MS. 16,363.1, vol. 26, container 10, pp. 87–88; also see Grattan's 20 February 1782 speech as recorded in ibid., vol. 24, container 9, p. 172, and in the *Parliamentary Register*, 1:258.

later, he was registering the same complaints about the empire that he had catalogued before April 1782. He still felt that Irish trade was disadvantaged, just as he still believed that the Crown and administration exercised too much influence in the Irish Parliament. Although "independent," that Parliament had not been freed of corruption, causing Grattan to grumble that "it is not even an aristocracy: it is an oligarchy."[20]

After all, the Catholic franchise meant little if Catholics were closed out of borough elections; in fact, in most cases they, like the majority of Protestant freeholders, were not voting burgesses. They had virtually no say in the election of some three-quarters of the M.P.s. And Catholics knew that what they had gained, the Irish Parliament had surrendered reluctantly. Grattan's sentiments in their favor were genuine enough, though he drew the line at the franchise; officeholding was not yet feasible, he felt. If Grattan was genuinely sympathetic, other leaders seemed to have supported relief only because they were pressured to do so by the administration, which in turn had been nudged along by the Pitt ministry. Pitt, for his part, supported Catholic relief as much to prevent domestic unrest in Ireland as to correct past injustices. He and many British and Irish politicians worried that the revolution begun in France in 1789 would spread to Ireland, uniting disgruntled Catholics and Protestant Dissenters into a popular movement that would threaten the imperial tie as well as the power of the Anglo-Irish elite.

Nevertheless, passage of the Catholic relief bill in 1793 was not just a political maneuver or a coordinated effort to prevent out-of-power Protestants and Catholics from banding together. The Pitt ministry, the Irish administration and the Irish Parliament never worked together smoothly enough to bring off concerted action on so divisive an issue. Grattan and John Philpot Curran urged their fellow M.P.s to approve Catholic relief because, if they did not, Pitt would use their failure as an excuse to press for a parliamentary union.[21] Memories of the failed commercial relief in 1785 and the regency crisis four years later were vivid enough to keep many M.P.s from trusting Pitt.[22]

M.P.s opposed to reform were not necessarily also opposed to the Catholic franchise. Grattan's old friend and author of *Baratariana*, Her-

20. *Parliamentary Register*, 13:159; and Grattan, ed., *Speeches*, 3:30–39.
21. Grattan, ed., *Speeches*, 2:368–70.
22. See James McLane Murphy, "The Pitt Administration and the Irish Roman Catholics, 1791–1801" (Ph.D. dissertation, Fordham University, 1968), for a sympathetic portrait of Pitt and a discussion of the complexities involved in adopting even a gradualist policy of Catholic emancipation. Also see O'Brien, *Anglo-Irish Politics*, 146–66.

cules Langrishe, had been one of the most vigorous supporters of the Catholic franchise as well as a steadfast opponent of parliamentary reform. Langrishe did not consider himself an "oligarch"; nor would it be fair to depict him and others like him as perpetrators of a carefully planned scheme to keep the people firmly under their thumb. Rather, Langrishe's position—neither duplicitous nor unreasonable from his perspective—was becoming increasingly untenable in the eyes of observers outside of Parliament. Those observers suspected that there was a conspiracy afoot to subvert their liberties, and the accusations of Grattan and other opposition leaders gave credence to their suspicions.

Grattan got along no better with Buckingham's successor, the earl of Westmorland, than he had with Buckingham. With the opening of each new parliamentary session from 1790 to 1794, Grattan found some reason to attack the administration for what he took to be its constitutional infractions. He could not fault Westmorland as he had Buckingham for liberally dispensing pensions and places, so he condemned him for not moving fast enough to reform the system that made such grants possible. He called for an inquiry into the conduct of government. He even accused the administration of having one purpose only in redesigning the gallery above the Commons chambers to seat fewer people: to challenge him and his allies, since traditionally the gallery had been filled with visitors (especially students from Trinity College) friendly to the opposition.[23]

With so much criticism of Parliament coming from within, and much of that from the man venerated as the "father" of parliamentary independence, it is small wonder that criticism from without also grew apace. Catholic reformers were not necessarily willing to let Grattan or Langrishe speak for them; more Protestants, too, began to look for their own spokesmen. Their search resulted in the creation of the United Irishmen. Grattan came to fear the Volunteers of the 1780s; he would be even more troubled by the United Irishmen of the 1790s. They advanced democratic politics and the ideal of a single national identity more insistently than the Volunteers ever had.

The United Irishmen were the offspring of a half century and more of Irish politics. They rose from the rubble of the Volunteer movement, and their founders included onetime Volunteers William Drennan and James Napper Tandy. Like the Volunteers, the United Irishmen took some of their inspiration from the American Revolution. They "walked

---

23. See, for example, Grattan's speech in Commons of 20 February 1790 in Grattan, ed., *Speeches*, 2:248; or the speech of 10 January 1783 in ibid., 3:1–16.

in the footsteps of the Americans in '74," claimed John Burk, a member before he fled Ireland in 1795 for the safety of the United States.[24] As they radicalized, they were even more influenced by the republican ideals of the French Revolution. In their criticism of the British Parliament and distrust of the Irish Parliament, they harked back to Charles Lucas. In their willingness to assert themselves politically, they expanded the demands and range of the patriot clubs formed in Lucas's era. They were, however, more skeptical that government could be changed, more aggressive in appealing to Catholics as well as Protestants, more unabashedly republican, and more inclined toward separatism than their forebears. Members of the gentry class and the Irish Parliament had not closed ranks against the patriot clubs of the 1750s. They had accepted— if reluctantly, in most cases—the Volunteers. The United Irishmen they disliked intensely and from the very start.

United Irishmen were exceedingly frustrated with the parliamentary opposition, supposedly the "voice" of the people. William Drennan had been willing to contemplate separation in 1785, telling his sister, "If I could think of politics it should be to persuade the people to a separation from England." Yet it would be another six years before Drennan decided that "nothing short of convulsion will throw off the incumbincy of our national, political, and civil grievances."[25] During the interval, Drennan saw members of the parliamentary opposition turn against the Volunteers and fail in their own efforts to carry any significant reform legislation. In 1787 and again in 1788, Grattan was even blocked in his attempts to ease tithe burdens on the peasantry. Grattan himself, Drennan eventually felt, did not go far enough in his popular politics. Indeed, while Grattan never abandoned the cause of parliamentary reform or Catholic relief, he stressed that the Catholics in particular "must avoid republican principles and French politics."[26]

Though Drennan found much to admire about Grattan, he had little faith in Grattan as a champion of reform and doubted that anything as loose and unstructured as whig clubs could make a difference. He concluded that neither the Dublin nor the Belfast societies had any "fellow-

24. John Burk, *History of the Late War in Ireland, with an Account of the United Irish Association* (Philadelphia: Francis and Robert Bailey, 1799), from the "Prefatory Remarks." Also see Joseph I. Shulim, "John Daly Burk: Irish Revolutionist and American Patriot," *American Philosophical Society. Transactions* (1964), pt. 6, pp. 5–60.
25. D. A. Chart, ed., *The Drennan Letters* (Belfast: His Majesty's Stationery Office, 1931), 34, and Colin P. Hill, "William Drennan and the Radical Movement for Parliamentary Reform, 1779–1794," 2 vols. (M.Litt. thesis, Trinity College, University of Dublin, 1967), 2:27, resp.
26. Grattan, *Memoirs*, 4:74, Grattan to a Mr. M'Can, 7 December 1792.

feeling with the people." Disillusioned with Grattan, the Whigs, and the entire Irish Parliament, he looked to the American and French examples and to the reformers in England to help men like him " cement the scattered and shifting sand of republicanism into a body."[27]

Drennan was like Charles Lucas in that he devoted more time to politics than to the practice of medicine. By 1790 he had moved to Dublin from Newry to take up politics full time. Drennan soon teamed with Theobald Wolfe Tone, son of a Dublin coach builder and young man on the make. Tone attended Trinity College and had recently returned from London, where he had studied law at the Middle Temple. Tone became a member of the Irish Bar, joined the Whig Club of Dublin, and was even approached by the Ponsonbys to stand for a seat in Commons. Tone later admitted that he was "a little dazzled with the prospect of a seat in Parliament, at which my ambition began to expand."[28] Expanding ambition took him away from both the Ponsonbys and the Whig Club, however, as he came to feel that parliamentary leaders like George Ponsonby and societies like the Whig Club failed to check the power of the administration or to articulate popular desires. He was bored with the law, having mastered very little of it even while at the Middle Temple, and he disliked the routine and hard work of a beginning lawyer's life. Thus he turned to politics as his creative outlet.

Tone's skills as an essayist had first brought him to the attention of the Whig Club; those same skills would be used in a more radical cause as Tone's restlessness and dissatisfaction grew. "I made speedily what was to me a great discovery, though I might have found it in Swift and Molyneux," Tone wrote later, "that the influence of England was the radical vice of our Government, and consequently that Ireland would never be either free, prosperous or happy, until she was independent,

27. Chart, ed., *Drennan Letters*, 55; also see ibid., 51–52, 53, 63, for Drennan's view of Grattan in 1790–91. Drennan had apparently not met Grattan by that time.

28. Barry O'Brien, ed., *The Autobiography of Theobald Wolfe Tone*, 2 vols. (London: T. Fisher Unwin, 1893), 1:25. Also see Frank MacDermot, *Theobald Wolfe Tone* (London: Macmillan, 1939); Marianne Elliott, *Wolfe Tone: Prophet of Irish Independence* (New Haven: Yale University Press, 1990); and Tom Dunne, *Theobald Wolfe Tone, Colonial Outsider* (Cork: Tower Books, 1982), which is brief but very good on Tone's political ideology. The biographical sketch in John Charles Molony, *Ireland's Tragic Comedians* (Freeport, N.Y.: Books for Libraries Press, 1970; orig. ed., 1934), 73–149, is also suggestive; the essay on Tone in Terence De Vere White, *The Anglo-Irish* (London: Victor Gollanz, 1972), 84–93, is much more critical. Froude, *English in Ireland*, 3:191, is not unkind to Tone, considering Froude's lack of sympathy for Tone's cause. *A Commentary on the Memoirs of Theobald Wolfe Tone* (Paris: Firmin Didot, 1828), apparently by Robert Johnson, an old Monk of St. Patrick and collaborator on "Causidicus" with Frederick Jebb, is very sympathetic to Tone. If Johnson (writing under the pseudonym Colonel Philip Roche Fermoy) was indeed the author, he was one of the few of the old Monk association who did not turn his back on popular politics.

and that independence was unattainable whilst the connection with England existed."²⁹ He began to look on the Whig Club "with great contempt" and lost his respect for most members of Parliament. He soon pressed beyond Molyneux and even Swift, feeling, nonetheless, that he simply followed the logic of their arguments.

Tone and Drennan joined with Joseph Pollock, Thomas Emmet, and a few others to found their own political club in 1790. It lasted only a few months and left behind "a puny offspring of about a dozen essays on different subjects."³⁰ Their club failed in part because its members were volatile and ambitious, but also because their differences—in temperament and in political and social objectives—were as powerful as the shared frustrations that had thrown them together.

Hearing that a group of Belfast merchants and tradesmen who had also been Volunteers had formed a democratic political club, Tone sent the members a set of three resolutions that he had drafted in July 1791. The resolutions stated that British influence in Ireland "was the great grievance of the country," that the most effective way to counter that influence was through parliamentary reform, and that no reform "could be just or efficacious" if it excluded the Catholics.³¹ These resolutions did not go as far as Tone would have liked. "I have not said one Word that looks like a wish for *separation*, tho I give it to you & to your friends as my most decided opinion that such an event would be a *regeneration* for this Country," he confided to his confederate, Thomas Russell. Tone the separatist realized that his was a minority view, even among those "radicals" of the Belfast club. The resolutions fell "short of the truth, but truth itself must sometimes condescend to temporise," he concluded.³²

Tone submitted his resolutions to the "Volunteers" of Belfast. By October 1791 they had re-organized themselves as the United Irishmen and within a month Drennan, working with Tone and James Napper Tandy (already prominent in Dublin municipal politics), had founded a group going by the same name in Dublin.

From their founding in 1791 until their proscription by the government in 1794, the various groups of United Irishmen were conscious of their tie to the all-but-defunct Volunteers. Like Volunteers, they took

29. O'Brien, ed., *Autobiography of Wolfe Tone*, 1:26.
30. Ibid., 1:34.
31. Ibid., 1:76.
32. Tone to Thomas Russell, 9 July (?) 1791, Peter Burrowes Papers, MS. 23 K53, RIA. For an interesting piece on Russell see C. J. Woods, "The Place of Thomas Russell in the United Irish Movement," in Hugh Gough and David Dickson, eds., *Ireland and the French Revolution* (Dublin: Irish Academic Press, 1990), 83–100.

Theobald Wolfe Tone, lightning rod of controversy from his day to our own, artist unknown. Courtesy of the National Gallery of Ireland.

some of their inspiration from the American Revolutionaries, trying to coordinate their activities through what were in effect committees of correspondence on the American model.[33] They were even more inspired by the early stages of the French Revolution, which Presbyterians of the north in particular followed enthusiastically. As with the Volunteers, the United Irishmen in Ulster, whether from their dissenting tradition or from their own experience with persecution, took the lead in urging Catholic emancipation and the spread of republican ideals. Presbyterian minister William Steel Dickson perhaps spoke for others in Ulster, not just those associated with the United Irishmen, when complaining that "rational republicanism" had never been given "a fair trial."[34] One group in County Antrim styling itself the "Friends of the French Revolution" sent a resolution to the French National Assembly in 1791, which read in part:

We believe that a nation has a right to form, maintain, and perfect its constitution, and to regulate at pleasure every thing relating to government. We believe a nation has an *inherent right* to change its constitution, and therefore we believe the Revolution in France to be founded in the *law of nature* and *of nations*, caused by tyranny and oppression, and sanctioned by dire necessity. We consider the enemies of this glorious Revolution, inimical to the rights of man; and its friends the *friends of civil and religious liberty*.[35]

The authors of this resolution equated the people with the nation. As the embodiment of the nation, the people took precedence over the constitution. These enthusiasts did not consciously pit themselves or the rest of the "people" against the constitution, however, and their characterization of events in France as a "glorious Revolution" was no stylistic accident or attempt at satire. They preferred to believe that revolution in France could lead to constitutional renovation at home, making the "people," in fact as well as in theory, the political nation. The United Irishmen of Dublin expressed similar sentiments when claiming that they were:

Instructed by the Genius of the Constitution, and the genuine spirit of the Laws, instructed of late, by all that has been spoken, or written or acted, or suffered

---

33. O"Brien, ed., *Autobiography of Wolfe Tone*, 1:82, for American committees as examples. See Rupert J. Coughlan, *Napper Tandy* (Dublin: Anvil Books, 1976), for Napper Tandy's career and a different perspective on the United Irishmen.
34. William Steel Dickson, *A Narrative of the Confinement and Exile of William Steel Dickson, D.D.* (Dublin: J. Stockdale, 1812), 5.
35. Resolutions of Political Meetings in Co. Antrim, 1763–1796, MS. 24 K2, RIA, from the resolution passed in July 1791 by the "Friends" in Ballymoney.

An End to "Independence"

in the cause of freedom; instructed by the late revolution in America, by the late revolution in Ireland, by the late revolution in France.[36]

National unity was the professed goal of the United Irish societies springing up around the country. Unity was the theme emphasized in the news of their proceedings, printed in papers like the Belfast-based *Northern Star,* which had been founded by local United Irishmen. Unity was the message conveyed in the Dublin-based *National Evening Star,* which carried on its masthead a Protestant, a Catholic, and a Dissenter shaking hands.[37] In the name of unity, the United Irishmen called for another grand national convention to assemble at Dungannon in 1793, and in the name of unity they submitted their proposal for parliamentary reform the next year. Under the sweeping changes proposed, members of Commons would be elected to represent three hundred entirely new electoral districts, with one M.P. each. Gone would be both borough and county representation, and in their place would be a system based "as nearly as possible" on population. Parliaments would be annual, there would be universal manhood suffrage, and anyone eligible to vote—Protestant or Catholic—could sit in Commons. Furthermore, because Commons would be opened to men of modest means, all M.P.s "should receive a reasonable stipend for their services."[38]

The proposal said nothing about abolishing the House of Lords, nor did it modify the relationship between Parliament and the administration; the House of Commons was its sole concern. Under it, all electors were expected to reside in the districts in which they voted, but candidates for Commons were required only to live somewhere "within the kingdom," and they were not expressly bound to vote as directed by their constituents. Even so, what the United Irishmen proposed was too much for members of Parliament—administration backers and opposition leaders alike. William Ponsonby could not carry his decidedly more modest reform bill; there was no chance at all for the United Irishmen plan. Ponsonby's bill was probably hurt by the fact that the United

---

36. *Proceedings of the Society of the United Irishmen of Dublin* (Philadelphia: Thomas Stephens, 1795), from an address issued by the United Irishmen on 26 October 1792.

37. J. T. Gilbert, *A History of the City of Dublin,* 3 vols. (Dublin: James Duffy, 1861), 2:61–62, for the *National Evening Star;* and Rosamond Jacob, *The Rise of the United Irishmen, 1791–1794* (London: George G. Harrap, 1937), 173–75, and O'Brien, ed. *Autobiography of Wolfe Tone,* 1:70–71, for the *Northern Star.*

38. Edward Curtis and R. B. McDowell, eds., *Irish Historical Documents, 1172–1922* (London: Methuen, 1943), 237–38, for the text of the United Irishmen parliamentary reform proposal (quote from p. 238); Dungannon resolutions of 1793 in Chart, ed., *Drennan Letters,* 136.

Irishmen had gone ahead with their own proposals. As Edith Johnston has observed, the times were not "propitious" for "moderate constitutional reformers who wished to keep a balance between the reactionary conservative and the incipient revolutionary."[39]

The parliamentary opposition was never tied to the United Irishmen in the way that it had been to the Volunteers, yet it took some time for the distance between them to widen. Thomas Conolly and Grattan met with Tone on occasion; Grattan even invited Tone to stay as a guest at his Tinnehinch home.[40] Tone and Catholic leaders like John Keogh were not unwelcome simply because they criticized parliament: Grattan had been doing that himself for over twenty years. Grattan was put off, however, by the increasingly threatening language used by the United Irishmen and Tone's eventual insistence that the "whole system" of government had to be altered or brought down by force. In Tone's view, the "Constitution of 1782" had been inadequate, especially in failing to free Catholics from "slavery" and in failing to check the power of the Ascendancy oligarchs. By the end of 1792, Grattan, the duke of Leinster, and several of their parliamentary associates had formed the Friends of the Constitution, Liberty and Peace to counteract the burgeoning influence of the United Irishmen. Hardly reactionaries, these "Friends" reaffirmed their attachment to the Crown, but they also made clear their support of limited parliamentary reform and the Catholic franchise.[41]

Not content to limit their activities to pamphleteering and protests, the United Irishmen attempted to resurrect the Volunteers and transform them into a National Guard, in imitation of the French. The Volunteers had begun as a military force and then were politicized; the United Irishmen began as a political lobby and then tried to build strength through military organization. They elected officers and formed units, as had the Volunteers. United Irishmen wearing old Volunteer uniforms assembled on 14 July 1792 in Belfast and Dublin to celebrate Bastile day. Napper Tandy labored mightily to turn the 4 November observance of the Glorious Revolution traditionally held in Dublin into a celebration of the French Revolution. With Tandy at their head, those who assembled wore green cockades instead of orange and refused to parade around William III's statue. Some wore new uniforms of dark green coats and green-and-white-striped trousers as well, to reinforce

---

39. Edith Mary Johnston, *Ireland in the Eighteenth Century* (Dublin: Gill and Macmillan, 1974), 174.
40. O'Brien, ed., *Autobiography of Wolfe Tone*, 1:106–7, 122.
41. Ibid., 1:147, for Tone and need for sweeping change; Grattan, *Memoirs*, 4:126–29, for the Friends of the Constitution.

their statement that they were Irish first and last. They also made a show of inviting Catholics as well as Protestants to join in. To all of this, Tone said "Bravo."[42]

The administration responded shortly after by banning any more such gatherings or martial displays. In order to impede extra-parliamentary politics, it forbade public meetings called "under pretense" of petitioning or influencing government. It had already taken steps to silence the popular press through censorship and prosecution. A very long and detailed militia law of 1793 was designed to protect government by empowering the governors of each county to compile and maintain militia rosters, with all members of the militia being sworn to uphold the king's law. This, it was hoped, would effectively eliminate the potential pool of recruits for new Volunteer or National Guard units.[43] All of this legislation built on what had been begun under Rutland in 1786 to diminish the threat posed by the Volunteers.

Grattan and a few supporters in Commons, with Charlemont and a handful in Lords, protested the passage of laws that they thought too sweeping; yet they too wanted to see the United Irishmen checked. By 1794 they had been and Tone, given the choice of exile or indictment, left for the United States—unchanged in his views but for the moment politically impotent. Napper Tandy also fled the country and ended up living not far from Tone during his brief exile. Tried for and acquitted of sedition in June 1794, Drennan chose to discontinue his political activism. Like Tone and Tandy he felt that the administration had undermined the United Irishmen while the parliamentary opposition turned away, too uncaring, too corrupt to act.[44]

Outlawed, the United Irishmen turned to France for help. They entered thereby a more radical, even revolutionary stage. Thomas Emmet and other leaders claimed that they had tried to democratize politics but had not insisted on a republic to replace mixed government, nor had they pushed for complete separation from Britain until *after* they were

---

42. O'Brien, ed., *Autobiography of Wolfe Tone*, 1:71–72, for Bastille Day in Belfast; ibid., 1:76, for the November 4 observance in Dublin. Also see Coughlan, *Napper Tandy*, 49–52; William Drummond, ed., *The Autobiography of Hamilton Rowan* (Shannon: Irish University Press, 1972; orig. ed., 1840), 154–55; and Jacob, *United Irishmen*, 148–53.

43. *Statutes at Large*, 16:794–95 (33 George III c. 29) for the law against popular assemblies, and ibid., 16:692–746 (33 George III c. 22) for the very detailed militia law. Also see Chart, ed., *Drennan Letters*, 164, 167, for Drennan's fear that government action would crush the United Irishmen. For a different perspective on the militia act, see Thomas Bartlett, "An End to Moral Economy: The Irish Militia Disturbances of 1793," in C. H. E. Philpin, ed., *Nationalism and Popular Protest in Ireland* (Cambridge: Cambridge University Press, 1987), 191–218.

44. O'Brien, ed., Autobiography of Wolfe Tone, 1:211–12; Chart, ed., *Drennan Letters*, 140.

dissolved by decree. In an affidavit submitted in August 1798, when they faced prosecution for complicity in an uprising that had broken out the previous spring, Emmet, Arthur O'Connor, and William James McNeven—all former leaders of the United Irishmen—swore that they had wanted to reform, not revolutionize, Irish government and that their objectives had changed only in 1794. Their earlier goal "went no further than a reform in parliament, only on more broad and liberal principles."[45] Because the government forced their hand, they claimed, they reluctantly became revolutionaries, looking to France to aid them in achieving independence from the British empire. Only then did they cease to identify their rights with those found in their constitution and theoretically protected by legal and historical precedent.

In truth, the goals of the United Irishmen had not been clear and they, like the Volunteers before them, did not speak consistently or with one voice. They were much more enthusiastic about recruiting Catholics than the Volunteers had been, and they did not object to the basic tenets of Catholic theology. Nevertheless, they distrusted the Catholic Church as a potential threat to their civil religion of a united Ireland. Even Tone seemed to be confused. He sometimes used the terms United Irishmen and Volunteers interchangeably, and, as a result, inappropriately mixed labels. The United Irishmen were not just an updated version of the Volunteers, although they experienced some of the same problems and had some of the same desires.

It took the United Irishmen almost a year after the 1793 Dungannon meeting to agree on their reform proposal and submit it to Parliament. Some wanted to give Catholics the franchise but keep them from sitting

---

45. The deposition is reprinted in John Gilbert, ed., *Documents Relating to Ireland, 1795–1804* (Dublin: Joseph Dollard, 1893), 147–62 (quote from 148). For the transformation of the United Irishmen into an avowedly republican and separatist group, see Nancy J. Curtin, "The Transformation of the Society of United Irishmen into a Mass-based Revolutionary Organization, 1794–6," *Irish Historical Studies* 24 (1985): 463–92; Marianne Elliott, "The Origins and Transformation of Early Irish Republicanism," *International Review of Social History* 23 (1978): 405–28; and idem, *Partners in Revolution* (New Haven: Yale University Press, 1982). Also see James Smyth, "Dublin's Political Underground in the 1790s," in Gerard O'Brien, *Parliament, Politics and People* (Dublin: Irish Academic Press, 1989), 129–48. Until recently most modern historians have been little interested in pursuing the argument made in Robert Clifford's *Application of Barruel's Memoirs of Jacobinism to the Secret Societies of Ireland and Great Britain* (London: E. Booker, 1798), to wit: that many United Irishmen were first brought together through Freemasonry, as were the Jacobins of France. Nancy J. Curtin, "Symbols and Rituals of United Irish Mobilisation," in Gough and Dickson, eds., *Ireland and the French Revolution*, 68–82, noted that Drennan saw the Masons as an organizational model for the United Irishmen. Also see A. T. Q. Stewart, *A Deeper Silence* (London: Faber and Faber, 1993), 164–78; and Jim Smyth, *The Men of No Property* (New York: St. Martin's Press, 1992), 45–46, 85–88.

in Parliament; others wanted to restrict the franchise to property holders rather than press for universal manhood suffrage; still others wanted to eliminate rotten boroughs but not completely restructure the basis of representation. Drennan never trusted Catholics as completely as did Tone. Neither man thought a republic in Ireland was presently feasible, although both espoused "republican" principles.[46]

Tone remains an enigma, a supposed republican who, like many of his associates, admired Thomas Paine but who also dismissed much of Paine's *Age of Reason* as "Damned trash!"[47] Easily bored and at times shamelessly lazy, Tone was a confusing blend of opportunist and romantic adventurer. When he tired of his studies at Trinity College, the young Tone wanted his father to buy him a commisssion in the British army so that he could go off and fight—against the rebellious Americans! He tried twice while at the Middle Temple to interest the British government in backing him as a filibusterer for the empire in "Cook's South Seas Islands." Snubbed both times, Tone was greatly aggrieved. His resentment burned so deep that some psycho-historian may someday attempt to explain Tone's later political career as a reaction to his unrequited love for empire. And while Tone professed to be a man of republican predilections, it is difficult to read his autobiography and not feel that he would have liked nothing better than to have been an aristocrat living a life of pleasure and ease.[48]

To his credit, Tone helped bring some Protestants and Catholics closer together. His 1791 pamphlet calling for Catholic emancipation impressed Protestant and Catholic reformers alike, and he was made a secretary to the Catholic Committee in recognition of his efforts. But

---

46. Tone's *An Argument on Behalf of the Catholics of Ireland* (1791) emphasized the corruption in Irish government resulting from British influence, the complicity of many Irish leaders, and the futility of any reform that excluded the Catholic franchise, but Tone did not come out for a clear overthrow of the Ascendancy; nor did he renounce ties to the king. It is difficult to know exactly when Tone made up his mind to be a separatist and a republican. In his autobiography he pushes the date back quite early—to 1791, when he wrote at least one separatist letter. Does this mean that the private Tone was more radical than the public Tone, or did Tone rewrite his own past in his autobiography? See O'Brien, ed., *Autobiography*, 1:55, for independence first, republic second (how could that be done?); for Drennan, see Chart, ed., *Drennan Letters*, 108, 122, 170. Also see R. B. McDowell, *Public Opinion 1750–1800* (London: Faber and Faber, 1944), 206–8.

47. O'Brien, ed., *Autobiography of Wolfe Tone*, 1:246.

48. For Tone's desire for a career in the British army, see ibid., 1:11; for his frustrated South Pacific plans, see ibid., 1:19, 31–32. Of Pitt's ignoring him when he applied the first time, a vengeful Tone wrote, "In my anger I made something like a vow, that, if I ever had the opportunity, I would make Mr. Pitt sorry, and perhaps fortune may yet enable me to fulfill that resolution" (1:19). Tone complained much about the Irish aristocracy and eventually vowed to show "no mercy" in bringing it down, yet through it all he seemed even more jealous that he could not change places with men like Thomas Conolly (Tone considered Conolly a fop).

neither he nor any other United Irishmen leader could quickly undo the damage of more than two centuries of religious division and misunderstanding. A government spy who infiltrated the Dublin United Irishmen reported that "there seems to be a very great distrust entertained by the protestants against the papists."[49] Sectarian jealousies burst from confinement even before the United Irishmen were banned by the government, with Catholic Defenders and Protestant Peep-O-Day boys going on destructive binges throughout Ulster. Catholics themselves were divided and the old Catholic Committee fragmented. Some members wanted to join with the United Irishmen; others wanted to continue the traditional policy of waiting for Parliament to legislate reform. Even those opting to go with the United Irishmen split, with some wanting to curtail agitation after Parliament passed the relief bill in 1793 and others wanting to press on without rest until full emancipation was attained.[50]

As damaging to Irish public life was the collapse of the parliamentary opposition. Grattan had hoped that Earl Fitzwilliam, Westmorland's replacement as lord lieutenant in early 1795, would be able to push through significant reform and undercut both the radicalized United Irishmen and the hidebound traditionalists in government. Fitzwilliam owned Irish land, was connected by marriage to the Ponsonbys, and had corresponded with Grattan before he accepted the post of lord lieutenant. Grattan had come around to supporting full Catholic emancipation. He agreed to work closely with Fitzwilliam, who also favored eliminating the remaining restrictions on Irish Catholics. For virtually the first time in his career, Grattan looked forward to a new parliamentary session where the Castle and opposition leaders would team to pass reform legislation.

49. R. B. McDowell, ed., "Proceedings of the Dublin Society of United Irishmen," *Analecta Hibernica* 17 (1949): 55, the comments of Thomas Collins in December 1792. Collins was a Dublin merchant who infiltrated the United Irishmen for the government.

50. For the moderate Catholic view, see *An Authentic and Copious Report of the Important Debate, at a Meeting of the Catholic Inhabitants of Dublin, on the 31 October Last; Relative to Obtaining the Elective Franchise, and the Right of Trial by Jury, for the Roman Catholics of this Kingdom* (Belfast: D. Blow, 1792); and *An Address from the General Committee of Roman Catholics to their Protestant Fellow Subjects* (Dublin: P. Byrne, 1792). Even this Catholic stand provoked a negative reaction among some Protestants—such as *Observations on the Declaration of the Catholic Society of Dublin* (Dublin: Henry Watts, 1792), by "A Protestant Whig" who also claimed to be a member of the Whig Club and to speak for the majority of his associates. This tract is sometimes attributed to Charles Francis Sheridan, though it is more inflammatory than Sheridan's usual style and may not have been written by him. Also see the general comments in Grattan, *Memoirs*, 4:53–70; O'Brien, ed., *Autobiography of Wolfe Tone*, 1:63–64; various letters in Chart, ed., *Drennan Letters*, from 1791 to 1793; and Smyth, *Men of No Property*, 100–120, for the Defenders and their polarization.

An End to "Independence" 217

Instead, the ministry recalled Fitzwilliam, and Grattan suffered the humiliation of seeing his bill for complete Catholic emancipation go down to resounding defeat in the 1795 parliamentary session. Fitzwilliam had overreached himself, going beyond what the Pitt ministry wanted when he backed immediate emancipation. He also alienated longtime administration supporters by removing the powerful and well-connected John Beresford from his revenue commission post. The earl of Camden replaced the disgraced Fitzwilliam and marshalled the pro-administration, pro-ministry forces to block Grattan's attempt at passing an emancipation bill in 1796. William Ponsonby's renewed effort to push through a parliamentary reform bill the next year suffered the same fate. Ponsonby's 1797 bill paired Catholic emancipation with a revised, more representative scheme for parliamentary districting—a last ditch, desperate effort to combine reform concerns that had long been kept distinct.

With Ponsonby's failure, Grattan resigned his seat and left Commons in disgust on 15 May 1797. He had warned beforehand that he and others would do just that if Ponsonby's bill failed, which he knew it would. "Having no hopes left to persuade or dissuade, and having discharged our duty," he said in a bitter, emotional farewell, "we shall trouble you no more, and after this day shall not attend the House of Commons."[51] Grattan had been sitting for the city of Dublin (his father's old constituency) since 1790 and tried to explain his actions in a published letter and public address to the electors. Having in mind the implementation of martial law in parts of Ulster as well as the blocking of reform and growing restrictions on the press, and speaking for those like John Philpot Curran and George Ponsonby who also resigned their seats, he explained:

Our opinion was, that the origin of the evil, the source of the discontent, and the parent of the disturbance was to be traced to an illstar'd and destructive

---

51. *Parliamentary Register*, 17:570. See pp. 530–70 for the debates and Ponsonby's defeat, 170 to 30, the vote for adjournment serving as a vote against reform. Ponsonby proposed that the counties be divided into voting districts of six thousand homes each, each district to return two M.P.s. All Catholic disabilities would be removed; all forty-shilling freeholders would vote. For the significance of the Fitzwilliam crisis, see Kennedy, "Irish Whigs, 1789 to 1793," 293–94; and Rex Syndergaard, "The Fitzwilliam Crisis and Irish Nationalism," *Eire-Ireland* 6 (Fall 1971): 72–82, which argues too hard for a new type of nationalism emerging from all of this. Also see Fitzwilliam's justifications of his actions in a letter to the (former lord lieutenant) earl of Carlisle of 23 March 1795 in HMC, *The Manuscripts of the Earl of Carlisle* (London: Eyre and Spottiswoode, 1897), 713–21; an example of popular support for Fitzwilliam by the freeholders of Antrim in "Resolutions of Political Meetings in Co. Antrim, 1763–1797," MS. 24 K2, RIA; and the accusations leveled at Grattan and Fitzwilliam for stirring the people up in Alexander Knox, *Essays on the Political Circumstances of Ireland* (London: J. Plymsell, 1799), essays II and III.

endeavour on the part of the Minister of the Crown to give the Monarch a power which the Constitution never intended: to render the King in Parliament every thing, and the People nothing; and to work the People completely out of the House of Commons, and in their place to seat and establish the Chief Magistrate absolute and irresistible.[52]

As Grattan explained many years later, the members of the opposition were trapped, with only one way out:

The reason why we seceded was, that we did not approve of the conduct of the United Men, and we could not approve of the conduct of the Government. We were afraid of encouraging the former by making speeches against the latter, and we thought it better in such a case, as we could support neither, to withdraw from both.[53]

To some observers, then and since, Grattan's resignation was a form of infanticide, or if not that, then a denial of paternity. "Grattan's Parliament" was never Grattan's to control, however, as Grattan's own actions testify. Not able to manage it completely, he quickly lost his ability even to influence it. Before he went off like Achilles to sulk in his tent, he left the impression that the Irish Parliament had been utterly corrupted. He could find no better explanation than that for the failure of his argument that the best way to prevent "revolution" was through "reformation."[54] "Do you imagine there is any man that would prefer the wild schemes of republicanism to the sober blessings of the English Constitution, if he enjoyed them?" Grattan asked.[55] The Whigs, whom he had helped to mobilize in 1789 as a political caucus—it would be claiming too much to say they were ever a party—had not held together. They soon, like the Monks of St. Patrick a decade before, lost what little strength they had.

Grattan seemed to possess a persecution complex; he even saw himself as a martyr in the cause of liberty. He had spent virtually all of his parliamentary career—some twenty-two years—as an opposition leader, an anti-administration outsider whose victory in April 1782 was temporary and more apparent than real. Most of the time he voted in the minority, struggling to find like-minded colleagues in Commons. His

---

52. Henry Grattan, *Mr. Grattan's Address to his Fellow-Citizens* (Dublin: Campbell and Shea, 1797), 10.
53. Grattan, *Memoirs*, 4:345.
54. Grattan, ed., *Misc. Works*, 62; and William Edward Hartpole Lecky, *A History of Ireland in the Eighteenth Century*, 5 vols. (London: Longmans, Green, and Co., 1913–16; orig. ed., 1892), 3:546–47, for the grim state of Irish affairs by 1796.
55. Grattan, ed., *Speeches of Grattan*, 3:263, from a speech on 17 October 1796, advocating complete Catholic emancipation. Also see ibid., 3:296–313, for a speech where Grattan returns to one of his favorite ploys: the American analogy.

old friend Hercules Langrishe had stood with him in the earliest days of his career, but then Langrishe, the administraton critic and advocate of imperial reform in the Townshend years, lost his Patriot zeal. He opposed Grattan on the issue of parliamentary reform in the 1780s. For a time he outstripped Grattan in his advocacy of Catholic reform, but in 1795 he balked at full emancipation and once again stood opposed to his friend. John Forbes, George Ogle, and Edward Newenham sided with Grattan on parliamentary reform and voted against him on Catholic emancipation. Had Henry Flood not died in 1791, he probably would have been aligned with them. Thus if Grattan managed to keep most of his friendships from succumbing to political differences and always found some men to back him, there still were times when he felt all but abandoned.

Grattan would have done well to remember that he too had not been perfectly consistent, either in his support of the Catholic cause or in his opposition politics. He had been slow to come around to full Catholic emancipation, being content before the mid-1790s that Catholics should exercise the franchise rather than sit in Parliament—a Parliament he fully expected to continue under Anglo-Irish Protestant domination. And while he condemned the administration for being too heavy-handed in squelching the United Irishmen and keeping peace in the countryside, he had not opposed passage of some acts designed to maintain law and order. Grattan's views had become especially problematic after 1792, when the French Revolution entered a more radical stage and the republicanism intrinsic in any drive for parliamentary reform at home became more pronounced.

Grattan's anti-Castle, anti-Pitt ministry comments were even more caustic in the 1790s than they had been in the 1780s, but they played to a different audience in the Irish Parliament. In the 1790s Grattan defended reform and emancipation as constitutional renovations rather than innovations, just as he had promoted parliamentary independence and then reform, without Catholic emancipation, in the early 1780s. When accusing Pitt of conspiring against Irish liberties in the 1790s he repeated charges first leveled during the commercial crisis of the preceding decade. His argument that the "connexion with Great Britain" should carry with it "perfect freedom" for all Irishmen seemed to reflect a qualified attachment to empire; he had said similar things before, when times were less desperate. And there is the key to Grattan's frustration and failure. The times had changed. Never popular with the most conservative leaders in Irish society, he had begun to lose many moderates as well.

Grattan's critics accused him of pushing Ireland toward the brink of revolution by his irresponsible insistence on reform in the midst of domestic and imperial crisis. During the Fitzwilliam controversy, numerous informal groups had seconded Grattan in opposing Fitzwilliam's recall. In responding to the protestations and resolutions sent to him by concerned citizens, Grattan emphasized that "some enemy" had thwarted them from reaching their goal of reform and emancipation, and he urged them not to give in but to continue asserting their rights. Speaking of Parliament, he proclaimed, "Let the people be the sole author of its existence, so they should be the great object of its care."[56] Grattan did not expressly urge people to take to the streets or join the United Irishmen, yet because he gave credence to already-existing fears of conspiracy, he had to bear some of the responsibility for the rioting and disillusionment with government that followed. Before he walked out of Commons in May 1797, he delivered a sweeping indictment of Parliament reminiscent of his April 1780 speech: Parliament, he charged, was inept and the tool of special interests. It had divided and paralyzed Irish society with penal codes and had acquiesced in its own emasculation with the Declaratory Act of 1720. It continued to resist reform even after achieving independence in 1782 and therefore still did not truly represent the people. Given the inflammatory nature of these views, one critic maintained that Fitzwilliam had committed political suicide by listening to Grattan. Insistence on reform had been an "act of madness" akin to casting a "firebrand" into a "combustible" country.[57]

Not all of Grattan's critics in the 1790s were dyed-in-the-wool administration men; some were old friends. Charles Francis Sheridan, critic of Blackstone and sometime member of the parliamentary opposition in the 1780s, used his pen for more conservative purposes in the following decade. He opposed full Catholic emancipation, contending that there was nothing wrong with keeping Catholics out of politics. He devised an argument to show that Catholics were entitled to membership in the "civil community" and complete rights to property ownership, employment, and religious freedom, but that they could not yet be trusted to become a part of the "political community." It would be enough for Catholics to be protected by the law; they did not have to have a hand in making it. Sheridan wanted Catholics to be content with a form of virtual representation and to accept restrictions that he had

---

56. Grattan, ed., *Misc. Works*, 63. Also see Grattan, *Memoirs*, 4:217–19, for Grattan's responses to those protesting Fitzwilliam's recall—responses that Froude, *English in Ireland*, 3:222–25, thought irresponsible, sowing the "seeds of disorder."
57. Knox, *Essays*, III, 26–28.

argued against in 1779 when defending the idea of Irish parliamentary independence. "I assert, that the *actual* representation of a part may be the *virtual* representation of the whole," wrote Sheridan, "because it may have precisely the same *efficacy* in securing the civil liberty of the whole community, than the *actual* representation of every individual member of it, could by possibility have."[58] His justification was that the Irish Parliament could fairly represent and protect Catholics under the rule of law, whereas the British Parliament could not for all of Ireland. Sheridan also advised against insistence on parliamentary reform or any attempt to alter the borough system so long as the French Revolution raged. "The spirit of salutary Reform is, in its progress, slow, mild, cautious, discriminating; it corrects with the tenderness of a parental hand," he counseled. A "fierce" and "undistinguishing" spirit of "Innovation" had been unleashed by "apostles of anarchy," spreading a dangerous spirit of democratic republicanism.[59] Sheridan therefore opposed Catholic relief in 1793 and the various reform bills introduced by William Ponsonby from 1793 to 1797.

Sheridan's old associate in the Monks of St. Patrick and erstwhile champion of the people, Joseph Pollock, also urged caution in the 1790s. Pollock had been an enthusiastic Volunteer and even joined the United Irishmen when they were first organized. By 1793 he was disillusioned with democratic politics. He feared that the United Irishmen were in danger of going the way of the French revolutionaries:

From the public political distrust of gentlemen, and of men of property,—as such,—to the destruction of *all ranks* and *all property,* and, with them, *all liberty and security,* the progress, in a revolution, is as necessary as the accelerated motion of a falling body; and the *reform* tht should *begin* on such principles, must *end,* not merely in a revolution, but in anarchy.[60]

---

58. Charles Francis Sheridan, *The Roman Catholic Claim to the Elective Franchise Discussed, in an Essay upon the True Principles of Civil Liberty and of Free Government* (Dublin: James Moore, 1793), 69. William Todd Jones, *A Letter to the Societies of United Irishmen of the Town of Belfast* (Dublin: J. Chambers, 1792), continued the crusade he had begun as a Volunteer to remove Catholic disabilities—citing Grattan's statement that Ireland would never be truly free until that happened—but he was drowned out by writers like Sheridan. See the critique of Jones in *Tracts on Irish Affairs* (Dublin: Richard White, 1791).

59. [Charles Francis Sheridan], *Some Observations on a Late Address to the Citizens of Dublin; with Thoughts on the Present Crisis,* 4th ed. (London: J. Debrett, 1797), quotes from pp. 3, 6. Like Grattan, Sheridan too made American allusions, this time to defend his anti-radical posture, whereas in earlier years it was to support his criticism of the empire.

60. Joseph Pollock, *Letters to the Inhabitants of the Town and Lordship of Newry* (Dublin: P. Byrne, 1793), 66. Also see *Thoughts on Liberty and Equality. By a Member of Parliament* (Dublin: James Moore, 1793), attributed to Laurence Parsons, one of the more liberal M.P.s, a man admired even by Wolfe Tone.

Theobald McKenna, onetime leader of the Catholic Committee and reform advocate, also feared that events were spiraling out of control. Echoing Charles O'Conor, who had worried that the "Intemperance" of some agitators in the 1780s pushed reform too far too fast, he warned against the delusive appeal of democratic republicanism. He did not agree with Pollock—much less Sheridan—on what, eventually, Catholics should be entitled to, but like them he reaffirmed his attachment to constitutional monarchy and the British imperial tie.[61] John Keogh, who had split with McKenna and the other Catholic moderates in order to join forces with the United Irishmen, after 1793 began to sound more like McKenna. They both feared that Ireland could tip toward democracy and to them—and to many others—democracy was the first step toward anarchy. Like Aristotle in his *Politics,* one pamphleteer warned that

> when the People, instead of destroying despotism, actually assume the place of the despot, and in lieu of his *will* substitute their own—There arbitrary Government appears in its most finished form; there it admits of no corrective—no palliative—its power is as unlimited as the will on which it depends is absolute—it is physically as well as politically supreme—and without being under the necessity of attending to those principles which are binding upon individual man, it exercises almost the omnipotence of God.[62]

With the exception of Fitzwilliam's brief lord lieutenancy the administration had opposed parliamentary reform and complete Catholic emancipation all along. Joined by moderates in Parliament fearful of revolution and separatism, governmental power grew through the 1790s. Watching politics from the sidelines by 1797, William Drennan noted that the "word of the administration is—Emancipation is Separation, and Reform a Republic."[63] Those in Parliament like Grattan who tried to counter that view failed; when they withdrew, Drennan remarked, they abandoned "all hopes of reforming the constitution by the constitution." Now outside the official channels of power, men like Grattan "must either unite with the people or be annihilated."[64]

Grattan could not bring himself to "unite" with the people in a grassroots movement to save the constitution or purge Irish society of lingering inequities. Losing ground with moderates in Parliament, he also

---

61. Theobald McKenna, *An Essay on Parliamentary Reform, and on the Evils Likely to Ensue from a Republican Constitution in Ireland* (Dublin: John Rice, 1793).

62. *Thoughts on the Will of the People* (Dublin: John Rhea, 1794), 10; sometimes attributed to Alexander Knox (see n. 51 above).

63. Chart, ed., *Drennan Letters,* 251; Drennan to his sister in February 1797.

64. Ibid., 260; Drennan to his sister, 1 August 1797.

lost popularity among the Protestant middle class. After resigning his seat in Commons, Grattan relegated himself to political impotency, since, by his own definition, government must be the final arbiter of change. He had not trusted the Volunteers as an independent political lobby, and he was happy to see them fade from power. The United Irishmen never met with his approval, even if he and Ponsonby had tried to find a way of working with some of them in the cause of reform.[65] He could not endorse the United Irishmen as a group; it would not have occurred to him to use them as a way of regaining power. The Volunteers of the early 1780s, at least, had possessed a modicum of deference and had included within their ranks more men of property and prominence. Yet even they could not be allowed to share power, Grattan decided.

By the time that Grattan left Parliament the United Irishmen, even though banned from public activity, had done the unthinkable: they had become revolutionaries and avowed separatists. They made it virtually impossible for Grattan and the old parliamentary opposition to characterize themselves as nationalists and defenders of the people. The United Irishmen discredited what those men saw as the real accomplishments of thirty years of "Patriot" politics. Grattan and most of his colleagues remained opposed to republicanism and separatism. Before the rise of the United Irishmen and the French Revolution, they had been able to cultivate a self-image that sustained them through the hurly-burly of shifting political alliances. Furthermore, before the 1790s they could criticize the many failings of the Irish Parliament without condemning the institution itself, because they could continue to believe that conditions would gradually improve. Likewise, they could profess their love for the king even as they condemned excessive Crown influence. When they had the American Revolution alone as their example, they could talk more easily about popular power and be more insistent about their constitutional claims.

The French Revolution brought a new frame of reference. It raised to the surface deepseated fears of popular power. Anglo-Irish politicians had always defended the idealized British constitution, even as the "Patriots" within their ranks criticized the way it had been applied to Ireland. In the 1790s the shortcomings of the constitution in practice seemed less important to most "Patriots," given the revolutionary radicalism in France. Some even concluded that Americans would have been better off staying in the empire and avoiding the excesses of democratic republicanism.[66]

65. Grattan, *Memoirs*, 4:285.
66. See, for example, McKenna, *Essay on Parliamentary Reform*, 34, 37.

The parliamentary opposition, never united for long and not sympathetic to a genuinely popular political movement, left the stage open to administration men more sure of themselves and more certain of the need for effective social control and stronger imperial ties. Grattan's influence reached low ebb in 1798 with the outbreak of rebellion. Refusing to accept his explanation for leaving Commons, the Dublin freemen denounced Grattan for abandoning them and the cause of reform. They turned on him because he had not done enough; the university shunned him because he had gone too far. A portrait of Grattan commissioned by Trinity College in 1782 and hung in the college theater was taken down and put in storage. A portrait of John Fitzgibbon, earl of Clare, was hung in its place.[67] Grattan had been politically eclipsed by Fitzgibbon some years before he left the Commons in 1797. With Fitzgibbon leading the way, Grattan's Parliament was soon to disappear, engulfed in a parliamentary union with Westminster.

Fitzgibbon had Old English and Catholic roots, but his father had become a Protestant, entered public life, and paved the way for his even more ambitious son. Fitzgibbon attended Trinity College, moved on to Oxford, was called to the Irish Bar, and entered Commons in 1778 as one of the university M.P.s. Hardly a slavish administration man, he did draw ever closer to the Castle. By 1783 he began sitting for the borough of Kilmallock, County Limerick. He became lord chancellor in 1789 and was named earl of Clare in 1795. He was just a few years younger than Grattan. The two men had known each other as youths in Dublin and as students at Trinity College. At one time friendly if not especially close, they formally broke over the regency crisis.

Fitzgibbon is a perplexing character, whose proper place in Irish history has been hotly debated. Critics derided him as an oligarch during his lifetime and dead cats were flung at his coffin when he died in 1802. He had, like most other prominent men, joined the Volunteers when they first formed but distanced himself from them as they became more politically demanding. He supported parliamentary independence unenthusiastically and adamantly opposed parliamentary reform and Catholic emancipation. He was awarded the chancellorship and a peerage in recognition of his efforts to counter the opposition Patriots and agitators outside Parliament. In effect he became the consummate law and order man, a staunch defender of governmental power. He was small, but he spoke with great force: hardheaded, direct, bruising in debate, and arrogant in manner.

67. Grattan, ed., *Misc. Works*, appendix, 240–41, 241n.; Chart, ed., *Drennan Letters*, 279–80, Drennan to his sister, 15 October 1798.

John Fitzgibbon, resplendent as lord chancellor and earl of Clare, by Hugh Douglas Hamilton. Courtesy of the National Gallery of Ireland.

To J. A. Froude he was the best politician and statesman ever produced by the Anglo-Irish elite, because he was a pragmatist, never letting reality become fogged in his mind—which Grattan, Froude determined, had not been able to do. Fitzgibbon opposed the cultivation of Anglo-Irish constitutional nationalism because he feared it would lead to a full-fledged Celtic-Catholic nationalism that rejected both the empire and the Anglo-Irish Ascendancy. Fitzgibbon was convinced that Ireland could prosper only if led by Anglo-Irish Protestants acting under British tutelage. To Froude, who felt the same even though he was writing three quarters of a century later, Fitzgibbon was a far-sighted champion of their shared cause.[68] For Fitzgibbon a parliamentary union made eminent sense; he bided his time, waiting for the proper moment.

Union was little discussed before the 1790s, although political economist Josiah Tucker had predicted in 1774 that the American colonies would be separated from the empire and that "a compleat union and incorporation with Ireland" would take place "within half a century." Accomplishment of one would hasten the advent of the other. He favored as well as predicted the parliamentary union; so did his critic, the radical reformer John Cartwright. Adam Smith also favored union and said as much in his *Wealth of Nations*.[69]

Union was not then popular in Ireland, and there was no great urgency in the matter anyway. There was some inclination to pursue the idea during Buckinghamshire's lord lieutenancy, especially with the commercial crisis in 1779. But the probable unpopularity of any such move in Ireland, combined with manifold concerns in the British Par-

---

68. Froude, *English in Ireland*, 2:50, 259–60, 482; echoed with only slightly less enthusiasm in Molony, *Ireland's Tragic Comedians*, 3–72. Also see the contemporary sketch in Falkland, *A Review of the Principal Characters of the Irish House of Commons* (Dublin, 1789), 14–17; and the very unflattering characterization in Grattan, *Memoirs*, 3:202, and sprinkled throughout.

69. Tucker in the *Hibernian Magazine* 4 (March 1774): 154–57; and Smith in *An Inquiry into the Nature and Causes of The Wealth of Nations*, ed. by Edwin Cannan (New York: Modern Library, 1937; orig. ed., 1776), 896–900. Cartwright disagreed with Tucker's conclusion that the British Parliament was sovereign over the American colonies and took Tucker to task in *American Independence, the Interest and Glory of Great Britain* (Philadelphia: Robert Bell, 1776; orig. ed., 1774). In Letter III, Notes & c., he concluded that "Humanity, wisdom, and virtue dictate an union" between Britain and Ireland. In 1785 Tucker still thought a union would be nice but at the moment infeasible, given the animosities sparked during the commercial crisis. See Tucker's *Reflections on the Present Matters in Dispute between Great Britain and Ireland* (London: T. Cadell, 1785), 34. Tucker had first predicted some twenty-five years before Lexington and Concord that the Americans would seek autonomy. James Kelly, "The Origins of the Act of Union: An Examination of Unionist Opinion in Britain and Ireland, 1650–1800," *Irish Historical Studies* 25 (1987): 236–63, surveys the gradual growth of unionist sentiments on both sides of St. George's Channel.

liament, prevented serious consideration of the measure.[70] The duke of Portland might have preferred union to the declaration of parliamentary independence pushed through by Grattan in April 1782, yet as lord lieutenant he made no real attempt to stop Grattan, nor did—nor seemingly could—the Rockingham ministry.[71] By the mid-1780s there were growing rumors that a union was in the offing, even if the idea of union was still unpopular among most Irish leaders. The duke of Rutland, at least in his official correspondence as lord lieutenant, had expressed his preference for union. Likewise in debates at Westminster, legislative union had been suggested as a solution to the British-Irish commercial conundrum.

The earl of Charlemont commented to Henry Flood on union rumors circulating in 1786, expressing hope that they were groundless. Any attempt to raise the question officially would "disgrace the movers" and "raise a flame in the country," he believed.[72] Charlemont's hostility to the notion notwithstanding, the idea of union would not go away. It is not clear exactly when Pitt the younger decided that union was the best

---

70. Arthur Young, *A Tour in Ireland*, 2 vols. (Dublin: George Bonham, 1780), 1:81–82, noted the unpopularity of union among the Irish in 1776, and vol. 2, pt. 2, 191–94, offered suggestions on how union could be accomplished (Young was not insistent here). For the possibility of union under Buckinghamshire, see Herbert Butterfield, *George III, Lord North, and the People, 1779–80* (London: G. Belland Sons, 1949), 104–9; Buckinghamshire's letters to George Germain of 20 August and 30 September 1779 in HMC, *Report on the Manuscripts of Mrs. Stopford-Sackville*, 2 vols. (London: Mackie, 1904–10), 1:258, 258, resp.; Lord Lucan to Edmund Sexton Pery, 21 August 1779, in HMC, *Eighth Report* (London: Eyre and Spottiswoode, 1881), pt. I, 202; and the pamphlets by [Joseph Pollock], *Letters of Owen Roe O'Nial* (Dublin: W. Jackson, 1779) and *Renovation without Violence Yet Possible* (Dublin: William Hallhead, 1779).

71. W. E. Hume-Williams, *The Irish Parliament: From the Year 1782 to 1800*, 2d ed. (London: Cassell, 1892), appendix, 114–19, reproduces the letters between Portland and Shelburne, where a union of some sort and Irish recognition of the superintending power of the British Parliament are suggested. The language was fairly cryptic. Hume-Williams was convinced that these men were contemplating a formal legislative union. It is just as likely that Portland had in mind an Irish recognition of British supremacy in external commercial and diplomatic affairs. Otherwise, it seems unlikely that Charlemont would have been friendly at all and the earl, according to Portland, was receptive to at least part of his plan. Hume-Williams (an Englishman) was himself pro-union—he thought it had been necessary and unavoidable.

72. Charlemont to Henry Flood, 12 November 1786, Henry Flood Correspondence, Add. MS. 22,930, BL. Also see Beresford, ed., *The Correspondence of the Right Hon. John Beresford*, 2 vols. (London: Woodfall and Kinder, 1854), 1:267–68, Lord Tyrone, older brother of John Beresford, letter of 15 June 1785, who favored union. Interestingly enough, John Jebb (like John Cartwright) also favored union, provided it was accompanied with real parliamentary reform, so that people in Britain as well as Ireland would be better represented. See John Disney, ed., *The Works Theological, Medical, Political, and Miscellaneous, of John Jebb, M.D., F.R.S. with Memoirs of the Life of the Author*, 3 vols. (London: T. Cadell, 1787), 1:203, Jebb to Henry Joy of Belfast, 28 November 1784.

policy. His ministry, organized near the end of 1783, was never unfriendly to the idea, but Pitt himself waited nearly a decade to make his pro-union sentiments widely known. The 1780s closed with pamphlets taking both sides of the issue. Pitt seemed to be inching toward a unionist policy by then, perhaps responding to the logic in warnings that "independent legislatures will produce independent states"; in other words, the tensions produced by *imperium in imperio* could not be endured forever.[73] Pitt repeatedly stressed during his pro-union speeches at Westminster in 1799 that he did not accept the 1782 settlement as any sort of "final adjustment," constitutionally or politically. His push for a commercial union in 1785 was a logical forerunner to his campaign for parliamentary union a decade later.

William Drennan observed in 1792 that "rumour of an Union" was spreading through Dublin; he predicted the next year, and again in 1796, that union was imminent and that Ireland would soon "be lost indeed."[74] Wrong about the timing, he was not wrong about the desire on both sides of the Irish Sea to bring an end to the arrangement formalized in 1782. Edmund Burke told Earl Fitzwilliam that he never liked it. Under it Ireland did not add "any security to its Liberty."[75] The Irish rebellion that erupted in the spring of 1798 pushed other M.P.s in Westminster and many leading Irishmen to concur with Burke.

Drennan and others had anticipated this rebellion.[76] One critic actually blamed Drennan for pushing the country into civil war by making government the scapegoat for all social evils, the "source of their woes." Drennan and the United Irishmen had ignited the fires of republicanism

73. From "Remarks on our Situation with respect to Ireland," an anonymous report written sometime between 1782 and 1798 in the Sydney Papers, vol. II, packet P, MS. 52, NLI. Was Pitt simply following the logic seen by his father many years before? Rumors that the elder Pitt wanted a union circulated in the American colonies back in 1773. See the *Virginia Gazette* (Purdie and Dixon) 1 April 1773. Also see the call for union by Englishman John Williams, *An Union of England and Ireland proved to be Practicable and equally Beneficial to each Kingdom* (London: G. Kennedy, 1787); another pro-union piece by "A Friend to Both Countries," *The Utility of Union between Great Britain and Ireland Considered* (Dublin: P. Byrne, 1787), and the retorts in *An Inquiry into the Justice and Policy of an Union between Great Britain and Ireland* (Dublin: P. Byrne, 1787) and *A Candid Review of the Most important Occurances that took place in IRELAND, during the last three years* (Dublin: P. Byrne, 1787).

74. Chart, ed., *Drennan Letters*, 91, Drennan to his brother-in-law, Samuel McTier, 29 September 1792; 145, Drennan to McTier again, 26 March 1793; and 235, Drennan to his sister in April 1796.

75. Burke to Fitzwilliam, 20 November 1796, in Thomas Copeland et al., eds., *The Correspondence of Edmund Burke*, 10 vols. (Cambridge: Cambridge University Press, 1958–78), 9:123; also see Burke's letter to Thomas Hussey of 18 May 1795, ibid., 8:245–51, for Burke's fear that Ireland was headed down the road to radicalism unless something was done to divert it.

76. Chart, ed., *Drennan Letters*, 235–36, Drennan to his sister, 18 April 1796.

and separatism, charged this accuser.[77] Drennan had dropped out of politics, but other United Irishmen did not. They continued meeting after the 1794 ban, and they added to their ranks. One estimate put their members at more than 80,000 in 1797.[78] They had finally come out for separation. They courted French aid in their quest for independence and welcomed the French fleet that arrived in 1796. Wolfe Tone was on board, back from his American exile with a commission in the French Army. The fleet did not stay long and landed no troops, but its appearance heartened those wanting to rebel, and it threw government into a panic. The government became more aggressive; the United Irishmen became even more resentful. By May 1798 some had rebelled, as had Catholic peasants here and there around the country.

The rebellion that began in the spring had been crushed by the summer. The French sent too little too late; the United Irishmen did not coordinate their resistance very well, and they were not able to join effectively with the Catholics. Indeed, sectarian violence had pitted Protestant "Orangemen" against Catholic "Defenders" for several years before the rebellion. A second French fleet was driven away, Tone was caught and sentenced to death, and the United Irishmen were scattered and ultimately vanished. The British dispatched thousands of regulars to restore order; they were assisted by the administration and a fairly united Parliament, as well as by the divisions within Irish society and the weakness of the French–United Irishmen alliance. Some Catholics who might have been sympathetic to revolt believed that France had become too radical, its turning on Catholicism tarnishing its image as an ally. Some Presbyterians in the north found France an unattractive partner not only because it was "atheistic" but because it had fallen into an undeclared naval war with the United States, now home for many of their friends and relatives. The French, for their part, did not really trust the United Irishmen, nor did they want to commit many men or resources to a risky enterprise. Only a handful of romantics among the Anglo-Irish ruling elite (like Edward FitzGerald, the duke of Leinster's younger brother) participated in the revolt; the vast majority of the rest thought the rebellion as unjustified and dangerous as the 1641 outbreak.

---

77. Knox, *Essays*, VIII, 62 (Drennan was not identified by name, though Knox probably knew Drennan had written the "Helot" letters).

78. John Blaquiere to Lord Liverpool, 3 February 1797, in the Blaquiere Letters, MS. 877, NLI. Blaquiere, like Beresford, was no friend to the United Irishmen. He and Beresford may well have exaggerated the numbers and popularity of the United Irishmen, but their estimate pales when compared with that of William MacNeven, who, in his testimony before a secret parliamentary committee, claimed there were over three hundred thousand by 1798.

Tone went to his death thinking himself an Irish nationalist, and there have been those who trace both modern Irish nationalism and the modern Irish revolutionary tradition to him and the United Irishmen. In his eyes he tried to do for the Irish what George Washington had done for the Americans. His only mistake, he felt, was that he failed. His associates also tried to employ the American revolutionary analogy, but to no avail.[79] To the men in power, they had been traitors whose acts were unconscionable. Grattan had nothing to do with the rebellion, though he sympathized with those he felt were driven to revolt by an unfeeling ministry and a corrupt administration. "The French and the United Irishmen together could never have made the people rebel, if both had not been assisted by the Administration," he later told the English historian Francis Plowden.[80] A few others shared Grattan's view that the Castle and Pitt ministry had been at fault, but they were a distinct minority.[81]

Rebellion gave Pitt the excuse he needed to call for a parliamentary union. During the fall of 1798 he solicited the views of Irish leaders, in an attempt to see how hard he could push for union in the new British and Irish parliamentary sessions that would open in January 1799. Longtime administration men like John Beresford and Sir John Blaquiere lined up in support, Blaquiere concluding that "nothing short of Legislative Union can secure this Kingdom to the Empire or to myself property or Life."[82] Opposition leader Barry Yelverton, now Lord Avonmore,

---

79. For Tone's Washington allusion, see O'Brien, ed., *Autobiography of Tone*, 2:359; for Thomas Emmet and William MacNeven's brief American allusions see Gilbert, ed., *Documents*, 164, 166, 178, 182. Knox, *Essays*, XVIII and XIX, drew on the American example—and specifically Washington—to condemn the democratic radicalism of the United Irishmen. For the rebellion itself, see Elliott, *Partners in Revolution*; Thomas Pakenham, *The Year of Liberty* (Englewood Cliffs, N.J.: Prentice-Hall, 1969); and the observations in R. R. Palmer, *The Age of the Democratic Revolution*, 2 vols. (Princeton: Princeton University Press, 1959, 1964), 2:236–38, 461, 491; McDowell, *Irish Public Opinion*, 202–19; and idem, "The Age of the United Irishmen: Revolution and the Union, 1794–1800," in Moody and Vaughan, eds., *New History of Ireland*, 4:339–73.

80. Grattan to Francis Plowden, 22 December 1803, in the Hardwicke Papers, vol. 347, Add. MS. 35,745, BL; the logical outgrowth of an attitude he began to shape at least as early as 1795, in the aftermath of the Fitzwilliam crisis and given his conviction that Irish freedoms were being conspired against in London as well as at Dublin Castle. See Grattan's letter to Edmund Burke of 14 March 1795 in Grattan, *Memoirs*, 5:562–63 (appendix).

81. A view advanced most vociferously in Jonah Barrington, *Rise and Fall of the Irish Nation* (New York: D. & J. Sadlier, 1885; orig. ed., 1833), 316, 337–39; also see Chart, ed., *Drennan Letters*, 288, Drennan to his sister, 8 February 1799.

82. Blaquiere to the duke of Rutland, 7 January 1799, Blaquiere Letters, MS. 877, NLI; this even though Blaquiere had admitted in a letter (in ibid.) to the earl of Liverpool, 29 July 1798, that the rebellion had not actually much disrupted the country after the initial shock wore off and the rebels were checked.

An End to "Independence"   231

favored union, as did sometime opposition member Thomas Conolly; both claimed to have preferred union all along, despite their support for Grattan in April 1782. Parliament in general had already shown that it was not as jealous of its prerogatives as it had been at other times, passing in the 1798 session a law granting the king greater leeway in calling parliaments. A similar bill proposed in 1759 had led to protest in Commons and riot without, and was withdrawn.[83]

Edward Cooke, undersecretary to the lord lieutenant, Charles, Earl Cornwallis, and M.P. for the borough of Leighlin, tried to clear the way with an ostensibly evenhanded, objective pamphlet contending that parliamentary union alone could solve the problem of *imperium in imperio*. With union, he contended, the Irish would more or less be doing what the Americans had done when they replaced the Articles of Confederation with the Constitution. Cooke appealed to as many interests as possible. To the Anglo-Irish elite he pointed out that union would preserve the Protestant Ascendancy by making Catholics less dangerous, because they would instantly become a minority group. To Catholics he held out the promise of quicker elimination of the remaining barriers restricting them, because they would be less feared and resented. To all he emphasized the improved trade resulting from full partnership in empire.[84]

Thus prepared, Cornwallis opened the Irish Parliament on 22 January 1799 with a carefully worded message urging a "permanent adjustment" that would better provide for the "common security" of the two kingdoms and consolidate "into one firm and lasting fabrick, the strength, the power, and the resources of the British Empire."[85] In other

---

83. See the 1798 law in the *Statutes at Large*, 18:791–93 (38 George III c. 20) and the 1759 incident in chap. 2.

84. [Edward Cooke], *Arguments For and Against an Union, between Great Britain and Ireland Considered* (London: J. Wright, 1798), 16–19; it provoked a response from George Barnes, *The Rights of the Imperial Crown of Ireland Asserted and Maintained, Against Edward Cooke, Esq.*, 3d ed. (Dublin: 1803; orig. ed., 1799), which also included the argument (made by William Saurin in September and December 1798 before the members of the Bar) that M.P.s were trustees of the people—arguments pushed by Plunket and Saurin in Commons debate. Barnes's appendix includes many protests against the union, including the protest of the Bar that passed overwhelmingly (166–32) on 9 December 1798. Barnes was a Bar member, as was Pemberton Rudd, whose *An Answer to the Pamphlet entitled Arguments For and Against an Union, &c. in a Letter to Edward Cooke, Esq., Secretary at War* (Dublin: J. Milliken, 1799), also attacked Cooke, especially for his feigned objectivity. So too did *The Union. Cease Your Funning; Or, the Rebel Detected* 5th ed. (Dublin: Edwards, Harris and Connor, 1799), attributed to Charles Kendal Bushe. Matthew Weld, *No Union! Being An Appeal to Irishmen* (Dublin: H. Fitzpatrick, 1798), had argued that if Americans could not reasonably be represented at Westminster, neither could the Irish.

85. *A Report of the Debate in the House of Commons of Ireland, on Tuesday and*

words, Cornwallis wanted the Irish Lords and Commons to vote in favor of union. He approached the subject gingerly, and it was well that he did, because the majority of M.P.s were not yet willing to legislate themselves out of existence. Debate over the issue took up most of the following three days.

Grattan was gone, but his old friend and powerful colleague George Ponsonby was back in Commons and took up the defense of parliamentary independence in his stead. William Conyngham Plunket and Francis Dobbs, both of whom sat for Charlemont's borough, sided with Ponsonby, as did many others. Though ailing, Charlemont himself led the outnumbered and outvoted anti-unionists in Lords. In Commons the anti-unionists were stronger, and Ponsonby wasted no time in proposing that the response to Cornwallis include a passage affirming "the undoubted birth-right of the people of Ireland to have a resident and independent Legislature, such as it was recognized by the British Legislature in 1782, and was finally settled at the adjustment of all differences between the two countries."[86] By one vote Ponsonby failed to carry his amendment, but he had the satisfaction of seeing Laurence Parsons, one of the few M.P.s Wolfe Tone had admired, carry a motion on 24 January that Commons should make no reference to union in its response to Cornwallis. Although Parsons's motion carried by only five votes and was not an explicit rejection of union, it did buy the anti-unionists some time.[87] Time, as it turned out, was not on their side. Ponsonby's failure to carry his motion in a second attempt, after Parsons's motion had passed, should have told anti-unionists just how tenuous their position was.

Arguments for and against union advanced during those three days of debates in Commons would be repeated in the next parliamentary session, and they anticipated the stands taken in sundry pamphlets (opposition newspapers had been all but silenced by the administration in 1798). Ponsonby, Plunket, Parsons, and other anti-union M.P.s argued

---

Wednesday the 22nd and 23d of January, 1799, on the Subject of an Union (Dublin: James Moore, 1799), 3.

86. Ibid., 14.

87. *A Report of the Debate in the House of Commons of Ireland, on the 24th, 25th, 26th, and 27th of January, 1799, on the Subject of an Union* (Dublin: James Moore, 1799), 155. The Lords accepted Cornwallis's message without amendment, 52 to 17 (proxies included), showing that the men there were not as averse to union as were many members of Commons (*Lords Journal*, 8:193). Still, fourteen of the Lords signed a "Dissentient" protesting a move toward union. Charlemont, Powerscourt, Arran, and Leinster were among the fourteen. Leinster voted for union the next year. Had he switched—and "sold out" as critics charged—or had he simply wanted to delay consideration in 1799, and in 1800 was ready to commit himself? Charlemont died before the 1800 session.

passionately, knowing that the vote would be close. The gallery was packed, one visitor commenting, "I never witnessed a debate in which the votes of so many members were decided by the eloquence of the speakers."[88] Anti-unionists stressed that it was not practical for Ireland to be represented at Westminster and that M.P.s sitting for Ireland would be too few adequately to protect Irish interests. Ponsonby charged that the British Parliament could not be trusted, that before 1779 its policies had been malevolently anti-Irish. Only Irish assertions of constitutional right, he stressed, had brought change. He and others contended that the Irish Parliament had proved itself to be an effective if imperfect organ of government.

Ponsonby and his colleagues did not stop with practical matters. Conflating the "Constitution of 1782" with the British constitution as it had been extended to Ireland, Ponsonby insisted that without an independent parliament the people and "their posterity" would be forever deprived of their most basic liberties.[89] Without mentioning Molyneux by name, Parsons dipped into the past to, in Molyneux fashion, instruct his listeners on how an independent Irish Parliament dated back to Henry II and the original introduction of English law. Plunket, who had been a student at Trinity College when the Volunteers were arguing that M.P.s were trustees and delegates of the people, resurrected that argument. He challenged the competency of Parliament even to consider the question of union. "You are appointed to make laws, and not legislatures. You are appointed to act under the constitution, not alter it."[90] He, Parsons, and Ponsonby thereby sought to make parliamentary independence untouchable and irreversible. Ponsonby stressed the permanence of what was wrought in 1782, making the constitution inseparable from parliamentary independence. Parsons gave an independent parliament the sanction of history. Plunket took the constitution and lodged it with the "people," beyond the reach of any parliament.

---

88. Gilbert, ed., *Documents*, 200.

89. *Report of the Debate*, 23 January 1799, 12; also see John Parnell, who also conflated the 1782 settlement with the Constitution (4), and Thomas Conolly, who claimed to have disliked the 1782 arrangement all along (14).

90. *Report of the Debate*, 24 January 1799, 95–96, for Parsons, and for Plunket, see David Plunket, *The Life, Letters and Speeches of Lord Plunket*, 2 vols. (London: Smith, Elder, 1867), 1:142 (and *Report of the Debate*, 23 January 1799, 20, for George Crookshank of Belfast, who said much the same). Those who are inclined to ignore these arguments as empty or cynical rhetoric ought to read John Dickinson's *Speech Delivered in the House of Assembly of the Province of Pennsylvania, May 24th, 1764* (Philadelphia: William Bradford, 1764), especially 25–26. Dickinson is greatly respected as a constitutionalist. As a politician he was also obliged to make arguments about representatives as delegates and constitutions as immutable, that, in other circumstances, could have proved embarrassing.

Francis Dobbs might not have had as high a regard for the Irish Parliament as these men, yet he sided with them because he continued to believe that 1782 was the "true date of Irish liberty." He did not simply resign himself to an independent parliament as the lesser of two evils. Like the others, he shared Grattan's vision of what Parliament, freed of Crown and administration influence and reformed to be more truly representative, could be. John Philpot Curran did not return to his seat in Commons and probably did not share Grattan's vision, yet he too continued to believe that a flawed independent Irish Parliament was better than no parliament at all. He had been much more sympathetic to the United Irishmen than Grattan had been; he might even have been inclined toward separatism; but he agreed with Grattan that it was unrealistic to think that Ireland could prosper outside the empire. Even William Drennan, grown cynical about Irish politics, preferred to keep an independent Parliament.[91]

Grattan himself added a dose of high drama to the debates when he returned to Commons for the 1800 session as M.P. for the borough of Wicklow. Too sick to stand unassisted, too frail to speak without his voice cracking, Grattan was like a parent rushing to the side of a misguided though still-loved youth. With permission to remain seated and wearing his old Volunteer uniform, he delivered an emotion-filled two-hour speech decrying union and bearing his "last testimony for the constitution of '82."[92]

Grattan was unpersuasive even if eloquent. Cornwallis already knew that his supporters could carry a motion for union in Lords, as they had the previous year. Parsons was not able to block him in Commons as he had before. Cornwallis therefore introduced a tentative plan of union for formal consideration in Commons on 5 February. Unable to prevent its discussion, the anti-unionists could only delay what had become inevitable. Many of them gave up and stayed away when Commons and Lords passed their joint union resolution on 27 March. The Irish Parliament met for the last time on 2 August, and as of 1 January 1801 it ceased to exist.

---

91. Dobbs in *Report of the Debate*, 23 January 1799, 37–40; and Dobbs's speech in this and the 1800 session printed in *Memoirs of Francis Dobbs, Esq.* (Dublin: J. Jones, 1800). For Curran see William Henry Curran, *The Life of the Right Honourable John Philpot Curran* (Chicago: Union Catholic Publishing, 1886; orig. ed., 1819), 318–19, and the contrast between him and Fitzgibbon in White, *The Anglo-Irish*, 94–110. For Drennan's cynical view of Irish politics and his opposition to union, see various letters written from 1798 to 1799 in Chart, ed., *Drennan Letters*, 280, 283, 284, 287.

92. Grattan to Richard Fitzpatrick, 14 February 1800, Charles James Fox Papers XIV, Fo. 213, MS. 47582, BL.

An End to "Independence"

Grattan was virtually harried out of the House before the terms of union were decided. He had been insulted by the chief secretary, Lord Castlereagh. As distressing, he had dueled with and wounded former friend and Monks of St. Patrick associate, Isaac Corry. A unionist, Corry had been made chancellor of the exchequer as a reward for his pro-government stands. More despondent than he had been since 1797, Grattan again withdrew to the isolation of the Wicklow woods and his home at Tinnehinch. The Castle had "bought the Parliament & dragooned the people," he protested, and brought about a union based on "hatred & contempt, perfidy & meanness."[93]

Grattan thought that Parliament had been betrayed, not only by the Pitt ministry and Cornwallis's administration, but by some M.P.s who changed their votes and chose union in 1800 when just the year before they had been opposed. Onetime Monk of St. Patrick, Whig Club member, and Grattan ally Arthur Browne switched sides in 1800, explaining that he had little choice because the Irish Parliament had lost "the affection of the Nation" and had become an inert mass. Grattan could forgive him; arch anti-unionist Jonah Barrington could not, calling Browne's "defection" the most "palpable case" of corruption. Barrington—himself a man of questionable integrity—was hardly being fair to the American-born Browne, who had studied at the school George Berkeley founded in Newport, Rhode Island, and then at Harvard before moving to Ireland and entering Trinity College, Dublin. Admitted to Lincoln's Inn and afterwards to the Irish Bar, Browne became a professor of Greek and canon as well as civil law at Trinity College. He had sat as M.P. for Trinity College from 1783 on and often showed his attachment to Irish constitutional rights. He was no political hack and it is unlikely that his vote could be bought. Sadly, in the heightened emo-

---

93. Ibid. Grattan's son, probably echoing his father, wrote in the *Memoirs*, 5:50, "Never in the annals of history can be found a greater combination of force, fraud, violence, bribery, and illegality." The younger Grattan fumed that "Unquestionably Lord Clare and Lord Castlereagh deserved to die" (ibid., 5:68). Characterizing the whole of British-Irish relations, he wrote, quoting his father, "The English government, in her strength, destroyed the Irish Constitution, in her weakness, she restored it, and on her recovery she took it back again" (ibid., 1:25). For a list of those compensated for lost boroughs, see Gilbert, *History of Dublin* 3:159–60; and the long indictment in Barrington, *Rise and Fall*, 383–460, and lists, 461–72, of who voted against and for union in 1799 and 1800. According to Barrington, the government bought off at least twenty-five M.P.s; thus corruption gave it the victorious edge. Also see the lists in Grattan, ed., *Speeches*, 3:345–47 (for 1799) and 373–75 (1800 vote), without editorial comment. Of the old Monks of St. Patrick sitting in Commons in 1799, five voted against union, and two for; in 1800, five were against, three were in favor (Arthur Browne, M.P. for Trinity College, changed his vote to "aye"); Ponsonby, Ogle, Francis Hardy, and "Lord" Kingsborough were opposed both times; Grattan, not present in 1799, voted "no" in 1800.

tions raised by the union debate, even men of good reputation could not safely change their minds.[94]

Grattan's old associate and mentor, Hercules Langrishe, was among those paid hefty sums as compensation for disestablished parliamentary boroughs that they had once controlled. It is quite possible that Langrishe and others like him voted for union in part to line their pockets. But there was more than money at stake. Grattan and Barrington's view notwithstanding, union was not just the result of a sell-out, even if there was a certain amount of "corruption."

Unionists had had a formidable arsenal of arguments, all of which they brought to bear. They argued that if Parliament—as opposition critics like Grattan had once charged—failed to protect public interest, it should be dissolved and they all should welcome union, as no doubt Molyneux would have done had Parliament failed his generation. If Parliament could not be trusted to reform itself, and the people could not be allowed to perform that task, what other option was there, they asked? Grattan and the anti-unionists, they continued, had behaved inconsistently, leaving Commons in a huff and then returning to save the very institution they had belittled as hopelessly corrupt. In an ironic twist, unionists who once defended the good name of Parliament against Grattan's diatribes and the condemnations of radicals now argued that Parliament was indeed beyond redemption. Their seeming flip-flop was no stranger nor necessarily any more disingenuous than that of anti-unionists, who now defended the institution they had once so roundly condemned. Unionists further noted that Plunket's argument that M.P.s were trustees was too conveniently applied, since many of the anti-unionists had objected to that characterization when the Volunteers and United Irishmen had made it. Besides, to argue that all power was literally vested with the people and reverted to them if the legislature were dissolved, unionists warned, was to court disaster. Given the recent rebellion, they did not have much trouble conjuring up fears of anarchy.

The anti-unionists, themselves a hodge-podge, united only—and that barely—in their desire to save Parliament, could not effectively counter any of these charges. Longtime administration men and members of the opposition had been shoved together in an uncomfortable alliance. Lacking solidarity and the ability to coordinate their own views as well

---

94. See Browne's speech (apparently before he had decided to switch) in *A Report of the Debate in the House of Commons of Ireland, on Wednesday and Thursday the 15th and 16th of January, 1800* (Dublin: James Moore, 1800), 86–87; and Barrington, *Rise and Fall*, 461, the "Original Red List," no. 14. Browne was named prime serjeant, though that does not mean he sold his vote.

as popular opinion, they fell prey to a better-organized group that turned the logic of their own arguments and the inconsistencies in their behavior against them.[95]

Parliament was deluged with resolutions and petitions from freeholders from most of the counties and many of the towns and cities, all protesting union. Members of the Bar had voted overwhelmingly against union on constitutional as well as practical grounds in December 1798, before the question was officially raised. They all made the same arguments, in various forms, that Ponsonby, Parsons, and Plunket made in Commons and that pamphleteers made in print. It would seem, then, that a majority of the Protestant electorate wanted to keep an independent parliament.

Writing pseudonymously as an "Irish Catholic," William MacNeven, from his Scottish prison cell, soft-peddled separatism. "Union and Separation are correlative terms," he declared; the Irish should "consider whether a provincial subjection to England, or a total independence,

---

95. G. C. Bolton, *The Passing of the Irish Act of Union* (Oxford: Oxford University Press, 1966), tells the story well enough. Also see J. T. Ball, *Historical Review of the Legislative Systems Operative in Ireland* (Dublin: Hodges, Figgis, and Co., 1889), 155–239, and Edward and Annie G. Porritt, *The Unreformed House of Commons*, 2 vols. (Cambridge: Cambridge University Press, 1903, 1909), 2:469–529. The 1800 speeches more or less repeat the arguments made in 1799. For drama, if not learned disquisition, it is interesting to compare Fitzgibbon's *The Speech of the Right Honourable John, Earl of Clare Lord High Chancellor of Ireland, in the House of Lords in Ireland, on a Motion Made by Him on Monday, February 10, 1800* (Dublin: J. Milliken, 1800) and the rebuttal from Commons by Grattan in *An Answer to a Pamphlet, entitled, The Speech of the Earl of Clare, on the Subject of a Legislative Union between Great Britain and Ireland* (London: George Grierson and J. Robinson, 1800). For the most detailed argument on M.P.s as trustees of the people, see William Saurin, *An Accurate Report of the Speech of William Saurin, Esq., in the Irish House of Commons, on Friday, the 21st of February, 1800, on the Question of a Legislative Union with Great Britain* (Dublin: J. Moore, 1800), where Saurin repeats the argument he and Joshua Spencer apparently had first made before the Bar in September 1798, repeated in December. Spencer cited John Locke as his authority and the drafting of the U.S. Constitution in 1787 as an example. For Saurin and Spencer, see Edward Cooke to Viscount Castlereagh, 10 September 1798, in the Marquess of Londonderry, ed., *Memoirs and Correspondence of Viscount Castlereagh, Second Marquess of Londonderry*, 12 vols. (London: Henry Colbourne, 1848–53), 1:343; and *A Report of the Debate of the Irish Bar, On Sunday, the 9th of December, 1798, on the Subject of an Union of the Legislatures of Great Britain and Ireland* (Dublin: J. Morre, 1799), 8–9. Also see the rebuttal to Saurin by Thomas B. Clarke, *The Doctrine of "An Appeal to the People and the Right of Resistance" as Laid Down by Mr. Saurin, in the Irish House of Commons, Considered and Confuted, in a letter to a Member of the Irish Parliament* (London: John Hatchard, 1800), and by William Cusac Smith (also a barrister and M.P.) in *Animadversions on the Speeches of Mr. Saurin and Mr. Bushe* (Dublin: Marchbank, 1800). Smith, arch-unionist, sat for borough Donegal, as did Charles Kendal Bushe, leading anti-unionist. That in itself says something for the vitality of Commons and the electoral system. Even though union advocates denied that Parliament was bound by the will of the people, they saw the need to take their arguments to the public—as their opponents were doing.

would be most conducive to the happiness of Ireland."[96] His suggestions had few if any takers. Prominent Catholics appear to have been friendlier to union, though it is noteworthy that Daniel O'Connell, in his first real try at politics, spoke in opposition. To O'Connell, abolition of Parliament was an undemocratic act whose outcome held little promise of a brighter future.[97]

Pro-unionists had some of the same advantages over anti-unionists as supporters of the U.S. Constitution had had over "Antifederalists" wanting to keep the Articles of Confederation. They were better organized, not simply because their votes had been lined up by the Castle and ministry, but because they were appalled by what had happened during the Irish equivalent of the "critical period" of the American 1780s. They wanted major changes, in order to prevent another crisis in the future. Like the "Federalists" who backed the Constitution, they also benefited from defections within the opposition ranks, notably Arthur Browne in Commons and the duke of Leinster in Lords, between the 1799 and 1800 parliamentary sessions. And like defenders of the Articles of Confederation, many anti-unionists (Grattan, for instance) played into the hands of their opponents by admitting that there were defects in the existing system. Finally, the dangers posed by union were hypothetical, while the shortcomings of the Irish Parliament were all too real.

Union came, unwelcomed by many and with some embarrassment to others. The Irish were given one hundred seats in the Commons at Westminster and thirty-two in Lords (twenty-eight temporal, four spiritual). The seats in Commons were divided among the thirty-two counties (two M.P.s each), two apiece for Dublin and Cork, one for Trinity College, and one each for thirty-one boroughs. The remaining boroughs were disenfranchised, thus finally and ironically eliminating the most "venal and corrupt" boroughs, whose extinction reformers had tried to arrange for three decades. To that extent Irish M.P.s more truly became repre-

---

96. An Irish Catholic, *An Argument for Independence, in Opposition to a Union* (Dublin: J. Stockdale, 1799) 44. William Steel Dickson confirmed MacNeven's authorship years later in his *Narrative*.

97. For O'Connell's speech see Grattan, *Memoirs*, 5:61–64; and the letter to O'Connell from his uncle of 30 January 1800 criticizing him for his anti-unionism, in Maurice O'Connell, ed., *The Correspondence of Daniel O'Connell*, 8 vols. (Dublin: Irish Manuscript Commission, 1972–80), 8:166–68. Also see Maurice O'Connell, "Daniel O'Connell and the Irish Eighteenth Century," *Studies in Eighteenth-Century Culture* 5 (1976): 475–95; and Murphy, "Pitt Administration," 167–96, on the anti-unionist failure with the Catholics. Grattan, *Memoirs*, 564–92 (appendix), reprints a few of the protests against union, and the *House of Commons Journal*, vol. 18, from January to April 1800, includes many protests against union from county and borough electors. Indeed, County Down was the only county to send a pro-union resolution to Commons—but it is difficult to ascertain from such documents the true sentiments of any electoral majority.

sentative. At the same time they were even more impotent because they were only 100 men added to the 558 M.P.s already in the Commons at Westminster.[98]

Resigning himself to defeat, Henry Grattan joined them in 1805, as did former House Speaker John Foster, George Ponsonby, Laurence Parsons, and others. William Conyngham Plunket also moved into this new parliamentary home. He rose higher, in fact, than he might have without union, ultimately to the Irish peerage and the office of lord chancellor. John Fitzgibbon, earl of Clare, did not prosper long, dying reviled by the people of Ireland and more or less ignored in England after he was named to the peerage there. Grattan and his son, even though both sat at Westminster, perpetuated the idea of a union bought through corruption and helped implant the nostalgic desire for a restoration of parliamentary independence. They also helped to mark Fitzgibbon and Pitt as traitors to Ireland's true cause. Though Fitzgibbon did not deserve all of the praise later lavished on him by J. A. Froude, neither did he deserve to be vilified. Likewise, Pitt might have put British interests ahead of those in Ireland, yet he was not the vile politico the Grattans made him appear. Others in the old Ascendancy were even more disgruntled than the Grattans and called for immediate repeal of the Act of Union.[99] Daniel O' Connell and the "Repealers" of the 1840s would take up that call, even as they pushed social changes that the old Anglo-Irish constitutional nationalists they eclipsed would have found too dangerous.

98. The text of the Act of Union is in *Statutes at Large*, 20:448–87 (40 George III c. 38).

99. George Barnes, *A Defence of the Parliamentary Institution of Ireland* (Dublin: H. Fitzpatrick, 1802), took up where Barnes's 1799 argument left off, defending the record of the Irish Parliament. George Sigerson, *The Last Independent Parliament of Ireland* (Dublin: M. H. Gill & Son, 1918) helped keep alive the Barnes view. *The Case of Ireland . . . Re-Stated* (Dublin: I. Colles, 1812), had argued vehemently for a restoration of parliamentary independence, making, as so many had before, an American comparison: that the Americans could not be represented at Westminster and neither could the Irish. See A. P. W. Malcomson, *John Foster* (Oxford: Oxford University Press, 1978), 351, for Foster's 1801 prediction that Irish Catholics would not rest until parliament was restored, that they would control it if it was, and that separatism would grow among them. Finally, it is interesting that English Catholic historian Francis Plowden would dramatically shift the emphasis of his *The History of Ireland, from Its Invasion under Henry II to its Union with Great Britain*, 2 vols. (London: C. Roworth, 1803), over the brief space of six years. In the 1803 original edition, he noted the many failings and inequities of British rule in Ireland and was much more sympathetic to Catholics than many historians of that era (he was, of course, a Catholic himself), but he also gave the British the benefit of the doubt and looked ahead to a brighter future through union. In 1809 he shifted the emphasis, arguing that union was a failure and that the Irish should have their parliament restored. Pro-union in 1803, he had become anti-union in 1809. His dissatisfactions anticipated those of more and more Irishmen, Protestant and Catholic, as the nineteenth century progressed.

The fight over union divided and weakened the Anglo-Irish elite and further disillusioned middle-class Protestants and many Catholics with their leadership. Several million pounds were spent by the government to reimburse those who surrendered parliamentary boroughs and, rightly or not, it was widely believed that pro-union M.P.s sold their votes in a corrupt bargain. Instead of symbolizing a new beginning, union increasingly came to represent old style power politics at their worst. For a later generation of Irish nationalists, the union would also be proof of Ireland's imperial entrapment.

Ireland outside of Ulster did not draw closer to Britain, but union did not bring the dire consequences that its opponents had prophesied. Although Irish trade did not suddenly flourish, neither did it collapse. Dublin did not suffer unduly because it was no longer a capital city. There was no mass exodus of emigrants or great leap in the tax rate. At the same time, there was no marked turnaround for the better. Pitt's "final" adjustment did not really solve basic domestic or imperial problems any better than had parliamentary independence—Grattan's "final" adjustment—in 1782. Catholics waited another twenty-nine years for the right to sit in parliament. Whether they would have sat earlier in an independent Irish parliament became moot.

Irish nationalism had been discredited only momentarily in 1800. It would gather strength in the following century, even as the Anglo-Irish Ascendancy was displaced. Irish nationalists over the centuries had gradually come to see an independent parliament as the prime defender of their constitutional rights. "Grattan's Parliament" was in one sense the fulfillment of a quest for those constitutional rights begun in the 1640s and intensified a century later. That quest was in turn based on claims first made by the Irish Parliament nearly two centuries before and on rights supposedly extended to Ireland by Henry II in the twelfth century. Yet in another sense Grattan's Parliament was a perversion of the quest. It was too exclusive and not truly autonomous; socially as well as politically it was fatally flawed.

By 1798 Parliament and constitutional nationalism were under a pall. Nonetheless, so long as Irish leaders continued to see themselves as a distinct group with their own interests that needed to be protected, nationalism and a desire for an independent legislature would re-emerge. By making their larger rights under their constitution indistinguishable from parliamentary rights, they had diminished the former while exaggerating the importance of the latter. At the same time it was also clear after 1800 that the best way to preserve those general rights was to have an independent parliament, and the constitutionalism that underlay Irish nationalist thought did not disappear with the Act of Union. Thus the political ideology that the Anglo-Irish had done so much to cultivate had an appeal that pre-dated the Ascendancy and would survive its passing. Daniel O'Connell (who admired Grattan) and the Repealers would not call for a restoration of Grattan's Parliament, which had been a Protestant preserve, but they did push for parliamentary independence and more political rights within the empire.

Building on what men like Patrick Darcy and the Irish Parliament and Catholic Confederates of his day had done, Anglo-Irish Protestants like Henry Grattan devised a sophisticated rationale not only for their power but for what they saw as Irish rights—under natural law, divine ordination, and an encompassing Irish constitution, itself an extension of the reverenced British constitution. Their political ideology, however, was full of incongruities and contradictions. They wanted to believe that Ireland was a true kingdom the equal of England, and later the United Kingdom of England and Scotland, but London never accepted their view. They tried to cast themselves as champions and representatives of the people, yet they took too long to include co-religionists of lesser means or unorthodox ecclesiastical views, and Catholics of all classes.

They never really understood the revolutionary implications of their constitutional nationalist creed. William Molyneux and Henry Grattan were alike in complaining about imperial rule, and yet they professed their attachment to empire. Grattan could utterly condemn the British Parliament and the union but still proclaim his love for the British constitution, so deep were his attachments. He and Molyneux managed to reconcile their differences with Britain. Ultimately there were others who could not. Grattan's constitutional nationalism, taken to its logical extreme, led to the republicanism and separatism of the United Irishmen. "Liberty, we say, with England, but at all events liberty," Grattan had exclaimed in his famous speech of 16 April 1782. For men like Tone and Drennan, it was impossible to have both.[100] Yet even the United Irishmen were reluctant revolutionaries. They too had difficulty dealing with some of the political and social implications of their arguments. Talk of national unity notwithstanding, the United Irishmen never fully embraced Catholics and Protestants, rich and poor, anglophobe and anglophile, separatists and advocates of imperial reform. Celtic revivalists and the vestigial Anglo-Irish Protestant elite of the next century had some of the same problems. Molyneux and Grattan passed on; their dilemma remained.

100. Irish Parliamentary Debates, vol. 26, container 10, p. 103.

CHAPTER 7

Ireland and the Rebellious American Colonies: A Comparison

The Dominion of Wealth, a commercial controul,
Founds a greatness of wealth on a meanness of soul,
Exults in a splendour, which, fatally bright,
Self destroying consumes that which gives it its light.
Not such were thy principles, Sparta; thy pride
Was, by Virtue, no less than in arms, to preside:
Hear ye statesmen, & blush, when a record ye find
That the poorest and best were the first of mankind.
                                    Daniel Webb, 1783[1]

Henry Grattan served in the parliament at Westminster from 1805 until his death fifteen years later, carrying on his fight for complete Catholic emancipation. Incongruously enough, Grattan first sat for an English borough after Earl Fitzwilliam arranged his election. He probably felt more comfortable after 1806, when he was representing the city of Dublin. Forgiven by electors who had turned on him less than a decade before, Grattan once again became a popular tribune. But old political wounds never healed completely. According to his son, he spent long spells at his beloved Tinnehinch, lost in melancholy. Here he had "rejoiced when gay" and here, "in moments of grief," he wept over Ireland's

---

1. Excerpt from a poem by Daniel Webb enclosed in a letter to Henry Flood of 7 November 1783, in the Henry Flood Correspondence, Add. MS. 22,930, British Library.

"division" and "downfall."[2] Grattan failed to win his battle for emancipation, but he ended his days as a respected elder statesman, so admired that when he died his remains were interred in Westminster Abbey. He objected to the burial site when first approached, preferring instead to lie in his native soil. He later relented, and his grave is marked by a simple plaque set in the floor of the Abbey's north transept. The spot is sometimes covered by chairs; when not, it is overshadowed by other monuments nearby—including one to the Elder Pitt—and by the majesty of the Abbey itself. In death as in life, Grattan became a small part of a much grander setting.

His memory lived on in Ireland but grew dim with the passing of the Ascendancy. Before he died, Trinity College rehung his portrait, not in the theater (where Fitzgibbon still looms), but in the dining hall, next to a portrait of Henry Flood. It is still there to be seen, although it is probably rarely noticed. Grattan's statue has stood in the middle of Dame Street, on what was once College Green, for over a century. Yet it somehow looks out of place, with Grattan gesturing futilely to motorists winding past the west entrance to Trinity. Grattan's Tinnehinch house, purchased with money bestowed by a grateful Irish Parliament, was auctioned in 1943; its contents were sold for a pittance and the house itself was razed not long after.[3]

Grattan in his glory years was celebrated as the "father" of Irish independence. Daniel O'Connell the "Liberator" now holds a better claim to that title. Thus if the "ghost of the Protestant Ascendancy walks still" in Ireland, that ghost does not really have a resting place.[4] Architecturally Dublin may be the most Georgian of any city in the old empire, but the buildings there are only a vague reminder of the Ascendancy. Leinster's mansion now houses the Irish Parliament; if it did not, it might have gone the way of Charlemont's townhouse, now an art gallery, or the once impressive Powerscourt home, now a shopping mall. Powerscourt manor in the Wicklow demesne was gutted by fire nearly two decades ago and may never by restored. Castletown is being refurbished, but ever so slowly. Although Russborough, Carton, and a handful of other estates survive, they do not serve the same symbolic function for

---

2. Henry Grattan, Jr., *Memoirs of the Life and Times of the Rt. Hon. Henry Grattan*, 5 vols. (London: Henry Colburn, 1849), 3:13.

3. *Irish Press*, 15 October 1943. Compare this brief note to the many newspaper notices of Grattan's death in 1820, included in Henry Grattan, Jr., ed., *The Speeches of the Right Honourable Henry Grattan*, 4 vols. (London: Longman, Hurst, Rees, Orme, and Brown, 1822), xxxvii–lxxxiv.

4. Quote from J. C. Beckett, *The Anglo-Irish Tradition* (London: Faber and Faber, 1976), 44.

the Irish as Mount Vernon and Monticello do for Americans. The men of Grattan's Parliament were not really Founders after all.

Washington, Jefferson, and the other American Founders had ambivalent feelings for Britain and the empire, and were hesitant to cross a political Rubicon. They certainly did not set out to become revolutionaries. As Hannah Arendt has observed, revolutions generally begin as "restorations or renovations."[5] Washington and the other American "revolutionaries" had not intended to do much more for their colonies than Grattan had wanted to do for Ireland. Hesitant or not, they eventually committed themselves to the revolutionary act of claiming—and fighting for—political independence. They thereby became the beneficiaries of a national myth-making apparatus that lionizes their accomplishments and explains away such things as their failure to abolish slavery or their lack of enthusiasm for egalitarian democracy. If Grattan and his associates had struck a blow for complete independence, perhaps they too would have been forgiven their shortcomings, and the attempts at celebratory myth-making by writers like Thomas Davis would have been more successful. But Grattan never wanted to become the founder of an independent nation because, like Edmund Burke, he feared that Ireland would be "wretched" and "undone" without its British tie. "I must rejoice at any thing which I conceive will benefit Ireland & which I imagine will not injure Great Britain," he once told Charles James Fox; he wanted to believe that Ireland and Britain could be "two nations, But in Fact one people."[6] To him, Catholic emancipation could be made safe only if Catholics agreed to accept Ascendancy leadership as the price of their political "freedom." Accordingly, perhaps it is not fair to compare Grattan with Washington or expect Grattan to be venerated in Ireland the way Washington is revered by many Americans. The mythical Grattan was never as potent a figure as the mythical Washington; even posthumously, Grattan could not stand as a symbol of national unity.

---

5. Hannah Arendt, *On Revolution* (New York: Viking Press, 1965; orig. ed., 1963), 30. See Gordon S. Wood, *The Creation of the American Republic 1776–1787* (Chapel Hill: University of North Carolina Press, 1969), 10–17, for how this was played out in the American Revolution.

6. Thomas Copeland et al., eds., *The Correspondence of Edmund Burke*, 10 vols. (Cambridge: Cambridge University Press, 1958–78), 9:257, letter of February 1797; and Grattan to Fox, 21 March 1785, Charles James Fox Papers XIV. Fo. 184, MS 47582, BL. Also see Seymour Martin Lipset, *The First New Nation* (New York: Basic Books, 1973), 62, and Lipset's observation that "all new nations must establish their own identities. But along with a self-conscious effort to establish a separate identity, which usually leads to a rejection of all things associated with the Mother Country, there continues to exist a deep-rooted admiration for its culture and values." Thus the American Founders were ambivalent about Britain, as were the Anglo-Irish, even if they followed a different course.

Ireland and the American Colonies

Unlike Washington, Grattan never ceased believing that his country and Great Britain could and should be formally tied together. He therefore did not push his criticisms or constitutional disputations to the point reached by Revolutionary Americans. His nationalism was more qualified, more circumspect. Men of Grattan's stamp assumed that it was possible to secure Irish liberties and constitutional rights without creating an independent nation.[7] They could in fact accept restrictions that strike students of modern nationalism as being illogical and inconsistent, disqualifying them as true "nationalists." But any form of nationalist thought, whether it be the more tentative constitutional nationalism of Henry Grattan or the full-blown, independence-seeking nationalism of Revolutionary Americans, is, as Hans Kohn noted, a "state of mind."[8] Grattan believed that Ireland was a distinct kingdom and thus in some sense an autonomous part of the British empire, to which it was joined by a non-resident king wearing two distinct crowns. History, not logic, told him that his belief was valid; that it could is a reminder that the Irish experience with, and place in, the empire differed from that of the American colonies.

The American colonies were not settled until after the spread of Protestantism to England. Normans arrived in Ireland during the twelfth century, when they and the indigenous population shared Catholicism.

---

7. "Nationalism is a term which lends itself to many definitions," observed Patrick Corish in "The Origins of Irish Nationalism," in Corish, ed., *A History of Irish Catholicism,* vol.3, no. 8 (Dublin: Gill and Son, 1968), 1. As Corish noted, "At least until fairly modern times, it has not necessarily demanded political independence" (ibid.). Similarly, Bernard Crick, *In Defence of Politics,* 2d ed. (New York: Pelican, 1982), noted that, after the French Revolution, "people who were oppressed felt that the solution was not, as the eighteenth-century Whigs thought, to gain a just constitution, but to gain a national state" (79). For still another view see Joep Th. Leersen, "Anglo-Irish Patriotism and Its European Context: Notes Towards a Reassessment," *Eighteenth-Century Ireland* 3 (1988): 7–24. Perhaps Grattan and his colleagues were holdovers from the older Whig ideal.

8. Hans Kohn, *Nationalism: Its Meaning and History* (New York: 1955), 9. In his *The Idea of Nationalism* (New York: Macmillan, 1944; rev. ed., 1967), Kohn argues (473) that Anglo-Irish nationalism fell short and was incomplete. By the standards he cites, it was not a true form of nationalism. The Anglo-Irish come up short as well by the standards set in Yehoshua Arieli, *Individualism and Nationalism in America* (Cambridge: Harvard University Press, 1964). Yet if nationalism is primarily a state of mind, the Anglo-Irish had grounds for believing they were somehow a "nation," as Owen Dudley Edwards contends in his essay "Ireland" in Owen Dudley Edwards et al., *Celtic Nationalism* (London: Routledge & Kegan Paul, 1968), 7–80. If one were to keep the distinction clear between reality and perception of reality, by the standards set forth in Boyd C. Shafer, *Nationalism: Myth and Reality* (New York: Harcourt, Brace, 1955), the Anglo-Irish did indeed qualify as "nationalists," at least in their minds; accordingly their "nationalism" cannot be dismissed as somehow unreal. As E. J. Hobsbawm (who in turn was building on the work of Ernest Gellner) put it, "Nationalism comes before nations. Nations do not make states and nationalisms but the other way around"; see *Nations and Nationalism since 1780* (Cambridge: Cambridge University Press, 1990), 10. Also see Benedict Anderson, *Imagined Communities* (London: Verso, 1991; orig. ed., 1983).

In the sixteenth century England joined the Reformation and dragged an unwilling, resentful Ireland along. The American colonies largely escaped the internal tensions that resulted from competition between Catholics and Protestants, and, among Protestants, between Dissenters and those in the Church of Ireland. Those tensions were occasionally expressed in violent outbursts that deepened sectarian animosities. Further, the sheer size of the mainland American colonies and their backcountry made it difficult if not impossible to impose any sort of religious orthodoxy for very long. Religious diversity was unavoidable, and with it came the rise of toleration.[9] Ireland was much smaller, and the religiously unorthodox could not practice in isolation. Finally, the great distance of the American colonies from Britain helped to keep the Anglican Church from becoming an effective arm of empire, and Anglican vestrymen like those in Washington's Virginia jealously protected local autonomy. More closely tied to the Anglican Church and the Irish administration, the Church of Ireland acted as a more effective extension of state power.

Ireland's proximity to Britain, an accident of geography, affected virtually all aspects of Irish life. The Irish themselves first drew ambitious Normans to their island. Once those Normans crossed the Irish Sea they usually stayed. Later generations of English and Scottish adventurers who followed them also remained. As the British empire took shape, so too did a more anglicized Ireland. Successive English plantations never completely transformed the island but spread to all but the westernmost reaches of Munster and Connacht. Ireland was consequently pulled into the mainstream of British politics.

So too, eventually, were the American colonies. They became for a time an even greater source of interest and yet the British reconciled themselves to letting thirteen of those colonies go in 1783. Until the twentieth century, Britain could not imagine doing the same with Ireland. If by the time of the American Revolution, Ireland had long since lost its appeal as the scene for new imperialist adventures, it nonetheless remained on Britain's exposed western flank. The British were convinced that they could not allow Ireland to be free of their control. An unfriendly, completely independent Ireland, especially an Ireland allied to Spain or France, could threaten the very life of Britain, or at least so British leaders feared. For eight years, they fought a rather foolish war to keep from losing what little control they exercised in the mainland

---

9. This is a point often made by American historians, such as in Thomas J. Curry's *The First Freedoms* (New York: Oxford University Press, 1986), 78–104.

American colonies below Canada.[10] Loss of Ireland was even more unthinkable, and the British would have fought more tenaciously to keep it. "Ireland is too great to be unconnected with us, and too near to be a foriegn state, and too little to be independent," wrote one Englishman to the duke of Rutland in 1784.[11] Rutland, then a harried lord lieutenant, did not dispute the veracity of such sentiments; neither did the men at Whitehall and Westminster who sent him to Dublin.

Because of its proximity and greater strategic importance, Ireland's political ties to Britain were always stronger than those of the American colonies. Ireland's Parliament, even before 1782, could claim more legitimacy and greater longevity than any colonial American legislature. And yet most of those legislatures, by their very distance from London, enjoyed more autonomy and therefore a de facto legitimacy denied the Irish Parliament, despite its greater claim to right by law. The Lords of Trade quickly retreated from their attempt in the late 1670s to apply the principles of Poynings' Law to the legislatures of Jamaica and Virginia, so vehement were negative reactions in those colonies.[12]

One of the more striking political distinctions between the American colonies and Ireland was the greater power of the lord lieutenant compared with that of royal governors. As Bernard Bailyn has shown, those governors were short on real power, having been granted more on paper than they exercised in practice. Insufficient patronage and a relatively broad franchise made politics difficult for them to manage.[13] Lords lieutenant could wield considerably more power, through the adroit awarding or withholding of places, pensions, and peerages. With the franchise restricted to a comparatively small number of Protestant electors, who were in turn checked by the borough system of parliamentary politics,

---

10. See my "Ending the War and Winning the Peace: The British in America and the Americans in Vietnam," *Soundings* 70 (1987): 445–74.

11. C. T. Grenville to Rutland, 3 December 1784, in Historical Manuscripts Commission, *The Manuscripts of His Grace the Duke of Rutland*, 4 vols. (London: Eyre and Spottiwoode, 1888–1905), 3:155.

12. Leonard Woods Labaree, *Royal Government in America* (New Haven: Yale University Press, 1930), 218–22. Also see the letter from Francis Bernard to Lord Barrington of 23 November 1765, in Edward Channing and Archibald Cary Coolidge, eds., *The Barrington-Bernard Correspondence* (Cambridge: Harvard University Press, 1912), 93–102, where Bernard, writing in the aftermath of the Stamp Act crisis, argued that Ireland served as an example of how to effectively bind a colonial dependency to the mother country. Bernard (even though governor of Massachusetts) little understood Irish or American affairs. He thought that Poynings' Law was working well in Ireland "without wanting the least Amendment of Fundamentals" (99).

13. Bernard Bailyn, *The Origins of American Politics* (New York: Alfred A. Knopf, 1968), 59–105.

lords lieutenant through most of the eighteenth century did not have to be as responsive to popular pressure as most colonial governors. For those same reasons, they were often better able to promote imperial interests. They never had enough patronage or power to ride roughshod; still, they had more to work with than their counterparts among royal governors in the American colonies.

Class lines in Ireland were hardly rigid, and it was possible for obscure men to rise to power and great men to fall. Irish society was nevertheless not as fluid or open as that of the American colonies, which, by virtue of their patterns of settlement, the character of the settlers, and the immensity of the wilderness those settlers set forth to tame, gave rise to a more dynamic culture. It was more difficult to perpetuate what Richard Bushman has called "monarchical politics" in an essentially "republican" social setting.[14] Nevertheless, there were American patriots still attached to the idea of monarchy as late as 1776, who fought against the king's government but not, they claimed, against the king himself. Anglo-Irish leaders would not go that far; they did not give up on George III, much less discard the idea of kingship. Nor did they relinquish their attachment to a more rigid hierarchy of power. Through the eighteenth century, at least, the Irish operated within the confines of aristocratic politics based on a traditional notion of the permanency of social divisions (although individuals could occasionally cross the lines separating them).

A successful lord lieutenant understood that one of his basic advantages was the dependence of the Anglo-Irish Ascendancy on British power. White Americans, especially those in the southernmost colonies, might have had a potential slave problem, but they did not need Britain to help them manage it. The Anglo-Irish were much less secure as a master class. Dispossessed and underprivileged Irish Catholics were not akin to the oppressed and enslaved Blacks in America. They were of the same race as the ruling class, they greatly outnumbered the Protestants, they were not chattels, and they had a historical claim to Ireland as their land. Ethnic and religious distinctions notwithstanding, the downtrodden in Ireland could not be treated as slaves, nor could Ireland be run under a formalized caste system.[15] Politically excluded for most of the eighteenth

---

14. Richard L. Bushman, *King and People in Provincial Massachusetts* (Chapel Hill: University of North Carolina Press, 1985). Also see Edwin G. Burrows and Michael Wallace, "The American Revolution: The Ideology and Psychology of National Liberation," *Perspectives in American History* 6 (1972): 167–306; and Jerrilyn Greene Marston, *King and Congress* (Princeton: Princeton University Press, 1987).

15. Although as Ned Lebow, "British Historians and Irish History," *Eire-Ireland* 8

century, Irish Catholics were not completely closed out of economic or social life. The Anglo-Irish elite as a whole lacked the inclination and wherewithal to keep them in such a reduced state. Catholics, and to a lesser extent and for a shorter period, Protestant Dissenters, were not members of the political culture, yet they were always a part of the larger society. Neither slave nor free, their peculiar status was just worrisome enough for the Anglo-Irish elite to want and need the support of a wealthier and more powerful Britain.

Necessity and fear do not alone explain the Anglo-Irish connection with Britain. Proximity also helped produce deep sentimental ties; Dublin and London were culturally as well as physically much closer than London and Boston. Americans too for most of their colonial experience professed great affection for Britain, yet the American filial tie was never as strong. The Anglo-Irish elite were much more closely linked to Britain through marriage and through countless less formal associations. Thomas Conolly and the first duke of Leinster both married daughters of the duke of Richmond, an English peer and parliamentary leader. Other English and Irish families were similarly connected. Those not related by blood were joined through socialization. The earl of Charlemont spent much of his time in London or Bath, and he was not unusual. Moreover, some prominent Irishmen owned estates in England, and there were even more Englishmen (most notably the marquess of Rockingham and his nephew, Earl Fitzwilliam) owning estates in Ireland. Some members of the Irish Parliament, in Lords and Commons, held seats at Westminster and vice versa.

Colonial Americans had traditionally professed a great reverence for and attachment to what they thought was the British constitution. But perhaps the British constitution was never quite as real to them as it was to the Irish. After all, they never enjoyed its protection as fully. The Irish had had Magna Carta and common law rights formally extended to them; their Parliament existed by right and, after 1782, with British recognition as a sovereign, independent body. They talked much more insistently about their constitution as the foundation of their rights than could Americans, who endeavored to dress their charters in the same garb. Technically, at least, every member of the Irish Bar was supposed to have spent a number of terms studying at one of the Inns of Court in London. Not all did, and even those who matriculated (like Henry

---

(December 1973): 3–38, and *White Britain and Black Ireland* (Philadelphia: Institute for the Study of Human Issues, 1976) contends, the Irish have been the victims of virulent racist stereotyping.

Grattan) did not overburden themselves with study. Even so, the Irish barristers who played such a crucial role in Irish parliamentary politics were more steeped in the British constitutional and legal tradition than were colonial American lawyers, most of whom did not have the same experience in law or politics. Perhaps it is no coincidence that some of those Americans who studied at one of the Inns of Court became (like John Dickinson) very reluctant revolutionaries or (like Daniel Dulany) eventually spurned revolution altogether.[16]

Nevertheless, there were centrifugal forces pulling Ireland away from Britain that almost balanced the centripetal forces that kept Ireland in the empire. In the eighteenth century they did not pull as strongly as they did in the rebellious American colonies, nor did they exert the force that they would in the following century, but they were undeniable if not yet irresistible. For all their differences, Ireland and the American colonies shared a simultaneous attraction and revulsion for the empire.

English expansion into Ireland predated sustained English settlement in the Americas by well over four hundred years, and yet both manifested some of the same problems. English expansionism was part of the great movement of European powers into outlying regions that Walter Prescott Webb called, simplistically, the interaction of peoples from the "metropolis" and "frontier." One does not have to share Webb's Turnerianism or his pride in this process to accept his view that this was a movement of prodigous sweep and with certain universal characteristics.[17]

More recent studies have substituted "core" and "periphery" for Webb's terms and have concentrated on the inherent problems of empire building, especially those of the English, imperialists before they had a clear sense of empire.[18] The Normans who waded ashore in Leinster in

---

16. "Perhaps" is in order because, of the Americans who studied at one of the Inns of Court before 1775 listed in E. Alfred Jones, *American Members of the Inns of Court* (London: St. Catherine's Press, 1924), actually more became Revolutionaries (sixty or so) than Loyalists (perhaps forty-five). John Murrin's note on Massachusetts "barristers"— a purely provincial designation *not* requiring matriculation at one of the Inns—in "Anglicizing an American Colony: The Transformation of Provincial Massachusetts" (Ph.D. dissertation, Yale University, 1966), 246–49, 311–13, is quite interesting. Of forty-six such "barristers" practicing in 1774, slightly more than half had Loyalist leanings.

17. Walter Prescott Webb, *The Great Frontier* (Boston: Houghton Mifflin, 1952).

18. For a geographer's perspective, see D. W. Meinig, *Atlantic America, 1492–1800* (New Haven: Yale University Press, 1986), 370–85; for that of a sociologist, see Michael Hechter, *Internal Colonialism* (Berkeley: University of California Press, 1975); and for a historian's view, see Jack P. Greene, *Peripheries and Center* (Athens: University of Georgia Press, 1986). Angus Calder's ambitious narrative, *Revolutionary Empire* (New York: E. P. Dutton, 1981) also discusses the larger problems of empire. For the growth of a separatist strain in the American colonies very early on, see J. M. Bumsted, "'Things in the Womb

the twelfth century were rather imperfect imperial agents. They were mercenaries recruited by a deposed king endeavoring to regain his throne. They, their descendants, and later English and Scottish adventurers developed their own interests and system of loyalties; sometimes they worked as extensions of English power, often they did not. They anglicized Ireland in fits and starts and not according to any carefully designed and implemented masterplan. At one time or another, most of Ireland was parceled out to them with the hope that their dominance over the natives would bring an end to the Irish problem. It did not. The Irish problem was never simply the Celts versus the English or the Protestants against the Catholics. Through intermingling and intermarriage, through evasion of the law and lax enforcement, Ireland managed to develop apart from English, and later British, wishes.

If a basic cause of an Irish sense of distictiveness was that England expanded before it had a blueprint for empire, not much had changed four hundred years later. The first tentative English expedition to the New World came only after Henry VII entered into a reciprocal arrangement with John Cabot, a Venetian adventurer. In exchange for title to whatever lands Cabot found and a share of the profits, Henry granted him protection under the English flag, monopoly rights, and a minimal amount of assistance. Nearly a century later, when Elizabeth I awarded a New World patent first to Sir Humphrey Gilbert and, after Gilbert drowned, to Sir Walter Raleigh, the mixture of public and private enterprise that underscored the original arrangement had not changed markedly. It could in fact be traced through virtually all of the subsequent subdivisions of title and charters granted through the eighteenth century. Quite simply, the English had an empire before they devised an imperial theory. Once they had a clearer notion of what they were about, they spent much of their time, in Ireland as well as the Americas, trying to get reality to conform to their idealized empire.

Even if the English had had a clear plan at the outset, and even if they had found a way to expand without entrusting overseas or cross-channel empire to adventurers, that does not mean that they could have had an empire free of growing pains. A certain amount of change was unavoidable as both the "core" and "periphery" evolved. Obviously England, like Ireland, was not the same in 1782 as it had been in 1172. Politically it had become Great Britain after two "revolutions," a "Restoration"

---

of Time': Ideas of American Independence, 1633–1763," *William and Mary Quarterly*, 3d ser., vol. 31 (1974): 533–64. For the evolutionary growth of revolutionary movements in general, see Lyford P. Edwards, *The Natural History of Revolution* (Chicago: University of Chicago Press, 1927).

between them, and an English-Scottish parliamentary union thereafter. Parliament had evolved from an advisory council to a sovereign body with power so great that Blackstone considered it coequal to the constitution. In no sense a maritime power in the twelfth century, Britain had the greatest overseas commercial empire in the world by the middle of the eighteenth century. Its sedentary, isolated agrarian existence had slowly been altered over the same period, and a new, more dynamic, even more industrialized society was beginning to emerge. Whatever guiding principle of empire the British followed, then, had to be adaptable, responsive to changes at home as well as in the American colonies and the "kingdom" of Ireland.

Peripheral areas like Ireland and the American colonies, in their own process of evolution, took ideas and institutions introduced by English adventurers and turned them to their advantage. They spoke the same language of law and politics, but not for the same ends. From the very beginning American colonists were concerned about protecting their interests and defining their constitutional rights; so were the Irish. And like the Americans for virtually all of their colonial period the Irish claimed their rights primarily as citizens of the empire.

Whenever the British were not responsive enough, the Irish attempted to force a change in policy by some of the same means employed by colonial Americans. Periodically, eighteenth-century Irish critics of the navigation system urged their countrymen to promote home manufactures and to boycott British goods. Jonathan Swift's pamphlets of the 1720s and 1730s anticipated the writings produced by Americans in the 1760s and early 1770s.[19] Americans evaded and protested the strictures laid down by the navigation acts, as did the Irish. Americans had no monopoly on smuggling.

American and Irish critics of empire called for greater public spiritedness and drew from history to show what happened to societies that ceased to be virtuous. Greece and Rome, argued Charles Lucas, fell because of "the *Faction* of the *Nobles*," the "*Corruption* of the *Commonalty*," and the "*Violence* of numerous *Standing Armies*." Lucas wrote for an Irish audience, but American readers would have understood what he meant when he attempted to draw lessons from the past, just as his solution to those problems in their contemporary guise would have sounded familiar. "Freedom is your BIRTH-RIGHT," proclaimed Lucas. "He that with-holds it from You, in any Point, in any Degree, *robs You, robs* the *Community, robs* the King. And he, that totally gives it

---

19. For the Revolutionary American home manufactures movement, see my *Mechanical Metamorphosis* (Westport: Greenwood Press, 1985), 8–36.

up, on the Demands of any Man, is a Slave and a Traitor."[20] Lucas's language might have been provocative and inflammatory, especially for 1749, when he wrote those lines, yet more and more Americans would echo him by the early 1770s. American pamphleteers characterized their dispute with Britain as a contest important to people everywhere, not just within the British empire. So did Anglo-Irish constitutional nationalists in their imperial disputes, notably when William Molyneux called his 1698 defense of Irish rights "the Cause of the whole Race of Adam."[21]

Charles Lucas wanted colonial Americans and fellow Irishmen in the 1760s to see how their causes were linked. Likewise for William MacNeven, even after the Americans won their independence and the Anglo-Irish elite denounced him and the other United Irishmen. "What was tyranny against the Americans, would necessarily be tyranny against the Irish," wrote MacNeven in 1807, a few years after he emigrated to the United States. What was "resistance so glorious in one country, could not be accounted a crime in the other," he pled. Those fleeing Ireland after the fiasco of 1798 and the Act of the Union, MacNeven contended, "were men who had proved on their native soil their adherence to the principles of the American declaration of independence." To his chagrin, MacNeven found that his new home was not necessarily a haven for failed Irish revolutionaries of the 1790s, perhaps because Americans—by his standards—had themselves been rather conservative revolutionaries back in the 1770s.[22]

Colonial Americans simultaneously professed their attachment to the British constitution and accused British ministers and the British Parliament of conspiring against their liberties. Similarly, Lucas and even Grattan (almost despite himself) made veiled threats against British rule and revealed a separatist streak. Like so many American agitators before 1776, Irish nationalists claimed that they wanted only to reform, not to dissolve, the empire. Patrick Darcy reminded Charles I in his 1643 *Argument* that no king was above the people; the authors of *Baratariana* offered a similar reminder to George III more than a century later. Irish Patriots sought to limit the king by reminding him that the imperial crown was distinct from the crown that he wore as king of Great Britain. Before rejecting monarchy altogether, American Revolutionaries often

---

20. Charles Lucas, *The Political Constitutions of Great-Britain and Ireland*, 2 vols. (London 1751), 472 and 477 resp. from the "Censor" V (1 July 1749).

21. William Molyneux, *The Case of Ireland Being Bound by Acts of Parliament in England Stated* (Dublin, 1698; reprint ed. Dublin: Cadenus Press, 1977), 24.

22. William James MacNeven, *Pieces of Irish History* (New York: Bernard Dornix, 1807), iii–iv.

made a similar argument: George III was their king only because of charters that were compacts between a free people and his predecessors. Anglo-Irish Patriot criticism of monarchical politics was muted by the standards Thomas Paine would set in 1776. Nevertheless, these "Patriots" were no less critical than American agitators before Lexington and Concord. Although most Irish parliamentary Patriots were more tied to older notions of social order and deferential politics than were Revolutionary Americans, they also believed in government by compact and in an elector's basic right to representation. They talked of a free people living in a free land, voluntarily tied to their king in compacts that, implicitly, they had the right to dissolve if violated. That the Anglo-Irish chose not to act on such a threat should not obscure this common belief.

Grattan and Lucas, in the tradition of Darcy and Molyneux, made history a battleground as they tried to put the past on their side. Disputes over questions of historical legitimacy were endlessly divisive. Commenting on the Norman invasion of Ireland in the twelfth century, Francis Plowden remarked that "the hour, which united the two kingdoms under one crown, gave birth to the national contest about the authenticity of the antient history of Ireland."[23] The passage of nearly seven centuries, he also observed, had only intensified the debate. The Irish divided among themselves, as well as from the British, on questions of historical interpretation. Key events such as the 1641 rebellion or the status of the Kilkenny confederation caused the spilling of much ink in historiographical warfare.

Like American patriots on the eve of their War of Independence, the Irish mixed constitutional and transconstitutional arguments. With both groups we see an attachment to a reified constitution that was virtually all-inclusive. Neither the Anglo-Irish nor the Revolutionary Americans before 1776 made a sharp or consistent distinction between constitutional and natural rights. They blended them together in their polemics. For Revolutionary Americans, the difference became clear only after the Declaration of Independence, when they formally rejected some aspects of British constitutionalism and pressed on to create their own, new traditions.[24] The Anglo-Irish, on the other hand, continued

---

23. Francis Plowden, *The History of Ireland from Its Invasion under Henry II to Its Union with Great Britain*, 2 vols. (London: Longman, Hurst, Rees, and Orme, 1809), 1:4.

24. That many American Revolutionaries, including some who framed the Constitution of 1787, still admired the British constitutional tradition has been stressed by various scholars, a point made succinctly in M. E. Bradford, *Original Intentions* (Athens, Ga.: University of Georgia Press, 1993), 17–33; and Michael Kammen, *A Machine That Would Go of Itself* (New York: Alfred A. Knopf, 1987), 156–84.

Ireland and the American Colonies   255

to adapt the British constitutional tradition to their needs. When history failed Molyneux or Grattan, they moved to higher notions of fundamental law—to what was "intended" under the constitution and to what all men were entitled to through divine ordination as well as natural right. The line separating these sources of fundamental law was vague, as was the understanding of what the unwritten British and Irish constitutions contained. Not only was the reality of fundamental law in doubt among British jurists and parliamentarians, but those who believed in its existence did not necessarily go along with the way that Anglo-Irish nationalists tried to apply it to their situation. Instead of bringing greater clarity, the search for rights further muddied the already murky questions of empire.[25]

For most of the eighteenth century, the Anglo-Irish identification with Ireland's Parliament was as strong as the attachment of colonial Americans to their assemblies. Both saw the legislature as the representative of the people and defender of the constitution, and both believed that their own legislatures were not subordinate to the British Parliament.[26] British imperialists of course disagreed. As a number of legal scholars have shown, it is fruitless to try and determine which view of the legislative rights of the British Parliament was "correct." The powers of that parliament increased dramatically over the seventeenth and eighteenth centuries, during the very years that the American colonies were settled and when Americans, like the Irish, were identifying their place in the empire and the rights to which they were entitled. The Revolutionary American or Anglo-Irish Patriot views were not necessarily wrong because they were different from the prevailing view in London, especially if they were based on an older conception of parliamentary power and subordination of the British Parliament to the British constitution.[27] Even British jurists with the express charge of determining

---

25. See Charles F. Mullett, *Fundamental Law and the American Revolution, 1760–1776* (New York: Columbia University Press, 1933); John Phillip Reid, *Constitutional History of the American Revolution*, 3 vols. (Madison: University of Wisconsin Press, 1986–), 1:9–15, 95, 237; idem, *In Defiance of the Law* (Chapel Hill: University of North Carolina Press, 1981); A. E. Howard, *The Road from Runnymede* (Charlottesville: The University Press of Virginia, 1968), 104–6; and Barbara A. Black, "The Constitution of the Empire: The Case for the Colonists," *University of Pennsylvania Law Review* 124 (1976): 1157–1211.

26. For American assemblies, see Jack P. Greene, *The Quest For Power* (Chapel Hill: University of North Carolina Press, 1963); Michael Kammen, *Deputyes and Libertyes* (New York: Alfred A. Knopf, 1969); and John Phillip Reid, ed., *The Briefs of the American Revolution* (New York: New York University Press, 1981).

27. H. T. Dickinson, "The Eighteenth-Century Debate on the Sovereignty of Parliament," *Transactions of the Royal Historical Society*, 5th ser., vol. 26 (1976): 189–210, discusses the question as it was debated from the latter part of the seventeenth century

what rights were extended to colonies did not always agree among themselves.[28]

Change over time complicated the search for rights on almost every level. It was difficult for Anglo-Irish constitutional nationalists to argue persuasively that the Irish had been granted the rights of Englishmen during the reign of Henry II when those rights to which they referred— under common law and a Magna Carta that was still forty years in the future—had not been clearly extended to Englishmen themselves. Moreover, Henry and his successors did not necessarily intend to set the precedents that later writers attributed to them. That was true as well for the Irish Parliament. For example, William Crawford argued in his 1782 *History* that Parliament had made a clear assertion of its legislative autonomy in 1537. The act that Crawford cited as evidence was actually designed to make the Irish Parliament an effective arm of protestantized England by controlling the Catholic Church in Ireland.[29] Crawford took the act out of context and, whether he realized it or not, indulged in a form of historical special pleading.

Crawford's mistake—and it could have been nothing more than an honest misreading of a document—illustrates the larger problem of how language often imperfectly reflects intent. The wording of documents can confuse rather than clarify issues, as American Revolutionaries learned after the Rockingham ministry knowingly used evasive language in the Declaratory Act of 1766. The confusion neither began nor ended there. Americans had also read in their colonial charters that they were entitled to the rights of Englishmen. London's view of what those rights

---

through the end of the eighteenth century. Also see A. Berriedale Keith, *Constitutional History of the First British Empire* (Oxford: Clarendon Press, 1930); Mullett, *Fundamental Law*; and Ball, *Legislative Systems*, for the changing face of empire and the difficulty for colonial Americans (discussed in Mullett) and the Irish (discussed in Ball) to ascertain and assert their rights.

28. See George Chalmers, ed., *Opinions of Eminent Lawyers on various points of English Jurisprudence, chiefly concerning the Colonies, Fisheries, and Commerce of Great Britain*, 2 vols. (London: Reed and Hunter, 1814) for an opinion offered in 1720 (1:202–15) that contrasted sharply with an opinion given in 1767 (1:200–202) on whether parliamentary statutes extended to the colonies even if the colonies were not mentioned by name.

29. William Crawford, *A History of Ireland*, 2 vols.(Strabane: John Bellew, 1783), 1:270; *Statutes at Large*, 1:142–57 (28 Henry VIII c. 19). Or what significance, if any, can one read into variations in the way that Ireland enjoyed "all its franchises and liberties," when such were "customary" and "ordained" and "established" by the Crown— meaning, had the Crown merely recognized existing rights or had it granted them in the first place? See the various possible readings of laws under Edward IV in Henry F. Berry, ed., *Statutes and Ordinances and Acts of the Parliament of Ireland*, 3 vols. (Dublin: Alexander Thom, 1907–14), 3:3, 41, 273, 651, 713. The wording was even trickier for the rights of the Catholic Church in Ireland at the same time.

Ireland and the American Colonies 257

encompassed differed from theirs, however, particularly on the question of whether or not colonial assemblies existed as a right or a privilege and, if they existed by right, if they had the sole authority to tax within their province's boundaries. Similarly, the Irish Patriots sifted through six hundred years of their past and found certainty in what was actually a very jumbled constitutional tradition.

Doubtless some Irish Patriots and American Revolutionaries contrived their arguments or rationalized their views, just as others made their arguments in all sincerity and with an honest attempt to be fair to the sources. Those arguments that were, with our advantage of hindsight, the most illogical or historically inaccurate were not necessarily because of that the least sincere.[30] With Ireland, as with the rebellious American colonies, the historical record was just vague enough for unresolvable disputes to creep in. Those who searched the past sometimes in their zealousness inappropriately and misleadingly made the historical record appear clearer than it was. That search would take Revolutionary Americans out of the empire, yet even as late as 1776 most American patriots wanted to believe that the empire could be reciprocal and that there was a place for them in it. Ultimately they could not sustain that belief. The Anglo-Irish did; they remained because they could better reconcile themselves to their place in the empire.

For those skeptics who see ideas as mere smokescreens behind which baser motives hide, both Anglo-Irish Patriots and American Revolutionaries were a calculating and needlessly contentious lot. To Townshend's chief secretary, George Macartney, the constitutional obsessions of the Irish parliamentary opposition did not make much sense. "Whether Ireland be a conquered country, or not, has been the subject of much idle disquisition," Macartney complained in 1773. "Every country under the sun has been conquered in its turn, and almost every region of the civilized world has undergone the revolutions of splendour and declension."[31] Macartney felt that the men behind *Baratariana* had irresponsibly roiled the waters during Townshend's administration. Theoretical rights or things as they once were—or perhaps even as they should have been—mattered little in the contemporary world. As Macartney saw it, Ireland was subordinate to Britain and powerless to change that fact; the Irish should reconcile themselves to reality. To persist in "idle disquisition" about theoretical rights was self-defeating.

Historian Charles Andrews was not as cynical as Macartney about

---

30. See Arthur Shaffer, *The Politics of History* (Chicago: Precedent Publishing, 1975), 31–36, for American writing during the Revolutionary era.
31. [George Macartney], *An Account of Ireland in 1773* (London, 1773), 54.

the role of ideas in society, but he did distinguish what he saw as the real world of rival interests and evolutionary social change from what he considered the more artificial, ethereal world of ideology. Ideas, he apparently concluded, were shaped by and subordinated to tangible, material concerns. After noting the debates between American pamphleteers and imperial apologists over the legislative prerogatives of the British Parliament, Andrews concluded that the "colonies would have gone ahead with their revolt, regardless of the conclusions of the intellectuals, for the impulses behind that movement did not originate in the question of parliamentary right." The debate, "though of great significance in the history of opinion touching the organization of the British empire, has but an academic interest in its relation to the progress of our revolution."[32]

But opinion is an expression of perceived reality, and because it can shape action, it is of more than just "academic" interest. Furthermore, ideology and interest are not easily separated, because interest is so often defined ideologically, as indeed Andrews's own research showed. Irish rummagings through the past and attempts at constitutional disquisition, like those of the Americans, were not simply calculated efforts to propagandize, to somehow justify what already had been decided. Thought and action, if not quite inseparable, were nevertheless interconnected. The search for constitutional rights was also a search for a social self, in Ireland as well as the American colonies. That search exacerbated imperial tensions and made conflict more rather than less likely, but it flowed from a natural impulse.

The Anglo-Irish of Grattan's Parliament did not push their arguments to the same point reached by Revolutionary Americans. Still, that does not mean issues of liberty and right concerned them any less.[33] They did

---

32. Charles M. Andrews, *The Colonial Background of the American Revolution* (New Haven: Yale University Press, 1958; orig. ed., 1924), 63–64. Andrews also wrote, however, that "the impact of convictions is one of the most frequent causes of revolution we must acknowledge" and that "primarily, the American Revolution was a political and constitutional movement and only secondarily one that was either financial, commercial, or social" in "The American Revolution: An Interpretation," *American Historical Review* 31 (1926): 221, 230, resp. Andrews did not deny a role to "ideas" in history, even if he felt that the particular issue of Parliament's right to tax the American colonies was not instrumental in bringing the American revolt. A great historian, he was still capable of contradicting himself and of not seeing the logic of his own arguments.

33. Raymond J. Barrett, "A Comparative Study of Imperial Constitutional Theory in Ireland and America in the Age of the American Revolution" (Ph.D. thesis, Trinity College, University of Dublin, 1958), contended that "despite the parallel historical situations, Irishmen did not view their problems, and therefore did not frame their justifications, as pre-eminently a matter of imperial constitutional theory, in contrast to what often seems a 'mass fixation' on this topic on the part of American patriots. It might not be fair to

Ireland and the American Colonies 259

not produce a sudden torrent of constitutional disquisition in the 1760s and 1770s, because they, unlike the Americans, already had an extensive array of titles from which to draw. Patrick Darcy, William Molyneux, and Jonathan Swift had already staked out the constitutional territory. Add to their writings the constitutional stands taken by members of the Irish Parliament. American patriots, lacking a central forum for debate, had a greater need for the press. Given the role played by the Irish Commons and the relatively small electorate, it is notable that the Irish produced as much polemical literature as they did.

Certainly the Anglo-Irish constitutional nationalists of the 1770s and early 1780s, at least those with any chance of winning a following, never went so far as to renounce all imperial connections. They produced no *Common Sense,* no Declaration of Independence, and they were wary of the implications of both documents—for themselves as well as for the rebellious Americans. American Revolutionaries eventually embraced Thomas Paine's condemnations of empire; even two decades later, Anglo-Irish parliamentary opposition leaders could not endorse Wolfe Tone's condemnations of empire.

Anglo-Irish Patriots and American Revolutionaries could not master the past, nor could they control the future. The American Founders did not intend to make their independent republic into a democracy. They were undoubtedly more democratic, by necessity if not always by choice, than their Anglo-Irish counterparts, but, despite their talk about the "people" as the source of power, they did not want popular sovereignty to displace deference to an elite. In their efforts to defend their notions of government, promote independence, and define a national mission, they fought among themselves as well as against the British, and they

---

assert that constitutional theory occupied a completely subsidiary place with Irishmen, but it is safe to say that it did not overshadow other considerations as it did in American thought" (26). George D. Boyce, *Nationalism in Ireland* (Dublin: Gill and Macmillan, 1982), 111, and Maurice R. O'Connell, *Irish Politics and Social Conflict in the Age of the American Revolution* (Philadelphia: University of Pennsylvania Press, 1965), 31, accepted Barrett's view; David Noel Doyle, *Ireland, Irishmen and Revolutionary America, 1760–1820* (Dublin: Mercier Press, 1981), 251, and Gerard O'Brien, *Anglo-Irish Politics in the Age of Grattan and Pitt* (Dublin: Irish Academic Press, 1987), 39–40, questioned it, and so do I. Barrett (an American), interestingly enough, drew heavily from Clinton Rossiter, *Seedtime of the Republic* (New York: Harcourt, Brace, 1953), to make his case, yet Rossiter, his admiration for the American Revolutionary generation notwithstanding, noted that the revolutionary pamphleteers did not produce much in the way of speculative political philosophy and tended to respond to practical issues of empire. Barrett argued that Charles Francis Sheridan's critique of Blackstone was an exception to his rule, yet Sheridan's tract would have been an exception to the rule among the Revolutionary Americans as well. Besides, with the Declaration of Independence, Revolutionary Americans moved beyond the old constitutionalism; by rejecting independence, the Anglo-Irish could not do the same.

drew the people into their contests. Popular participation moved beyond what the old elite considered acceptable bounds, and the independent American republic was politically reshaped. The political culture that emerged was not what the Founders had in mind and was something over which they had little control.[34]

Irish politics were even more elitist, and yet leaders of the Anglo-Irish Protestant Ascendancy experienced some of the same pressures as the American Founders. The logic of their own arguments pushed them down a road they did not really want to travel. Most opposition leaders in Grattan's Parliament assumed that they could be nationalists without becoming republicans or revolutionary separatists. They complained about the empire, they denounced Dublin Castle, and they promoted themselves as representatives of the people, protectors of the public interest, and guardians of the constitution. One Irish barrister, arguing against parliamentary union in a hastily assembled meeting of the Irish Bar in December 1798, had pledged his loyalty to Britain and the empire even as he accused Pitt of conspiring to bring down the Irish constitution. In a fervent plea that drew the applause of many colleagues, he proclaimed:

> I am enabled, by the visible and unerring demonstrations of nature, to assert, that Ireland was destined to be an independent nation. Our patent to be a state, and not a shire comes direct from Heaven. The Almighty has, in magestic characters, signed the grand charter of our independence. The great Creator of the World has given unto our beloved country, the gigantic outlines of a kingdom, and not the pigmy features of a province. God and Nature, I say, never intended that Ireland should be a province; and, by God, she never shall.

He uttered this within minutes of stating that "this nation, from her situation, language, and constitution, ought to be, and must ultimately be, a part of Great Britain."[35] He believed that Ireland could be a kingdom even though it was not free to choose its king, nor was its legislature really independent. He called it a nation even though, at that moment, its people seemed hopelessly divided. He could reconcile the tensions

---

34. Robert H. Wiebe, *The Opening of American Society* (New York: Alfred A. Knopf, 1984), 3–125; also see Edmund S. Morgan, *Inventing the People* (New York: W. W. Norton, 1987); and Gordon S. Wood, *The Radicalism of the American Revolution* (New York: Alfred A. Knopf, 1992). For the phenomenon in Ireland see Eric Strauss, *Irish Nationalism and British Democracy* (New York: Columbia University Press, 1951), 276–80.

35. The argument of "Mr. Goold" in *A Report of the Debate of the Irish Bar on Sunday, the 9th of December, 1798, on the Subject of an Union of the Legislatures of Great Britain and Ireland* (Dublin:. J. Moore, 1799), 47, 46 resp.

Ireland and the American Colonies 261

and seeming inconsistencies in his argument; there were others who could not.

During one of those seemingly interminable debates in Commons on pensions and places, and only after he made the usual, almost obligatory professions of allegiance, Laurence Parsons attacked the notion that the "Constitution of 1782" had changed Irish life for the better. "We are an independent kingdom, true. We have an imperial crown distinct from England, true," noted Parsons. "But it is a metaphysical distinction—a mere sport for speculative men," he scoffed. And, he warned prophetically, the people would grow increasingly disillusioned and might someday insist on cutting the imperial tie.

> The depraved policy with which this country was governed before the American war, will not be tolerated now. If such policy was to have been continued, the concessions of that time should never have been made. Government should either undo what it then did, which is impracticable, or it should cease to do what it is now doing. To arm a country with power first, and to treat it afterwards, as if it were impotent, is the most preposterous folly. Why was it, that the people required those concessions which were made during the American War? Because they expected to be governed better in consequence of them. Do you think then they will be satisfied to find they are not? Those concessions on the part of the English parliament, I grant were as ample as they well could be, for they were every thing short of separation. Let ministers then beware what conclusions they may teach the people, if they teach them this, that the attainment of every thing short of separation, will not attain for them good government.[36]

Beginning with Charles Lucas in the 1740s and spreading to the Volunteers of the 1780s and United Irishmen of the 1790s, there were more and more "people" unwilling to curb their criticism of the empire and Dublin Castle, and they were less and less willing to defer to the Patriots in Parliament as their spokesmen. Some, like Wolfe Tone, became political revolutionaries, calling for independence and denouncing the "nationalism" of the parliamentary opposition as too lukewarm and indecisive. These political revolutionaries in turn were pressured to be-

---

36. Parsons spoke in support of Ponsonby's motion, seconded by Grattan on 15 February 1790, to complain about places and pensions. The motion went down to a resounding defeat (*The Parliamentary Register*, 17 vols. [Dublin: James Moore, 1782–1801] 10:245, 246). Parsons, I should add, proves again the disjointed nature of the Irish Patriots. He was close to Flood and traded insults with Grattan in the Commons on 3 March 1789. Parsons accused Grattan of acting "from private pique when it was his duty to have acted from public principle"; moreover, Parsons added, "What great public measure did he ever undertake, that he did not blunder?" (ibid, 9:154, 155). For Parsons's career in the Irish Commons see N. D. Atkinson, "Sir Laurence Parsons, Second Earl of Rosse, 1758–1841" (Ph.D. thesis, Trinity College, University of Dublin, 1962), 65–178.

come social revolutionaries, to accept a broader definition of political culture that included Catholics as well as Protestants, people of modest means as well as those in what could pass as the Irish middle class. Not all of them made the second transition, and they ended up being too moderate and therefore too conservative, the very things that they accused parliamentary "oligarchs" of being.

The American Founders could not have fought, much less won, their War of Independence without at least some popular backing; without popular support, Grattan and the other Irish constitutional nationalists could not have forced free trade or a formal recognition of parliamentary independence. Yet the "people" in both lands developed a political identity of their own. In the 1789 Commons debates over John Forbes's place and pension bill, Arthur Browne noted that both those representing the Castle and the king and those more jealous of the power of the local aristocracy had appealed to the people. Given the prevailing assumption that there were three estates in society and that they manifested themselves as monarchy, aristocracy, and people, Browne observed, it was unavoidable that one estate would combine with another to check the power of the third. The Irish House of Commons, in theory the "democratical part" of government, could act as a "counterpoise" to the other "two powers." This arrangement was "the surest safeguard of the welfare and liberties of the people," when the system worked. The people often got what they wanted because the politics of self-interest were turned to their advantage, and to the greater good of the nation.[37] The king (through the Castle) and the aristocrats had no choice but to cater to the popular will.

Browne mentioned in passing something that Alexis de Tocqueville would explore in greater depth a half century later. Speaking of the three estates in France from the twelfth to the nineteenth centuries, Tocqueville concluded:

In the course of these seven hundred years it sometimes happened that the nobles, in order to resist the authority of the crown or to diminish the power of their rivals, granted some political power to the common people. Or, more frequently, the king permitted the lower orders to have a share in the government, with the intention of limiting the power of the aristocracy.[38]

---

37. Browne in a Commons debate on 9 March 1789, *Parliamentary Register*, 9:287–88. Disillusioned with the system by 1800, Browne voted for union.

38. Alexis de Tocqueville, *Democracy in America*, 2 vols., (New York: Alfred A. Knopf, 1980; orig. ed., 1835, 1840), 1:4. In *A Memorial Addressed to the Sovereigns of America* (London: J. DeBrett, 1783), Thomas Pownall showed how far he had gone since

The irony is that the aristocracy and the monarchy lost rather than gained power in the long run, their dabbling in democratic politics resulting in the promotion of an egalitarian strain inimical to their very existence. Tocqueville was ambivalent about all of this, knowing full well the shortcomings of the *ancien régime* but fearing a future where the popular will always prevailed.

Tocqueville might have seen egalitarianism as an irresistible force in nations where it had been unleashed, but he was not such a determinist that he believed egalitarianism would make all societies it touched indistinguishable. Indeed, on his one trip to Ireland he complained, "If you want to know what can be done by the spirit of conquest and religious hatred combined with the abuses of aristocracy, but without its advantages, go to Ireland."[39] The Ireland that Tocqueville visited in 1835 was hardly staggering under the weight of egalitarian excess.

Irish conditions did not mirror those in France. Irish chieftains and "kings" and Anglo-Norman lords during the Middle Ages built alliances in order to gain and hold power. They exchanged guarantees of right for obligations of service, a feudalistic arrangement that carried some of the same implications about freedoms and prerogatives that would also be claimed under the common law, Magna Carta and, ultimately, the "constitution." At the very moment that competing factions in medieval Ireland attempted to coalesce power, they had to justify their actions and identify certain rights. Rights claimed by Irish "kings" or Anglo-Norman lords could be claimed by rival groups and, much later, by people of the more middling sort who had virtually no organized political voice before the eighteenth century. What was true for Ireland was true for Britain as well. The vaunted British constitution was defined and redefined through political accommodation; Crown prerogative, parliamentary suzerainty, and popular sovereignty were constantly reworked in response to social change.[40] "In the eighteenth century," John

---

advocating a "grand marine dominion" in the 1760s (see supra, chapter 3). Pownall not only accepted American independence, he accepted an American "imperium" based on popular sovereignty. Pownall's guarded optimism for the American political experiment anticipated that of Tocqueville. Pownall worried that the "spirit of liberty" would be crushed by factionalism; Tocqueville worried more about the crushing weight of egalitarianism.

39. Alexis de Tocqueville, *Journeys to England and Ireland* (New Haven: Yale University Press, 1958), 122.

40. A theme traced, for example, in David Lindsay Keir's *The Constitutional History of Modern Britain since 1485*, 8th ed. (New York: D. Van Nostrand, 1966), although Keir strained to find consistency amidst all the changes.

Phillip Reid has observed, "the constitution was not the measure of what was lawful but the standard of what should be. The British constitution was whatever could be plausibly argued and forcibly maintained."[41]

The Irish in the eighteenth century were more manageable than Revolutionary Americans because of their different social climate and their different experience with empire, not because of British-imposed law and order. The lord lieutenant had more power than colonial governors, but no amount of power or patronage would have sufficed to keep the peace if the general population had become too hostile.[42] Whether from genuine love for the empire or fear of upheaval if the imperial tie were cut, most members of the Anglo-Irish Protestant Ascendancy resisted the drift toward independence, even as they attempted to protect their interests and define their constitutional rights. Many Catholics and other second-class citizens, for their own reasons, were likewise not ready to rebel. At the same time, Ireland was changing. It would never have precisely the same "republican" social setting as the United States, but republican notions did become more influential. The Irish were not, as J. A. Froude claimed in the 1870s, congenitally incapable of asserting their will.[43] Although the Anglo-Irish Ascendancy disappeared, the nationalistic emphasis on Irish liberties that it promoted and the revolutionary strain that it resisted survived.[44] Combined they would help produce an independent nation.

41. John Phillip Reid, *The Concept of Representation in the Age of the American Revolution* (Chicago: University of Chicago Press, 1989), 8. "There had never been anything fixed or static about the English constitution," cautioned Goldwin Smith in *A Constitutional and Legal History of England* (New York: Charles Scribner's Sons, 1955), 155.

42. John Phillip Reid's *In A Defiant Stance* (University Park: Pennsylvania State University Press, 1977), is a very suggestive comparison of the conditions of law in Massachusetts and Ireland on the eve of the American Revolution. I fear, however, that Reid exaggerated the amount of power wielded by the British directly or indirectly through Dublin Castle in Ireland. See the comments by Jack P. Greene, "From the Perspective of Law: Context and Legitimacy in the Origins of the American Revolution," *South Atlantic Quarterly* 85 (1986): 62–63. For the restricted power of lords lieutenant, see Johnston, *Great Britain and Ireland,* passim.

43. James Anthony Froude, *The English in Ireland in the Eighteenth Century,* 3 vols. (London: Longmans, Green, and Co., 1872–74).

44. See, for example, the 1886 speech by J. E. Redmond, Irish barrister, M.P. at Westminster, and home rule advocate, "Irish Protestants and Home Rule," in John J. Clancy, ed., *Essays and Speeches on the Irish Question* (London: The Irish Press Agency, 1888), vol. 1, no. 11.

Bibliographical Note

I will not attempt to include here all of the sources, published and unpublished, primary and secondary, that I consulted and that are important to the periods and subjects touched in this book. For those, the reader is referred to the detailed chapter notes. I should make it clear, however, that my research was much more extensive on Ireland between 1750 and 1800 than in earlier periods. The constitutional and political crisis of the empire came to a head then; I searched the literature on preceding eras to find antecedents for issues that proved most divisive during those years.

For general context, D. George Boyce's *Nationalism in Ireland* (Dublin: Gill and Macmillan, 1982) was indispensable. J. B. Archer's brief essay, "Necessary Ambiguity: Nationalism and Myth in Ireland," *Eire-Ireland* 19 (Summer 1984): 23–37, reviewed recent writing on Irish nationalism, including Boyce's book. Owen Dudley Edwards, "Ireland," in idem et al., *Celtic Nationalism* (London: Routledge and Kegan Paul, 1968), was very useful, as were Donnchadh Ó Corráin, "Nationality and Kingship in Pre-Norman Ireland," in T. W. Moody, ed., *Nationality and the Pursuit of National Independence* (Belfast: Appletree Press, 1978), and R. F. Foster's *Modern Ireland, 1600–1972* (London: Allen Lane, 1988). Marxist historian T. A. Jackson's *Ireland Her Own* (London: Cobbett Press, 1947) was provocative. Oliver MacDonagh's *States of Mind* (London: George Allen & Unwin, 1983) was suggestive, but MacDonagh, like Sean Cronin, *Irish Nationalism* (Dublin: Academy Press, 1980), and Tom Garvin, *The Evolution of Irish Nationalist Politics* (Dublin: Gill and Macmillan, 1981), focused on developments after 1800. The same can be said of Robert Kee's popular *The Green Flag* (London: Weidenfeld and Nicholson, 1972).

Angus Calder's sweeping narrative, *Revolutionary Empire* (New York: E. P. Dutton, 1981), puts Ireland into the larger picture of British expansionism, covering roughly from the Tudor period through the American Revolutionary era. Michael Hechter, *Internal Colonialism* (Berkeley: University of California Press, 1975), provides a different perspective and carries the author's theme from 1536 to 1966. Keith Robbins's "Core and Periphery in Modern British History," *Proceedings of the British Academy* 70 (1984): 275–97, urges caution in using such labels. Nicholas Canny's *Kingdom and Colony: Ireland in the Atlantic World, 1500–1800* (Baltimore: Johns Hopkins University Press, 1988) is also very insightful. Jack P. Greene, *Peripheries and Center* (Athens: University of Georgia Press, 1986), and D. W. Meinig, *Atlantic America, 1492–1800* (New Haven: Yale University Press, 1986), focus on American affairs but do allude to Ireland and offer insights into imperial problems on both sides of the Atlantic. Both

Greene and Meinig moved well beyond the oversimplified discussion in Walter Prescott Webb's *The Great Frontier* (Boston: Houghton Mifflin, 1952).

Historians now treat the debate between Charles Howard McIlwain, *The American Revolution: A Constitutional Interpretation* (New York: Macmillan, 1923), and Robert Livingston Schuyler, *Parliament and the British Empire* (New York: Columbia University Press, 1929), as unresolvable. That it is illustrates the difficulty of reconstructing the past and, at the same time, shows how American Revolutionaries and Irish Patriots, on one side, talked past British imperialists on the other. Schuyler and McIlwain are thus still worth reading, if not for having precisely reconstructed the past, then for demonstrating how futile it was in the seventeenth and eighteenth centuries—no less than in our own—to use history to establish precedent. A. Berriedale Keith, *Constitutional History of the First British Empire* (Oxford: Clarendon Press, 1930) covers much of the same ground as McIlwain, with whom Keith disagreed. J. T. Ball, *Historical Review of the Legislative Systems Operative in Ireland* (Dublin: Hodges, Figgis, and Co., 1889), and the first two chapters in Alfred Gaston Donaldson, *Some Comparative Aspects of Irish Law* (Durham: Duke University Press, 1957), trace the strengthening of ties between Ireland and Britain from 1172 to 1800 and the difficulty of finding clear precedents for Irish assertions of right.

Readers lacking a legal background would be well advised to peruse John Phillip Reid's studies of constitutionalism in the eighteenth-century British empire, notably his comparisons of colonial American and Anglo-Irish conditions in *Constitutional History of the American Revolution*, 3 vols. (Madison: University of Wisconsin Press, 1986–), and *In a Defiant Stance* (University Park, Pa.: The Pennsylvania State University Press, 1977). Marie Therese Flanagan, *Irish Society, Anglo-Norman Settlers, Angevin Kingship* (Oxford: Clarendon Press, 1989), is especially good on the problem of defining "kingship" in Ireland, before as well as after Henry II's arrival. G. O. Sayles and H. G. Richardson, *The Irish Parliament in the Middle Ages* (Philadelphia: University of Pennsylvania Press, 1952), examine the Irish Parliament's transition from an advisory council to a true legislative body. Brendan Bradshaw, *The Irish Constitutional Revolution of the Sixteenth Century* (Cambridge: Cambridge University Press, 1979), concentrates on the emergence of Irish constitutionalism during the reign of Henry VIII. J. G. Swift MacNeill's *The Constitutional and Parliamentary History of Ireland til the Union* (Dublin: Talbot Press, 1917) discussed the Irish Parliament, but it was also intended as a history "of the salient features of the rise and progress of the Irish Constitution." Edward and Annie G. Porritt, *The Unreformed House of Commons*, 2 vols. (Cambridge: Cambridge University Press, 1903, 1909), 2:183–529, cover the changing nature of Irish parliamentary politics before 1800.

J. C. Beckett and the late J. G. Simms can be counted among the best twentieth-century Irish historians, and early on I went to their works—most notably Beckett's *The Making of Modern Ireland* (New York: Alfred A. Knopf, 1969) and *The Anglo-Irish Tradition* (New York: Faber and Faber, 1976), and Simms's *Colonial Nationalism, 1689–1776* (Cork: Mercier Press, 1976) and *Jacobite Ireland, 1685–1691* (London: Routledge and Kegan Paul, 1969). Simms also wrote *William Molyneux of Dublin, 1656–1698* (Dublin: Irish Ac-

Bibliographical Note

ademic Press, 1982; edited by P. H. Kelly) and edited the most accessible copy of Molyneux's famous 1698 tract as *The Case of Ireland Stated* (Dublin: Cadenus Press, 1977). Two copies of Molyneux's "The Case of Ireland's Being Bound by Acts of Parliament in England Stated" are in the Trinity College, Dublin, collections (MS. 890), along with Sir William Domvile's never-published "A Disquisition touching that great Question Whether an Act of Parliamt made in England shall binde ye Kingdome, & people of Ireland without their Allowance & Acceptance of such Act in the Kingdome of Ireland" (1660). Isolde Louise Victory's "Colonial Nationalism in Ireland, 1692–1725: From Common Law to Natural Right" (Ph.D. dissertation, Trinity College, University of Dublin, 1985) discussed Molyneux as well as Swift, but Victory, I feel, tried too hard to show the evolution of arguments that were jumbled together throughout the period she covered and the longer span that I examined. I found James Ivan McGuire, "Politics, Opinion and the Irish Constitution, 1688–1707" (M.A. thesis, University College, Dublin, 1968), more persuasive.

Trinity College, Dublin, also has two manuscript copies (MSS. 647 and 843) of "A Declaration setting forth how and by what meanes the Lawes and Statutes of England from time to time came to bee of force in Ireland," written in 1643 or early 1644, and first published in Walter Harris, ed., *Hibernica* (Dublin: John Milliken, 1747, 1750), Part II, along with a rebuttal by Samuel Mayart. Patrick Darcy might not have written that "Declaration," but copies of his no less important *An Argument* (Waterford: Thomas Bourke, 1643) have survived. The notes to Chapter 1 explain the controversies surrounding the "Declaration" and Molyneux's *Case*, both on questions of authorship (in the case of the "Declaration") and valid argumentation (particularly in the *Case*). Also see William O'Malley's "Patrick Darcy, Lawyer and Politician, 1597–1668" (M.A. thesis, University College, Galway, 1973). John T. Gilbert, ed., *History of the Irish Confederation and the War in Ireland*, 4 vols. (Dublin: M. H. Gill & Son, 1882–1888), includes Richard Bellings's narrative as well as other documents dealing with Irish unrest in the 1640s.

Naturally I could not go very far without reading James Anthony Froude's *The English in Ireland in the Eighteenth Century*, 3 vols. (London: Longmans, Green, and Co., 1872–74) and William Edward Hartpole Lecky's *A History of Ireland in the Eighteenth Century*, 5 vols. (London: Longmans, Green, and Co., 1913–16; orig. ed., 1892). Froude's writing was colored by his confidence in English cultural superiority and his belief that "the superior part has a natural right to govern; the inferior part has a natural right to be governed." Froude dropped the Irish into the latter category. Froude's pontificating and Social Darwinism aside, he occasionally offered insightful criticisms of the British navigation system and the Anglo-Irish Protestant Ascendancy. Lecky, himself Anglo-Irish, was of course more sympathetic to the Ascendancy, even as he echoed Froude's critique of British mercantilism. For the biases of both men, see Anne Wyatt, "Froude, Lecky and 'the humblest Irishman,'" *Irish Historical Studies* 19 (March 1975): 261–85.

The essays in T. W. Moody and W. E. Vaughan, eds., *A New History of Ireland*, vol. 4 (Oxford: Clarendon Press, 1986), especially those by J. L. McCracken and by R. B. McDowell, helped me, as did the detailed bibliography compiled by David Dickson. I also read the essays in volume 2 of that same Oxford series, edited by Art Cosgrove and covering 1169–1535, and volume 3, edited by T. W. Moody, F. X. Martin, and F. J. Byrne (covering 1534–1691). R. B. McDowell's *Ireland in the Age of Imperialism and Revolution, 1760–1801* (Oxford: Clarendon Press, 1979) has a fine bibliography; McDowell's *Irish Public Opinion, 1750–1800* (London: Faber and Faber, 1944) lists, by year, many of the more important Irish political pamphlets written between 1698 and 1800. David Dickson's *New Foundations: Ireland, 1660–1800* (Dublin: Helicon Ltd., 1987) is an excellent overview. So is Edith M. Johnston's *Ireland in the Eighteenth Century* (Dublin: Gill and Macmillan, 1974). Johnston's *Great Britain and Ireland, 1760–1800* (Edinburgh: Oliver and Boyd, 1963) is a meticulous institutional and administrative history. These works should be supplemented with Francis Godwin James's *Ireland in the Empire, 1688–1770* (Cambridge: Harvard University Press, 1973); Robert E. Burns, *Irish Parliamentary Politics in the Eighteenth Century*, 2 vols. (Washington, D.C.: The Catholic University of America Press, 1989–90), which stresses the complexity of the undertaker system and the power of such Anglo-Irish leaders as Henry Boyle and Archbishop George Stone; Maurice O'Connell, *Irish Politics and Social Conflict in the Age of the American Revolution* (Philadelphia: University of Pennsylvania Press, 1965); Gerard O'Brien, *Anglo-Irish Politics in the Age of Grattan and Pitt* (Dublin: Irish Academic Press, 1987); Thomas Bartlett's incisive discussion, "The Catholic Question, 1690–1830," in *The Fall and Rise of the Irish Nation* (Savage, Md.: Barnes & Noble, 1992); S. J. Connolly, *Religion, Law, and Power* (Oxford: Clarendon Press, 1992); the essays in Thomas Bartlett and D. W. Hayton, eds., *Penal Era and Golden Age* (Belfast: Ulster Historical Foundation, 1979), and Gerard O'Brien, ed., *Parliament, Politics and People* (Dublin: Irish Academic Press, 1989); an armload of articles by Thomas Bartlett and A. P. W. Malcomson, cited at appropriate places in the notes; and Part Two of Foster's *Modern Ireland*, pp. 167–286.

For Ireland and the American Revolution, O'Connell's book and his essay "The American Revolution and Ireland," *Eire-Ireland* 11 (Summer 1976): 3–12, are most useful, as are Owen Dudley Edwards's "The American Image of Ireland: A Study of Its Early Phases," *Perspectives in American History* 4 (1970): 199–282, and "The Impact of the American Revolution on Ireland," in *The Impact of the American Revolution Abroad* (Washington, D.C.: Library of Congress, 1976); David Noel Doyle, *Ireland, Irishmen and Revolutionary America, 1760–1820* (Dublin: Mercier Press, 1981); and Theresa Margaret O'Connor, "The More Immediate Effects of the American Revolution on Ireland, 1775–1785" (M.A. thesis, Queen's University of Belfast, 1938). All are effective antidotes to Michael Kraus's overenthusiastic "America and the Irish Revolutionary Movement in the Eighteenth Century," in Richard B. Morris, ed., *The Era of the American Revolution* (New York: Columbia University Press, 1939). Raymond J. Barrett, "A Comparative Study of Imperial Constitutional Theory in Ireland and America in the Age of the American Revolution" (Ph.D. thesis, Trinity College, University of Dublin, 1958) erred, I am convinced, in two crucial ways: by exaggerating the "system" of constitutional thought among

Revolutionary Americans and by downplaying too much the Anglo-Irish concern with constitutional questions.

Lawrence Henry Gipson, *The British Empire before the American Revolution*, 15 vols. (New York: Alfred A. Knopf, 1936–70), 1: 197–237, and 13: 3–32, placed Ireland within the larger imperial crisis of the 1760s and 1770s. R. R. Palmer, *The Age of the Democratic Revolution*, 2 vols. (Princeton: Princeton University Press, 1959, 1964), touches but lightly on Irish developments between 1760 and 1800. Richard Koebner devotes a chapter to Ireland during roughly the same period in *Empire* (New York: Grosset & Dunlap, 1961). Irish reformist urges during the 1780s are discussed in much more detail in Daniel H. Smyth, "The Volunteer Movement in Ulster: Background and Development, 1784–5" (Ph.D. dissertation, Queen's University of Belfast, 1974), and in two works by James J. Kelly: "The Irish Parliamentary Reform Movement: The Administration and Popular Politics, 1783–5" (M.A. thesis, University College, Dublin, 1981) and "The Search for a 'Commercial Arrangement': Anglo-Irish Politics in the 1780s," 2 vols. (Ph.D. dissertation, University College, Dublin 1985). Nancy J. Curtin traced the growing radicalism of the next decade in "The Transformation of the Society of the United Irishmen into a Mass-based Revolutionary Organization, 1794–6," *Irish Historical Studies* 24 (1985): 463–92. Marianne Elliott's "The Origins and Transformation of Early Irish Republicanism," *International Review of Social History* 23 (1978): 405–28, served as a précis for *Partners in Revolution* (New Haven: Yale University Press, 1982). Jim Smyth, *The Men of No Property* (New York: St. Martin's Press, 1992), and A. T. Q. Stewart, *A Deeper Silence* (London: Faber and Faber, 1993), dig to the roots of the United Irish movement.

If, as Thomas Jefferson once lamented to John Adams, a complete history of the American Revolution could not be written because so much had been lost, the same applies to the history of eighteenth-century Irish politics. The leaders of Grattan's Parliament did not leave the large body of correspondence that has survived from the American Revolutionary generation. That could be one reason that Irish "Patriots" have not held the place in Irish memories enjoyed by American Revolutionaries among Americans of the present generation. The Henry Flood Correspondence (Add. MS. 22,930) at the British Library does not include much by Flood; snippets of Grattan's correspondence can be found at the British Library and the National Library of Ireland (hereafter BL and NLI). The earl of Charlemont's thirty volumes of papers (MS. 12R) at the Royal Irish Academy (hereafter RIA) are the exception proving the paucity rule for the Grattan group. Almost all of the significant Charlemont papers in that collection on political affairs have been published in the Historical Manuscripts Commission (hereafter HMC), *The Manuscripts and Correspondence of James, First Earl of Charlemont*, 2 vols. (London: Eyre and Spottiswoode, 1891, 1894). A. P. W. Malcomson's *John Foster* (Oxford: Oxford University Press, 1978) is one of the few full-scale biographies of recent vintage, but then Foster left a substantial body of papers. Little survives for John Fitzgibbon and many other leading members of the Irish Parliament. Robert Burns reviewed Fitzgibbon's career through the regency crisis of 1789 in "The Rise of John Fitzgibbon: A Study of Anglo-

Irish Politics during the Age of the American Revolution" (Ph.D. dissertation, Harvard University, 1960). The correspondence of other Irish politicians is scattered through various HMC collections; for example, the letters of House Speaker Edmund Sexton Pery were gathered in HMC, *Eighth Report*, Part I (London: Eyre and Spottiswoode, 1881), pp. 173–208, and continued in HMC, *Fourteenth Report* (London: Eyre and Spottiswoode, 1895), Appendix, Part IX, pp. 155–99.

Most of the more detailed biographies of Grattan-era Irish leaders were written by contemporaries or family members and include selections from correspondence that had passed into their hands and stayed there. Grattan's son, Henry Grattan Jr., wrote *Memoirs of the Life and Times of the Rt. Hon. Henry Grattan*, 5 vols. (London: Henry Colburn, 1849), which reproduced the text of many Grattan letters. The younger Grattan also edited both *The Speeches of the Right Honourable Henry Grattan*, 4 vols. (London: Longman, Hurst, Rees, Orme, and Brown, 1822), and the *Miscellaneous Works of the Right Honourable Henry Grattan* (London: Hurst, Reese, Orme, and Brown, 1822). Stephen Gwynn's *Henry Grattan and His Times* (London: George S. Harrap and Co., 1939) is not quite as celebratory but is still sympathetic and does not add much to what Grattan's son had already revealed. Gerard O'Brien, "The Grattan Mystique," *Eighteenth-Century Ireland* 1 (1986): 177–94, reviews Grattan biographical historiography and the larger problem of reconstructing Patriot politics. In "Illusion and Reality in Late Eighteenth-Century Irish Politics," *Eighteenth-Century Ireland* 3 (1988): 149–55, O'Brien offered a rebuttal to W. J. McCormack's "Vision and Revision in the Study of Eighteenth-Century Irish Parliamentary Rhetoric," *Eighteenth-Century Ireland* 2 (1987): 7–35. Francis Hardy remains the primary biographer of his friend Charlemont, based on his *Memoirs of the Political and Private Life of James Caulfield, Earl of Charlemont*, 2 vols. (London: T. Cadell, 1810). Maurice Craig's *The Volunteer Earl* (London: Cresset, 1948), like Gwynn's study of Grattan, does not add much that cannot be found in Hardy—although Craig struck a more scholarly stance. William Henry Curran wrote his father's biography in *The Life of the Right Honorable John Philpot Curran* (London: Longman, Hurst, Reese, Orme, and Brown, 1819). Thomas Davis's brief *The Life of the Right Hon. John Philpot Curran* (Dublin: James Duffy, 1846) borrows heavily from that earlier study, as does Leslie Hale's *John Philpot Curran* (London: Jonathan Cape, 1958). Much of what the younger Grattan and Curran knew about their fathers went with them to the grave. Likewise with Warden Flood, author of the *Memoirs of the Life and Correspondence of the Right Hon. Henry Flood, M.P.* (Dublin: John Cumming, 1838). Jonah Barrington's *Rise and Fall of the Irish Nation* (New York: D. & J. Sadlier, 1885; orig. ed., 1833) and *Personal Sketches of His Own Times* (New York: W. J. Widdleton, 1853) probably tell us as much about Barrington's quirks as they do about the men of Grattan's generation. Marianne Elliott's *Theobald Wolfe Tone* (New Haven: Yale University Press, 1990) shows how Tone did—and in other ways did not—break with Grattan and those of his ilk.

The views of Dublin Castle and the various ministries in London are easier to decipher, through the State Papers (Ireland) 63 at the Public Record Office (hereafter PRO) in London (from 1558 to 1782) and the Home Office Papers 100 at the PRO branch in Kew (1782 to 1800). These can be supplemented with letters to and from lords lieutenant and chief secretaries in numerous HMC collections (which include papers for the earl of Buckinghamshire, the earl of Carlisle, and the duke of Rutland); and, at the BL, the Northington Letter-Book, 1783–1784 (Add. MS. 38,716), the Marquis of Buckingham Letter-Books, 1782–1789 (Add. MSS. 40,177–40,180, 40,733), and the Auckland Papers, vols. 6 and 7 (Add. MSS. 34,417–34,418), which contain letters from William Eden, 1780–1782; the John Blaquiere Letter Books, 1772–1776, in the PRO State Papers (Ireland) 63, vols. 437A and 437B; the Harcourt Papers (MSS. 73 and 74) at the Gilbert Library, Dublin City Library; and the Harcourt Letters, 1772–1775 (MS. 5161), at the NLI. Most of Harcourt's letters are printed in Edward William Harcourt, ed., *The Harcourt Papers*, 12 vols. (Oxford: James Parker, 1880–1905). The Heron Papers (MSS. 13,034–13,063) include letters when Heron was chief secretary to the earl of Buckinghamshire. The papers of Thomas Orde, chief secretary to the duke of Rutland, are also at the NLI (MSS. 16,350–16,370).

The *Printed Records of the Parliament of Ireland, 1613–1800* (New York: Trans-Media Publishing, 1975) have been reproduced on 46 reels of microfilm, along with a guide by Dermot Englefield, *The Printed Records of the Parliament of Ireland, 1613–1800* (London: Lemon Tree Press, 1978). This collection contains the published House of Commons journal (1613–1800), the published journal for the House of Lords (1634–1800), separately published votes and proceedings of Commons (1692–1800), the *Parliamentary Register* of Commons debates (1781–1797), supplementary volumes for House debates on union (1799–1800), and, finally, *The Statutes at Large* (1310–1800). Virtually all of these were first printed at one time or another during the last two decades of the 18th century, but they are brought together here most conveniently. Henry F. Berry, ed., *Statutes and Ordinances and Acts of the Parliament of Ireland*, 3 vols. (Dublin: Alexander Thom & Co., 1907–14), collected parliamentary statutes recorded through the reign of Edward IV, many of which are not among the *Statutes at Large*. Commons debates before as well as after the advent of the *Parliamentary Register* in 1781 were often summarized in newspapers like the *Hibernian Journal: Or, Chronicle of Liberty* (beginning in 1771), the *Dublin Journal* (1751–1801), and *The Public Register: Or, Freeman's Journal* (1763–1801). The NLI has microfilm copies of all three; the Library of Congress has the latter two (nos. 428 and 432, resp.). The rare book room at the Library of Congress also has a complete run of Walker's *Hibernian Magazine* (1771–1811), a Dublin periodical as politicized as the leading newspapers.

There are also two manuscript sources that deal with the history of the Irish Parliament, and these are too little used. The first is a history of debates in the Irish Commons from 18 June 1776 to 21 April 1789 (MS. 16,363.1) in the Library of Congress and attributed to M.P. Sir Henry Cavendish. This eighty-two-volume collection is divided into forty-five volumes of "verbatim" shorthand notes and thirty-seven volumes of longhand transcriptions. There are large gaps in the record and almost nothing for 1786–88; even so, this is a useful supplement to other accounts. For the collection and the question of authorship, see Peter D. G. Thomas "The Authorship of the Manuscript Irish Parliamentary Diary (1776–1789) in the Library of Congress," *English Historical Review* 77 (1962): 94–95.

The other source is a history of the Irish Parliament from its origins until 1773 by Hugh Howard in the Gilbert Library, Dublin City Library (MSS. 88 and 89). Howard apparently did most of the work on this study from 1772–74, then left it virtually untouched until making a final note in 1797. Perhaps he gave up because of age or because parliamentary proceedings were starting to be published in the 1780s. In any event, it is an interesting attempt at reconstituting the past by working through statutes and other public records. Howard seems to have accepted the Molyneux view of Irish parliamentary and constitutional rights. J. T. Gilbert discussed Howard's history briefly in HMC, *Third Report* (London: Eyre and Spottiswoode, 1872), appendix, pp. 432–34.

A notable exception to the scanty record in some areas is the preservation of most if not all of the important political pamphlets written from the 1740s through 1800. The Charles Haliday Pamphlet Collection at the RIA, indexed by date and topic in a two-volume guide by J. T. Gilbert, is exceptional. The RIA has other pamphlets in a general, separately indexed collection. The NLI also has a good collection of pamphlets, and a fair number of Irish tracts—including those by Charles Lucas, a man too often neglected by historians—can be found at the BL. I drew heavily from these collections; individual titles are cited in the notes.

Some of the pamphlets in all of those collections were published anonymously. In a few cases authorship can be determined by internal evidence or by references made in contemporaneous writings. In other cases authorship was assigned years later by archivists or librarians. They may have been right; they may also have been wrong. This, joined to the fact that the official records and newspaper accounts did not give precise, word for word accounts of parliamentary debates, makes reconstructing the Irish past difficult. The published journals for the Irish Commons and Lords are very sketchy and give the misleading impression that Parliament House was a placid place. The *Parliamentary Register* shows that this was not the case (in Commons, at least), but the debates printed there were reported in the third person by those who kept the record, and those recorders sometimes editorialized—for example, describing John Philpot Curran as speaking in a "very ludicrous manner" (*Parlimentary Register,* 17:554); and the *Parliamentary Register* did not catch everything—hence the need for letters, journals, and other accounts to find out what happened in Parliament. That men like Henry Grattan later revised, even bowdlerized, their speeches further exacerbates the problem. For Grattan and his editorial emendations, see Richard Koebner, "The Early Speeches of Henry Grattan," *Bulletin of the Institute of Historical Research* 30 (1957): 102–14, and the essays by Gerard O'Brien and W. J. McCormack noted above. Historians should not take Grattan at his word; moreover, they should stop to consider if what was written was what was spoken. The same caution should be used for all sources—advice routinely passed on to students by professors, but advice often forgotten by the professors in their own research and writing.

Index

Act of Union in 1800, 6, 53, 202, 234, 253; terms of, 238–39
Adams, John: Irish-American analogies, 90–91, 103–4, 105
Adams, Randolph: problem of sovereignty, 2
American Revolution: impact on Ireland, 1–2, 105–8; Irish link, 252–56; limited democratic urge, 259–60, 262. *See also* constitution; Volunteers
Andrews, Charles: on ideology and interest, 257–58
Anglo-Irish Protestant Ascendancy: concern for rights, 1; elitist limitations, 5; undercut by constitutionalism, 6–7; Catholics removed from the constitutional tradition, 18, 34–35, 68; Molyneux's *Case* defines that tradition, 19–21, 29; danger of being removed from it, 191–92; too narrow appeal, 241; attachment to Britain, 245–50; disappears, 264
Annesley v. Sherlock: alienates Irish Parliament, 41–42
Archdall, Nicholas: pamphlet opposed to union, 56, 57–58
Arendt, Hannah: on revolution, 244
Aristotle: governmental forms, 195–96, 222

Bailyn, Bernard: on conspiracy, 86; royal governors in colonies, 247
Baratariana, 122, 253; oppose Townshend, 79–82, 85
Barré, Isaac: takes sons of liberty appellation from Charles Lucas, 86
Barrett, Raymond: Anglo-Irish constitutionalism, 258n–259n
Barrington, Jonah: reminiscences, 122n, 125n; anti-unionist, 235, 236
Becker, Carl: on appeal of ideas, 4
Beckett, J. C.: on Constitution of 1782, 144

Bentham, Jeremy: critiques Blackstone, 116
Beresford, John: dislikes Volunteers, 163–64; removed from post, 217; for union, 230
Berkeley, George: defense of Irish rights, 49–51; wants Catholics to become Protestants, 71, 191
Blackstone, William: parliamentary sovereignty, 84–85, 252; views critiqued, 116–19, 153; on representation, 153–54
Blaquiere, John: controversial, 96; blocks pro-Americans in Commons, 99; estimates numbers of United Irishmen, 229n; for union, 230
Bolton, Richard: possible author of 1644 "Declaration," 16, 16n
Boyle, Henry, earl of Shannon: undertaker, 52; in 1750s controversies, 54; elevated to peerage, 66
Bradshaw, Brendan: on sixteenth-century Irish constitutional revolution, 11
Brinton, Crane: on historical explanation, 3
Bristol, Frederick Augustus Hervey, fourth earl of and bishop of Derry: at Volunteer national convention, 177
Brooke, Henry: Anglo-Irish view of Irish past, 70; shares ideas with Charles O'Conor, 73
Browne, Arthur: changes vote on union, 235–36, 238; on political estates, 262
Brownlow, William: parliamentary reform, 179, 181, 186
Buckingham, Richard Nugent-Grenville-Temple, first marquess of: lord lieutenant as earl Temple, 173; return and struggles, 196–200
Buckinghamshire, John Hobart, second earl of: lord lieutenant, 110–11, 226; plays politics, 130; allows Volunteers to form, 148, 163; disturbed by them, 163–64

273

Index

Burgh, James: on imperial crisis, 88; critiques Blackstone, 116

Burgh, Walter Hussey: pro-American speech, 101; criticizes British trade policy, 114; Monks of St. Patrick, 121; backs Grattan, 126, 132, 138; seeks office, 141–42

Burke, Edmund: disdain for Charles Lucas, 65; Ireland to benefit from American Revolution, 97; disappointment, 100; favors trade concessions, 113; opposes parliamentary independence, 136, 228; Ireland needs Britain, 244

Burns, Robert: on Irish politics, 51–52

Burrowes, Peter: ease Catholic restrictions, 191

Bushe, Gervase Parker: *Baratariana* essays, 79–82; pamphlet on imperial affairs, 82; pro-American, 98, 107; desires moderation, 115; opposes Grattan, 126; perpetual mutiny bill dispute, 129–30; against parliamentary reform, 179, 181; for Catholic emancipation, 189; regency crisis, 200

Bushman, Richard: on republican culture, 248

Cabot, John: explorer, 251

Cambrensis, Sylvester Giraldus (Gerald of Wales), 19

Camden, John Jeffreys Pratt, second earl of: lord lieutenant, 217

Carlisle, Frederick Howard, fifth earl of, lord lieutenant, 130–31; accepts Volunteers, 148

Carteret, John, first marquess of Granville: lord lieutenant, 51

Carton estate, 52, 243

Cartwright, John: parliamentary reform, 183; predicts union, 226

Cary, Edward: holds seat in Commons, 162

Castlereagh, Robert Stewart, viscount: insults Grattan, 235

Castletown house, 52, 158, 243

Catholic emancipation, 107, 189; Catholic hopes for, 40, 73, 194; Volunteer interest in, 174–84 passim; 1793 gains, 203; United Irishmen and, 208, 210–11, 214–15, 241; Fitzwilliam fiasco, 216–17; post-union, 240; slavery analogy, 248–49

Catholics and constitutional tradition, 6; written out of, 17–18, 34–35, 68–69, 72, 191–92; O'Conor and Curry restore them to, 68–71, 73; likewise William Todd Jones, 190; and William Crawford, 190–91. *See also* Patrick Darcy; Daniel O'Connell; Hugh Reilly

Cavendish, Henry: notes on Commons debates, 112n

Charlemont, James Caulfield, first earl of: on 1750s constitutionalism, 55; criticizes octennial act, 76–77; connection of Ireland to America, 85, 98, 101; Monks of St. Patrick, 121; Society of Granby Row, 121; distressed by Flood-Grattan split, 138–40; commander of the Volunteers, 149; borough patron, 156; wants Volunteers out of politics, 165, 169; Volunteer convention in 1783, 176–77; regency crisis, 197, 199; opposes union, 227, 232, 232n; attachment to Britain, 249

Charles I: struggles, 12–13, 15

Charles II: does without Irish Parliament, 27

Clare, earl of. *See* John Fitzgibbon

Clarke, Aidan: on Poynings' Law, 12

Coke, Sir Edward: his inconsistency, 36n

commercial relief: and American war, 109–10, 112–15; postwar complaints, 145–46, 196

Conolly, Thomas, 197; pro-American, 98; advises Buckinghamshire, 110, 111; against Grattan, 126; would have supported union in 1782, 143, 146; motion to thank Volunteers, 149; retains seat in Commons, 158, 162; opposes parliamentary reform, 181; Wolfe Tone's disdain for, 215n; for union, 231; tie to duke of Richmond, 249

constitution: creation of constitutional tradition, 4–5; caught in political disputes, 6–7; as understood by Anglo-Irish, 19–26; and parliamentary independence, 107–8; Constitution of 1782, 124–45; 1782 settlement inadequate, 188, 212, 228, 231; threatened in regency crisis, 196–200; in union debates, 232–35; American analogy, 238. *See also* Patrick Darcy; Henry Grattan; Charles Lucas; William Molyneux; nationalism; Charles O'Conor; revolutionary impulse

Continental Congress: seeks Irish connection, 90, 93; gives up, 104

Cooke, Edward: pro-union, 231

Cornwallis, Charles, first marquess: lord lieutenant: for union, 231–32, 234

Corry, Isaac: duels Grattan, 235

Cox, Richard: Irish rights and union, 34

Index

Crawford, William: nationalistic *History*, 190–91; flaws in, 256
Curran, John Philpot: Monks of St. Patrick, 122; for parliamentary reform, 181; animosity toward John Fitzgibbon, 200; for Catholic emancipation, 204; resigns from Commons, 217; anti-union, 234
Curry, John, 189: restores Catholics to constitutional tradition, 68–71

Daly, Denis: resolution supporting Crown, 110; criticizes British mercantilism, 112; wants moderation, 115; warns against popular politics, 115; Monks of St. Patrick, 121; impressive library of, 122; opposes Grattan, 126; borough patron, 156; Commons represents the people, 160; supports Catholic emancipation, 189
Darcy, Patrick: defense of Irish rights, 13–15; 1643 *Argument*, 15–16; basis for later constitutional arguments, 26; and Walter Harris, 73; *Argument* reprinted, 87; noted by Hercules Langrishe, 135n; in constitutional tradition, 241, 253, 259
Davies, Sir John, 31
Davis, Thomas: on Monks of St. Patrick, 120; mythmaking of, 244
Declaration of Independence: unenthusiastic Anglo-Irish reaction to, 102–3, 254–55, 259
"Declaration" of 1644: on Irish rights, 16, 24, 26; finally printed, 118
Declaratory Act of 1720: Irish subordination and alienation, 41, 42, 48, 53, 141; condemned by Charles Lucas, 62; danger in imperial context, 86–87; problem of language, 87n; criticized by Charles Francis Sheridan, 117; and by Grattan, 120; and William Crawford, 190; repealed and renounced, 136
Declaratory Act of 1766: problem of, 86–87, 87n, 256
Defenders, Catholic, 216, 229
Dickinson, John: links Irish and American affairs, 87–88; Friendly Sons of St. Patrick, 105n; reluctant revolutionary, 250
Dickson, William Steel: champions Volunteers, 163; supports republicanism, 210
Dissenters: discrimination against, 40, 249; extended the franchise, 156
Dobbs, Arthur, 51

Dobbs, Francis, 165, 183; American war and Ireland, 109; on Irish rights, 116; 1782 *History*, 146–47; background, 170–72; popular politics, 172–73; proposes parliamentary reform, 175; pulls back from radical politics, 175, 192; and English reformers, 183; anti-union, 234
Domvile, Sir William: 1660 "Disquisition" and Irish rights, 19–20, 22, 199; position undercut, 24
Drennan, William: background, 170–72; popular politics, 172–73, 183, 241; *Orellana* letters, 188, 189, 192; United Irishmen, 205–14; as separatist, 206; withdraws from politics, 213; predicts union, 228; opposes it, 234
Dulany, Daniel: rejects revolution, 250

Eden, William: chief secretary under Carlisle, 130–31
Edwards, Owen Dudley: on Irish sympathy for Americans, 95
Elizabeth I: New World patents, 251
Emmet, Thomas: and Wolfe Tone, 208

Filmer, Robert: mentioned, 36
FitzGerald, Edward: in 1798 revolt, 229
Fitzgibbon, John, earl of Clare: reluctantly for parliamentary independence, 143; regency crisis and peerage, 199, 200; rises to power, 224–26; fades, 239
Fitzwilliam, William Wentworth, second earl, 228; as lord lieutenant, 216–17, 222; arranges election for Grattan, 242; Irish estate, 249
Flood, Henry, 114, 157, 219, 227; political rise, 79–80; *Baratariana* essays, 79–82; unlikely "Junius" author, 89n; joins the administration, 96; alliance with Grattan, 107, 132–33; renunciation and break with Grattan, 136, 138; seeks seat at Westminster, 140, 177; in the Volunteers, 149–52; for parliamentary reform, 176–82
Forbes, John: Monks of St. Patrick, 121–22; supports Grattan, 126, 132, 219; at 1783 Volunteer convention, 176; reform bill, 201–2
Foster, John: anti-union, but later sits at Westminster, 238–39; predicts Catholic dominance, 239n
Fox, Charles James, 244; favors trade concessions, 113; likes Charles Francis Sheridan's tract, 116; does little for parliamentary reform, 185

Franklin, Benjamin: on Irish-American similarities, 91–93, 103–4
Friendly Sons of St. Patrick: and American Revolution, 104
Froude, James Anthony: criticizes the Anglo-Irish, 100–101, 141; admires John Fitzgibbon, 226, 239; Irish disunited, 264

Gardiner, Luke: anti-Volunteer resolution, 182
George II, 76, 78; in 1753–1755 controversy, 53–54
George III, 140; loss of American colonies, 74; Charles Lucas on, 78; rebuked in *Baratariana*, 81; criticized elsewhere, 97; Anglo-Irish critics of empire loyal to him, 110, 119, 248, 253–54; accepts Irish parliamentary independence, 135; awarding of Irish peerages, 158; regency crisis, 196–97
Gilbert, Sir Humphrey: New World patent, 251
Gordon, Thomas: as commonwealthman, 49, 63
Grattan, Henry:, on 1750s controversies, 55; *Baratariana* essays, 79–82; not likely "Junius" author, 89n; alliance with Flood, leadership of Patriots, 107–8; resolution supporting the Crown, 110; rise in Irish politics, 112–24; wants trade concessions, 113–14; Monks of St. Patrick, 121; 1780 Declaration of Right fails, 124–28; tries again, 132; difficulty of reconstructing speeches, 125n, 134n–135n; April 1782 speech and victory, 134–35, 150–51; father of Irish independence, 135; battles Flood over renunciation, 136–38; in the Volunteers, 149–52; danger of democratic politics, 152; unforeseen implications of appealing to the people, 165–68; supports parliamentary reform, 179–82; turns on Volunteers, 182; criticized in *Orellana*, 188; for limited Catholic emancipation, 189; regency crisis, 197–201; placemen reform bill, 202–3; for Catholic franchise, 203–4; dislikes United Irishmen, 205; in Fitzwilliam crisis, 216–17; resigns from Commons, actions assessed, 217–20, 222–23; back in Commons to fight union, 234–35; feels betrayed by Pitt, 194, 239; duel with Isaac Corry, 235; in Westminster parliament, 239, 242–43; as constitutional nationalist, 241; attachment to the empire, 244–45; use of history, 125–26, 254, 255
Grenville, George: right of British Parliament to tax Ireland and American colonies, 86, 122
Guatimozin essays. *See* Frederick Jebb

Handcock, William: appeals to electors, 161
Harcourt, Simon, first earl: lord lieutenant during the American war, 95–100, 104, 107, 110–12, 147
Harrington, William Stanhope, first earl of: unimpressive lord lieutenant, 52
Harris, Walter: antiquarian and critic of Catholics, 70; printing of the 1644 "Declaration," 73
Hartstonge, Henry: Monks of St. Patrick, 121
Hearts of Steel: depredations, 106
Hely-Hutchinson, John: opposes Townshend, 76, 77; pamphlet against British mercantilism, 114–15; as greedy officeseeker, 140
Henry II, 256; deals with Irish kings, 6; in Darcy's *Argument* and the 1644 "Declaration," 17, 27; in Domvile's "Disquisition," 20–22; and Molyneux's *Case*, 24–28; in *Guatimozin*, 118; and Crawford's *History*, 190
Henry VII: sends Edward Poynings as lord deputy, 10; patent to John Cabot, 251
Henry VIII: recognizes Ireland as kingdom, 2, 10–11; not important to Molyneux's *Case*, 26–27, 199
Hudson, Edward: Monks of St. Patrick, 121

Ireland: definitional problem as kingdom, 2–3; kingdom and constitutional tradition, 8–9. *See also* constitution; nationalism; revolutionary impulse

James, Francis Godwin: rising power of legislatures, 52
James II: as symbol of Stuart oppression, 18, 37
Jebb, Frederick, *Guatimozin* and "Causidicus" letters, 118–19; Monks of St. Patrick, 121; becomes administration man, 141; danger of democratic message, 152
Jebb, John: parliamentary reform, 183–84
Jefferson, Thomas: as founding father, 244

Index

John I: as lord and king of Ireland, 22, 24, 28
Johnson, Robert: "Causidicus" letters, 118–19; sympathy for Wolfe Tone, 207n
Johnston, Edith Mary: on the 1790s, 212
Johnstone, George: Irish sympathetic to Americans, 94
Jones, William Todd: supports reform, 182–83; Catholics not dangerous, 190; regency crisis, 198
"Junius" essays: on imperial crisis, 88–89

Kelly, James J.: on Volunteers, 182
Kildare, Gerald FitzGerald, seventh earl of: removed and reinstated as lord deputy, 10
Kilkenny Confederates: defend Irish rights, 15–16, 17, 241, 254; Anglo-Irish disregard, 35
King, William, bishop, Anglo-Irish constitutional nationalist, 30; ideas problematical, 36–38
Knox, William: imperial reform, 82–84; warned about Volunteers, 149
Kohn, Hans: on nationalism, 245

Langrishe, Hercules: *Baratariana* essays, 79–82; mentor to Grattan, 80; essay on imperial affairs, 82; drifts from Patriots, 107; against Grattan, 126, 218–19; opposes parliamentary reform, 179, 181, 186; supports limited Catholic emancipation, 189; for Catholic franchise, 204–5; pro-union, 236
Latouche, James Digges: Dublin politics, 72
Lecky, William Edward Hartpole, tensions in eighteenth-century Ireland, 39, 40–41; Irish sympathize with Americans, 94–95; celebrates Constitution of 1782, 144
Leinster, James FitzGerald, first duke of, 96, 98, 101, 114, 212; Volunteer involvement, 149, 170; regency crisis, 197, 200; changes vote for union, 232n, 238; tie to duke of Richmond, 249
Leland, Thomas: pro-Protestant history, 70; but shares with Charles O'Conor, 73
Leslie, Charles: critique of Anglo-Irish Protestant nationalism, 36–38
Limerick, Treaty of: punishes Catholics, 40
Littleton, Thomas, English jurist, 27

Locke, John, 36; friend of Molyneux, 19; ideas used by Charles Francis Sheridan, 117
Lucas, Charles, 107, 157, 161, 191, 207, 254; stormy career, 59–68; ideas beyond: Swift, 60; Molyneux, 60, 63; and Domvile, 65; his popular politics, 72, 261; critic of Townshend, 78–79; connection to Grattan group, 80; sees conspiracy against Irish and American liberties, 86, 252–53; implications for popular power, 152, 166

Macartney, George: criticizes Patriots, 257
McKenna, Theobald: rejects radicalism, 222
MacNeven, William James, United Irishman, 214; calls for separation, 237; on shared Irish and American experiences, 253
Madden, Samuel: call for union, 50; defense of Irish rights, 50–51; Catholics should become Protestants, 71, 191
Madison, James: Ireland benefits from American rebellion, 106
Magna Carta: and fundamental Irish rights, 26, 249, 256, 263
Malone, Anthony, prime sergeant, 54; chancellor of the exchequer, 66
Mansfield, William Murray, first earl of, lord chief justice: hears Irish case on appeal, 138, 191
Martin, Richard: Monks of St. Patrick, 121
Mason, John Monck: against parliamentary reform, 181
Maxwell, Henry: treatise on union, 31
Mayart, Samuel: critique of 1644 "Declaration," 17, 28
Mervin, Audley: defense of Irish rights, 13
Metge, Peter: supports Grattan, 126
Molesworth, Robert: commonwealthman, 48
Molyneux, William, his *Case*: 18, 19, 108, 126, 189, 190, 199, 233, 236, 254, 259; importance to Irish constitutional tradition, 8; as synthesis, 19; its position and its critics, 23–29, 35–36; tradition that it was burned, 28n–29n; and Jonathan Swift, 46; reprinted, 87; owned by Benjamin Franklin, 91–92; endorsed by Charles Francis Sheridan, 117; noted by Hercules Langrishe, 135n; problem with constitutional nationalism, 241; Irish rights and a

Molyneux, William *(cont.)*
  higher cause, 253; use of the past, 255. *See also* nationalism
Monks of St. Patrick, or Monks of the Screw, 201, 218, 235; membership and political bent, 120–22; drift apart, 141
Mornington, Richard Colley Wellesley, second earl of: critical of Flood and renunciation, 138; borough patron, 156; objects to politicized Volunteers, 178
Morris, Richard B.: exaggerates similarity of Irish and American conditions, 93–94
Mutiny bill: center of controversy, 129–30; altered, 136

Napper Tandy, James: revolutionary tendencies, 194; United Irishman, 205, 208; flees into exile, 213
nationalism: limited Anglo-Irish form of, 6, 245; problematical, 35–38; moderate tone, 48–51; under pall with union, 240–41. *See also* constitution; Patrick Darcy; Henry Grattan; William Molyneux; revolutionary impulse
Newenham, Edward: tribute to Charles Lucas, 65; pro-American, 98; Monks of St. Patrick, 121; backs Grattan, 126, 219; with Volunteers, 176; for parliamentary reform, 179, 181
North, Frederick, Lord: criticized in *Baratariana*, 81; criticized elsewhere, 94, 97; attempts to keep Ireland in line, 110–11, 112–13, 115–16; Hely-Hutchinson anecdote, 140
Northington, Robert Henley, second earl of: lord lieutenant, 145, 178, 181; on controlling Irish Patriots, 186; warned that people stirring, 187

O'Connell, Daniel, 238; as constitutionalist, 239, 240; and "Liberator," 243
O'Connell, Maurice: on mutiny bill dispute, 130
O'Connor, Arthur, United Irishman, 214
O'Conor, Charles, 222; defends Catholics in constitutional tradition, 69–71; opposition to radicalism, 189; dream of united society unrealized, 191
Octennial Act: dispute over, 76–77
O'Leary, Arthur: Monks of St. Patrick, 121
O'Nial, Letters of Owen Roe. *See* Jospeh Pollock
Orangemen, 229
Otis, James: on Ireland and imperial crisis, 88

Paine, Thomas: limited appeal of *Common Sense* to Anglo-Irish, 102–3, 254, 259; *Age of Reason* belittled by Wolfe Tone, 215
Palmer, R. R.: on democratic revolutions, 3
Parliament, British: Commons condemns Molyneux's *Case*, 28–29; purportedly orders it burned, 28n–29n; avoids constitutional issues, 42–43; lack of clear Irish policy, 75–76; mistreats Ireland, 117–18, 190; criticized by Irish Patriots, 124–44 passim; cannot control Patriots, 152; in Irish politics, 197
Parliament, Irish: asserts legislative autonomy, 8, 9; as defined in Anglo-Irish constitutional tradition, 13–26; willing to consider union, 32; alienated by Declaratory Act, 41–42; pride of, 52–53; in 1750s controversies, 53–57; position on the American rebellion, 96–102; in battle for Constitution of 1782, 124–44; illusion of independence, 144–45; Commons not representative, 155–57; Commons' growing power, 158–61; disbanded with union, 230–39
Parliament House: source of pride, 52–53; gallery redesigned, 205
parliamentary reform movement: in England, 154–55; in Ireland, 155–94; small gains, 202–3. *See also* popular sovereignty; Volunteers
Parsons, Laurence: anti-union, 232–33; but sits at Westminster, 238; derides Constitution of 1782, 261; Patriots divided, 261n
patriot clubs of the 1750s, 58, 67–68
Patriot Parliament of 1689: dismissed by Anglo-Irish, 18
Patriots, Irish Parliament: concern for rights, 1; rise in 1750s, 53–55; dabbling in democratic politics, 59, 152; rebirth in 1760s, 74–75; sympathy for Americans, 98–102; unite with American rebellion, 107–8; split in 1783, 138–44; and later, 261n; discredited, 223. *See also* Henry Grattan
Peep-O-Day boys, 216
Pery, Edmund Sexton: Irish Parliament politicized, 55
Pitt, William (the elder), 107; interest in union, 228n
Pitt, William (the younger): commercial crisis of 1785, 145–46; abandons parliamentary reform, 185; criticized in *Orellana*, 188; desire for union, 194,

228, 230; regency crisis, 199; distrusted, 204; vilified, 239
Plowden, Francis, 230; critical of union, 239n
Plunket, William Conyngham: anti-union, 232–33, 236; sits at Westminster, 239
Pocock, J. G. A.: on reconstructing the past, 4
Pole, J. R.: on doctrine of instruction, 184
Pollock, Joseph: *Letters of Owen Roe O'Nial*, 118–19; unforeseen implications of his message, 152; *Letters* inspire William Drennan, 188; with Wolfe Tone, 208; rejects radicalism, 221
Ponsonby, George, 96, 98; Monks of St. Patrick, 121; Grattan as father of independence, 135; regency crisis, 199, 200; resigns from Commons, 217; anti-union, 232–33; in Westminster parliament, 239
Ponsonby, John: opposes Townshend, 76, 77
Ponsonby, William: reform bill, 202, 211–12, 217, 221
popular sovereignty: implicit in Darcy's *Argument*, 14; in ideas of Charles Lucas, 62–64, 66–67, 78–79; in patriot clubs of 1750s, 67–68; rise of popular politics, 72; linked to Volunteers, 151, 162, 192n–193n; threat to elite control, 152; challenge to Commons, 160–62; in union debates, 231n, 233, 237n; American founders and Anglo-Irish ambivalent about, 259–64. *See also* Charles Lucas; William Saurin; United Irishmen; Volunteers
Portland, William Henry Cavendish Bentinck, third duke of: lord lieutenant, 131, 134, 135, 178; unenthusiastic about parliamentary independence, 143, 227; regency crisis, 196
Postlethwait, Malachy: book stirs controversy, 55–56
Powerscourt demesne, 52, 243
Pownall, Thomas: advocates imperial reform, 83–84; on *imperium in imperio*, 146
Poynings, Edward: lord deputy, 10
Poynings' Law: subordination of Irish Parliament, 10, 53; suspended, 11; challenged, 33; aimed at Irish executive, 41; criticized, 55, 62, 190; move to revise, 110; 1557 modification, 128–29; revised, 136; failed attempt to apply to Jamaica and Virginia, 247

Pym, John, 13

Raleigh, Sir Walter: New World patent, 251
regency, crisis of 1788–89, 196–200
Reid, John Phillip: on rights in the empire, 1; on the British constitution, 263–64; Irish-American comparison, 264n
Reilly, Hugh: on Irish rights, 18–19
republicanism: fears of in the 1750s, 58. *See also* popular sovereignty; revolutionary impulse
revolutionary impulse: resisted, 5, 35, 66–67, 72, 194; linked to nationalism, 35–36, 38, 241, 264; United Irishmen embrace, 213–14. *See also* nationalism; United Irishmen
Richard I: and Ireland as kingdom, 22, 24
Richmond, Charles Lennox, third duke of, 249
Robbins, Caroline: on commonwealth tradition, 48
Rockingham, Charles Watson-Wentworth, second earl of: and Declaratory Act of 1766, 86–87, 87n, 258; trade concessions for Ireland, 113; flexible with Irish demands, 134; annoyance with Patriots, 135
Rowan, Archibald Hamilton: urges use of force, 192
Russborough estate, 52, 243
Russell, Thomas, United Irishman, 208, 213
Rutland, Charles Manners, fourth duke of: lord lieutenant, 145, 181, 247; against parliamentary reform, 185–86; wants union, 193–94, 227; law and order emphasis, 196

Saurin, William: anti-unionist, on popular sovereignty, 231n, 237n
Schuyler, Robert Livingston: on Molyneux's *Case*, 24, 24n
Scott, John: fears Volunteers, 163–64
Sharp, Granville: on imperial crisis, 88
Shelburne, William Petty, first earl of: wants union, 30–31; on 1750s unrest, 54; favors trade concessions, 113; approves of Charles Francis Sheridan's tract, 116
Sheridan, Charles Francis: critiques Blackstone, 116–18; Monks of St. Patrick, 121; against Grattan, 126; on Patriot split, 140–41; office seeker, 142; opposes Volunteers, 169; report possibly

Sheridan, Charles Francis *(cont.)*
by, 187n; regency crisis, 197–98, 200; against radicalism, 220–21
Sheridan, Richard Brinsley, 117
Sheridan, Thomas: proposes union, 30
Smith, Adam, 130; advocates union, 221
Society of Granby Row, 121
Stone, George, Archbishop of Armagh: undertaker, 52
Strafford, earl of. *See* Thomas Wentworth
Swift, Jonathan, 72, 108, 124, 189, 190, 259; nationalist writings, 43–48, 252; not representative of Anglo-Irish nationalists, 48

Temple, Earl. *See* Marquess of Buckingham
Tisdal, Philip: purported *Baratariana* authorship, 80n
Tocqueville, Alexis de: on rising egalitarianism, 262–63
Tone, Theobald Wolfe: revolutionary tendencies, 194, 241; United Irishmen and, 205–14; assessed, 215–16; admires Laurence Parsons, 234; with French invasion and execution, 229–30; unpalatable to Anglo-Irish elite, 259
Townshend, Charles, 75, 88
Townshend, George, fourth viscount, 147; problems as lord lieutenant, 75–81; leaves with majority in Parliament, 95; honorary member of Monks of St. Patrick, 120n
Trenchard, John, commonwealthman, 49, 49n, 63; favors union, 50
Tucker, Josiah: predicts union, 226

Union: proposed in 1677, 30; Molyneux considers, 30n; lukewarm Anglo-Irish desire for in 1703, 32; attractive to some in 1720s, 49–50; fears of in 1750s, 56–57; rumors of in 1770s, 95n; events leading to, 226–37
United Irishmen: as republican separatists, 5; beyond Anglo-Irish constitutionalists, 38; embodiment of popular will, 195–96; rise of, 205–14; French Revolution and radicalism, 213–14, 223, 261; limited appeal of, 241

Volunteers: misread by Americans, 105; rise with American war, 106; politicized, 147–52, 163–66, 261; 1782 Dungannon meeting, 150–51, 168; challenge Patriots, 172–74; 1783 national convention, 175–79; 1784 and 1785 meetings, 181–82; divided, 192; links to United Irishmen, 195–96, 208–9

Walpole, Horace: rumors of Irish sympathy for Americans, 94; Irish restive, 115
Walpole, Robert: Walpolean politics, 48, 51
Washington, George: Wolfe Tone compares himself with, 230; in American founding myths, 243–44
Webb, Walter Prescott: on European expansion, 250
Wentworth, Thomas, first earl of Strafford: precipitates constitutional crisis, 12–13, 14, 69
Westmorland, John Fane, tenth earl of: lord lieutenant, 205
Whig Club, 200–201
Whiteboys: depredations, 106, 147, 187, 193
Wilkes, John: Charles Lucas compared with, 64, 67; in Hell-Fire Club, 120; Irish interest in, 154, 155, 162
Wilson, James: links Irish and American affairs, 88; critiques Blackstone, 116
Wood, William: halfpence controversy, 47, 51
Woolens Act, 29, 49, 190

Yelverton, Barry: purported *Baratariana* author, 80n; 1778 resolution supporting Crown, 110; drive to revise Poynings' Law, 110, 129–32; Monks of St. Patrick, 121; backs Grattan, 126, 138; office seeker, 141–42; would have agreed to union in 1782, 143, 146; election to multiple seats, 158; Commons and the people, 160; opposes parliamentary reform, 179–80; regency crisis, 198; for union, 230–31

Neither Kingdom Nor Nation: The Irish Quest for Constitutional Rights, 1698–1800 was composed in Sabon by Brevis Press, Bethany, Connecticut; printed and bound by Thomson-Shore, Dexter, Michigan; and designed by Kachergis Book Design, Pittsboro, North Carolina.